The Challenge of Modernity

Social History, Popular Culture, and Politics in Germany
Geoff Eley, Series Editor

Cities, Sin, and Social Reform in Imperial Germany, Andrew Lees

The Challenge of Modernity: German Social and Cultural Studies, 1890–1960,
Adelheid von Saldern

Exclusionary Violence: Antisemitic Riots in Modern German History,
Christhard Hoffmann, Werner Bergmann, and Helmut Walser Smith, editors

Languages of Labor and Gender: Female Factory Work in Germany, 1850–1914,
Kathleen Canning

That Was the Wild East: Film Culture, Unification and the "New" Germany,
Leonie Naughton

Anna Seghers: The Mythic Dimension, Helen Fehervary

*Staging Philanthropy: Patriotic Women and the National Imagination in Dynastic
Germany, 1813–1916,* Jean H. Quataert

Truth to Tell: German Women's Autobiographies and Turn-of-the-Century Culture,
Katharina Gerstenberger

The "Goldhagen Effect": History, Memory, Nazism—Facing the German Past,
Geoff Eley, editor

Shifting Memories: The Nazi Past in the New Germany, Klaus Neumann

Saxony in German History: Culture, Society, and Politics, 1830–1933,
James Retallack, editor

*Little Tools of Knowledge: Historical Essays on Academic and Bureaucratic
Practices,* Peter Becker and William Clark, editors

*Public Spheres, Public Mores, and Democracy: Hamburg and Stockholm,
1870–1914,* Madeleine Hurd

*Making Security Social: Disability, Insurance, and the Birth of the Social
Entitlement State in Germany,* Greg Eghigian

*The German Problem Transformed: Institutions, Politics, and Foreign Policy,
1945–1995,* Thomas Banchoff

*Building the East German Myth: Historical Mythology and Youth Propaganda in the
German Democratic Republic, 1945–1989,* Alan L. Nothnagle

Mobility and Modernity: Migration in Germany, 1820–1989, Steve Hochstadt

Triumph of the Fatherland: German Unification and the Marginalization of Women,
Brigitte Young

*Framed Visions: Popular Culture, Americanization, and the Contemporary German
and Austrian Imagination,* Gerd Gemünden

The Imperialist Imagination: German Colonialism and Its Legacy,
Sara Friedrichsmeyer, Sara Lennox, and Susanne Zantop, editors

Contested City: Municipal Politics and the Rise of Nazism in Altona, 1917–1937,
Anthony McElligott

(continued on last page)

The Challenge of Modernity

*German Social and
Cultural Studies, 1890–1960*

ADELHEID VON SALDERN

*Translated by Bruce Little
With a Foreword by Geoff Eley*

Ann Arbor

THE UNIVERSITY OF MICHIGAN PRESS

Copyright © by the University of Michigan 2002
All rights reserved
Published in the United States of America by
The University of Michigan Press
Manufactured in the United States of America
♾ Printed on acid-free paper

2005 2004 2003 2002   4 3 2 1

A CIP catalog record for this book is available from the British Library.

Library of Congress Cataloging-in-Publication Data

Saldern, Adelheid von.
    The challenge of modernity : German social and cultural studies,
  1890–1960 / Adelheid von Saldern ; translated by Bruce Little ; with a
  foreword by Geoff Eley.
        p.   cm.
    Includes bibliographical references and index.
    ISBN 0-472-10986-3
    1. Germany—Social conditions.   2. Germany—Social life and customs.
  3. Germany—Politics and government.   I. Title

  HN445 .S25   2002
  306'.0943—dc21   2002019083

For Manfred

Contents

Foreword

Geoff Eley

Adelheid von Saldern is one of the most interesting historians currently working in Germany. Since the mid-1960s, beginning with a monograph on the collapse of the Weimar Republic, she has steadily amassed a remarkable bibliography on central questions of Germany's history in the twentieth century. Her major interests range from social histories of urbanization and the rise of the labor movement, through extensive studies of the housing question in Germany and elsewhere, to analyses of popular culture between the wars and a pioneering project on radio under Nazism and the GDR.[1] Her work also includes studies of local government, a rich portfolio of publication specifically on Hanover, and an underappreciated book on the Mittelstand under the Third Reich.[2]

---

1. For Adelheid von Saldern's first book, see *Hermann Dietrich: Ein Staatsmann der Weimarer Republik* (Boppard, 1966). It was followed by *Vom Einwohner zum Bürger: Zur Emanzipation der städtischen Unterschicht Göttingens 1890–1920: Eine sozial- und kommunalhistorische Untersuchung* (Berlin, 1973); *Auf dem Wege zum Arbeiter-Reformismus: Parteialltag in sozialdemokratischer Provinz: Göttingen 1870–1920* (Frankfurt, 1984); *Neues Wohnen: Wohnungspolitik und Wohnkultur im Hannover der Zwanziger Jahre* (Hanover, 1993); and *Häuserleben: Zur Geschichte städtischen Arbeiterwohnens vom Kaiserreich bis heute* (Bonn, 1995). See also the following edited volumes: *Stadt und Moderne: Hannover in der Weimarer Republik* (Hamburg, 1989); with Sid Auffarth, *Wochenend und schöner Schein: Freizeit und modernes Leben in den Zwanziger Jahren: Das Beispiel Hannover* (Berlin, 1991); with Inge Marßolek, *Zuhören und Gehörtwerden,* vol. 1, *Radio im Nationalsozialismus: Zwischen Lenkung und Ablenkung* (Tübingen, 1998); vol. 2, *Radio in der DDR der 50er Jahre: Zwischen Lenkung und Ablenkung* (Tübingen, 1998); with Inge Marßolek, *Radiozeiten: Herrschaft, Alltag, Gesellschaft (1924–1960)* (Potsdam, 1999).

2. For the work on local government, see, for example, "SPD und Kommunalpolitik im Deutschen Kaiserreich," *Archiv für Kommunalwissenschaften* 23 (1984): 193–214; "Geschichte der kommunalen Selbstverwaltung in Deutschland," in Roland Roth and Hellmut Wollmann (eds.), *Kommunalpolitik: Politisches Handeln in den Gemeinden* (Opladen, 1994), 2–19; and "Kommunale Verarmung und Armut in den Kommunen während der

If this impressive inventory seems to reflect the profession's passage from the critical social histories of the 1970s to the new cultural history of the last decade, this is because Adelheid von Saldern played a vital role in pioneering those very innovations. Her *Vom Einwohner zum Bürger,* published in 1973, was an excellent case study in the social and political dynamics of urbanization in the central German university town of Göttingen between the Kaiserreich and the Weimar Republic, which captured admirably the new potentials of the upsurge in social history already under way. Ten years later, *Auf dem Wege zum Arbeiter-Reformismus* then became the companion study, complementing the earlier social history with an analysis of the Göttingen SPD, whose local minute book von Saldern was lucky enough to have discovered.

But this did more than simply extend the previous picture by resting a study of the labor movement's "politics" on top of the previously assembled "material foundations." In the early 1980s, that approach was still the commonest one among labor historians in Germany, who continued to base their arguments about the strengths and weaknesses of Social Democracy before 1914 on structural accounts of industrialization, living standards, and material conditions of life, combined with the repeatedly reiterated claims about the political system's unreformed authoritarianism, the notorious Sonderweg thesis about Germany's peculiarities compared with the "West." In this prevailing approach, the one — the dynamism of German capitalism — created the conditions for the emergence of a modern labor movement, while the other — the political backwardness of an illiberal and repressive imperial state — prevented that labor movement from developing the healthy reformist proclivities of, say, the Labour Party in Britain. Instead, the authoritarian state denied the labor movement such "normal" opportunities for political participation and kept it artificially beholden to a Marxist radicalism more easily superseded or marginalized elsewhere.[3]

großen Krise 1928 bis 1933: Am Beispiel der Finanz- und Wohnungs(bau)politik," *Soziale Bewegungen: Jahrbuch 3* (Frankfurt, 1987), 69–110. For an indication of the work specifically on Hanover, see the references in footnote 30 of the introduction to this volume. For the book on the Mittelstand, see *Mittelstand im "Dritten Reich": Bauern, Handwerker, Einzelhändler* (Frankfurt and New York, 1979); and "The Old *Mittelstand,* 1890–1939: How 'Backward' were the Artisans?" *Central European History* 25, no. 1 (1992): 27–51.

3. For a critique of the Sonderweg thesis, see David Blackbourn and Geoff Eley, *The Peculiarities of Germany History: Bourgeois Society and Politics in Nineteenth-Century Germany* (Oxford and New York, 1984). The locus classicus for the labor history variant of the approach is now the multivolume *Geschichte der Arbeiter und der Arbeiterbewegung in Deutschland seit dem Ende des 18. Jahrhunderts* (Bonn), edited by Gerhard A. Ritter for the SPD-affiliated Friedrich Ebert Foundation. See especially Jürgen Kocka's two volumes, *Weder Stand noch Klasse: Unterschichten um 1800* and *Arbeitsverhältnisse und Arbeiterexistenzen: Grundlagen der Klassenbildung im 19. Jahrhundert* (Bonn, 1990); and

In the strongest versions, this approach became linked to further arguments about the cohesiveness of the labor movement's underlying "social-moral milieu," shaped by interlocking structures of residence, employment, sociability, and subcultural organization, which closed working-class sociopolitical identity against the outside.[4] From the early 1960s, this fashioning of a structural explanation for the distinctiveness of German labor history — based on the combination of industrializing modernity, political backwardness, and subcultural defensiveness — became established as one of the fixed referents for the wider historiography of the Kaiserreich, with profound implications for the period after 1914–18. In practice, this dominant system of explanation also severely narrowed the latitude for local studies or studies of particular aspects of the working class, for these were mainly harnessed to the established metanarrative described earlier. Complicating the latter — especially by cultural or ethnographic readings, interpretive approaches to everyday life, or symbolic analysis — might have been academically interesting, it was suggested, but scarcely altered the overriding power of structural determinations, which tragically defined the fate of German labor during the Weimar Republic and the Third Reich.

This began to change in the late 1970s, when a few independent voices started questioning the sufficiency of this dominant framework. As with all major intellectual movements with cross-cutting connections to a wide array of academic contexts and broader cultural and political publics, this was a complicated story, whose ramifications I am necessarily oversimplifying here. But creative nodules of historical work began developing at the new universities of Konstanz and Essen around Dieter Groh and Lutz Niethammer, with further links to the Ruhr University in Bochum, in a growing critical distance from the freshly minted social science history then consolidating its West German ascendancy. Equally important, Alf Lüdtke and Hans Medick, two research scholars at the Max Planck Institute of History in Göttingen, began their patient and tireless

Gerhard A. Ritter and Klaus Tenfelde, *Arbeiter im Deutschen Kaiserreich 1871 bis 1914* (Bonn, 1992). For a useful summary statement in English, see Jürgen Kocka, "Problems of Working-Class Formation in Germany: The Early Years, 1800–1875," in Ira Katznelson and Aristide R. Zolberg (eds.), *Working-Class Formation: Nineteenth-Century Patterns in Western Europe and the United States* (Princeton, 1986), 279–351. For further critical discussion, see Geoff Eley, "Class, Culture, and Politics in the Kaiserreich," *Central European History* 27 (1994): 355–75.

4. See especially M. Rainer Lepsius, "Parteiensystem und Sozialstruktur: Zum Problem der Demokratisierung der deutschen Gessellschaft," in Gerhard A. Ritter (ed.), *Die deutschen Parteien vor 1918* (Cologne, 1973), 56–80; and Peter Lösche, "Is the SPD Still a Labor Party? From 'Community of Solidarity' to 'Loosely Coupled Anarchy,'" in David E. Barclay and Eric D. Weitz (eds.), *Between Reform and Revolution: German Socialism and Communism from 1840 to 1990* (New York, 1998), 531–45.

advocacy and over the longer term helped decisively shift this historio-graphical agenda.[5] These, then, were the endeavors that von Saldern's study of the SPD's local everydayness also pushed forward, presaged by her pioneering essays on municipal socialism and distinguished by the nicely bounded concreteness that the Göttingen materials allowed.[6]

Adelheid von Saldern and her fellow advocates wanted to move social history away from the primacy of structural analysis — the "big structures, large processes, huge comparisons" unremittingly celebrated by the social science historians — but without recurring to the older ground of an institutionally or politically limiting labor history.[7] Instead, they called for a more "qualitative" appreciation of the circumstances under which ordinary people lived their lives, including not only the material conditions of daily existence but the interior world of popular experience in each of those contexts too. By pushing historical analysis into these experiential or subjective domains, they argued, the concep-tual and instituted boundaries between the "public" and "private" might be broken down and new ways of connecting the political and cultural realms worked out. This was the really difficult but ultimately decisive terrain of historical investigations, if problems of democratic political culture and the rise of fascism were to be effectively addressed.

Although the mainstream of the West German profession did its best to marginalize these new efforts, they converged with important directions elsewhere and found much sustenance in international arenas of discussion. By the early 1990s, the "new cultural history," historical anthropology, and cultural studies were all encouraging such trans-national conversations in the United States, whose interdisciplinarity further emphasized the importance of going outside the immediate disci-plinary boundaries in Germany.

---

5. See especially Lutz Neithammer and Franz-Josef Brüggemeier, "Wie wohnten Arbeiter im Kaiserreich?" *Archiv für Sozialgeschichte* 16 (1976): 61–134; Jürgen Reulecke and Wolfhard Weber (eds.), *Fabrik—Familie—Feierabend: Beiträge zur Sozialgeschichte des Alltags im Industriezeitalter* (Wuppertal, 1978); Dieter Groh, "Base-Processes and the Problem of Organisation: Outline of a Social History Research Project," *Social History* 4 (1979): 265–83; Hans Medick, "The Proto-Industrial Family Economy: The Structural Function of Household and Family during the Transition from Peasant Society to Indus-trial Capitalism," *Social History* 1 (1976): 291–315; Alf Lüdtke (ed.), "Bedürfnisse, Erfahr-ung und Verhalten," *Sozialwissenschaftliche Informationen für Unterricht und Studium (SOWI)* 6 (1977): 147–96.

6. Adelheid von Saldern's *Auf dem Wege* provides the kind of book-length exemplifi-cation that the essays edited by Alf Lüdtke in *The History of Everyday Life: Reconstruct-ing Historical Experiences and Ways of Life* (Princeton, 1995; original German edition, Frankfurt, 1989) programmatically project.

7. See Charles Tilly, *Big Structures, Large Processes, Huge Comparisons* (New York, 1984).

Finally, the growth of Alltagsgeschichte in the 1980s had larger political inspirations. At first, the bulk of practical research occurred beyond the official profession in a wider domain of public history, embracing museums, exhibitions, further education, and the programs of local government cultural offices, as well as the mass media, local publishing, and local research projects in schools. This grassroots activity became loosely coordinated through a West German history workshop federation, whose emergence also interacted with the peace movement and the launching of the Greens during the late 1970s and early 1980s. A preponderance of interest in the Third Reich — in uncovering the character of popular experience and coming to terms with the impact of Nazism — sharpened this unmistakable political edge.[8] Adelheid von Saldern was centrally involved in these organizational histories, one of the few tenured professors of history behind the efforts eventually producing the new journal *WerkstattGeschichte*.

Everyday-life historians created a "third space" *between* the older institutional accounts of labor history and the structural approaches to industrialization and working-class formation preferred by social science historians. In *Auf dem Wege zum Arbeiter-Reformismus* and her writings on housing that immediately followed, von Saldern wanted to dig beneath the organized party, trade-union, and associational activity, which had usually identified working-class agency and consciousness, to examine the behaviors and attitudes of ordinary working people themselves. In the informal settings of working-class everydayness, in families, households, streets, neighborhoods, bars, and recreational spaces, as well as in the manifold contexts of the workplace, she and her colleagues argued, specific patterns of sociability and subjectivity were generated that crucially shaped the possible forms of politics. In other words, to understand the strengths and weaknesses of the German labor movement, historians needed to look beyond the established antinomy between the modern industrial economy and backward authoritarian state, which supposedly shaped the character of German labor history in such ironclad ways. Moreover, if that structural framework limited the development of the labor movement, the latter's institutions themselves acted on the potentials of working-class culture in selective and limiting ways. Once the implications of this insight were grasped, differences and conflicts between the labor movement and the working class could then be properly faced.

---

8. For detailed discussion, see Geoff Eley, "Labor History, Social History, *Alltags-geschichte:* Experience, Culture, and the Politics of Everyday Life: A New Direction for German Social History?" *Journal of Modern History* 61 (1989): 297–343, especially 297–300 and 315–21; and idem, "Nazism, Politics, and the Image of the Past: Thoughts on the West German *Historikerstreit,* 1986–87," *Past and Present* 121 (1988): 171–208.

Given the broadly progressive inclinations of most labor historians, the importance of such conflicts has been extraordinarily difficult to acknowledge, particularly when socialist politicians or trade unionists appeared in less than democratic lights. Yet for the duration of its history, the socialist tradition has defined itself negatively in relation to many aspects of working-class existence, despite its abstract centering of collective working-class agency as the source of forward-moving historical change and progressive good. The self-improving and moralizing aspects of socialist philosophy always validated certain kinds of workers — and certain attributes of working-classness — over others. The socialist image of the class-conscious proletarian usually projected a manual worker in handicrafts or industry, formed by the dignity of labor and workplace cultures of skill, living by values of sobriety and self-improvement in settled working-class communities, with a respectable family life — all of which, of course, was heavily male defined. Obversely, this positive category of the worker also left out a lot of negatively perceived working-class experience — notably, the roughness and disordered transience of much working-class living, with its dependence on informal economies, casualized labor markets, improvised domestic arrangements, and crime. Entire categories of workers barely figured in the positive ideal at all, including ethnic minorities, the religiously devout, and especially women.

In all of these ways, working-class everydayness became the starting point for a more sophisticated appraisal of the potentials and difficulties of progressive politics. But this was the opposite of a naively romanticized construction of an "alternative" or "real" working class, whose authentic radicalism the labor movement had misrecognized or betrayed. Everyday-life historians certainly argued for the existence of needs and desires — elementary and informal structures of working-class solidarity — whose democratic potentials were tragically neglected, whether in and before 1914, in the German Revolution, or in the failure to head off the rise of Nazism. Yet they also pointed to equally self-interested and narrowly defensive aspects of working-class culture, including the short-term calculus of survivalism and "making it through"; forms of collective intolerance militating against the achievement of broadly based democratic unity; and the structural hierarchies of skill, age, region, ethnicity, religion, and especially gender, which divided the working class and fragmented the efforts at solidarity.[9]

---

9. See especially Alf Lüdtke, "What Happened to the 'Fiery Red Glow'? Workers' Experiences and German Fascism," in idem (ed.), *The History of Everyday Life: Reconstructing Historical Experiences and Ways of Life* (Princeton, 1995), 198–251; "The Appeal of Exterminating 'Others': German Workers and the Limits of Resistance," in Michael Geyer and John W. Boyer (eds.), *Resistance against the Third Reich, 1933–1990* (Chicago, 1994), 53–74.

Gendered cultures of patriarchal and work-related masculinity were the most persistent of these internal systems of difference. But although Alltagsgeschichte and gender history possessed natural affinities in this regard, the actual convergence of these interests was very slow to occur: during the 1980s, very few of Alltagsgeschichte's practitioners noticed the absence of women's experience from their writing and research or began addressing the masculinity of their working-class subjects. Likewise, the most important advances in women's history tended to come from elsewhere.[10] For example, Lüdtke's highly original concept of Eigensinn showed how the complex forms of workers' self-affirmation in the workplace, including pride in skill and the dignity of labor, could become a source of depoliticizing consolation in times of fascist political repression, so that the best resources for a positive working-class identity linked to democracy, consistently celebrated by labor historians, came to promote acquiescence and even complicity in the antidemocratic public culture of the Third Reich.[11] Yet this analysis was not pushed further to explore the prerequisites of patriarchal and sexualized masculinity these constructions of work-defined positive identity also entailed. The coherence and efficacy of identities in the workplace could certainly be linked to egalitarian family relationships between women and men, but they more often presumed gendered inequalities of domestic and sexual power.

These brief reflections should make the importance and originality of Adelheid von Saldern's work much clearer. During the 1980s and 1990s, she became one of the best practitioners of the approaches Alltagsgeschichte helped to pioneer, in ways that both realized some of their best purposes and pushed them into new and exciting terrain. Thus, her study of the Göttingen SPD in *Auf dem Wege zum Arbeiter-Reformismus* was not just an excellent account of the vagaries of socialist organizing in the unpromising environment of a small provincial town dominated by the official culture of university and garrison, with a "traditional" social structure and little developed industry. It was far more an attempt to understand the rigidities of a socialist subculture that failed to work with those limitations. Faced with the challenge of its local circumstances, von Saldern argues, the Göttingen SPD turned inward, taking refuge in the party's overarching ideology and national program and evading the tasks of local strategy. But while preserving a seemingly radical class-political

10. For one key exception, see Dorothee Wierling, "A History of Everyday Life and Gender Relations: On Historical and Historiographical Relationships," in Alf Lüdtke (ed.), *The History of Everyday Life: Reconstructing Historical Experiences and Ways of Life* (Princeton, 1995), 148–68.

11. See the essays in Alf Lüdtke, *Eigen-Sinn: Fabrikalltag, Arbeitererfahrungen, und Politik vom Kaiserreich bis in den Faschismus* (Hamburg, 1993).

vision, this blocked the party from intervening effectively in the local arena or from developing an effective grassroots political style. Even more, this retreat into the abstract territory of the SPD's formal revolutionism immunized local activists from addressing their politics to the everyday actualities of living under capitalism—to the practical, personal, and experiential dimensions of ordinary working-class life.[12]

In other words, von Saldern's book was one of the earliest attempts to get inside the tense and difficult relationship between the SPD and its putative working-class supporters, which traditional labor historians had tended all too easily to obscure. By exploring the gaps between SPD practice and its idealized constituency, her analysis inserted itself *between* the social history of working-class formation and the rise of the labor movement, in ways intended to pose that relationship as a difficult and open-ended problem rather than an assumed causality or foregone conclusion. After conducting one of the earliest local studies of the labor movement's social history in *Vom Einwohner zum Bürger,* therefore, von Saldern also became one of the first to respond to the Alltagsgeschichte's new possibilities. Through a variety of publications, she then translated the resulting insights into a general argument about the labor movement's historiography, for which the first two chapters in this volume are excellent illustrations.

By exploring the areas of tension linking and separating the Social Democrats and their working-class supporters, von Saldern prized open the concept of the "social-moral milieu" on which so much of the social history of German politics in the late nineteenth and early twentieth centuries relies. In the resulting analytical space, she reclaimed the area of "everydayness" for its political significance, pushing past the classical Marxist dismissals of everyday environments as the scene of unconsciousness and alienation and reevaluating their place in working-class subjectivity. Here, the housing question became an ideal context of study—simultaneously a classic object of socialist analysis and concern, a growth area of the new social history since the 1970s, and an undertheorized site of political action, whose neglect the emergent everyday-life histories were trying to address.

Once again, von Saldern moved from more orthodox treatments of SPD local government politics and programmatic practice, through studies of housing reform and new working-class housing developments in the 1920s, to imaginative and searching analyses of domestic culture and

---

12. In other words, *Auf dem Wege* becomes far more than a local party history based on the exceptional source of the SPD's local minute book, because von Saldern reads that local archive against the theoretical, interpretive, and ethnographic possibilities Alltagsgeschichte had started to provide.

the broader definitional contests over the meaning of home.[13] In this context, her work converged with another area of exciting innovation during the 1980s, namely, the study of "social rationalization" during the Weimar Republic and the Third Reich. As a broader discourse of modernizing social reform, encompassing large-scale industrial planning, the structure of the firm, the priorities of social policy, and efforts at molding family and domestic life, social rationalization became the focus of pioneering work in German women's history during the 1980s, with exceptionally fruitful collaborations between West Germany and the United States.[14]

In common with the latter, von Saldern developed a sophisticated double analytic of power and contestation in order to investigate this important area. On the one hand, she captured the clear neo-Foucauldian or disciplinary logics recognizable in government interventions; in the developing machinery of social work practice; and in the social policy initiatives of industrial firms, trade unions, and other private agencies. But on the other hand, she saw equally clearly the room for conflict and the ability of those targeted by the new policies to bend and reshape them to their own ends—what her own introduction to this volume, which follows, calls the "subjective appropriation process" of "compliance, refusal, subversion, or a complex combination of attitudes." As she says, social rationalization was the opposite of a fixed term or closed concept. As in her earlier study of the SPD's local practice, Alltagsgeschichte afforded the tools for opening up the gaps and dissonances between the implementation of policies and their encounter with the complex cultural resources of the people affected. While the reformists' vision of a "clean modernity" motivating the Social Democratic housing policies of the 1920s proved insensitive to many of the actual needs of their working-class recipients, the coordinates of daily life also remained disconnected from political culture.

At the same time, the social agenda of housing policies had some profound long-term effects. On the positive side, definite material improvements for limited sections of the working class combined with a new sense of entitlement to welfare during the Weimar Republic to

13. In addition to the chapters in this volume, see the two books *Häuserleben* and *Neues Wohnen* and the edited collection *Stadt und Moderne;* also see "The Workers' Movement and Cultural Patterns on Urban Housing Estates and in Rural Settlements in Germany and Austria during the 1920s," *Social History* 15 (1990): 333–54.

14. See Atina Grossman, "Gender and Rationalization: Questions about the German/American Comparison," *Social Politics* (1997): 6–18; Dagmar Reese, Eve Rosenhaft, Carola Sachse, and Tilla Siegel (eds.), *Rationale Beziehungen? Geschlechterverhältnisse im Rationalisierungsprozess* (Frankfurt, 1993); Mary Nolan, *Visions of Modernity: American Business and the Modernization of Germany* (New York and Oxford, 1994).

broaden the understanding of rights and citizenship. On the other side, of course, these progressive potentials were brutally cut off by the Nazi seizure of power in 1933. More insidiously, the new moralizing talk of cleanliness and hygienic living blurred into more authoritarian discourses of social order and social hygiene, where the racialized versions of the Nazis were already working aggressively away. If the new pedagogies of improvement and orderliness in the 1920s remained profoundly different from the fascist social policy regime that supplanted them, they also contrasted with the repressive systems of policing and social administration under the empire before 1914. In common with other recent studies of the Weimar welfare state, von Saldern's work provides a much-needed basis for thinking these specificities through.[15]

Thus the second section of this collection, "Social Rationalization and Gender," brings together fascinating treatments of the interrelations among housing reform, domestic culture, social policy, women's history, and the mundane dynamics of working-class life. Here, von Saldern makes good Alltagsgeschichte's neglect of women, not only bringing domestic space into public view but also clarifying the political significance of domestic culture in its gendered dimensions, while retrieving women's everydayness from the narrowly constructed histories of family where it has been conventionally subsumed. She also offers a necessary comparative perspective, posing the differing valencies of social rationalization in Germany and the United States.

The final section of this volume, "Popular Culture and Politics," shows a further broadening of Alltagsgeschichte toward the study of commercialized and mass-mediated popular culture, using the approaches usually summarized these days as "cultural studies."[16] The new mass culture of the 1920s, crystallizing around movies, dance halls, spectator sports, radio, advertising, cosmetics, and fashion, proved deeply antithetical to the established socialist ideals of "ennobling" the working class by expanding its access to existing cultural goods. Indeed, mass culture was perceived by socialists as steadily undermining the labor movement's organized culture of self-improvement. For the high-minded architects of cultural socialism, the emergent cultures of consumption were the new enemy, threatening "traditional" working-class values, corrupting

---

15. See especially Young-Sun Hong, *Welfare, Modernity, and the Weimar State, 1919–1933* (Princeton, 1998); David F. Crew, *Germans on Welfare: From Weimar to Hitler* (New York and Oxford, 1998); Greg Eghigian, *Making Security Social: Disability, Insurance, and the Birth of the Social Entitlement State in Germany* (Ann Arbor, 2000).

16. Here see Geoff Eley, "Problems with Culture: German History after the Linguistic Turn," *Central European History* 31 (1998): 197–227.

popular taste, and seducing the young with cheap thrills and superficial pleasures.

As von Saldern points out, this implies a manipulative concept of popular culture. In the historiography of Nazism, it encouraged simplified understandings of ideology, in which the Third Reich's cultural policies were viewed reductively as emanations from the regime's basic drive for control, instrumentalized into machineries of conformity and propaganda. For many years, this model of ideology pervaded approaches to the "massified" popular culture of the Nazi regime, whether through Cold War notions of totalitarianism or their left-wing mirror image in arguments influenced by the Frankfurt school about the culture industry. The new interdisciplinarity of cultural studies, reinforced by an interest in the ideas of Pierre Bourdieu, has clearly been helpful in transcending these older approaches. Arguments about the growing centrality of cultural distinctions of consumption and style under the conditions of late capitalism have usefully influenced discussions of the earlier-twentieth-century contexts.[17]

In von Saldern's work, they conjoin creatively with the impulse coming from Alltagsgeschichte, itself reworked through the impact of feminist theories of gender. The sequence of chapters in the final part of this collection—a case study of the local politics of leisure in the early years of the Weimar Republic, two treatments of the highly contested public discourse surrounding popular culture on Left and Right, and a fascinating discussion of radio and its pedagogies in the GDR—beautifully maps the territories where future work on popular culture and politics will have to be done. All the key themes are present, including the broadening of historical horizons to new subject matters and the requisite interdisciplinary approaches; the need to integrate studies of popular culture and leisure into the general social and political histories of the twentieth century; the complex interrelations between politics and entertainment under the violently contrasting regimes of democratic capitalism, fascism, and state socialism; the importance of bringing the

---

17. See Alf Lüdtke, Inge Marßolek, and Adelheid von Saldern (eds.), *Amerikanisierung: Traum und Alptraum in Deutschland des 20. Jahrhunderts* (Stuttgart, 1996), 213–45; Scott Denham, Irene Kacandes, and Jonathan Petropoulos (eds.), *A User's Guide to German Cultural Studies* (Ann Arbor, 1997); Kate Lacey, *Feminine Frequencies: Gender, German Radio, and the Public Sphere, 1923–1945* (Ann Arbor, 1996). And for three pioneering studies of the postwar era: Erica Carter, *How German Is She? Postwar West German Reconstruction and the Consuming Woman* (Ann Arbor, 1997); Heide Fenhrenbach, *Cinema in Democratizing Germany: Reconstructing National Identity after Hitler* (Chapel Hill, 1995); Uta Poiger, *Jazz, Rock, and Rebels: Cold War Politics and American Culture in a Divided Germany* (Berkeley, 2000).

histories and historiography of popular culture into dialogue with labor history; popular culture's centrality to questions of political order, both under democratic political systems and in resisting the totalizing ambitions of dictatorship; and the need to read these questions for their gendered assumptions and meanings.

There is much more to be said in contextualizing the chapters in this volume, and these brief remarks cannot substitute for the commentaries in von Saldern's own introduction, still less for the excellence of the chapters themselves. The author's importance in pioneering new approaches, in the institutional and intellectual environs of a West German historical profession persistently hostile to them, cannot be emphasized too strongly. For many years, she was one of only a very few women holding full professorial positions in German history departments. She also played a key role in the early organizing efforts of the history workshop movement during the 1980s and the subsequent establishment of the journal *WerkstattGeschichte*. During the 1980s and 1990s, she responded creatively to the rise of gender history. In all of these ways, her work is distinguished by a willingness to take intellectual risks by responding to new historiographical challenges.

In her early work on the SPD and the labor movement; in the fashioning of a powerful corpus of theory, methodology, and empirical scholarship for the emergent claims of Alltagsgeschichte; in opening up the entire domain of popular culture as well as particular subjects like sports and radio; and in demonstrating the unavoidable necessities of gendered analysis — in all of these respects, Adelheid von Saldern has become one of the most challenging and experimental twentieth-century historians currently working in Germany. Social History, Popular Culture, and Politics in Germany is delighted to bring this excellent historian's work into wider circulation.

Acknowledgments

Grateful acknowledgment is made to the following authors, publishers, and journals for permission to reprint previously published materials.

Chapter 1, "Party Centers and Party Hinterlands: The Trend to Centralization and Hierarchism in the Wilhelminian SPD," first appeared as "Parteizentren und Parteiprovinzen: Zentralisierungs- und Hierarchisierungstendenzen innerhalb der Wilhelminischen SPD" in *Internationale Wissenschaftliche Korrespondenz zur Geschichte der deutschen Arbeiterbewegung (IWK)* 28, no. 1 (1992): 226–59.

Chapter 2, "Workers' Parties, Class Identity, and United Action: Experiences, Social Constructs, and Myths in the Weimar Republic," first appeared as "Arbeiterparteien, Klassenidentität, und Aktionseinheit: Erfahrungen, soziale Konstruktionen, und Mythen in der Weimarer Republik" in Adelheid von Saldern (ed.), *Mythen in Geschichte und Geschichtsschreibung aus polnischer und deutscher Sicht,* 197–227 (Münster, 1996).

Chapter 3, "Instead of Cathedrals, Dwelling Machines": The Paradoxes of Rationalization under the Banner of Modernity," first appeared as "Statt Kathedralen die Wohnmaschine": Paradoxien der Rationalisierung im Kontext der Moderne" in Frank Bajohr, Werner Johe, and Uwe Lohalm (eds.), *Zivilisation und Barbarei: Die widersprüchlichen Potentiale der Moderne: Gedenkschrift für Detlev J. K. Peukert,* 168–92 (Hamburg, 1991).

Chapter 4, "How Should Linoleum Floors Be Cleaned? A Contribution to Alltagsgeschichte and the Social History of the 1920s," first appeared as "Wie säubere ich einen Linoleumboden?" Ein Beitrag zur Alltags- und Gesellschaftsgeschichte der Zwanziger Jahre" in Berliner Geschichtswerkstatt (ed.), *Alltagskultur, Subjektivität und Geschichte,* 235–53 (Münster, 1994).

Chapter 5, "The Social Rationalization of Domestic Life and House-work in Germany and the United States in the 1920s," first appeared as "Social Rationalization of Living and Housework in Germany and United States in the 1920s" in *History of the Family: An International Quarterly* 2, no. 1 (1997): 73–97.

Chapter 6, "The Poor and Homeless of Hanover in the Weimar Repub-lic: The World of Gertrude Polley," first appeared as "Arme und Obdachlose in Hannover" in Hans-Dieter Schmid (ed.), *Hannover: Am Rande der Stadt,* 221–55 (Bielefeld, 1992).

Chapter 7, "A Sensation Comes to Naught": Gertrude Polley at the Cen-ter of a Discourse" by Adelheid von Saldern, Karen Heinze, and Sybille Kuster, first appeared as "Eine Sensation stößt ins Leere": Gertrude Polley im Mittelpunkt eines Diskurses" in Adelheid von Saldern, *Neues Wohnen in Hannover: Wohnungspolitik und Wohnkultur im Hannover der Weimarer Republik,* 69–95 (Hanover, 1993).

Chapter 8, "Sports and Public Culture: The Opening Ceremonies of the Hanover Stadium in 1922," first appeared as "Sport und Öffentlich-keitskultur: Die Einweihungsfeier des hannoverschen Stadions im Jahre 1922" in Hans-Dieter Schmid (ed.), *Feste und Feiern in Hannover,* 173–211 (Bielefeld, 1995).

Chapter 9, "Popular Culture: An Immense Challenge in the Weimar Republic," first appeared as "Massenkultur im Visier: Ein Beitrag zu den Deutungs- und Einwirkungsversuchen in der Weimarer Republik" in *Archiv für Sozialgeschichte* 33 (1993): 21–58.

Chapter 10, "Art for the People": From Cultural Conservatism to Nazi Cultural Policies," first appeared as "Kunst für's Volk": Vom Kul-turkonservatismus zur nationalsozialistischen Kulturpolitik" in Harald Welzer (ed.), *Das Gedächtnis der Bilder: Ästhetik und Nationalsozialis-mus,* 45–104 (Tübingen, 1995).

Chapter 11, "Entertainment, Gender Image, and Cultivating an Audi-ence: Radio in the GDR in the 1950s," first appeared as "Unterhaltung, Geschlechterbilder, Hörerverbindung: Zur Geschichte des Rundfunks in der DDR der fünfziger Jahre," in Adelheid von Saldern *Politik—Stadt—Kultur: Aufsätze zur Gesellschaftsgeschichte des 20. Jahrhunderts,* 205–29 (Hamburg, 1999), ed. Inge Marßolek and Michael Wildt.

Every effort has been made to trace the ownership of all copyrighted material in this book and to obtain permission for its use.

Introduction: The Challenge
of Modernity

Books and articles are always written in particular contexts — the contexts of one's own way of thinking and of developments in historiography in general. There is a complex relationship between the evolution of one's own work and the evolution of the profession as a whole, and I will look more closely in retrospect at some aspects of it in my own case. Over the years, there are many breaks and discontinuities in one's own historical writings and those of the profession. As a result of the passage of time, the past must be reconstructed "in order to take possession of a reality that no longer exists."[1]

Most of the chapters in this volume are set in the Weimar Republic but not all. The first chapter, "Party Centers and Party Hinterlands," deals with Wilhelminian Germany. Chapter 10, "Art for the People," looks at the Third Reich, while chapter 11, "Entertainment, Gender Image, and Cultivating an Audience," focuses on the German Democratic Republic (GDR) in the 1950s. Seen with historical perspective from the late twentieth century, all these politically very different states and societies between 1900 and 1960 seem to have had at least one thing in common: they felt profoundly challenged by modernity; saw great opportunities and dangers in it; and wanted to select what they wished from all that was new, mold it, and adapt it to themselves.[2] Similar

---

1. Reinhart Kosellek, *Vergangene Zukunft* (Frankfurt, 1984), p. 282ff.; cf. also Georg Iggers (ed.), *The Social History of Politics: Critical Perspectives in West German Historical Writing since 1945* (New York, 1985); for another view of historical writing in the Federal Republic, see Bernd Faulenbach, "Deutsche Geschichtswissenschaft nach 1945," *Tijdschrift voor Geschiedenis* 94 (1981): 29–57. I am grateful to Inge Marßolek and David F. Crew for their advice and criticism.

2. The modernizing impulses have again become very rapid and intense since the 1960s, and they changed the Federal Republic considerably.

impulses existed beforehand and afterward, of course, but one of the basic tenets of this work is that the attempts to shape and channel cultural modernity were particularly intense between 1900 and 1960 and characteristic of the societies of this time.[3]

There are certainly some problems with the term *modernity*. Like many other labels, it is fuzzy and ill defined. We need to distinguish between "modernity" in the broad sense, stretching back to the Enlightenment,[4] and a more narrow sense that sets the beginnings of "modernity" around the turn of the last century (1880–1930).[5] The latter origins, which are particularly relevant here, have been described as follows: "The modern world, which still shapes the society in which we live, emerged in the decades between 1880 and 1930, when the mood varied between a euphoric belief in progress and the melancholy conviction that the world was bound to collapse. The rise of modernity pitched contemporaries into a very different world, in which new ways of perceiving and behaving were emerging."[6] Modern art forms developed in a reciprocal relationship with the deep-seated social changes, as well as a host of unfamiliar cultural practices that were often considered the height of fashion and very American — for instance, jazz. What some saw as a creative cultural departure, others perceived as a challenge and a threat, especially the older generations, which felt unsettled by cultural modernity and wanted to channel and shape it in accordance with their own views. Some people even equated cultural modernity with a great social crisis. The disputes over cultural modernity were never so divisive as in the 1920s, and they climaxed during the all-enveloping crisis (*Gesamtkrise*) in the final years of the Weimar Republic. The Bauhaus movement, for instance, became

---

3. Although in a weakened form compared with efforts in the 1950s and 1960s, firm direct attempts to guide modernity continued in the GDR in the following decades, in contrast to the situation in the Federal Republic. This is another indication of the separate path taken by the GDR since the 1960s.

4. Cf. in this regard Max Horkheimer and Theodor W. Adorno, *Dialectic of Enlightenment* (New York, 1944).

5. Cf. also the title of the educational radio broadcast "Jahrhundertwende: Der Aufbruch in die Moderne 1880–1930" and the eponymous two volumes (Reinbek, 1990), edited by August Nitschke, Gerhard A. Ritter, Detlev J. K. Peukert, and Rüdiger vom Bruch.

6. (Text on the flap of the book jacket of "Jahrhundertwende," mentioned in footnote 5.) For the various conceptions of modernity (and postmodernity) see as well for instance Wolfgang Welsch, *Unsere postmoderne Moderne* (Mannheim, 1987), especially 77; cf. Geoff Eley, "Die deutsche Geschichte und die Widersprüche der Moderne: Das Beispiel des Kaiserreiches," in Frank Bajohr, Werner Johe, and Uwe Lohalm (eds.), *Zivilisation und Barbarei: Die widersprüchlichen Potentiale der Moderne: Gedenkschrift für Detlev J. K. Peukert* (Hamburg, 1991), 17ff.

embroiled in a cultural war that is virtually incomprehensible today, in which symbolism played a major role.

The Nazis benefited in the end from all the cultural infighting and offered what passed for their own synthesis. "Reactionary moderniza- tion," in Herf's words, or "the pathology of modernity," in the words of Peukert, were attempts to find a term to describe these developments. Terms like these can only be acceptable under two conditions. First, there must be some recognition of the fact that historical writing be- comes cramped and limited if it works with a loaded concept of "moder- nity," that is, one that is closely associated with the ideals of the Enlight- enment and therefore entirely positive. Expressed the other way around and with particular reference to the Third Reich, modernity was *insepar- ably* bound up with barbarism.[7] Historians no longer see the Holocaust as a result of irrational, premodern barbarism. Modernity itself is thought now to harbor many possibilities, one of which is certainly barbarism. In light of their experiences with National Socialism in the 1940s, Theodor W. Adorno and Max Horkheimer pointed long ago to the danger of instrumental reason falling into the service of totalitarian governments. More recently, Zygmunt Bauman in particular has studied the ambiva- lent effects of the zeal for planning and doing all that can be done.[8] Second, it is not very helpful to think in terms of opposites: modernity here and antimodernity there. Usually we face blends and amalgams that are specific to particular times and social systems and must be thoroughly studied in their own right. The chapters in this volume are a contribution to this end.[9]

I

The initial two chapters fall into the category of the history of the labor movement. We look first at the Social Democratic Party (SPD) in Wil- helminian times, especially its social milieus and organizational culture. The differing paces of modernization in the party's centers and hinter- lands are studied—a result of the asynchronous evolution of the econ- omy, society, cultures, and mentalities. We also look at the extent to

---

7. Eley, "Die deutsche Geschichte"; David F. Crew, "General Introduction," in David F. Crew (ed.), *Nazism and German Society 1933–1945* (London and New York, 1994), 24.

8. Horkheimer and Adorno, *Dialectic of Enlightenment;* Zygmunt Bauman, *Dialek- tik der Ordnung: Die Moderne und der Holocaust* (Hamburg, 1992).

9. The following comments refer solely to those of my research interests that are apparent in the chapters in this volume. Missing most notably is my research into the middle class and National Socialism.

which the SPD adopted the trend toward centralization, bureaucracy, and hierarchy in the hope of increasing its efficiency, although the results seem only mixed and ambivalent when viewed from our present perspective.

The second chapter concentrates on how the leaderships of two major parties, the Social Democrats and Communists, perceived and responded to the beginnings of the modernization of work and everyday life, social milieus, and politics in the 1920s. We also look in this connection at the divisions in the labor movement and its efforts at united action and compare our conclusions with those of contemporaries. It is obvious that central aspects of the history of the labor movement must also be reappraised in light of German reunification. How this reappraisal will ultimately turn out remains to be seen.[10]

The two chapters on the history of the labor movement represent one of my long-standing areas of interest, going back to the 1960s.[11] At that time, only a few studies were beginning to emerge on the topic.[12] The student movement of 1968–69 sparked greater interest in the history of the labor movement on both my part and that of historians in general.[13]

---

10. Two questions are up for discussion. First, should the especially well-developed socialism under the German Empire be interpreted primarily as a reaction to the petrified, undemocratic conditions prevailing at the time, or was socialism not only a reaction but a social utopia as well? The former point of view is advocated by Klaus Tenfelde, *Die Geschichtsschreibung über die deutsche Arbeiterbewegung am Ende des 20. Jahrhunderts: Bestandsaufnahmen, Probleme, Perspektiven* (brochure, in press). Similar thoughts are expressed in Tenfelde, "Europäische Arbeiterbewegung im 20. Jahrhundert," in Dieter Dowe (ed.), *Demokratischer Sozialismus in Europa seit dem Zweiten Weltkrieg,* 9–41 (Bonn, 2001). Second, how should the Communist labor movement of the 1920s be accommodated in general German history? In Tenfelde's paper, the Communist movement is marginalized and portrayed only in very general form. See in this regard the different approach of Klaus-Michael Mallmann, *Kommunisten in der Weimarer Republik: Sozialgeschichte einer revolutionären Bewegung* (Darmstadt, 1996). Mallmann writes political social history "from below," which puts the Communist movement in a new light.

11. I had been working on *Vom Einwohner zum Bürger: Emanzipation der städtischen Unterschicht 1890–1920: Eine kommunal- und sozialhistorische Untersuchung* (Berlin, 1973) since 1967. The idea for this book was taken from Gerhard A. Ritter, *Die Arbeiterbewegung im Wilhelminischen Reich: Die Sozialdemokratische Partei und die Freien Gewerkschaften 1890–1900,* 2d ed. (Berlin, 1963). Prior to Ritter's study, the labor movement almost never appeared in the literature as a subject in its own right.

12. Besides Ritter, *Arbeiterbewegung,* see also Eberhard Kolb, *Die Arbeiterräte in der deutschen Innenpolitik 1918–1919* (Düsseldorf, 1962); Helga Grebing, *Geschichte der deutschen Arbeiterbewegung* (Munich, 1968); Hans-Christoph Schröder, "Sozialismus und Imperialismus: Die Auseinandersetzung der deutschen Sozialdemokratie mit dem Imperialismusproblem und der 'Weltpolitik' vor 1914" (Ph.D. diss., Cologne, 1966); Hans-Joseph Steinberg, *Sozialismus und deutsche Sozialdemokratie: Zur Ideologie der Partei vor dem 1. Weltkrieg* (Hanover, 1967).

13. I probably would not have written a second book about the labor movement if not for a lucky find in the sources: the internal minutes of local SPD meetings. It took

Here was a topic that could provoke the historical establishment of the day and distance one from the dull anti-Communism of the Cold War, a topic that was associated with many kinds of political hopes and through which one could explore, with mounting self-confidence, intellectual traditions well off the beaten track.[14] Workers and the labor movement were seen potentially as crucial subjects in the history of the transformation of capitalist, industrial societies into democratic, socialist ones, and Karl Marx was considered a great pioneer in the analysis of class society. The student movement caused a boom in the market (!) for left-wing socialist and unorthodox Marxist literature, which radically changed the literary culture of the Federal Republic in the late 1960s and early 1970s.[15] The impulses that it generated extended far beyond the political Left, although the "guild" of professional historians remained relatively unmoved by the changes in what people were reading and discussing. Nevertheless, the "guild" was sufficiently influenced by the student movement to accept the history of the labor movement as a serious subject and respectable area of interest. This probably would have happened eventually without the students but presumably in a slower and more limited way. The type of Marxist-oriented histories of the labor movement being written in the English-speaking countries remained definitely beyond the pale, however, and certainly not career enhancing. Any Marxist-oriented histories of the labor movement that did appear in the Federal Republic were written in the main by political scientists[16] and were regarded by

longer to evaluate them than originally planned because they were hard to decipher. Adelheid von Saldern, *Auf dem Wege zum Arbeiterreformismus: Parteialltag in sozialdemokratischer Provinz: Göttingen 1870–1920* (Frankfurt, 1984). For a short version: idem, "Latent Reformism and Socialist Utopia: The SPD in Göttingen 1900–1920," in Eric D. Weitz and David E. Barclay (eds.), *Between Reform and Revolution: Studies in the History of German Socialism and Communism from 1840 to 1990* (Oxford and Providence, 1998), 195–221.

14. Limitations of space prevent further discussion here of the other topic that raised a storm within the historical guild before the advent of the student movement, namely, Fritz Fischer's theories on responsibility for the outbreak of the First World War. Fritz Fischer, *Germany's Aims in the First World War* (London, 1966); originally published as *Die Kriegszielpolitik des kaiserlichen Deutschland 1914/18* (Düsseldorf, 1961).

15. In my book on the middle classes in the Third Reich I took a hard look at Marxist-oriented views and compared them with empirical findings. Adelheid von Saldern, *Mittelstand im "Dritten Reich": Bauern, Handwerker, Einzelhändler* (Frankfurt and New York, 1979); idem, "The Old *Mittelstand*, 1890–1939: How 'Backward' Were the Artisans?" *Central European History* 25, no. 1 (1992): 27–51; idem, "Mittelschichten und Konservatismus in historischer und aktueller Perspektive," in Heinrich Espkamp et al. (eds.), *Die neokonservative Verheißung und ihr Preis* (Cologne, 1989), p. 66–104.

16. For instance before the student movement: Wolfgang Abendroth, *Aufstieg und Krise der deutschen Sozialdemokratie* (Frankfurt, 1964); Georg Fülberth and Jürgen Harrer, *Die deutsche Sozialdemokratie* (Darmstadt and Neuwied, 1974). It was also primarily

West German historians as far too crude for them. The historians avoided the debates and clash of scholarly opinions over Marxism, especially the unorthodox variety, by throwing themselves into exceedingly painstaking empirical studies. If West German historians dealt with Marxism at all, it was with that practiced in the GDR, from which they could easily distance themselves.[17] More intellectual effort would have been needed to take issue with the kind of unorthodox Marxism emerging in England, but it was assiduously ignored for the most part. As late as 1980, Dieter Groh could still comment on the astounding lack of response in Germany to Eduard P. Thompson's *The Making of the English Working Class* (Harmondsworth, 1963). At the time even less notice was taken of Perry Anderson, Raymond Williams, Stuart Hall, Christopher Hill, and Eric Hobsbown.[18]

In the late 1970s, interest shifted from the political history of the labor movement to the history of the workers' cultural movement.[19] Insofar as my own research was concerned, Raymond Williams contributed enormously to expanding my concept of culture in connection with the history of the labor movement, despite the danger of pushing it too far. As I wrote at the time: "Workers' culture refers on the one hand to everyday life, to how workers lived and dressed, and to what they did in their spare time, and on the other to alternative 'ideas about the nature of social relations' and to the development of alternative political prac-

---

political scientists who studied fascism from a Marxist perspective, for example, Reinhard Kühnl, *Formen bürgerlicher Herrschaft* (Reinbek, 1971); Eike Henning, *Bürgerliche Gesellschaft und Faschismus in Deutschland: Ein Forschungsbericht* (Frankfurt, 1977).

17. Sometimes, though, literature from the GDR was read for its empirical value. This was especially true of the research into the resistance to National Socialism.

18. Groh was one of the great exceptions: Dieter Groh, "Zur Einführung," in Eduard P. Thompson (ed.), *Plebeische Kultur und moralische Ökonomie: Aufsätze zur englischen Sozialgeschichte des 18. und 19. Jahrhunderts* (Frankfurt, 1980), 5ff.

19. Gerhard A. Ritter, "Arbeiterkultur im Deutschen Kaiserreich: Probleme und Forschungsansätze," in idem (ed.), *Arbeiterkultur* (Königstein, 1979), 15–39. A first version of this article was published as "Worker's Culture in Imperial Germany: Problems and Points of Departure for Research," *Journal of Contemporary History* 13, no. 2 (1978): 165–89; Brigitte Emig, *Die Veredelung des Arbeiters: Sozialdemokratie als Kulturbewegung* (Frankfurt, 1980): see Adelheid von Saldern, "Arbeiterkulturbewegung in Deutschland in der Zwischenkriegszeit," in Friedhelm Boll (ed.), *Arbeiterkulturen zwischen Alltag und Politik: Beiträge zum europäischen Vergleich in der Zwischenkriegszeit* (Vienna, 1986), 29–71. At the same time and in the following years, there were more and more studies of individual groups of workers. Miners were probably the most studied group. See in this regard Klaus Tenfelde, *Sozialgeschichte der Bergarbeiterschaft an der Ruhr im 19. Jahrhundert* (Bonn, 1977); Franz-Josef Brüggemeier, *Leben vor Ort: Ruhrbergleute und Ruhrbergbau 1889–1919*, 2d ed. (Munich, 1984); for longshoremen and shipyard workers see Michael Grüttner, *Arbeitswelt an der Wasserkante: Sozialgeschichte der Hamburger Hafenarbeiter 1886–1914* (Göttingen, 1984).

tices arising from the need of workers to make major changes to their living and working conditions."[20] The formation of organizations such as the Social Democratic Party, labor unions, and the various workers' cooperatives and associations was therefore a *cultural* achievement. From this perspective, I found the organizational history of the labor movement beginning to mesh with its cultural history, as can be seen in chapter 1. At the same time, my awareness of public proletarian culture was growing. Already sensitized by Habermas's *Strukturwandel der Öffentlichkeit*,[21] I was influenced by the book of Oskar Negt and Alexander Kluge[22] and undertook to study proletarian publics as a part of the political culture and relate them to the hegemonic culture (Antonio Gramsci's term). As I said in 1983: "The measure to use in assessing the maturity of a proletarian public is . . . the initiatives that connect all areas of life with each other."[23] Elsewhere I said: "Workers adopt some of the forms and substances of the hegemonic culture and appropriate them."[24] My awareness at the time of the complexity of the appropriation process and the variety of possible interpretations and explanations saved me from the widespread concept of embourgeoisement[25] and later served me well in the reception of "cultural studies" in the English-speaking countries.

II

Some of the chapters presented here fall into the category of urban history. My interest in urban history goes back to the mid-1960s, when there was still some question about whether it could be a fit subject for serious historians. It was considered especially dubious when the particular subject was not yet included in the regular canon of professional historians, for instance, the history of the labor movement.[26] However,

---

20. Von Saldern, *Auf dem Wege,* 130. Raymond Williams, *Culture and Society 1780–1950* (London, 1958).

21. Jürgen Habermas, *Strukturwandel der Öffentlichkeit: Untersuchungen zu einer Kategorie der bürgerlichen Gesellschaft* (Darmstadt and Neuwied, 1962).

22. Oskar Negt and Alexander Kluge, *Öffentlichkeit und Erfahrung: Zur Organisationsanalyse von bürgerlicher und proletarischer Öffentlichkeit* (Frankfurt, 1972).

23. Von Saldern, *Auf dem Wege,* 163.

24. Ibid., 130.

25. According to embourgeoisement concept, particular social strata, in this case workers, adapt their lifestyles and cultural interpretations of the world to those of the bourgeoisie.

26. Examples of histories of local labor movements from the early days are the following: Hugo Eckert, *Liberal- oder Sozialdemokratie: Frühgeschichte der Nürnberger Arbeiterbewegung* (Stuttgart, 1968); Karl-Ernst Moring, "Reformismus und Radikalismus in der Sozialdemokratischen Partei Bremens von 1890–1914" (Ph.D. diss., Hamburg,

urban history quickly established itself and by the 1970s could no longer be omitted in the Federal Republic from social and economic history; political history; and most of all, the history of the resistance.[27]

The "dig where you stand" movement[28] began around 1980 and was soon subsumed by the idea of history workshops.[29] In the late 1980s, I attempted to incorporate history workshops into our everyday life at the university and, as part of our practice-oriented history curriculum at the University of Hanover, initiated a project with students that lasted for several years and took the form of various modules. A number of students were undertaken of the topic "urban culture and different milieus in Hanover in the early twentieth century."[30] These research modules

---

1968); Heinrich Karl Schmitz, *Anfänge und Entwicklung der Arbeiterbewegung im Raum Düsseldorf* (Hanover, 1968). Finally, in 2000 an association of urban history was founded that should create an interdisciplinary network among urban historians.

27. A good example because not narrowly confined to the resistance: Inge Marßolek and René Ott, *Bremen im Dritten Reich: Anpassung, Widerstand, Verfolgung* (Bremen, 1986).

28. The book was written by the Swede Sven Lindquist (Studier av halka pêa vägar [Goteburg, 1979]). See in this regard Hannes Heer and Volker Ullrich (eds.), *Geschichte entdecken: Erfahrungen und Projekte der neuen Geschichtsbewegung* (Hamburg, 1985), which was the first overview published after the great History Workshop Fest in Berlin in 1984.

29. The direct lead-up to the history workshop movement, in which I was personally involved, was closely connected to the history department of the University of Hanover. The idea, advanced primarily by Hans Heinrich Nolte, of founding a critical, leftist historical journal did not rally enough support in the end at two rather small meetings in Hanover and Bremen around 1980. Instead, it was decided to build up a network using a newsletter system. After the network was established, the West German History Workshops were established at a meeting in Göttingen in November 1982 as a federation of the numerous history workshops operating successfully on the local level. The history workshop movement is not as prominent now as it used to be in many places, while the journal *WerkstattGeschichte* (Hamburg) has consolidated itself in a more professional form than earlier workshop journals and gained a consistent readership.

30. In addition to an exhibition on leisure culture in the 1920s, the project "Lebenswelten und Stadtkultur im Hannover des frühen 20. Jahrhunderts" has generated the following publications: Geschichtswerkstatt Hannover (ed.), *Alltag zwischen Hindenburg und Haarmann: Ein anderer Stadtführer durch das Hannover der 20er Jahre* (Hamburg, 1987); Adelheid von Saldern (ed.), *Stadt und Moderne: Hannover in der Weimarer Republik* (Hamburg, 1989); Sid Auffarth and Adelheid von Saldern (eds.), *Wochenend und schöner Schein: Freizeit und modernes Leben in den Zwanziger Jahren: Das Beispiel Hannover* (Berlin, 1991); Adelheid von Saldern and Sid Auffarth (eds.), *Altes und Neues Wohnen: Linden und Hannover im frühen 20. Jahrhundert* (Seelze-Velber, 1992); Adelheid von Saldern, *Neues Wohnen: Wohnungspolitik und Wohnkultur im Hannover der Zwanziger Jahre* (Hanover, 1993); the sound and slide show *Frieda* (with accompanying booklet); Richard Birkefeld and Martina Jung, *Die Stadt, der Lärm, und Licht: Die Veränderung des öffentlichen Raumes durch Motorisierung und Elektrifizierung* (Seelze-Velber, 1994). Many of the studies were coheaded by the architectural historian Sid Auffarth of the University of Hanover, whom I want to thank for fruitful cooperation.

were also intended to ease the way of graduate students into the life of professional historians.[31] One module in this local history project that stands out in particular was the fictitious story *Frieda*, a sound and slide show for schools.[32] It attempted to highlight the implications of the fact that all historical writing is fictitious[33] (an insight/ideal/consideration that was much discussed at the time), while also pointing out the differences from pure fiction. A story was constructed that seemed believable but never actually happened. It could have, though, because the problems raised and various facts included were taken from a solid study of historical sources and the literature. The clash of various (sub)cultures in Hanover in the 1920s was depicted through the main character, "Frieda," her parents, brother, and friends. The clashing subcultures included labor movement culture, popular culture, traditional middle-class culture, and the everyday culture of working people.

Alongside the various studies of local social and cultural history, I returned again and again to the subject of municipal government, its accomplishments and its failings.[34] The study *Vom Einwohner zum Bürger* (From inhabitant to citizen), begun in the late 1960s, focused largely on the roles played by the class-based organizations formed by workers in the municipality of Göttingen in Wilhelminian times.[35] I also attempted to piece together the areas in which workers were allowed to participate in finding solutions to municipal problems. This topic has again become current under the heading of "citizenship." My case study showed that if municipal governments took any interest at all in social problems in Wilhelminian times, they adopted a very paternalistic approach. Although municipalities in Prussia were more resistant than those in southern Germany to the extension of voting rights, they

31. It was especially informative to develop and carry out the exhibition, which was connected with practical training as an integral part of the curriculum for the Magister Artium degree in history at the University of Hanover.

32. Lending no. 1540225/26; twenty-four minutes, eighty slides; accompanying booklet: Adelheid von Saldern et al., *Ein Tag im Leben der Frieda: Eine Fiction-Story,* ed. NLVwA-Landesmedienstelle Hannover (Hanover, 1991).

33. See in this regard Kosellek, *Vergangene Zukunft.*

34. For the most recent study, see the following overview: Adelheid von Saldern, "Geschichte der kommunalen Selbstverwaltung in Deutschland," in Ronald Roth and Hellmut Wollmann (eds.), *Kommunalpolitik: Politisches Handeln in den Gemeinden* (Opladen, 1994), 2–19; see also Adelheid von Saldern, "Kommunale Verarmung und Armut in den Kommunen während der großen Krise 1928 bis 1933: Am Beispiel der Finanz- und Wohnungs(bau)politik," in *Soziale Bewegungen: Jahrbuch 3* (Frankfurt, 1987), 69–110.

35. Von Saldern, *Vom Einwohner zum Bürger.* Cf. idem, "Wilhelminische Gesellschaft und Arbeiteklasse: Emanzipations- und Integrationsprozesse im kulturellen und sozialen Bereich," *Internationale Wissenschaftliche Korrespondenz zur Geschichte der deutschen Arbeiterbewegung (IWK)* 13, no. 4 (1977): 469–506.

proved more receptive to industrial conflict resolution, that is, to the institutionalization of industrial relations. Committees were established and chaired by a government official, with equal representation of management and labor.[36] Municipal governments, however, showed little interest before 1914 in solving the housing problem.[37] The altogether very limited opportunity for workers to participate in municipal politics, especially in Prussia, strengthened the tendency in the SPD to focus all its hopes for gaining power on Reich politics rather than on municipalities.[38] The inclination of the party grass roots to concentrate on Reich politics was confirmed by my second microstudy of Göttingen.[39]

III

I gravitated toward Alltagsgeschichte (the history of everyday life) and Milieugeschichte (the history of various milieus) from two starting points, namely, local history and the history of the labor movement. My book *Auf dem Wege zum Arbeiterreformismus* (1984) reconstructed daily life within the Social Democratic Party on the local level and was therefore a particular kind of Alltagsgeschichte. As a result of the strong social disapproval of the SPD in Wilhelminian times, there was a tension between everyday life in general and life within the party. Anyone who joined the SPD was breaking traditional patterns and taking an extraordinary step,[40] around which his interests and needs would start to revolve. Once they became members, many men included organizational work for

36. We should mention the trade courts and arbitration committees in this connection. For the ability of municipal governments to modernize, see George Steinmetz, *Regulating the Social: The Welfare State and Local Politics in Imperial Germany* (Princeton, 1993).

37. I wrote various articles about this, including "Kommunalpolitik und Arbeiterwohnungsbau im Deutschen Kaiserreich," in Lutz Niethammer (ed.), *Wohnen im Wandel: Beiträge zur Geschichte des Alltags in der bügerlichen Gesellschaft* (Wuppertal, 1979).

38. "Die Gemeinde in Theorie und Praxis der deutschen Arbeiterorganisation 1863–1920," in *IWK* 12, no. 3 (1976): 295–353.

39. Von Saldern, *Auf dem Wege*.

40. I relied primarily at the time on a concept of everyday life, as developed by Antonio Gramsci and Agnes Heller and in Germany by people of the critical Left such as Thomas Leithäuser. The everyday activities of subjects were depicted as full of alienation, routine, and cliché. The thought patterns of the vast majority of people were often assumed to be "petty, hostile to change, and conservative." Cf. von Saldern, *Auf dem Wege*, 20–22. Later, the "thoughts and activities of everyday life" were seen in a more neutral or even positive light, just as subjectivity received a value in itself and a new emphasis. See also Alf Lüdtke, "Einleitung: Was ist und wer treibt Alltagsgeschichte?" in Alf Lüdtke (ed.), *Alltagsgeschichte: Zur Rekonstruktion historischer Erfahrungen und Lebensweisen* (Frankfurt and New York, 1989), 9–48.

the SPD in their regular routines. Women were not allowed to join political parties until 1908, but those who joined the SPD thereafter experienced even more difficulty than the men because of the added problem of having to reconcile their interests and everyday experiences as women with the interests and life of the party. The SPD also often had strained relations with individual workers, who were inclined to be rough and engage in behaviors that conflicted with the everyday norms of the party, for instance, in regard to discipline and order.

The relationship between everyday life and the party organization is often treated in historical studies under the heading "social-moral milieus."[41] Various milieus were heavily influenced by particular religions, regional traditions, economic situations, and cultural orientations. The assumption is that similar experiences in life and similar convictions fostered similar political orientations and vice versa. The study of reciprocal influences breathes life in the truest sense of the word into sociological studies and studies of the history of political parties, as well as the history of the labor movement. The disadvantage of the term *social-moral milieu* is that the strains that often existed between everyday life and particular political organizations tend to be overlooked, in addition to the tensions that erupted when different organizations, such as the KPD (Communist Party of Germany) and SPD, attempted to take the same social milieus under their wings. Another question that is generally disregarded is how relevant the workers' parties and cultural associations actually were to the everyday lives of working people, in particular women, in the 1920s.[42]

Since the 1980s issues of this kind led me to the history of housing and domestic culture and made me especially receptive to the ways in which space was appropriated in everyday life.[43] The change of topic

---

41. Especially influential was the article by M. Rainer Lepsius, "Parteiensystem und Sozialstruktur: Zum Problem der Demokratisierung der deutschen Gesellschaft," in Gerhard A. Ritter (ed.), *Die deutschen Parteien vor 1918* (Cologne, 1973); Mallmann, *Kommunisten;* Adelheid von Saldern, "Sozialmilieus und der Aufstieg des Nationalsozialismus in Norddeutschland (1930–1933)," in Frank Bajohr (ed.), *Norddeutschland im Nationalsozialismus* (Hamburg, 1993), 20–52.

42. A controversy erupted over this question, especially in regard to the influence of the workers' cultural associations. Adelheid von Saldern, "Sozialmilieus und Massenkultur in der Zwischenkriegszeit: Das Beispiel Hannover," in Karljosef Kreter and Gerhard Schneider (eds.), *Stadt und Überlieferung: Festschrift für Klaus Mlynek* (Hanover, 1999), 183–200.

43. See especially Paul-Henry Chombart de Lauwe, "Aneignung, Eigentum, Enteignung," *Arch+* 9, no. 34 (1977): 2–6; Orvar Löfgren, "Trautes Heim (The sweetness of home): Veränderung des Familienideals in Schweden des 20. Jahrhunderts," in Peter Borscheid and Hans J. Teuteberg (eds.), *Ehe, Liebe, Tod: Zum Wandel der Familie, der Geschlechts- und Generationsbeziehungen in der Neuzeit* (Münster, 1983), 91ff. Michel de

proved fruitful as new and different questions emerged, oversimplifica-
tions were exposed, and domestic culture was understood as a complex
appropriation of the available spaces and objects, the meaning of which
had to be determined. One gains a sense of intimacy with spaces
through the appropriation of them. This means that spaces often have
to be reinterpreted and aligned to some extent with one's subjective
imagination of them. Feelings of estrangement fade as particular colors,
shapes, sounds, smells, and patterns of light and shadow are repeatedly
perceived. Spaces are also appropriated through the communications
carried on within them, including conflicts. There are not only social
aspects to the shaping and appropriation of spaces but gender and generational aspects as well. The appropriation of spaces and the objects in
them plays an important role in social integration, social distinctions,
and the formation of one's identity.[44]

The research still reflects the fact that housing and domestic life
were, and often still are, seen as private matters. Some pioneering studies
appeared in the late 1970s,[45] but for the most part, professional historians
did not take much interest in the history of the home.[46] Housing and
domestic life were included in the long-established history of the family,[47]
although here too they tended to be marginalized. The situation changed
as the history of women came to the fore, and the work and everyday life
of mothers and housewives were studied, although the home itself did not
figure especially prominently. The home can be seen as the intersection of
a host of interests, whether private or public, political or social, group or

---

Certeau, *L'intervention de quotidien: Arts de faire* (Paris, 1980); Lüdtke, "Einleitung";
Geoff Eley, "Geschichte der Arbeiterbewegung — Sozialgeschichte — Alltagsgeschichte:
Erfahrung, Kultur, und die Politik des Alltags: Eine neue Richtung für die neue deutsche
Sozialgeschichte," in Geoff Eley, *Wilhelminismus, Nationalismus, Faschismus: Zur historischen Kontinuität in Deutschland* (Münster, 1991), 269–79; David F. Crew, "Alltagsgeschichte: A New Social History 'from Below'?" *Central European History* 22, no. 3–4
(1989): 394–407.

44. There are some remarkable attempts now in German cities to provide support
for the appropriation of living quarters and, in doing so, to encourage citizen initiatives
and self-organization. One example is the second City Forum I organized in Hanover,
which was held on June 21, 1996.

45. Lutz Niethammer with Franz-Josef Brüggemeier, "Wie wohnten Arbeiter im
Kaiserreich?" *Archiv für Sozialgeschichte* 16 (1976): 122–34; Niethammer, *Wohnen im
Wandel.*

46. One exception is Special Research Area 164, "comparative historical urban
research," at the University of Münster. Some studies were also carried out here of the
history of housing and domestic life, and conferences were organized. See for instance
Clemens Wischermann, *Wohnen in Hamburg vor dem Ersten Weltkrieg* (Münster, 1983).

47. See Tamara K. Hareven, "The History of the Family and the Complexity of
Social Change," *American Historical Review* 96, no. 1 (1991): 95ff.

individual. A five-volume history of the home[48] perhaps is a first great milestone in this core area of Alltagsgeschichte.[49] This study and others like it will highlight the historicity of housing and domestic life, capture the breaks and continuities and the complex interactions between subjects and their social surroundings, make a start on describing the multifarious appropriation processes, and help to define what was private and what was public at the time. The discussion surrounding the formation and disintegration of social classes is affected, and light is cast on the numerous ideological and social policy implications of domestic life and the construction of housing, especially in the modern era.

IV

My research interests shifted again when cultural aspects of the situation became apparent and challenged social history. Critical social history became firmly established in the early 1970s and was long thought by many, including myself, to epitomize the progress in historical writings since the 1950s and 1960s.[50] While social history emphasizes structures and processes and tends to disregard social agents and subjectivities, new cultural history highlights cultural practices and individual subjects, in what they did and how they saw the world. In some instances, social history is now edging closer to cultural history (and vice versa), and power relationships, for instance, are being studied not only as social phenomena but as cultural phenomena as well.[51] The distance that mainstream German historiography has traveled since as recently as the mid-1980s can be seen, for example, in Heinrich August Winkler's criticisms of my book on the middle classes in the Third Reich.[52] He vehemently attacked the section on social climbing, rituals, and honors, which I based on Bourdieu's insights and where I concluded that these factors

48. The overview of the history of housing and domestic life *Geschichte des Wohnens:* vol. 3, *1800–1918: Das bürgerliche Zeitalter,* ed. Jürgen Reulecke (Stuttgart, 1997); vol. 4, *1918–1945: Reform, Reaktion, Zerstörung,* ed. Gert Kähler (Stuttgart, 1996); vol. 5, *Von 1945 bis heute,* ed. Ingeborg Flagge (Stuttgart, 1999).

49. Cf. as well Adelheid von Saldern, *Häuserleben: Zur Geschichte städtischen Arbeiterwohnens vom Kaiserreich bis heute* (Bonn, 1995).

50. See Ute Daniel, "'Kultur' und 'Gesellschaft': Überlegungen zum Gegenstandsbereich der Sozialgeschichte," *Geschichte und Gesellschaft* 19, no. 1 (1993): 69–100.

51. See in this regard Alf Lüdtke, "Einleitung: Herrschaft als soziale Praxis," in idem (ed.), *Herrschaft als soziale Praxis* (Göttingen, 1991); Nicholas B. Dirks, Geoff Eley, and Sherry B. Ortner (eds.), *Culture/Power/History: A Reader in Contemporary Social Theory* (Princeton, 1994); David F. Crew, *Germans on Welfare: From Weimar to Hitler* (New York and Oxford, 1998).

52. Von Saldern, *Mittelstand.*

may well have influenced people in ways favorable to the National Social-ist regime.[53]

Thanks to the stimulus of research in the fields of cultural sociology and social anthropology, historians are now taking the influence of sym-bols seriously, even in the apparently very rational modern era. New cultural history attributes symbolic value even to the ordinary objects of everyday life. Automobiles, flowerpots, furniture, and radios are no longer studied just as objects; researchers are now interested in the ways that people relate to these objects and the ways in which objects function as media for communication between people.[54] The wide-spread theories in Germany of embourgeoisement are strictly phenome-nological in outlook and overlook gendered interpretations and the interpretations of particular social strata.[55] The insights of the French cultural sociologist Pierre Bourdieu into "subtle distinction"[56] cannot simply be transferred without significant alteration to other times and societies, including Germany. However, I found his work very stimulat-ing, especially his thoughts about the transfer of various "kinds of capi-tal." The different activities and areas of one's life, from family to occupation, from income to pastimes, and from education to consump-tion, form a nexus that determines, reflects, and reproduces one's social status (i.e., that of men)[57] and their families. In other words, historians of the twentieth century are also beginning to take an interest in the interaction among economics, cultural practices, education, and one's position in society. The sensitivity to subtle distinction has generally increased. In modern twentieth-century societies, where almost all cul-tural products and articles of consumption are available to everybody, at least theoretically, and where choices are based "solely" on price and personal taste, the symbolic languages that cement one's social identity and differentiate social strata and groups become increasingly subtle.[58] Finally, Bourdieu's thoughts about habitus have helped us to under-

53. See the discussion in *Geschichte und Gesellschaft* 12, no. 2 (1986): 235–43; and 12, no. 4 (1986): 548–57, here 557; von Saldern, *Mittelstand,* 213ff., 226; Pierre Bourdieu, *Zur Soziologie der symbolischen Formen* (Frankfurt, 1974). More recent researchers are inclined to think that Nazi integration strategies were more successful than Winkler thought at the time not only in regard to tradespeople and farmers but also to workers.

54. See for instance Wolfgang Ruppert (ed.), *Fahrrad, Auto, Fernsehschrank: Zur Kulturgeschichte der Alltagsdinge* (Frankfurt, 1993).

55. It is very surprising in this regard that there are hardly any empirical studies of the cultural history of the petite bourgeoisie in the twentieth century.

56. Pierre Bourdieu, *Distinctions: A Social Critique of the Judgement of Taste* (Cam-bridge, MA, and London, 1984).

57. Bourdieu disregards gender, and his approach must therefore be expanded.

58. Bourdieu, *Distinctions.*

stand how it arises and how enduring it is, although little light is shed on when and how habitus can and does change.[59]

New cultural history has contributed not only to the discovery of the inconspicuous and unspectacular, of symbols, and of subtle distinction but also to the broadening of our horizons as historians. General historians are taking more and more interest in architecture, urban planning, music, art, sports, movies, radio, and so forth—all domains that were previously the preserve of specialists in art history or in architecture, sports, or the movies. The interests of historians now frequently infringe on those of cultural sociologists, social anthropologists, and ethnologists. This leads to problems of competence and discipline overlap, which the traditional university structures frequently do not accommodate as well as possible. Nevertheless, the benefits of broadening horizons clearly outweigh the drawbacks as historians examine the historical sources from new angles and take a direct interest in the work of neighboring disciplines. The opportunities for interdisciplinary cooperation have increased immeasurably as a result.

Our task now is to integrate the history of popular culture and leisure more fully into the general social and cultural history of the twentieth century. This kind of integration is also necessary in regard to the Third Reich, because the dominant explanations of the Nazis' success with the mass media concentrated exclusively on manipulation and instrumentalization. This approach was well suited to the theory of totalitarianism, which was so prevalent during the Cold War,[60] while more leftist historians who used similar terms could invoke the authority of the Frankfurt school. Only slowly did historians begin to entertain other approaches, such as those developed in connection with cultural studies in the English-speaking countries, especially in regard to the relationships among the media, power, and the public, which naturally differed between dictatorships and democracy.[61] In looking at popular culture as a contested area in democracy, we ought to stress that the various social classes and groups did not have equal influence on the production of this culture, not only because of the large amounts of investment capital

---

59. Pierre Bourdieu, *Outline of a Theory of Practice* (1977). The concept of habitus is more precise than the concept of mentalities. However, the softer word *mentality* has become more entrenched in the literature than *habitus*.

60. The theory of totalitarianism generally has two distinguishing features: first, the research focuses on the phenomenological similarities between left-wing and right-wing dictatorships, for example, between Nazi Germany and the Soviet Union, and second, the claim to total power is implicitly assumed to be fully effective.

61. See Lawrence Grossberg, Carry Nelson, and Paula Teichler (eds.), *Cultural Studies* (London and New York, 1992); Dirks, Eley, and Ortner, *Culture/Power/History*.

needed but also because of the better chances for those who created and reproduced dominant values and norms.

Another question to be addressed is how the public appropriated popular culture. There are two important aspects. First, the cultural products had to reflect at least some of the perceptions, experiences, and interests of the purchasers or consumers in order to attract their interest. Second, we must recognize that popular culture was appropriated in very different and complex ways, which varied considerably from one person to the next. Although cultural artifacts were obviously not open to any interpretation at all, they could be seen in a variety of lights depending upon one's social class, ethnicity, gender, generation, and personal situation or mental predisposition. Objective artifacts, including media products, and the subjective appropriation of them are no longer considered separate matters but a complex duality riddled with the tensions that run throughout all human activity, including everyday life, power structures, and the media.

New cultural history entered my work primarily through my interest in popular culture and leisure. Until recently, researchers in this area usually worked in a discourse isolated from the discourse used in respect to the workers' cultural movement. The only contacts were those products of popular culture that were embraced by the workers' cultural movement, for instance socially critical films such as *Kuhle Wampe* or the sports taken up by the workers' athletic movement. It was difficult for me and presumably many others to realize that numerous young workers, especially women, greatly preferred trashy movies to union meetings. Once I had noticed this fact, I discovered many sources attesting to it, such as the following complaint from labor unions in 1928: "Many of our members look for leisure activities that will give them some pleasure in life in other areas that . . . lead them away from the life of the union."[62]

Another difficulty with researching popular culture and leisure in the 1920s was the fact that the discussion of important phases of modernization in the twentieth century tended to focus attention upon the 1950s and 1960s. Although this tendency is justified in hindsight, it is much less justified when seen from the viewpoint of the perceptions and experiences of the people at the time. A sense of rapid change depends on one's past experiences, and it is clear that people in the 1920s felt that they were living through a time of immense cultural upheaval. The most important factor in this feeling was the takeoff of popular culture and new leisure activities (chap. 9).

---

62. Quoted in von Saldern, "Arbeiterkulturbewegung," 62.

It is also difficult to entertain two apparently contradictory ideas at the same time, namely, the obvious poverty of many workers as a result of the economic crises in Germany and yet their mounting consumption of popular culture. My collaboration with Dietrich Mühlberg's group at the Berlin Humboldt Universität on the cultural history of the labor movement proved very helpful in this regard. Mühlberg was looking at the "new interests of changed people" in the wake of the modernization of work and everyday life after the turn of the century. Our lively discussions led finally, under the cultural agreement between East and West Germany[63] that came into effect shortly before the Wende, to official visits back and forth, the holding of two conferences in East and West, the exchange of two exhibitions,[64] and the publication of an article that we coauthored.[65]

The chapters in this volume about popular culture and leisure between 1920 and 1960 concentrate on four areas. Chapter 8, "Sports and Public Culture," looks at the relationship among athletics, municipal government, and the public, using a local microstudy of the early 1920s. We see class conflict, gender differences, conservative militaristic traditions, a certain athletic ethos, and attempts to invoke a sense of national identity despite the lost war. Chapter 9, "Popular Culture," examines the public stances on popular culture adopted by various political movements in the Weimar Republic. What is particularly striking is the enormous resentment that was felt for popular culture when it was considered void of anything "worthwhile." Although the views of all the larger political parties and groups are represented, the emphasis is on the relationship between cultural conservatism[66] and National Socialism, which is discussed in chapter 10, "Art for the People." To what extent, we ask, did cultural conservatism pave the way for the cultural policies of the Nazis, and which cultural practices were still allowed under the Third Reich? We often think of cultural life in the Third Reich in terms of extremes: either suppression or full conformity with the party line. On the one hand, there were the defamation and suppression of the

63. With the support of the Volkswagen Stiftung (Foundation).

64. The exhibitions were on the history of leisure culture.

65. The texts were not published, however, until after reunification. Adelheid von Saldern, "Der Wochend-Mensch," *Mitteilungen aus der kulturwissenschaftlichen Forschung* 15, no. 30 (1992): 5–34; Adelheid von Saldern and Dietrich Mühlberg, "Kontinuität und Wandel der Arbeiterkultur: Ein Forschungsaufriß," *Mitteilungen aus der kulturwissenschaftlichen Forschung* 15, no. 30 (1992): 226–60.

66. See also chapter 10 and Adelheid von Saldern, "Überfremdungsängste: Gegen die Amerikanisierung der deutschen Kultur in den zwanziger Jahren," in Alf Lüdtke, Inge Marßolek, and Adelheid von Saldern (eds.), *Amerikanisierung: Traum und Alptraum im Deutschland des 20. Jahrhunderts* (Stuttgart, 1996), 213–45.

artistic avant-garde, Jewish artists, the workers' cultural movement, and various clubs, as well as attempts to repress particular forms of popular culture, such as jazz. On the other, there were women doing their officially approved round dances or gymnastic exercises with clubs, bombastic exhibitions of "folk culture," and the propagandistic Kraft durch Freude (Strength through Joy) trips. Between these extremes, however, were many cultural practices about which we still know too little: parish fairs, various sports, pub life, club life, fire-brigade and archery festivals, going to the movies, reading magazines, technological exhibitions, dances, shows, light music, expeditions in small groups, private tours, private parties in one's home or gardening plot, and listening to the radio.[67] Research into these activities may well help to answer the question of why many Germans apparently felt quite comfortable in the Third Reich (at least until 1939–41) and did not turn their minds nearly as often as we think to politics, terror, and dictatorship.[68] Despite the *Gleichschaltung* (coordination) of clubs, associations, and cultural life in general, enough latitude remained that most Germans did not feel so culturally deprived as one would often assume from reading the literature.[69] We still have much to learn about the role that politics played in the everyday lives of most people. We also need to revive the discussion about whether many Germans actually looked with much favor before 1933 on the artistic, avant-garde, "unbridled" popular culture and the "Americanization" of German culture and everyday life. The main analytical interest in all this lies in linking Nazi rule to society and cultural history to political history. Chapter 10 summarizes the empirical research in this regard, points out gaps in the research, and encourages further work.

The last chapter is based on the project "Radio and the Gender Order 1930–60," funded by the Volkswagen Stiftung.[70] As a modern medium, radio provides excellent insights into the relationship among

---

67. See for instance Adelheid von Saldern, "Cultural Conflicts, Popular Mass Culture, and the Question of Nazi Success: The Eilenriede Motorcycle Races, 1924–1939" *German Studies Review* 15, no. 2 (May 1992): 317–38.

68. The desire to put the audience in a happy frame of mind played a role at the time in radio programming. It was felt that this would help to integrate people into Nazi society.

69. The mention of a certain latitude should not be understood as implying that there was any freedom. It means only that the regime did not have total control over everyday culture.

70. The group consisted of Inge Marßolek, Adelheid von Saldern, Daniela Münkel, Monika Pater, and Uta C. Schmidt. See Inge Marßolek and Adelheid von Saldern (eds.), *Zuhören und Gehörtwerden*: vol. 1, *Radio im Nationalsozialismus: Zwischen Lenkung und Ablenkung* (Tübingen, 1998); vol. 2, *Radio in der DDR der 50er Jahre: Zwischen Lenkung und Ablenkung* (Tübingen, 1998).

the power structures, society, and everyday life. With the advent of radio, a public medium intruded into the private world of the home in a totally unprecedented way. Public life and private life became inseparable. This chapter looks at radio in the GDR in the 1950s, often with a gender-specific perspective. The history of radio at that time is marked by the diverging desires of ordinary listeners and the political authorities. The disagreements were particularly evident in the area of politics and entertainment. The state wanted "joyful socialism," to be sure, but felt that the best way of achieving it was to have entertainment programming that was not just amusing and that contained interspersed political or educational insights. In adopting this approach, the GDR was resurrecting to some extent ideas developed by the labor movement in the Weimar Republic, especially by the Communists, who were convinced that people could be educated to socialism. However, educating people by radio proved very difficult because they could simply switch stations or turn the radio off altogether, even in the dictatorship of the GDR.

We look further, in this general context, at how the relationship between the sexes was portrayed on East German radio, concentrating for the most part on entertainment programming. It turns out that many traditional ideas continued to be purveyed despite the break with the past in 1945, at least in broadcasts that were not primarily political. These ideas often stood in curious contrast to official government statements about the equal place of men and women in socialist society.[71] This chapter is intended as a contribution to the history of mentalities.[72]

V

Some of the chapters discuss acculturation efforts and other practices on the part of the authorities that are often described as "social engineering" or "social rationalization." Whether the concept of "social rationalization" has enough analytical merit to serve as an important key to government practices and acculturation attempts in the modern age remains an open question. There are some indications that it might.

---

71. See in this regard Inge Marßolek and Adelheid von Saldern, "Radio and NS-Gesellschaft: Prolegomena zu einer Rundfunkgeschichte als Sozial- und Kulturgeschichte," in Marlis Buchholz, Claus Füllberg-Stolberg, and Hans-Dieter Schmid (eds.), *Nationalsozialismus und Region: Festschrift für Herbert Obenaus zum 65. Geburtstag,* (Bielefeld, 1996), 227–95; Inge Marßolek and Adelheid von Saldern, "Massenmedien im Kontext von Herrschaft, Alltag, und Gesellschaft: Eine Herausforderung an die Geschichtsforschung," in Inge Marßolek and Adelheid von Saldern (eds.), *Radiozeiten: Herrschaft, Alltag, Gesellschaft (1924–1960)* (Potsdam, 1999), 11–39.

72. Cf. Peter Dinzelbacher (ed.), *Europäische Mentalitätsgeschichte* (Stuttgart, 1993), especially Dinzelbacher's introduction.

Driven by studies done by Michel Foucault, Norbert Elias, Max Weber, Detlev J. K. Peukert, Jonas Frykman, Orvar Löfgren, Zygmunt Bauman, and Tilla Siegel, "social rationalization" seems to be developing into a theoretical and conceptual nexus[73] to which empirical results can be tied. It seems useful as a concept because individual research results from a variety of ideological and political contexts can be integrated under it at a moderately abstract level.

Of particular importance in this connection are contemporary discourses, the analysis of which requires close attention to text and language in order to highlight the prevailing thought patterns and methods of argument, concepts of humanity or worldviews, and overt or covert desires to gain power. When I came upon the Polley scandal in the files one day, I had a concrete opportunity to experiment with "discourse analysis," together with Karen Heinze and Sybille Küster (see chap. 7). Consistent with the course of the international discussion (although German historians had hardly been involved), we too debated at length whether social reality could be adequately understood solely through the reconstructions provided by newspaper articles, that is, texts, or whether, for basic methodological and conceptual reasons, other historical sources needed to be studied as well. We decided upon the latter course, searched the sources for information about Polley, and attempted to understand something about the environment in which she lived. Our emphasis was on poverty, welfare, and homelessness (cf. chap. 6).[74]

Various acculturation efforts seem to fall under the heading "social rationalization," including attempts to lead people in a socialist direction, at least on a verbal level. Many aspects of the concept of the "new man" (*der neue Mensch*), an idea that encompassed both men and women and that emerged in connection with the cultural socialism of the 1920s, reflected the widespread desire to rationalize human behavior. For instance, the "new man" was supposed to be well disciplined — although not from blind obedience but rather from his or her own insight and understanding, which could be nurtured through an appropriate education. "Proletarian discipline needs people to fit in, not subordinate themselves (*Proletarische Disziplin will Einordnung, nicht Unterord-*

---

73. Michel Foucault, *Discipline and Punish: The Birth of the Prison* (1979); Detlev J. K. Peukert, *Max Webers Diagnose der Moderne* (Göttingen, 1989); Norbert Elias, *Über den Prozeß der Zivilisation* (Frankfurt, 1976); Jonas Frykman and Orvar Löfgren, *Culture Builders: A Historical Anthropology of Middle-Class Life* (New Brunswick and London, 1987); Bauman, *Dialektik;* Tilla Siegel, "Das ist nur rational: Ein Essay zur Logik der sozialen Rationalisierung," in Dagmar Reese et al. (eds.), *Rationale Beziehungen? Geschlechterverhältnisse im Rationalisierungsprozeß* (Frankfurt, 1993), 363–97.

74. See also von Saldern, *Neues Wohnen.*

nung). It needs insight and understanding in the service of the whole, thinking for oneself, and a sense of shared responsibility."[75] A very broad view was taken of the kind of training and education that the "new man" would need. As was stated at a union meeting in 1925: "as mechanization progresses — and it will progress — unions have a duty to develop not only wage policies but cultural policies as well. They must concern themselves not only with the *what* of housing, clothing, food and recreation but the *how* as well."[76]

Social rationalization was not only a socialist concept but very much a part of middle-class culture as well. In the nineteenth century, the middle-class desire for social rationalization could be largely satisfied through proper etiquette and strict rules of behavior. As Kocka has pointed out, this kind of rationalization was deeply ingrained in bourgeois culture in Germany. After the First World War, though, it could no longer be sustained in the face of Americanization and the rise of popular culture. Proper etiquette began to crumble as its outer shell, best symbolized perhaps by restrictive female clothing based on the corset, withered away. If traditional social rules and codes were to be followed at all, it would have to be in response to inner conviction. It was no coincidence that the reform movement developed its new pedagogy at this time, with an emphasis on the education given to children and youth from an early age in the hope of raising a new kind of human being. Educators would no longer thrash young people for their misdeeds but would empathize with them and feel the way into their souls in order to instill a deep-seated devotion to "proper behavior" and the needs of the community.

Efforts to rationalize society and discipline the population go back, of course, as far as the Renaissance.[77] However, the methods are always peculiar to the times, and the question of interest here is what was typical of the 1920s. Of the various innovations in this period that played important roles in social rationalization, the two that are emphasized are welfare and the construction of publicly subsidized housing.

Reformers believed that the people could be greatly influenced through the spaces in which they lived and the material faits accomplis with which they were confronted. Therefore the process for changing them would be very calm and peaceful. "Instead of cathedrals, dwelling machines," demanded Oskar Schlemmer. What this meant is discussed in chapter 3. We might just add, by way of introduction, that the reference

75. Cf. for instance Paul Franken, *Vom Werden einer neuen Kultur: Aufgaben der Arbeiterkultur- und -sportorganisationen,* (1930; reprint, Münster, 1989), 53ff.

76. Cited in von Saldern, "Arbeiterkulturbewegung," 50.

77. Elias, *Zivilisation.*

to machines was not incidental. By the 1920s, the debate no longer revolved around machines per se but around a new symbiosis between the machine and the individual — a symbiosis that was realized in what was called "Fordism." Machines, by their very nature, force people to be rational and disciplined, a fact that was probably not lost on the thinkers pondering the relationship between people and spaces. This relationship was certainly worth investigating since the new publicly subsidized housing program was providing an unprecedented opportunity to shape the homes of thousands of people and, to a certain extent, plan how they would live their lives. In the end, about 2 million publicly subsidized homes were built.

Welfare policy afforded another opportunity to rationalize society by pushing people in the "right" direction. We enter the world of welfare through the case of Gertrude Polley, discussed in chapter 7. She was hardly a model recipient from the viewpoint of the welfare authorities, and their attempts to push her in the right direction failed to have the desired effect. Over the course of time, Polley became known as a perpetual complainer and crank, that is, as someone who did not internalize the psychological pressures exerted by the welfare authorities and who behaved in unacceptable ways in their eyes. We see in this case the helplessness of individuals vis-à-vis powerful public officials "just" doing their jobs in routine ways by insisting on socially rationalized behavior from poor people dependent on welfare. Feeling mistreated by government agencies, Polley reacted to her experiences and took unique action.[78] One of the distinguishing features of the Weimar Republic[79] (and later of the Federal Republic) was the feeling among many impoverished people that they had a *right* to government assistance, a feeling that did not exist in this form under either the empire or the Third Reich.

There is a host of possible misunderstandings, concerns, and qualifications that should be noted in regard to the concept of "social rationalization," of which we will mention a few. First, it would be erroneous to conclude that "social rationalization" refers to a closed, narrow concept of society with definite strategies for implementing it. The opposite was the case. There was an abundance of ideas and movements, which are only bundled together in retrospect under the heading "social rationalization" as an analytical construct. The various concepts and discourses revolved around a broad variety of subjects ranging from sexual ethics to family planning, from "good taste" to proper hygiene, from eugenics to racial policies, from the construction of housing to

---

78. For the experience dimension see Victor W. Turner and Edward Bruner (eds.), *The Anthropology of Experience* (Urbana, 1986).

79. See in this regard the striking examples in Crew, *Germans on Welfare*.

children's playgrounds, from reform pedagogy to education through the media, and so on.

Second, the fact that particular concepts and discourses are discussed in connection with social rationalization does not mean that the people who were targeted necessarily acted in the desired ways. Our approach to social rationalization should always make clear, in the area of housing for instance, that various rooms and spaces were appropriated by individuals in their own way. As I concluded from my studies of the new housing estates in the 1920s, "the widespread kinds of appropriation that determined everyday culture consisted both of conformity to the behavioral norms established by the housing estates and of moderate circumvention or subversion of these norms when they were considered unreasonable or unjustified. In addition, people gave their own estates a positive (re)interpretation (including the successful repression of hopes that had proved unattainable)."[80] The aging people whom I interviewed in the late 1980s, in what had been "new" estates in Hamburg, Berlin, and Frankfurt, appropriated their homes in the 1920s (and still do today) in ways that enabled them to develop a positive relationship with their social surroundings. The homes and the people in them were as neat and clean as the housing reformers of the 1920s could have hoped; however, the kind of furniture that people chose would have set Walter Gropius spinning in his grave. From a socioanthropological point of view, this furniture demonstrates individuality and independence of mind in the subjective appropriation process.[81] Because of the limited sources we could not study this process in sufficient breadth and depth in the chapters on housing; only Gertrude Polley's unconventional response to the welfare bureaucracy could be studied in detail in chapter 7.

In regard to the general problems of Wirkungsforschung (research into the appropriation process), researchers have to be satisfied with what seems likely when interviews are no longer possible. Situations and dispositions can be pointed out that make certain behaviors seem likely, such as compliance, refusal, subversion, or a complex combination of

---

80. Adelheid von Saldern, "Die Neubausiedlungen der Zwanziger Jahre," in Ulfert Herlyn, Adelheid von Saldern, and Wulf Tessin (eds.), *Neubausiedlungen der 20er und 60er Jahre: Ein historisch-soziologischer Vergleich* (Frankfurt and New York, 1987), 69; See also Adelheid von Saldern, "Bauen und Wohnen: Ein Thema für die 'Geschichtswissenschaft'?" in Adelheid von Saldern (ed.), *Bauen und Wohnen in Niedersachsen Während der fünfziger Jahre* (Hanover, 1999), 11–53, here 8. A misleading interpretation appears in Mary Nolan, *Visions of Modernity: American Business and the Modernization of Germany* (New York and Oxford, 1994), 236.

81. See Peter Gorsen, "Zur Dialektik des Funktionalismus heute: Das Beispiel des kommunalen Wohnungsbaus im Wien der zwanziger Jahre," in Jürgen Habermas (ed.), *Stichworte zur "Geistigen Situation der Zeit"* (Frankfurt, 1979), 2:688–707.

attitudes. Researchers also need to consider attachments to particular milieus and environments. Sources have to be read against the grain: a multitude of admonishments and exhortations, for instance, is indicative of considerable noncompliance or even refusal, as can be seen in chapter 4. Ultimately, there are clear limits to what historians can accomplish in their studies on processes of appropriations, just as there are in research into the historical effects of the media.

Long-term effects remain a special problem. Mentalities are particularly resistant to change and have a time structure of their own. However, Norbert Elias has shown very clearly for previous centuries that mentalities do change eventually, and his studies should be continued for the twentieth century. Cleanliness is one area in which a huge acculturation process has been at work over the last hundred years. Behaviors have changed not only in reaction to new technologies, mounting awareness of the importance of hygiene, and other health-related concerns but also because of new social norms that have become established over time through public discourse, education, and socialization. This process should not be seen as especially hierarchical or top to bottom; here too, we need to be aware of the complex ways in which new ideas are created and appropriated and the reciprocal influence of social norms and actual practices. In any case, the ultimate outcome is clear: hygienic practices have changed considerably over the decades.

Another criticism of the concept of "social rationalization" is that the methodologies are not specific enough to the issue at hand and therefore lack precision and can easily go astray. The overstated continuity "from Weimar to the Holocaust" gained some adherents because of the many continuities that did exist, especially on the level of discourse and concepts. However, it is very misleading to ignore all the ruptures with the past in 1933. As is well known, these ruptures included the following: (1) the monopoly imposed on certain discourses, for instance the discourse about race; (2) the suppression or elimination of all viewpoints based in fundamental ways on a different concept of society and humankind; and (3) the imposition of radical Nazi views by means of a dictatorship, which was then able to carry out the Holocaust largely in the shadow cast by the war.

The nebulous nature of the term *social rationalization* is also apparent in a comparison of Germany and the United States (see chap. 5). Ideas for rationalizing society emerged in the United States as well but in a different social context. Here these ideas were mere specks in a society in which "proper taste" and living habits were largely determined by capitalism and the free market. In Germany on the other hand, the cultural influence of the state and government agencies was far greater.

In addition, ideas about educating the masses in the United States tended to focus on issues related to ethnic minorities and how to Americanize them. In chapter 5, we outline some of the similarities and differences in the attempts to rationalize housing and domestic life in Germany and the United States, thereby engaging in some comparative history.[82]

VI

Some chapters fall under the general heading "gender history," which in Germany is going through tense and exciting times. There is still quite a rigid gender division in the research and discourse in Germany, and this kind of history is usually seen as the exclusive preserve of women. The grotesque result is that most male professors and even many younger male academics remain blissfully unaware of both the German and foreign literature on gender history.

Gender history is now reaching the third stage in its evolution. After focusing primarily on the history of women, and then expanding in its second stage to gender history, it has now reached a third stage where well-established and often cited research results are again being questioned. For example, some doubts are now being raised about the effects of the concept of polarized gender characteristics since the late Enlightenment, which used to be accepted as one of the standard truths of the history of women. According to the critics, normative concepts about polarized gender characteristics and the attribution of gendered social tasks were implicitly but wrongly assumed to capture the full historical reality. "From the beginning, there was little ability to take a 'differentiated view' of the relations between the sexes and perceive the differing manifestations at a given time, to appreciate all the variability that existed in 'being a women' and 'being a man.'"[83] In short, the polarization of the sexes, as previously portrayed in the research, is criticized as exaggerated and often contrary to the social reality.

The role of women in the Third Reich has also become quite controversial as a result of a debate conducted under the polarized heading

---

82. A comparative view of Austria and Germany can be found in Adelheid von Saldern, "The Workers' Movement and Cultural Patterns on Urban Housing Estates and in Rural Settlements in Germany and Austria during the 1920s," *Social History* 15, no. 3 (October 1990): 333–55.

83. Anne-Charlott Trepp, *Sanfte Männlichkeit und selbständige Weiblichkeit: Frauen und Männer im Hamburger Bürgertum zwischen 1770 und 1840* (Göttingen, 1996), 16; here, too, there is an account of the discussion.

"victims or perpetrators?"[84] The discussion revolves primarily around the question of whether there was a private sphere dominated by women that had very little to do for the most part with the crimes of the Nazi regime. Another question that arises is whether most German women should be considered victims of the Nazi regime on the grounds that it clearly discriminated against them. These and other controversies show that gender history and the history of women have become normal subjects of historical research, within which different views, approaches, opinions, and prejudices are openly debated. Gender history and the history of women have outgrown their early political and educational motivations and their need to establish an identity and have now opened themselves to controversy.

Particularly noteworthy, as well, is the ever more insistent attempt to establish gender history as an integrating principle, which is to say that the gender aspect of a subject permeates and shapes the whole. "No more isolation, part of general history" is the slogan. In the words of Hanna Schissler: "Gender history as a program aims therefore not only to include both men and women but also to view women as an integral part of society, and not just as another subsystem."[85] Nevertheless, history that focuses primarily on women (or men) remains a legitimate area of interest, which can be especially informative when used as an opportunity for sophisticated accounts of social and power relationships.[86]

The innovative women's and gender research conducted on the international level prompted me to take gender issues increasingly into account in my own work, sometimes specifically and sometimes in a more integrated fashion.[87] The scandal surrounding Gertrude Polley

---

84. See in this regard the overview by Adelheid von Saldern, "Victims or Perpetrators? Controversies about the Role of Women in the Nazi State," in David F. Crew (ed.), *Nazism and German Society 1933–1945* (London and New York, 1994), 141–66. I found especially helpful the insights of Ernst Fraenkel, *The Dual State: A Contribution to the Theory of Dictatorship,* 2d ed. (New York, 1941).

85. Hanna Schissler (ed.), *Geschlechterverhältnisse im historischen Wandel* (Frankfurt and New York, 1993), 17.

86. See for instance Ute Frevert, *Ehrenmänner: Das Duell in der bürgerlichen Gesellschaft* (Munich, 1991).

87. Early beginnings: Adelheid von Saldern, "Die Situation der Frau im Dritten Reich," in Historisches Museum (ed.), *1933 und danach* (Hanover, 1983); more recent works by von Saldern: "Victims or Perpetrators?"; "'Nur ein Mädchen': Geschlechtergeschichte am Beispiel hannoverscher Quellen aus den zwanziger Jahren," in Horst Kuss and Bernd Mütter (eds.), *Geschichte Niedersachsens neu entdeckt: 10 Kapitel aus der Geschichte des 19. und 20. Jahrhunderts* (Braunschweig, 1996); "Modernization as Challenge: Perceptions and Reactions of German Social Democratic Women," in Helmut Gruber and Pamela Graves (eds.), *Women and Socialism/Socialism and Women in Interwar Europe,* 95–135. (New York and Oxford, 1998), and chapters 7 and 11 in this volume.

shows, for instance, how gendered the concept of social rationalization really was. A woman with a "loose" lifestyle, who was also in a weak social position because of poverty, could easily find herself in grave difficulties, as we see in our study in chapter 7 of the Polley case.

The efforts to educate and inform the public about domestic life were also highly gendered (chaps. 4 and 5). Both advertisers and reformers of domestic life directed their messages primarily at housewives, who were considered responsible for maintaining neat, attractive homes and who usually embraced this role since they lacked sufficient occupational or other responsibilities. Women were inundated with advice to the effect that "the only right way to live is the rationalized way."[88] Family life, housekeeping, and the home were considered an inseparable whole. If housekeeping was neglected, the family was allegedly endangered, and since the family was considered the foundation of society and the state, the housekeeping duties attributed to women through the family became a social and political concern.

How compatible was social rationalization with the greatly lauded concept of "motherhood" inside and outside the home? Were these not contradictory principles? One might think so at first glance, especially if social rationalization is thought to be predicated solely on reason and is considered the polar opposite of emotion, which is attributed to women while reason is reserved for men. However, the concept of social rationalization included emotional activities as well, although gendered and confined to certain times, places, and situations and always within certain limits. From a conceptual standpoint, motherhood of this kind could easily serve rational, utilitarian purposes. Motherhood was considered the necessary emotional compensation for the adoption of economically oriented rationalization, which ultimately served the education and improvement of the labor force.[89]

VII

The chapters arose in different contexts and emphasized different things, and the strength of my own background in the research varied considerably. However, there is one common denominator: "modernity." A few key words could serve as a guide to their contents. Party organization is

---

For integrated approaches by von Saldern, see for instance *Häuserleben;* "Latent Reformism"; "Gesellschaft und Lebensgestaltung: Sozialkulturelle Streiflichter," in Gerd Kähler (ed.), *Geschichte des Wohnens* (Stuttgart, 1996), 4:45–183.

88. Siegel, "Das ist nur rational," 368.

89. Cf. Siegel, "Das ist nur rational," 375. It would be wrong, though, to view the principle of motherhood solely from a rational, utilitarian viewpoint.

discussed (chaps. 1 and 2), as well as bureaucratization (chaps. 1 and 7). The differentiation of society and participation in political life and the related changes in perceptions and interpretations are addressed (chap. 2). Social rationalization is discussed (chaps. 3–7), especially in regard to welfare and the construction of modern housing and with due consideration for national idiosyncrasies and contexts (chap. 5). Sometimes the complexity of individual or group appropriation processes is emphasized, along with the ways in which people complied with or resisted rationalization (chap. 7). The rise of modernity was also apparent in the advent of popular culture, for instance in sports and radio (chaps. 8 and 11). Popular culture became one of the most contentious issues of the time (chaps. 9 and 10). Could it be suppressed, channeled, or transformed? Could alternatives to it be encouraged, or could traditional values be instilled in it, especially in respect to gender relations (chap. 11)? Modernity was certainly felt at the time to be an extremely complex issue. It opened up new opportunities, refined the mechanisms through which power could be exercised, catalyzed the development of society, and posed considerable acculturation challenges in everyday life. The chapters in this volume attempt to capture some aspects of this multidimensional process.

The concepts, approaches, and methods I used in my research evolved in the context of the discussions and debates of the times. Critical social history certainly provided the foundation, but I was subject to various influences over the years. Neighboring disciplines provided important inspiration, particularly political science, the history of architecture, cultural sociology, and social anthropology.[90] My love of experimentation led me to combine new conceptual and methodological approaches with conventional empirical research.[91] I derived great intellectual pleasure from this and found the work very stimulating. There is a fine line, of course, between necessary receptiveness to new ideas and excessive eclecticism. However, if historiography is the reconstruction of realities that can only be approximated and never fully captured, one can and should approach them from a number of different angles, using various methods.

Not only my methods varied but my subjects as well. There were many reasons for this, mostly related to my social policy interests at the time and my hopes for the future. However, in my early days as a researcher, I also felt a certain alienation from the subjects of my work,

90. Especially important for me were all the years of working with Sid Auffarth of the Institute for Art History and the History of Architecture, Hanover University.

91. See for instance Inge Marßolek and Adelheid von Saldern, (eds.), "Diskurs-Experimente," *WerkstattGeschichte* 3, no. 7, special issue, (1994), with various contributions from Karen Heinze, Sabine Guckel-Seitz, and Philipp Sarasin.

together with a great curiosity about what I could discover through my own efforts. This was especially true of my research into workers and the petite bourgeoisie. I turned to other factors such as urban culture, popular culture, and housing and domestic life because I had the impression that there was much more to say about them than could be found in the literature. Sometimes I was influenced in my selection of subjects by an external impetus, or grants beckoned.[92] These changes in topic helped to renew my excitement over my research — a feeling that stimulated my day-to-day work.[93] I have also always regarded research processes as vast learning experiences in their own right, and occasional changes in topics and methods were beneficial from this point of view as well.

Finally I would like to acknowledge the inspiration I received from the English-speaking countries, especially from my colleagues in the United States and Canada. They showed particular interest in my work. I found the culture of discussion there particularly stimulating and motivating, especially the receptiveness to new approaches and questions — a receptiveness that was previously unknown to me.

I would like to take this opportunity to thank my American colleagues, colleagues, and friends. This volume is dedicated to them.[94] I am especially grateful to Geoff Eley and David Crew for the support they have given to this project.

---

92. This was especially true of the interdisciplinary project on the construction of new housing in the 1920s and 1960s, a historical sociological comparison, and of the project mentioned previously on radio and gender from 1930 to 1960. Both projects were supported by the Volkswagen Stiftung, and a total of seven young scholars could therefore be employed for the duration of the two projects.

93. My dissertation (under Franz Schnabel, Munich) was entitled *Hermann Dietrich: Ein Staatsmann der Weimarer Republik* (Boppard, 1996). Hermann Dietrich (German Democratic Party, later German State Party) was the Reich minister of finance under Brüning.

94. Leora Auslander, Kenneth D. Barkin, Paul Betts, David Blackbourn, Kathleen Canning, Jane Caplan, Jack Censer, Roger Chickering, Abby Collins, Kathleen Neils Conzen, David F. Crew, Belinda Davis, Geoff Eley, Gerald D. Feldman, Peter Fritzsche, Michael Geyer, Victoria de Grazia, Pamela M. Graves, Atina Grossmann, Helmut Gruber, Miriam Hansen, Tamara K. Hareven, Jeffrey Herf, Young-Sun Hong, Georg Iggers, Wilma Iggers, David Imhoof, Peter Jellavich, Anton Kaes, Stefan Kalberg, Michael Kater, Alice Kessler-Harris, Rudy Koshar, Lawrence W. Levine, Vernon Lidtke, Peter Loewenberg, Charles S. Maier, Andy Markovits, Frederick McKitrick, Sonja Michel, David Montgomery, Mary Nash, Mary Nolan, Susan Pennybacker, Klaus Petersen, Uta Poiger, Anson Rabinbach, Bill Rader, Nancy Reagin, Jerry Sider, George Steinmetz, Louise A. Tilly, Judith Vichniac, Eric D. Weitz, Bernd Widdig, and Leora Wildenthal.

THE DYNAMICS OF THE WORKING-CLASS MOVEMENT IN SOCIETY

CHAPTER 1

Party Centers and Party Hinterlands: The Trend to Centralization and Hierarchism in the Wilhelminian SPD

Introduction

Anyone who examines the economic, social, and cultural development of various regions of Germany in the nineteenth century cannot fail to notice how different the conditions were. Strong disparities persisted despite the movement toward greater political unity after the founding of the German Empire in 1871 and the creation of a single national market and a relatively uniform legal system. It still made an enormous difference whether one lived in Berlin, Hamburg, or Leipzig or in Göttingen, Tübingen, or Marburg.[1]

The differences in regional development were due largely, though not exclusively, to the asynchronous expansion and intensification of capitalism and the market economy. Asynchronous development is an important characteristic of modernity. It is caused not only by differences in flows of capital and trade but also by the tenacity of old mentalities and habits. The use of the term *asynchronous* does not imply that development moves in linear fashion. There are tendencies of course toward uniformity and standardization in modern, capitalist societies, between regions, for example, or between town and country.

---

1. See in this regard the exemplary study Gert Zang (ed.), *Provinzialisierung einer Region: Regionale Unterentwicklung und liberale Politik in der Stadt und im Kreis Konstanz im 19. Jahrhundert: Untersuchungen zur Entstehung der bürgerlichen Gesellschaft in der Provinz* (Frankfurt, 1978); Rainer Fremdling and Richard H. Tilly (eds.), *Industrialisierung und Raum: Studien zur regionalen Differenzierung im Deutschland des 19. Jahrhunderts* (Stuttgart, 1979); Jürgen Bergmann et al., *Regionen im historischen Vergleich: Studien zu Deutschland im 19. und 20. Jahrhundert* (Opladen, 1991).

However, these tendencies are not the product of linear predispositions but rather of dialectical processes that can generate peculiar conditions in each case. These "peculiar conditions" need to be explored further in order to determine how people both shaped them and were shaped by them.

Various organizations played a role in this shaping process. The labor movement developed in the nineteenth century along very different lines in different places and regions. Centers of industry and commerce generally spawned regional or local labor movements, thereby becoming potential party centers as well, at least insofar as the local authorities were not especially effective at suppressing the labor movement or the workers did not remain closely attached to a Catholic milieu, as in the Ruhr.

The labor movement in Germany did not develop and spread from one central location but rather from a number of different locales, especially the Leipzig, Berlin, Hamburg, and Braunschweig areas.[2] It tended therefore to be organized in a polycentric way. In the early decades of the German Empire, Berlin did not play an especially prominent role in the Social Democratic Party,[3] although it was an important center of innovation, much as Mannheim became in later days for southern Germany. The Socialist Laws (1878–90) reinforced the polycentrism of the party.[4] With the end of these laws in 1890 and the rescinding of the ban in Prussia on freedom of association, the situation changed, although not very dramatically. Henceforth, a powerful party apparatus could be developed with the full sanction of the law, and this incipient process tended to magnify the importance of the imperial capital of Berlin within the SPD. However, the generally polycentric structure of the party did not change, and the expansion of the party bureaucracy tended in fact to strengthen the regional centers and thus reinforce polycentrism.[5]

The terms *party centers* and *party hinterlands* are nothing more than vague constructs used here to facilitate our analysis. They are employed in both a broad sense, in reference to general sociocultural differences, and a narrow sense, in reference to more organizational differences. The purpose is to detect general trends, although counterexamples can usu-

2. Cf. Dieter Kramer, "Das Neue in der Geschichte der Arbeiterkultur: Berliner Beispiele und ihre überregionalen Wirkungen," in Theodor Kohlmann and Hermann Bausinger (eds.), *Großstadt: Aspekte empirischer Kulturforschung* (Berlin, 1985), 332ff.

3. Cf. Kramer, "Das Neue," 332.

4. For the early labor movement see Hartmut Zwahr, "Die deutsche Arbeiterbewegung im Länder- und Territorienvergleich 1875," *Geschichte und Gesellschaft* 13, no. 4 (1987): 448ff.

5. For instance, the Bremen SPD kept Karl Radek in the party, even though the executive had expelled him. I am grateful to Feliks Tych for pointing this out.

ally be found that qualify and differentiate the trends. Although the "party centers" and "hinterlands" were often the same in both the socio-cultural and organizational senses, some differences did exist. In other words, local associations that were sociocultural hinterlands did not usu-ally develop into organizational centers, but they did in some cases when there was no alternative. Conversely, local associations that were socio-cultural centers usually became organizational centers as well, although there were some exceptions in highly industrialized regions such as Saxony and the Ruhr, where a number of towns in close proximity were in the running to become the district organizational center and a choice had to be made.

We will look now at how the relationship between party centers and hinterlands developed in Wilhelminian times. This line of research was prompted by the realization that the evolving organization of the Social Democratic Party[6] must be seen in connection with the processes at work in society as a whole. For instance, communications of all kinds were improving, from railroads to mass-circulation newspapers, provid-ing new ways to intensify the contacts between party centers and hinter-lands and paving the way for a more hierarchical party structure. In practical terms, the issue boils down to whether the sociocultural differ-ences between party centers and hinterlands and the organizational de-pendencies between them intensified or weakened during those years of mounting urbanism and the rapid organizational rise of the party. Did the party hinterlands become more reliant on the developing regional centers? What role did "urbanity" or various concepts of "urbanity" play in this, particularly in a party such as the SPD, which was considered not only a party of highly industrialized areas but also of big cities and urban culture?[7]

We look subsequently at developments in the relationship between party centers and hinterlands from the point of view of party member-ship, organization, and sociocultural infrastructure; the various proletar-ian publics; labor unions and strikes; and the working-class milieus that developed in particular areas of cities.

---

6. Cf. for England Gareth Stedman Jones, "Working-Class Culture and Working-Class Politics in London 1870–1900," *Journal of Social History* 7 (1973–74): 460–508.

7. For more about the strength of the SPD in comparison with the size of the city see Gerhard A. Ritter, "Die Sozialdemokratie im Deutschen Kaiserreich," *Historiche Zeit-schrift* 249 (1989): 347ff. The heavily industrialized rural municipalities in the Kingdom of Saxony were an exception. See the pertinent study by Gerhard A. Ritter, "Das Wahlrecht und die Wählerschaft der Sozialdemokratie im Königreich Sachsen 1867–1914," in Ger-hard A. Ritter with Elisabeth Müller-Luckner (eds.), *Der Aufstieg der deutschen Arbeiter-bewegung: Sozialdemokratie und Freie Gewerkschaften im Parteiensystem und Sozialmilieu des Kaiserreichs* (Munich, 1990), 49ff.

Party Membership

In both its centers and hinterlands, the SPD was definitely a proletarian party from the point of view of the membership,[8] of which 80 to 90 percent was workers.[9] However, some differences can still be seen between the members in the centers and in the hinterlands.[10] For instance, worker-farmers were much more common in the hinterlands,[11] where the party had a more rural, plebeian character, while the centers were more urban proletarian. We assume, therefore, that the new values of capitalist, industrial society were mixed up in the party hinterlands with the precapitalist, more plebeian values of the "moral economy,"[12] forming a synchronous-asynchronous blend that differed from the values of the party centers.[13]

Petits bourgeois, especially self-employed tradesmen, shopkeepers, and lower-level salaried employees, accounted for only a small percentage of party members in both the centers and the hinterlands.[14] However, petits bourgeois members were still much less frequent in the hinterlands.[15] For instance, they accounted for only 4.3 percent of all

8. See also in this regard Adelheid von Saldern, "Wer ging in die SPD? Zur Analyse der Parteimitgliedschaft in Wilhelminischer Zeit," in Gerhard A. Ritter with Elisabeth Müller-Luckner (eds.), *Der Aufstieg der deutschen Arbeiterbewegung: Sozialdemokratie und Freie Gewerkschaften im Parteiensystem und Sozialmilieu des Kaiserreichs* (Munich, 1990), 161ff.

9. Cf. Dieter Fricke, *Handbuch zur Geschichte der deutschen Arbeiterbewegung 1869 bis 1917* (Berlin, 1987), 2:334.

10. Helga Grebing speaks about how the history of the SPD gave it a dual nature, on the one hand a populist party and on the other a working-class party. See Helga Grebing, *Arbeiterbewegung: Sozialer Protest und kollektive Interessenvertretung bis 1914* (Munich, 1985), 7.

11. For Württemberg see Jörg Schadt and Wolfgang Schmierer, *Die SPD in Baden-Württemberg und ihre Geschichte: Von den Anfängen der Arbeiterbewegung bis heute* (Stuttgart, 1979), 109.

12. For the term *moral economy* used here, see the standard work by Eduard P. Thompson, *The Making of the English Working Class* (Harmondsworth, 1963). Individual empirical examples can be found in my local study *Auf dem Wege zum Arbeiterreformismus: Parteialltag in sozialdemokratischer Provinz: Göttingen 1870–1920* (Frankfurt, 1984), 494.

13. We can assume that in the party hinterlands the subsistence economy was still not close to being as thoroughly supplanted by the consumption and transportation economy as in the party centers in the big cities.

14. The relatively small percentage of petty bourgeois in the SPD is an indication of the receptiveness of this class in Germany to right-wing parties and organizations.

15. Cf. Robert Michels, "Die deutsche Sozialdemokratie: Mitgliedschaft und soziale Zusammensetzung," *Archiv für Sozialwissenschaft und Sozialpolitik* 23 (1906): 509; Fricke, *Arbeiterbewegung*, 249ff.; Adelheid von Saldern, *Vom Einwohner zum Bürger: Zur Emanzipation der städtischen Unterschicht Göttingens 1890–1920: Eine sozial- und*

members in Göttingen, 4.4 percent in Marburg, and 5.7 percent in Frankfurt in comparison with 8.6 percent in Nuremberg and 7.2 percent in Harburg (excluding the salaried employees of the labor unions and the SPD itself). In Munich, a city with relatively little heavy industry, petits bourgeois accounted for 21.6 percent of all members in 1906, although Munich was an anomaly and the differences between party centers and hinterlands were usually not so pronounced. In general, however, it is apparent that relatively few petits bourgeois joined the party in the hinterlands, and the connection they provided between the working and middle classes was therefore relatively weak. As a result, the social and political confrontation between these classes tended to be sharper in the hinterlands.

Unskilled workers, on the other hand, accounted for a relatively high percentage of party members in the hinterlands. In the party center of Nuremberg, only 9.3 percent of members were listed as unskilled workers in 1894, in comparison with 25 percent in Göttingen in 1906–7 and 21 percent in Celle in 1898.[16] The fact that unskilled members were more common in the hinterlands probably weakened their position within the party as a whole, which was more influenced by skilled workers and tended to reflect their interests more. There were, however, some exceptions to the rule. In Harburg, a "Social Democratic city" and therefore a potential party center, unskilled factory workers made up 22 percent of all members and were therefore strongly represented in the local association.[17]

Another difference between the party centers and hinterlands was in the number of members from the middle and upper bourgeoisie, especially academics and intellectuals. If they joined the party at all, it was almost always in the centers and only rarely in the hinterlands, even in university towns such as Tübingen or Göttingen. This was due primarily to the fact that the middle-class academics in the universities tended to share the generally illiberal, anti–Social Democratic views that predominated there. In the big cities, there were other kinds of intellectuals

---

kommunalhistorische Untersuchung (Berlin, 1973), 114; for Harburg see Peter-Christian Witt, "Die Entstehung einer 'sozialdemokratischen' Stadt," in Gerhard A. Ritter with Elisabeth Müller-Luckner (eds.), *Der Aufstieg der deutschen Arbeiterbewegung: Sozialdemokratie und Freie Gewerkschaften im Parteiensystem und Sozialmilieu des Kaiserreichs* (Munich, 1990), 281.

16. For Nuremberg, see Dieter Rossmeisl, *Arbeiterschaft und Sozialdemokratie in Nürnberg 1890–1914* (Nuremberg, 1977); for Göttingen see von Saldern, *Auf dem Wege,* 115. The extent to which different methodologies play a role in this must remain an open question. I am grateful to Andreas Brundiers for pointing out this and what follows about Celle.

17. Witt, "Entstehung," 281.

as well, such as writers, artists, and newspaper editors, who in some cases were quite sympathetic to the SPD. The party centers therefore had more "cultural capital" (Pierre Bourdieu's term) at their disposal than the hinterlands. Writers and artists often encouraged the development of labor movement culture or sought to ensure that the working classes had as much opportunity as possible to partake of middle-class culture. The presence of members from the intelligentsia in the party centers helped to instill confidence in the cultural potential of the labor movement, despite all the conflicts, and this cultural confidence tended to rub off on political matters as well when conditions were right. Jewish intellectuals played a particularly prominent role in the party centers. Finding themselves cultural outsiders to some extent on a personal level, they were often particularly critical of contemporary manifestations of Germany's militaristic, bureaucratic, imperialistic, and capitalist society. This led them to oppose the system and embrace alternatives, especially socialism and Social Democracy.

There was also a gender aspect to the differences between the party centers and hinterlands. Although the Associations Act of 1908 had enabled women to join the party, it continued to be male dominated. The percentage of female members tended to be higher however in the hinterlands, such as in Göttingen and Göppingen, where women accounted for as many as one-third of the members, in comparison with only 13.4 percent in the party as a whole.[18] In party strongholds such as Hamburg, where there were three associations, women made up less than 10 percent of the members in 1907–8.[19] The preceding comments about the effects of the concentration of unskilled party members in the hinterlands apply as well to women. The higher proportion of female members in the hinterlands did little to enhance the influence of their sex in the party centers and was disadvantageous in view of the male dominance of the party as a whole.

The party centers and hinterlands differed as well, to some extent, in the occupations of most of their members. Some party centers, for instance Düsseldorf, were dominated by metalworkers because of the concentration of metalworking industries in the area. In 1907, metalworkers accounted for 35 percent of the members in this city.[20] These

---

18. Von Saldern, *Auf dem Wege*, 43; for Göppingen see Dieter Wuerth, *Radikalismus und Reformismus in der sozialdemokratischen Arbeiterbewegung Göppingens 1910–1919* (Göppingen, 1978). Further research needs to be done into the reasons why women participated at differing low rates in the prewar SPD.

19. Fricke, *Arbeiterbewegung*, 1:433.

20. For this and what follows see primarily Mary Nolan, *Social Democracy and Society: Working-Class Radicalism in Düsseldorf 1890–1920* (Cambridge, 1981), 104. There were similar results in Berlin as well.

workers had a distinct social profile because their work still had not been de-skilled to any great extent and they often enjoyed a relatively high degree of independence on the job. They tended therefore to have a strong sense of self-worth and progressive views of the future, which distinguished them from the general run of workers. In addition, metalworkers were often recruited from skilled workers who had intentionally abandoned their social and cultural roots in the countryside and wanted to work in industry and live in the city. They had broken with traditional rural life and moved to the city as young workers, and they were open to fresh ideas. Their occupational skills, cultural orientations, and relatively strong position in the social world of the factory led them to identify strongly with being workers.

In the party hinterlands, it was usually not metalworkers who led the way but construction and lumber workers. In Celle, for instance, they accounted for 50 percent of the SPD members. Construction and lumber were still not heavily industrialized, and construction in particular was very vulnerable to the vagaries of the economy. Many small lumber companies were having a hard time competing with larger companies and the machinery those competitors could afford. We can assume that the dismal prospects of the smaller companies affected their employees, who faced much darker or at least more uncertain futures than workers in the metal industries. Construction workers still often had many ties to rural life, not least of all because of the short-term contracts they usually had, and therefore did not identify as easily as metalworkers with the strongly urbanized labor movement.[21]

Another important difference between the party centers and hinterlands lay in the proportion of workers who joined the SPD. In Göppingen, for instance, only 6 percent of all workers were members in 1910, and in Augsburg, only 3.9 percent were members in 1908 and 5.5 percent in 1911.[22] The highest proportions could be found in Greater Berlin, where 11.6 percent of all workers had joined by 1906.[23] The relatively

---

21. Witt, "Entstehung," 281. However, there have been other findings as well, for instance in Harburg. Here metalworkers accounted for a large share of the party (24 percent in 1907), as did workers in the timber and construction sectors (34 percent).

22. Wuerth, *Radikalismus,* 54. Ilse Fischer, *Industrialisierung, sozialer Konflikt, und politische Willensbildung in der Stadtgemeinde: Ein Beitrag zur Sozialgeschichte Augsburgs 1840–1914* (Augsburg, 1977), 334.

23. Dieter Fricke, "Die Parteiorganisation der deutschen Sozialdemokratie," in Gerhard A. Ritter with Elisabeth Müller-Luckner (eds.), *Der Aufstieg der deutschen Arbeiterbewegung: Sozialdemokratie und Freie Gewerkschaften im Parteiensystem und Sozialmilieu des Kaiserreichs* (Munich, 1990), 157; cf. Ritter, "Sozialdemokratie," 323ff. Here there is an overview of the percentage of the inhabitants of various agitation districts who were also party members.

high percentage of members in some cities becomes even more apparent in light of the average for the entire Reich. According to the official statistics for 1895 and 1907 respectively, 1 percent and 4.5 percent of all workers were members of the SPD. The figures for artisans and industrial workers were respectively 2 and 7 percent.[24] A more crucial issue than the proportion of workers who joined the party was whether their absolute number in a given city, together with workers who joined only the union, was enough to create a potential or actual counter-force to the hegemony of the bourgeoisie.[25] It made a real difference whether the local SPD had only about 200 members, as in Göttingen in 1908; 6,693 members as in Munich in 1900; or 11,000 members as in just the sixth Berlin constituency association in 1905.[26] The disparities between regions were as striking as the disparities between cities. Some regions were party backwaters, such as Posen, West Prussia, Pomerania, and East Prussia. These four regions together accounted for only 2.58 percent of all party members in 1914. On the other hand, 28.4 percent of all party members lived in just Greater Berlin, Hamburg, Dresden, and Schleswig-Holstein. On the level of constituency organizations, this concentration meant that more than one-third of all party members (36.53 percent) belonged to the eighteen largest organizations.[27] The number and size of the organizations in various regions led to pronounced differences in the importance of these regions to the party as a whole.

Another important distinction between party centers and hinterlands lay in the proportion of Social Democratic voters who were also party members.[28] In the regional party center of Hanover, for instance, 34.6 percent of the men who voted for the SPD were also party members in 1912. Only a few constituencies in the Reich could boast a higher percentage, including Constituency III in Hamburg with 39.9 percent and Altona with 42.6 percent. In the party hinterlands, these percent-

---

24. Fricke, *Partieorganisation,* 156; cf. Ritter, "Sozialdemokratie," 323ff.

25. This possibility existed in the party hinterlands only when various groups of people who were suppressed or deprived of their rights could be successfully approached. Cf. above all Schadt and Schmierer, *SPD.*

26. Fricke, *Arbeiterbewegung,* 1:306. The SPD had only 15 members in Tübingen in 1895; cf. DGB Tübingen (ed.), *Arbeitertübingen: Zur Geschichte der Arbeiterbewegung in einer Universitätsstadt* (Tübingen, 1980), 19. It can be said in general that the development of the labor movement was obstructed to a large extent in the party hinterlands after 1890, and this had a considerable effect on the number of members. However, there were also differences between various hinterlands. For instance, the Celle standard already had 264 members in 1898.

27. Fricke, "Parteiorganisation," 157.

28. A corresponding overview by agitation district can be found in Ritter, "Sozialdemokratie," 323ff.

ages were much lower because of the social opprobrium attached to being a member of the SPD. Many people who voted for the party therefore shied away from becoming members. In the Hanover constituency of Goslar-Zellerfeld, only 5.5 percent of SPD voters were also party members. In Göttingen, only 4 percent were members in 1907 and 13.2 percent in 1913. Even in constituencies where the Social Democratic candidate was victorious in the Reichstag elections of 1912, for instance the Hanover constituencies of Hildesheim and Hameln (including Limmer) and the constituency of Holzminden-Gandersheim, party membership was often low. In Hameln, only 19.8 percent of SPD voters were party members, in Hildesheim 15 percent, and in Holzminden-Gandersheim 23 percent. In contrast to the situation in the party centers, the potential counterforce to the hegemony of the bourgeoisie remained nameless in the hinterlands. The historian Karl Rohe examined this question in the Ruhr area and determined that in 1912 only 19.1 percent of SPD voters in the Dortmund constituency were party members, 13.4 percent in the Duisburg constituency, 12.3 percent in the Essen constituency, and 11.9 percent in the Bochum constituency. The average for the entire Reich was 22.8 percent.[29] Rohe went one step further and analyzed elections to the Landtag as well because there was no secret ballot and voting was public. He used the number of people prepared to support the SPD openly in order to gauge the strength of a local SPD-inspired political culture. He examined the Landtag election of 1913 and the sharp contrast between Dortmund and Essen. In this election, only 19.7 percent of the voters in Essen openly supported the SPD, in comparison with 35 percent in Dortmund, but in the election of 1912 to the Reichstag, held under a secret ballot, the SPD was spectacularly successful in Essen.[30]

In general, the SPD did not garner many votes in the party hinterlands.[31] Its supporters could be found primarily in Berlin and Potsdam, Breslau, Magdeburg, Wiesbaden, Düsseldorf, Braunschweig, and the

---

29. See in this regard the pioneering study of Karl Rohe, "Die Ruhrgebietssozialdemokratie im Wilhelminischen Kaiserreich und ihr politischer und kultureller Kontext," in Gerhard A. Ritter with Elisabeth Müller-Luckner (eds.), *Der Aufstieg der deutschen Arbeiterbewegung: Sozialdemokratie und Freie Gewerkschaften im Parteiensystem und Sozialmilieu des Kaiserreichs* (Munich, 1990), 329. The strong fluctuations in membership also need to be taken into account.

30. Ibid., 330.

31. At the time, party hotbeds were considered to be places where the SPD's share of the vote reached 30 to 60 percent of the total. Peter Steinbach, "Sozialdemokratie im Spiegel der historischen Wahlforschung," in Gerhard A. Ritter with Elisabeth Müller-Luckner (eds.), *Der Aufstieg der deutschen Arbeiterbewegung: Sozialdemokratie und Freie Gewerkschaften im Parteiensystem und Sozialmilieu des Kaiserreichs* (Munich, 1990), 9.

cities of the Hanseatic League.[32] For lasting success at the polls, the SPD needed social milieus favorable to it, just as the Center Party needed Catholic milieus. These social milieus provided an atmosphere in which voting patterns could become entrenched and quite consistent. The SPD found itself in a rather unusual situation in the Ruhr Valley because many of the people among whom it tried to gain support had migrated from the rural eastern provinces of the Reich and never felt fully at home in milieus dominated by the SPD. To the extent that the miners who had grown up in the Ruhr voted for the Social Democrats at all instead of the Center Party, they did so more as a result of the influence of "a relatively closed social milieu of fellow miners, which was independent of the SPD."[33]

Party Organization

In general, the labor movement spread into the party hinterlands much later than into its great centers, in many cases not until the 1890s or even after the turn of the century.[34] After the Socialist Laws were rescinded, a number of Reichstag constituencies were combined to form party agitation districts (*Agitationsbezirke*), each under an "agitation committee." In the words of Dieter Fricke: "In practical terms, the agitation committees were institutions standing between the central leadership and the individual constituency organizations."[35] Later they came to be called district associations (*Bezirksverbände*). In southern and central Germany, these regional groups came together to form statewide SPD organizations, for instance in Saxony, Bavaria, and Baden.[36] The Jena Articles of Association of 1905 stated that "The Social Democratic associations join together to form district associations and state-wide organizations (*Landesorganisationen*), which manage the party's affairs according to their own bylaws. The party executive must be informed of these bylaws and they may not contradict the Articles of Association of the party as a whole. The local executives must report their election results to

32. Ibid., 11.

33. Rohe, "Ruhrgebietssozialdemokratie," 327ff.

34. The SPD was not established in Göttingen until 1891 and in Tübingen until 1906. Steps were taken to found a Lassallean organization in Göttingen in the early 1870s but mostly by people new to the area. It quickly disintegrated under local pressures, and this kind of development was broken off. In Celle, on the other hand, various continuities can be found.

35. Fricke, *Arbeiterbewegung*, 1:235. For the organizational history see the older work by Thomas Nipperdey, *Die Organisation der deutschen Parteien vor 1918* (Düsseldorf, 1961).

36. See Fricke, *Arbeiterbewegung*, 1:275ff.

the party executive."[37] Under the Articles of Association governing the prewar SPD, the regional party centers gained considerable independence, which they soon learned how to exploit vis-à-vis their own hinterlands. An essential precondition for the accumulation of power on the regional level was the creation of a modern party apparatus, at least for the times, with salaried party secretaries. The effects of the bureaucratization and professionalization of party functions could be seen primarily in the decade preceding the outbreak of the First World War.[38] Friedhelm Boll commented in regard to the regional centers of Braunschweig and Hanover that the hiring of party secretaries and formation of statewide and local organizations strengthened the hand of the various regional centers in comparison with the constituency organizations. The emergence of district associations was the organizational precursor of new kinds of dependency, and it is not surprising that protests mounted in some party hinterlands, such as Hameln, Peine, Einbeck, and Hanover-Münden, against the political dominance of the party center in Hanover and its press.[39]

For a more detailed look at the trend toward hierarchism, we will turn now to the history of the Göttingen SPD. The organizational center in Hanover that was responsible for Göttingen gained more and more influence over the local association. This was due mainly to the local association's own receptivity to advice and influence. The local party acted in such a docile way because it had few members and little electoral support in comparison with the regional center and these were the only factors that seemed to matter in the eyes of the party bureaucrats. The local party organization was also very aware that it lacked certain experiences that could be gained in larger centers, for instance the appearance of a strong proletarian public in times of strikes and demonstrations. The party hinterland attempted to compensate for its lack of experience by appropriating the experiences of others, particularly the party center.

The Göttingen SPD was also much inclined to spend its time poring over great issues of national or even international importance, while paying little attention to local or regional affairs. In this way, it simply avoided the practical problems of the SPD in the hinterlands. This attitude was certainly encouraged by the limited electoral franchise at the time, which ensured that the SPD could not have much direct influence

---

37. Quoted in ibid., 1:258.

38. Fricke, "Parteiorganisation," 155.

39. Friedhelm Boll, *Massenbewegungen in Niedersachsen 1906–1920: Eine sozialgeschichtliche Untersuchung zu den unterschiedlichen Entwicklungstypen Braunschweig und Hannover* (Bonn, 1981), 104.

over municipal politics in any case. In view of the generally difficult situation in the hinterlands, party activists probably felt that it was more effective to concentrate on gaining power on the national level by winning elections in the party centers and then using the power of the national government to change municipal bylaws and increase their influence on the local level.[40] In addition, if the local party members had taken a strong interest in the immediately surrounding area, they would have had to interpret local circumstances and events for themselves, and they did not generally feel adequate to this task. Hegemonic middle-class culture was by far the most powerful force in the hinterlands,[41] and local SPD members had little faith in their ability to swim against the tide.

In some cases though — for instance in Celle — party members in the hinterlands drew quite different conclusions and turned their backs almost entirely on broad national issues in order to concentrate on local affairs, regardless of how petty. At one point, the local party members even resolved not to bother discussing the national party program at all because, in the words of the minutes, "we can't do anything about it anyway." This attitude, like that of the Social Democrats in Göttingen, was probably rooted in the endemic feeling of impotence in the hinterlands, although the party members in Celle had the advantage over those in Göttingen of looking back on a strong SPD tradition in the local area. Perhaps Göttingen and Celle were two sides of the same coin: flight into great national issues or flight into purely local concerns, often with little connection to developments in society as a whole or the basic principles of the party program. The current state of the research does not enable us to determine the extent to which the regional party centers tried to grapple with local failings and weaknesses. In the case of Göttingen, though, there are strong indications that the party center in Hanover did not do much to counteract the disregard for local issues.

In general, party hinterlands such as Göttingen suffered increasingly from a lack of confidence in their own abilities. Their mounting feelings of insecurity were only exacerbated by the party officials in

40. The SPD was more involved in municipal politics in south German states such as Württemberg, where the opportunities for participation in the political process were greater. See Schadt and Schmierer, *SPD,* 109; in general for this topic see Adelheid von Saldern, "Die Gemeinde in Theorie und Praxis der Arbeiterorganisationen 1863–1920," *IWK* 12, no. 3 (1976): 295–353.

41. The authorities even kept the workers' cultural associations under surveillance and harassed them. For Göttingen see von Saldern, *Auf dem Wege,* 127ff.; for Lahr see Walter Caroli and Robert Stimpel, *Geschichte der Lahrer SPD: Ein Beitrag zur politischen Entwicklung in der Stadt Lahr* (Lahr, 1970), 92. In addition, religious affiliations must be considered, which were probably stronger in the party hinterlands than in its centers. See in this regard von Saldern, *Auf dem Wege,* 31f.

Hanover, who repeatedly told the local members how inadequate their organization and efforts at political agitation were. Officials in Hanover offered the Göttingen association practical assistance in what the party center considered to be the key areas of "agitation and organization." This assistance gradually undermined the autonomy of the hinterland and its psychological freedom as well. Gradually, the regional party center gained the ability under certain circumstances to steer or even determine the position that the hinterland adopted on the political directions that the party should take.

The regional party centers did not gain this ability in all cases, however, as can be seen in the relationship between the party center in Stuttgart and the subordinate Göppinger association. Despite the trend toward regional centralization, the prerequisites were apparently lacking in this case for the hinterland to fall into line. The experiences of the Göppingen members were apparently so different from those in the regional center that they simply could not go along with the reformist direction that it adopted. Much depended as well on the particular people involved, especially the party secretaries. The more dynamic and persuasive they were, the more success they usually had at unifying the views of the organizations in their hinterlands. The trend toward greater centralization and hierarchism could be seen as well within the party hinterlands themselves. For instance, the party association in the small town of Hannoversch-Münden chafed under the increasing domination of the Göttingen association.[42]

The harmonization of the political approaches within various districts was furthered by the spread of "Kautskyism," or the belief that the revolution would eventually happen if one just waited. Kautskyism left the party grass roots in a very unstable position, caught between reform and more radical solutions. Local party associations could easily swing one way or the other.[43] The direction that eventually won out depended not least of all on the mentalities and dispositions of the local party members. When Karl Rohe studied the Dortmund SPD, he came to the conclusion that the local Social Democrats were not deeply alienated from the life and culture around them and were more disposed toward

---

42. For hierarchism within the party hinterlands see as well the work on Bielefeld. Karl Ditt, *Industrialisierung, Arbeiterschaft, und Arbeiterbewegung in Bielefeld 1850–1914* (Dortmund, 1982), 248.

43. Cf. the views advanced in Adelheid von Saldern, "Arbeiterradikalismus–Arbeiterreformismus: Zum politischen Profil der sozialdemokratischen Parteibasis im Deutschen Kaiserreich: Methodisch-inhaltliche Bemerkungen zu Vergleichsstudien," *IWK* 20, no. 4 (1984): 483–98. This chapter builds in some ways on the older article but in light of more recent research.

reform. Party members were often more radical in areas where there were many migrants who had not been integrated very well into the local working-class milieu, whether for reasons of religious conflict or other reasons.[44] Rohe argues that working-class radicalism and reformism should both be further subdivided to reflect a more social orientation and a more political orientation. He even goes so far as to postulate a mental affinity between "social radicalism" and "social reformism," with only the social position differing in each case. "Social radicalism" is best understood, according to Rohe, as a product of particular "marginalized" positions. It often led to relatively spontaneous radical actions provoked by particular circumstances. In contrast, both "political radicalism" and "political reformism" required a certain amount of education and a long-term view of politics. The same could be said of working-class reformism. Rohe finally postulates that "the culturally significant boundaries apparently worked against a distinction between 'working-class radicalism' and 'working-class reformism.'" However, "political reformism" could also develop from "social reformism," and "political radicalism" could develop from "social radicalism."[45] In order to test this hypothesis more thoroughly, further empirical comparative studies are needed. One would assume that "political reformism" and, though less common, "political radicalism" were found more frequently in the party centers than in the party hinterlands.

Social Democratic Infrastructures

The party centers and hinterlands differed as well in the number of Social Democratic self-help organizations and friendly societies that they had. These included offices for dispensing relief and advice for workers; child protection and poor-relief commissions; various kinds of workers' cultural associations, such as gymnastics groups and choral societies; co-op consumer groups; building societies; people's theater; and the "people's insurance" (*Volksfürsorge*). The presence of Social Democratic infrastructures strengthened the sense of comradeship, improved the lives of many working-class families, expanded the number of party supporters, and helped to develop a social milieu supportive of

44. Rohe, "Ruhrgebietssozialdemokratie," 336. Rohe points for example to the Catholic milieu around Essen, which proved quite unreceptive to the mostly Protestant migrants.

45. Cf. also the comment about "the dispositional closeness between working-class reformism and radicalism" in von Saldern, "Arbeiterradikalismus," 493. Rohe's view avoids the one-sidedness still to be found in Erhard Lucas's study, which gives the impression there were only various forms of radicalism. Erhard Lucas, *Arbeiterradikalismus: Zwei Formen von Radikalismus in der deutschen Arbeiterbewegung* (Frankfurt, 1976).

the party.[46] In Harburg, for instance, the Volkswohl Sport and Play Ground, GmbH., was established thanks to funding from the labor unions and SPD. The local county manager, an avowed opponent of the labor movement, scolded the municipal authorities for not taking a similar initiative themselves and commented: "There is no denying that the creation of a public park like the Volkswohl goes a long way toward meeting the needs of the working population for rest and relaxation. It is very regrettable, though, that it was left to the Social Democrats and labor unions sympathetic to them to bring about this kind of project. Its purpose is not only indirectly to draw the masses of workers more closely to the Social Democratic Party but also to serve directly for party functions (meetings, summer festivals, May Day celebrations, etc.) and therefore serve the political class war. In my view, other methods should have been found to build a facility of this kind, for instance through the city administration with support from industrial circles."[47]

In the party hinterlands, not many associations and organizations were affiliated with the SPD. There was also a shortage of funding, culture talent, and skilled personnel. For instance, in all of Singen before the First World War, there was only one of the life-skills associations (*lebenspraktische Vereine*) affiliated with the SPD.[48] Although Singen was unusual in this respect, this illustrates the inability of the party hinterlands to develop Social Democratic milieus. They were far more likely to emerge in the party centers, if at all. However, there was not always a dearth of self-help organizations in the party hinterlands, as can be seen again in the example of Celle, where a strong Social Democrat consumer co-op emerged and where the party gained substantial influence over the local building and savings association. In addition, three workers' choral societies and three workers' athletic clubs provided for leisure and cultural activities. Celle also boasted a proletarian freethinkers association, a "Humor Club," a hall-building association, and an office to provide advice for workers.

Despite the counterexample of Celle, workers in the party hinterlands were generally far more dependent on middle-class and municipal institutions. They usually had much less confidence, therefore, in their

---

46. See for example in this regard, Witt, "Entstehung," 273, 287ff.

47. This letter from 1912 is quoted in Witt, "Entstehung," 290. For the development of bourgeois- and church-dominated labor associations see Adelheid von Saldern, "Wilhelminische Gesellschaft und Arbeiterklasse: Emanzipations- und Integrationsprozesse im kulturellen und sozialen Bereich," *IWK* 13, no. 4 (1977): especially 487ff.

48. Gert Zang, "Die Entstehung des sozialistischen Lagers: Die verspätete Entdeckung lebenspraktischer Hilfen: Der Milchvertriebsverein 1912," in Gert Zang (ed.), *Arbeiterleben in einer Randregion: Die allmählich Entstehung der Arbeiterbewegung in einer rasch anwachsenden Industriestadt Singen a.H. 1895–1933* (Konstanz, 1987).

ability to get along by helping each other. Since workers in the hinterlands had less experience at creating and operating organizations of their own, or organizations close to the SPD, and remained more dependent on middle-class or municipal institutions, they were more likely to adapt to the hegemonic bourgeois culture and to behave respectfully toward its representatives.

The party centers and hinterlands differed as well in the ease with which they could find space for party meetings. For many years, even after the legislation of 1890, the SPD remained dependent on innkeepers who were willing to allow their facilities to be used. In the large cities, some innkeepers could usually be found who considered Social Democrats valuable customers and were willing to accommodate them. Occasionally, though, a boycott had to be threatened in order to "persuade" particular innkeepers to cooperate.[49] On the other hand, there were often innkeepers in the big cities who felt close to the SPD or had even joined it. In Leipzig, for example, 3.4 percent of the party members were innkeepers.[50]

In the party hinterlands, though, the hegemony of the bourgeoisie was very strong, and the SPD had difficulty finding space for its meetings. In Göttingen, for instance, the police warned innkeepers not to accommodate the SPD or else officers would ensure that no students or military personnel ever patronized their establishments again. Many innkeepers bowed to this kind of informal pressure.[51] In later years, labor unions began building union halls and "halls of the people," but they were primarily in the party centers and especially in big cities such as Hamburg or Berlin. By 1906 there were twenty-seven union halls and halls of the people in the Reich, and by 1914 there were seventy-six.[52] These halls became very important symbols of the power of the labor movement — at least in the party centers. The Social Democrats in Celle attempted to build a union hall by themselves, but the attempt collapsed in 1905 for lack of funds.

Proletarian Publics

The labor movement demanded in vain a "right to the street" for public demonstrations. However, in large cities and party centers it succeeded

---

49. James S. Roberts, "Wirtshaus und Politik in der deutschen Arbeiterbewegung," in Gerhard Huck (ed.), *Sozialgeschichte der Freizeit* (Wuppertal, 1980), 128.

50. Michels, "Die deutsche Sozialdemokratie," 509.

51. Stefan Goch reports on a lack of space in the Gelsenkirchen area as well in *Sozialdemokratische Arbeiterbewegung und Arbeiterkultur im Ruhrgebiet: Eine Untersuchung am Beispiel Gelsenkirchen 1848–1975* (Düsseldorf, 1990), 118f.

52. Authors collective led by Dietrich Mühlberg (ed.), *Proletariat: Kultur und Lebensweise im 19. Jahrhundert,* 206 (Leipzig, 1986).

sometimes under the proper conditions in simply seizing that right, for instance on the occasion of strikes or of demonstrations for peace or electoral reform or on May Days. In big centers, the police often refrained from action against illegal outdoor demonstrations in order not to highlight social conflicts at an inopportune moment. No one knew for sure, though, what would happen at particular events because mounted police or even the army were sometimes called up to disperse the crowds.

Despite the inherent risk in any outdoor demonstrations, party centers were occasionally prepared to take a chance. Impressive outdoor demonstrations were sometimes organized, for example the demonstration in Berlin in January 1907 in favor of reforms to the Prussian electoral laws.[53] In addition, workers wended their way through the streets of Berlin every year on March 18 to the graves of the so-called Märzgefallenen, or martyrs who had lost their lives in the March uprising of 1848. The police took action in 1892 but succeeded only in prompting even more workers to make the pilgrimage the next year. We should recall the large demonstrations through the streets of downtown Hamburg at the time of the "theft of the right to vote" in 1905–6. These demonstrations were extremely tense and finally escaped the control of the Social Democratic organizers.

In the party hinterlands, the SPD could not afford such tests of strength on the open streets.[54] Even on May Day it did not dare to claim a "right to the street."[55] At no time did the Göttingen SPD, for instance, hold an event out of doors. The hinterlands of southern Germany were somewhat more tolerant, especially about May Day parades. Events of this kind were legalized in Württemberg, and people were able to parade openly on the streets here and even in party hinterlands such as Tübingen, at least after 1910.[56] In Prussia, though, May Day parades remained generally verboten. In such places as Celle and the Gelsenkirchen area, May Day "strolls" were therefore often held instead.[57]

The SPD usually followed the May Day rules laid down by the

---

53. Eduard Bernstein, *Die Berliner Arbeiter-Bewegung* (Berlin, 1910), 3:193.

54. A striking example is provided by Süchteln on the left bank of the Lower Rhine. Three Social Democratic choral associations wanted to parade through the streets but were broken up by troops with drawn sabers. Norbert Pies, "Hetzer wohnen hier verhältnismäßig wenige," in Günter Pätzold and Karl-Heinz Schlingmann (eds.), *Geschichte der Arbeiterbewegung am linken Niederrhein* (Marburg, 1989), 70f.

55. For the history of May Day celebrations see Inge Marßolek (ed.), *100 Jahre Zukunft: Zur Geschichte des 1. Mai* (Frankfurt and Vienna, 1990).

56. DGB Tübingen, *Arbeitertübingen,* 102; Schadt and Schmierer, *SPD,* 114; Wuerth, *Radikalismus,* 57.

57. For the Gelsenkirchen area see Goch, *Sozialdemokratische Arbeiterbewegung,* 128f.

police, even in party centers. Whether in Berlin or the hinterlands, the celebrations were held in large inns. There were some differences, though, between the big city and the hinterlands. Eduard Bernstein described a May Day celebration in Berlin as follows: "In 1894, the labor unions in Berlin found that 12,000 people turned up to celebrate, and by 1905 it was 50,000 or 60,000. Several hundred thousand, though, took part in the afternoon and evening festivities of the constituency organizations. And what enthusiasm burst forth again and again at these festivities alongside all the entertainment and high jinks! What jubilation and cheering greeted the melodies of workers' songs, and with what fervor people joined in the mass sing-alongs. The speeches, which were the real purpose of the festivities, were greeted with stormy applause!"[58] May Day in the hinterlands was celebrated as well, with speeches, songs, and entertainment. There were far fewer participants, though, and workers did not dare to take a day off. In the Göttingen area, for instance, May Day was always a regular workday.

Social Democratic centers and hinterlands differed as well insofar as party newspapers were concerned.[59] Party centers and local areas of strength, such as Harburg, usually had SPD newspapers,[60] which carried some reports from the hinterlands but not many. The party press played a very important role as the potential foundation of a counterpublic. Mass communications in class-specific publications familiarized workers on a daily basis with the collective nature of their fate, with broader connections among the problems facing them, and with a more general view of their individual experiences and interpretations of them. However, complaints often arose in the hinterlands that the reporting about them was rather poor. For instance, the Social Democrats in Göttingen expressed their dissatisfaction with the quality of the reports in the *Volkswille,* which was published in Hanover.[61] Shortly before the First World War, they even discussed a plan to create their own party press, arguing that "we need an organ that takes our backward situation into account. Most important, local conditions have to be discussed in light of our program. Only in this way can we appeal to the broad masses of

---

58. Bernstein, *Berliner Arbeiter-Bewegung,* 430.

59. Besides mentioning newspapers and magazines, we should also point to journeymen in various trades and migrant factory workers who moved from region to region as "agents of innovation"; Kramer, "Das Neue," 332.

60. The party newspapers were also organized originally in a polycentric way. Before the passage of the Socialist Laws, the party's two largest publishing houses were not in Berlin but in Leipzig (Genossenschafts-Buchdruckerei) and Braunschweig (Wilhelm Bracke). However, the SPD's new central organ, *Vorwärts,* was published in the imperial capital of Berlin; for Harburg see Witt, "Entstehung," 285.

61. von Saldern, *Auf dem Wege,* 187.

people, who are still unenlightened."[62] According to the Göttingen association, the *Volkswille* was totally unsatisfactory because it was tailored to conditions in the big city. In addition, the *Volkswille* was regarded as too high-flown for many workers "in our area." The cultural disparity between the urbanized party centers and the hinterlands of towns and small cities clearly came to the fore here. According to the Göttingen association, women were especially eager to read about local news, which the *Volkswille* did not cover.[63] Dissatisfaction with the *Volkswille* was also frequently voiced in Celle and elsewhere in the party hinterlands. As a result, many people continued to read the local bourgeois newspapers instead. The level of satisfaction with Social Democratic newspapers was therefore very different in the party centers and the hinterlands. Party newspapers were not published in the hinterlands until after the First World War.

Labor Unions and Strikes

Labor unions were the most abundant source of recruits for the SPD,[64] and local party organizations needed them in the area in order to expand and possibly make inroads into the hegemony of the bourgeoisie, despite the large number of union members who did not become party members. In Prussia, labor unions were at first most solidly entrenched in Berlin and the provinces of Hanover, Schleswig-Holstein, Brandenburg, and Hessen-Nassau. The heavily industrial areas in Saxony, the Rhineland, and Westphalia did not boast the most members until after the turn of the century.[65] As time passed, union members tended to become more evenly distributed around the Reich, and the strong disparity between northern and southern Germany abated.[66]

Local union councils, which linked all unions of a given city or town and thus were an indication of the number of individual unions in the area, became increasingly frequent in cities and towns. There were 820 such councils in 1914, up from 353 in 1901.[67] At the same time, various occupational groups professionalized their administrations. The number

62. *Volkswille,* July 15, 1914.
63. von Saldern, *Auf dem Wege,* 188.
64. Cf. Ritter, "Sozialdemokratie," 332.
65. Klaus Schönhoven, "Die regionale Ausbreitung der deutschen Gewerkschaften im Kaiserreich 1890–1918," in Gerhard A. Ritter with Elisabeth Müller-Luckner (eds.), *Der Aufstieg der deutschen Arbeiterbewegung: Sozialdemokratie und Freie Gewerkschaften im Parteiensystem und Sozialmilieu des Kaiserreichs* (Munich, 1990), 355. However, the author abstains from seeking analytical explanations.
66. Ibid., 357.
67. Ibid.

of union functionaries rose five times as fast as the number of members between 1898 and 1914. As the unions professionalized their organizations, "regional managements were set up to recruit members and attend to them."[68] As in the Social Democratic Party, this meant greater centralization and hierarchism at the regional level, while local union organizations suffered. Double memberships in both the union and the SPD remained limited, with party members often accounting for only a small proportion of the union members. In Frankfurt am Main, about 9 percent of union members were also party members in 1925, in Marburg (a party hinterland) 23 percent, and in Göttingen 14 percent. In Greater Berlin, only 16.4 percent of union members were also members of the SPD in 1906.[69]

In view of the limited membership in the SPD, whether in party centers or the hinterlands, the presence of labor unions was essential for the formation of proletarian publics, especially in strike situations. Masses of striking workers were primarily an urban phenomenon. In Berlin and the cities of the Hanseatic League, according to Friedhelm Boll, two to four times as many workers went on strike on average, including lockouts, as in the rest of the Reich.[70] However, if one looks at the number of labor disputes rather than the number of strikers and employers engaging in lockouts, the situation was quite different. Mecklenburg-Schwerin, Schleswig-Holstein, East Prussia, Alsace-Lorraine, and Pomerania led the way in this regard, following at some distance by the provinces of Saxony and Hanover and the small state of Thuringia. These were regions in which the labor movement was still relatively underdeveloped.[71] There were also many labor disputes in the municipalities surrounding the Hanseatic cities, medium-size industrialized cities, and smaller municipalities in central Germany.

Northern and southern Germany differed quite sharply. Apart from isolated islands such as Nuremberg and Augsburg, where labor disputes were quite frequent, the social climate in the south was usually better than in the north, and strikes were less common. In northern and central Germany, a strong correlation often existed between the number of union members and the number of workers who participated directly in labor disputes, for instance in the cities of Hanover, Frankfurt, Dresden,

---

68. Schönhoven, "Ausbreitung," 357, 358.
69. Information in Michels, "Die deutsche Sozialdemokratie," 489ff., 499ff.; von Saldern, *Vom Einwohner zum Bürger,* 173; Ritter, "Sozialdemokratie," 332. For figures for the Ruhr area, see Rohe, "Ruhrgebietssozialdemokratie," 328.
70. Boll, *Massenbewegungen,* 400.
71. Ibid., 400ff.

and Leipzig.[72] The experiences gained in labor disputes apparently often made workers want to become union members. However, other reactions could be seen as well, especially in agricultural areas, the Prussian provinces that had considerable heavy industry, and the Reichsland of Alsace-Lorraine. Here workers tended to become involved in labor disputes much more frequently than they joined a union.[73] In small cities and towns, according to Friedhelm Boll, there were often relatively high participation rates in strikes and elections but low participation rates in unions.[74] This leads one to conclude that the workers were permanently suppressed by various power structures. Strikes heightened workers' awareness of themselves and society and strengthened feelings of solidarity and community. Learning processes were initiated, especially when strike meetings stimulated thought and action. The great miners' strike of 1889, for example, induced whole villages and areas of towns that had voted mostly liberal in 1887 to switch en masse to the Social Democrats in the Reichstag elections of 1890. The strike had evidently destroyed faith in traditional company paternalism.[75]

It was hard to create bands of militant strikers in the party hinterlands. Here the strikers often worked for different companies or at different jobs, and many organizational problems arose as a result. In addition, the strikers frequently filtered back to their villages of origin to find work in the fields or at odd jobs because of the temporary loss of their regular employment, especially bricklayers, construction workers, and carpenters. Other strikers simply left the region entirely.[76] Under these conditions, it was difficult to form bands of striking workers for extended periods. However, there is always the counterexample of Celle, where bricklayers walked out in 1907 on a strike that was well supported and lasted for a year. The problems experienced in the hinterlands were not unknown in the big cities and party centers. Here too, striking workers sometimes left town for other locations, seeking to solve the problem on an individual basis. This reaction was more

---

72. Ibid., 406.

73. Ibid., 408.

74. Friedhelm Boll, "Arbeitskampf und Region: Arbeitskämpfe, Tarifverträge, und Streikwellen im regionalen Vergleich 1871–1914," in Gerhard A. Ritter with Elisabeth Müller-Luckner (eds.), *Der Aufstieg der deutschen Arbeiterbewegung: Sozialdemokratie und Freie Gewerkschaften im Parteiensystem und Sozialmilieu des Kaiserreichs* (Munich, 1990), 380.

75. Rohe, "Ruhrgebietssozialdemokratie," 322ff.

76. Typical of this was the course of the tobacco workers' strike in Eschwege in 1890. Konrad Homeister, *Die Arbeiterbewegung in Eschwege (1885 bis 1920): Ein Beitrag zur Kreis- und Stadtgeschichte* (Kassel, 1987), 21f. Many of the strikers simply left Eschwege.

debilitating in the hinterlands, though, where organized labor was already relatively weak.[77]

Most strikes in the hinterlands were agreed upon in advance with the union's district association and were aimed at rectifying the particularly low wages paid in outlying areas. Union officials made a special effort after the turn of the century in particular to reduce the large wage gap between the centers and hinterlands. In outlying areas, the labor movement generally lacked self-confidence and was inclined to trust district associations to assess the situation and make the right decisions, even if the workers' demands were not met in full and compromises had to be struck with the employers. The reliance on help "from above," that is, from district associations, did little to help workers in outlying areas develop any faith in themselves, especially since they also often realized the weakness of their position vis-à-vis the companies because of the high, though hidden, levels of structural unemployment. Companies in the provinces accordingly found it easy in many cases to replace striking workers with more compliant employees.[78] In conclusion, we can assume that the weakness of labor unions in outlying areas and their relative strength in bigger centers undermined the self-confidence of local SPD groups.

Local Milieus

M. Rainer Lepsius introduced the concept of "socio-moral milieus" in his description of society under the empire. These milieus were characterized by particular religions, regional traditions, economic conditions, and cultural orientations.[79] The term was used in investigations of the "socially transmitted everyday environments of individuals or social groups."[80] It turned out that social milieus were often quite small in size, frequently just a neighborhood or part of a neighborhood.

The urbanization process in big cities led to social segregation and the formation of working-class areas. Although these areas were not inhabited exclusively by working-class families, workers clearly dominated the social and cultural life. Towns and small cities were not free

---

77. von Saldern, *Auf dem Wege,* 199.

78. Ibid., 109; for Lahr cf. Caroli and Stimpel, *Lahrer SPD,* 48.

79. M. Rainer Lepsius, "Parteiensystem und Sozialstruktur: Zum Problem der Demokratisierung der deutschen Gesellschaft," in Gerhard A. Ritter (ed.), *Die deutschen Parteien vor 1918* (Cologne, 1973), 56–80, here 68.

80. Karl Gabriel, "Die Erosion der Milieus: Das Ende von Arbeiterbewegung und politischem Katholizismus?" in Heiner Ludwig and Wolfgang Schroeder (eds.), *Sozial- und Linkskatholizismus* (Frankfurt, 1990), 242.

from this kind of social segregation, but the working-class neighborhoods lacked the physical and cultural density found in larger centers. Many working-class families still lived in the bourgeois-dominated centers of towns and small cities such as Göttingen, although only in decaying older buildings. In the big cities, working-class neighborhoods crystallized either in the large apartment block districts built at the time or in the transitional zones of old housing on the fringes of the town centers. According to one study of the working-class area in the west end of Munich: "People knew each other at work and also met after work in the neighborhood. . . . The inhabitants were not very mobile and could almost always be found in their particular milieu, which developed a social profile of its own. The inhabitants tended to be similar in age and to have similar experiences. All the prerequisites were in place for very intensive communications."[81] The Social Democrats benefited in these areas from the politicization of people who had previously not bothered to vote. The west end of Munich also absorbed many of the workers streaming into the city from elsewhere. The newly arriving people "were immediately integrated into the Social Democratic political culture of the area. . . . Its particular social and geographic environment facilitated a quick, mass orientation in a socialist direction."[82] The intense social communications fostered the emergence of special cultural practices.[83] The west end of Munich contrasted in this regard with towns in the Ruhr where, according to Rohe, new migrants were not very well integrated into the local milieu. The important role played by Social Democratic milieus in attracting support from the petite bourgeoisie can be seen in the barbers, innkeepers, grocers, and independent tradesmen in these neighborhoods who sympathized with the party or even openly supported it.[84]

---

81. Stephan Bleek, "Ein Wählermilieu in der Großstadt: Bemerkungen zum Durchbruch der SPD in einem Münchner Arbeiterviertel," in Gerhard A. Ritter with Elisabeth Müller-Luckner (eds.), *Der Aufstieg der deutschen Arbeiterbewegung: Sozialdemokratie und Freie Gewerkschaften im Parteiensystem und Sozialmilieu des Kaiserreichs* (Munich, 1990), 140; see also Stephan Bleek, *Quartierbildung in der Urbanisierung: Das Münchner Westend 1890–1933* (Munich, 1991).

82. Bleek, "Wählermilieu," 142ff.; cf. Dieter Hertz-Eichenrode, "Parteiorganisation und Wahlkämpfe der Sozialdemokratie in Berlin," in Gerhard A. Ritter with Elisabeth Müller-Luckner (eds.), *Der Aufstieg der deutschen Arbeiterbewegung: Sozialdemokratie und Freie Gewerkschaften im Parteiensystem und Sozialmilieu des Kaiserreichs* (Munich, 1990), 140; cf. Karl Heinrich Pohl, *Die Münchener Arbeiterbewegung: Sozialdemokratische Partei, freie Gewerkschaften, Staat und Gesellschaft in München 1890–1914* (Munich, 1992).

83. See in general Vernon L. Lidtke, *The Alternative Culture: Socialist Labor in Imperial Germany* (New York and Oxford, 1985).

84. See Ritter, "Sozialdemokratie," 329.

Summary

It was very difficult to develop Social Democratic milieus in the party hinterlands. Many people who felt inclined to the SPD preferred to provide anonymous support, for instance in secret ballots in elections to the Reichstag, rather than support it openly by becoming a member or voting publicly for it in elections to the Prussian Landtag. This behavior shows that SPD voters were either reluctant to break radically with the traditional life and culture around them or were afraid to do so because of hostile reactions from employers or the authorities.

Already under the German Empire, the power of the regional union and SPD administrations increased as they became more professional and bureaucratic. The new regional structures brought greater centralization and hierarchism to the party hinterlands, despite the polycentric nature of the party as a whole. The regional party or labor union centers made it possible to bring strong, lasting pressure to bear on the local organizations or constituency associations.

The social and cultural disparities between the party centers and hinterlands widened in many ways in Wilhelminian times, largely because of the greater opportunities in urban areas. Intellectuals played a far more important role in the party centers, and the party's cultural infrastructure was also much more developed. The social and cultural disparities were further exacerbated by the emergence of regional organizations and the new hierarchies that they brought. The result in the hinterlands was the "peculiar conditions" mentioned at the beginning of this chapter, as the hinterlands were caught up in the modern trend toward centralization, bureaucracy, and hierarchism, while at the same time some typically provincial structures remained intact.

The trend in the prewar SPD toward regional centralization, bureaucracy, and hierarchism should not be seen simply as a case of the regional centers riding roughshod over the hinterlands. Much valuable assistance was provided, especially in respect to organization and agitation. The labor union centers also helped with strikes and wage negotiations. Although centralization and hierarchism always meant that the regional centers gained a certain control over the hinterlands, some freedom of action remained on the local level. The regional party centers often attempted to harmonize the political choices within "their" districts but again without complete success. In order to be fully successful, the party centers would have to change the prevailing mentalities and predispositions at the local and constituency levels, in addition to providing assistance and displaying their power.

The trend toward greater centralization, bureaucracy, and hierarchism in the regions was very much a part of the modern development of organizations. In assessing it, we must consider both the help that was provided and the external and internal dependencies that resulted. The trend was certainly a two-edged sword. As the regional party centers expanded, they provided organizational help to the hinterlands, broadened the horizons of local party organizations, and offered new and different interpretations of reality. On the other hand, the trend toward centralization and hierarchism must have often had a debilitating effect in the hinterlands. They could easily conclude that agitation and organization were all that mattered and that local and constituency associations could no longer rely on their own political and cultural resources. Henceforth, the hinterlands only developed party profiles based on local concerns to the extent that was essential for electoral success. When local problems did arise, it was relatively easy to import outside speakers from higher up the party hierarchy. The regional party centers apparently did not give sufficient thought to the appropriate amount of internal and external autonomy for the hinterlands and to helping them learn how to help themselves. If this had been done, the hinterlands would have learned how to understand and interpret their own situations better without losing sight of general party policy and society as a whole. It was all too easy for broad chasms to emerge between everyday experience in the hinterlands and the experience of the party. Once again, though, the example of Celle shows that the party hinterlands could develop different images. It would therefore be very informative if future research could analyze and characterize not only the party centers but various hinterlands as well.

Large political parties need a reasonable amount of homogeneity, that is, an internally consistent party image, as much as they need organization, centralization, and professionalization. The issue is always how far to go. Historical studies have long emphasized the "excessive" organization and bureaucratization of the Wilhelminian SPD and the reliance of local and constituency organizations on help from above. The development of regional party centers and the associated trend toward centralization, bureaucracy, and hierarchism resulted in a party that was too well disciplined. This lent Social Democracy in Germany a particular flavor of its own. One is left to ponder the general questions of how a balance could best be struck between party unity and local autonomy and how a mutually beneficial exchange of ideas could be established between party centers and party hinterlands, without leaning so much toward centralization that grassroots democracy suffered or so much toward autonomy that the party became weak and divided. This has always been a difficult balancing act.

CHAPTER 2

Workers' Parties, Class Identity, and United Action: Experiences, Social Constructs, and Myths in the Weimar Republic

Introduction

Discussions about the term *working class* have again come to the fore in light of the social developments in the second half of the twentieth century. Klaus Tenfelde spoke of a "society of renters and consumers . . . beyond class,"[1] and André Gorz bid "farewell to the proletariat,"[2] which had become, in his view, a privileged minority of jobholders with correspondingly conformist social behaviors. The end of the proletariat was also noted by Josef Mooser.[3] Ulrich Beck emphasized the "individualization" of lifestyles and life circumstances and the consequent disregard of social rank and class, despite the survival of social distinctions at elite levels (the elevator effect).[4]

I am grateful to Klaus-Michael Mallmann, Inge Marßolek, Herbert Obenaus, Monika Pater, Uta C. Schmidt, Klaus Tenfelde, and Hartmann Wunderer for their suggestions and criticisms.

1. Klaus Tenfelde, "Überholt von der demokratischen Massengesellschaft," *Frankfurter Allgemeine Zeitung*, no. 56, March 7, 1988, p. 7.

2. André Gorz, *Abschied vom Proletariat: Jenseits des Sozialismus* (Frankfurt, 1980).

3. Josef Mooser, *Arbeiterleben in Deutschland 1900–1970: Klassenlagen, Kultur, und Politik* (Frankfurt, 1984).

4. Ulrich Beck, "Jenseits von Klasse und Stand? Soziale Ungleichheiten, gesellschaftliche Individualisierungsprozesse, und die Entstehung neuer sozialer Formationen und Identitäten," in Reinhard Kreckel (ed.), *Soziale Ungleichheiten* (*Soziale Welt*, special volume 2) (Göttingen, 1983), 35–74; idem, *Risikogesellschaft: Auf dem Weg in eine andere Moderne* (Frankfurt, 1986).

Gerhard Schulze, for his part, studied the "experience (*Erlebnis*) society."[5]

Underlying all these attempts to characterize the society of today is the question of how the history of the proletariat and workers' parties should be written or rewritten.[6] The interest in this issue has increased considerably since the historic events of 1989–90, and a definite political twist has been added. In Klaus Tenfelde's view, it has become clearer since the fall of the Berlin Wall that the German labor movement is developing in the long run along the same lines as the labor movements in the other "Western" countries with constitutional governments. It has generated a modern *Volkspartei*, or broadly based political party, despite some major setbacks and delays, especially under the Nazi dictatorship. The transformation into a broadly based party really began after 1945, according to Tenfelde, and was based on "greater political participation," the erosion of social classes, and the emergence of the modern welfare state.[7] Peter Lösche and Franz Walter provided further support for this view in their book on the history of the Social Democratic Party. According to them, "the Weimar SPD's understanding of parliament and parliamentarism was still strongly affected by the experience of Bismarckian constitutionalism. In actual practice, though, the SPD had begun to transform itself into a broadly based party (*Volkspartei*) within a system of parliamentary government."[8] In the passages that follow, the authors examine the SPD primarily from the point of view of these questions. All historical writing has a particular perspective, of course, and serves current intellectual interests, whether directly or indirectly. The issue that arises is whether the perspective that is taken imposes unnecessary

---

5. Gerhard Schulze, *Die Erlebnisgesellschaft: Kultursoziologie der Gegenwart,* 4th ed. (Frankfurt, 1993). One should not forget, however, in all these studies of the present day that individuals find themselves in "the social realm of society," that the inequalities between social strata (and classes) not only exist from an objective point of view but are experienced subjectively, even though social positioning has become much more complex and difficult to determine than used to be the case.

6. The three volumes by Henrich August Winkler are considered standard works on the labor movement in the Weimar Republic: *Von der Revolution zur Stabilisierung: Arbeiter und Arbeiterbewegung in der Weimarer Republik 1918–1924; Der Schein der Normalität: Arbeiter und Arbeiterbewegung in der Weimar Republik 1924–1930; Der Weg in die Katastrophe: Arbeiter und Arbeiterbewegung in der Weimar Republik 1930–1933* (Bonn, 1984–90). There are more suggested readings here.

7. Klaus Tenfelde, "Die politische Rolle der deutschen Arbeiterbewegung" (paper presented at the Eighteenth International History Conference in Montreal, August 27–September 3, 1995).

8. Peter Lösche and Franz Walter, *Die SPD: Klassenpartei—Volkspartei—Quotenpartei: Zur Entwicklung der Sozialdemokratie von Weimar bis zur deutschen Vereinigung* (Darmstadt, 1992), 11ff.

conceptual limitations. The impulses in the SPD toward a broadly based Volkspartei can only be studied if the question of the "working class" and experiences of class society are addressed at the same time. Jürgen Kocka coined the term *Klassen-Entbildung*[9] (disintegration of the classes) in reference to the changes after 1945 in the lifestyles of workers and in the organizations and social aspirations of the lower social strata,[10] but it is also relevant to a central issue in the Weimar Republic. We should explore the processes tending to strengthen or dissolve the social classes and determine the extent to which the Weimar Republic was perceived at the time as a class society. There are no simple answers, and these key issues need to be explored on three levels, namely, structures and processes, the collective state of mind, and concrete actions.[11]

"Gender research," which was an offshoot of labor movement research, has contributed enormously to the realization that analytical categories such as "gender" are basically social constructs. What is true of the category "gender" must logically also be true of the category "class." Perry Anderson says, for instance, that the "working class" must be understood as a conceptual and cultural construct, although he hastens to add that this construct is based on real experience of social and economic proletarianization. "Reality" and "constructs" of it are interrelated in very complex ways, and the research has begun to turn therefore to "the reciprocal historical processes of the subjective and objective evolution of reality and of behaviors and conditions."[12] Gone forever are the days when one could speak glibly about "the workers," implicitly reducing the diversity and complexity of their lives to a single common denominator. The days are also gone when one could imply that working people saw themselves at all times and in all situations as "workers."[13]

---

9. This term appears in Jürgen Kocka, *Lohnarbeit und Klassenbildung* (Berlin and Bonn, 1983), 11ff.

10. Adelheid von Saldern and Dietrich Mühlberg, "Kontinuität und Wandel der Arbeiterkultur: Ein Forschungsaufriß," *Mitteilungen aus der kulturwissenschaftlichen Forschung* 30 (1992): 227.

11. According to Jürgen Kocka at the Eighteenth International History Conference in Montreal, August 27–September 3, 1995.

12. Regina Becker-Schmidt and Gudrun-Axeli Knapp, *Das Geschlechterverhältnis als Gegenstand der Sozialwissenschaften* (Frankfurt, 1995), 8; cf. also Kathleen Canning, "Gender and the Politics of Class Formation: Rethinking German Labor History," *American Historical Review* 97 (June 1992): 736–68. However, "reality" cannot be distinguished quite so neatly from the "social constructs of reality," especially since "social constructs" can help to create "realities."

13. Cf. Perry Anderson, *Arguments within Marxism* (London, 1980), 16ff. Patrick Joyce, "Work," in F. M. L. Thompson (ed.), *The Cambridge Social History of Britain 1750–1950* (Cambridge, 1990), 2:192ff. The interests of researchers have been changing in recent years as a result. No longer do they focus on the relative unity of an emerging

Most of these people had a number of identities, as they did in earlier historical periods as well, and considered themselves also for instance Berliners, parents, women, Germans, or freethinkers.

The questions that arise are, under what circumstances did their identity (as class-conscious) workers take priority over their other social identities and for what proportion of them was this true? Such questions are easy to ask but hard to answer, apart from some vague conclusions predicated on certain "facts." What usually emerges are snapshots of particular moments that can easily obscure the underlying trends "before" and "after." In any case, a stable, enduring sense of "class consciousness" had become obsolete by this time. It is important that this matter be clarified so that we do not approach the historical sources with exaggerated ideas of "class" and "class relations." Eduard P. Thompson once said: "When we speak of a class we are thinking of a very loosely-defined body of people who share the same congeries of interests, social experiences, traditions and value system, who have a disposition to behave as a class, and to define themselves in their actions and in their consciousness in relation to other groups of people in class ways."[14]

Social constructs bind many different individual experiences and identities together in broad, homogenized social-cultural configurations, or "classes." "Class emerged as a set of discursive claims about the social order seeking to order the latter in terms of itself."[15] Highly active members of the "working class," especially intellectuals and party leaders, often played major parts in the social construct of it.[16] Under certain conditions, social constructs can lead to joint undertakings in the real world. Gareth Stedman Jones pushed this idea to the limit in his book *Languages of Class* (1983), in which he ascribed exclusively to language as the carrier of the discourse about "class" the power to generate coherent class thought and action. He was concerned primarily with dissociating

---

"working class," but rather they study all sorts of largely occupational groups. However, we still know very little about the thought patterns and activities of the "apolitical" unorganized workers.

14. Eduard P. Thompson, "The Peculiarities of the English," in Ralph Miliband and John Saville (eds.), *Socialist Register 1965* (London, 1966), 357. For the extent to which this approach can be applied to other countries, see the introduction by Ira Katznelson in Ira Katznelson and Aristide R. Zolberg (eds.), *Working-Class Formation: Nineteenth-Century Patterns in Western Europe and the United States* (Princeton, 1986), 11ff.

15. Nicholas B. Dirks, Geoff Eley, and Sherry B. Ortner (eds.), *Culture/Power/History: A Reader in Contemporary Social Theory* (Princeton, 1994), 30.

16. We need to determine in this connection whether and to what extent certain "social constructs" can be instilled "from above" when there are many corresponding experiences to which the discourse can refer. I am grateful to Klaus Tenfelde for pointing this out.

"the ambition of a theoretically informed history from any simple pre-judgment about the determining role of the 'social' . . . as something outside of, and logically . . . prior to its articulation through language."[17] Nowadays at least, he is preaching to the converted in his criticism of a deterministic perspective — though not in regard to the extent to which social constructs and discourses must be predicated on social and economic processes and structures that can be experienced in the real world in order to have much effect. Those researchers who are persuaded by these kinds of interconnections and reciprocal relationships will find that studies of social constructs and discourses always point to social analysis — and vice versa.[18]

When the social construct of the "working class" becomes too far removed from its foundations in actual experience, when it takes on a life of its own and becomes fraught with symbols and rituals, a myth begins to take shape. Individuals are identified totally with particular classes, and social and world history are seen in deterministic fashion as leading to the eventual victory of the "working class." The mythologization of the "working class" arose, to be sure, from a deep-seated need in many workers. The mythology illustrated and suggested enormous might and instilled feelings of strength and self-confidence in the members and functionaries of working-class organizations. It helped to awaken slumbering potential and provided the political and ideological glue that helped to hold working-class milieus together. The concepts developed by Marx in his dialectical interpretation of history took on a life of their own in later decades, lost their dialectical force, and were popularized. In this form, they lent meanings to history, became a kind of mythology and incantation, and determined symbols and imaginary significations. The imaginary became a creative, shaping force, and every use of the myth only served to repotentiate it.[19] All the ideologically charged festivals and celebrations and all the symbols and inflated rhetoric illustrate the process by which the social construct of the "working class" was transformed into myth.[20] It was easy, we must remember, for

17. Gareth Stedman Jones, *Languages of Class: Studies in English Working-Class 1832–1982* (Cambridge, 1983), 7.

18. Cf. in this regard the criticism of Peter Schöttler, introduction to Gareth Stedman Jones, *Klassen, Politik, und Sprache,* ed. Peter Schöttler (Münster, 1988), 27.

19. For the importance of the imaginary in general see Cornelius Castoriadis, *The Imaginary Institution of Society* (Cambridge, 1987).

20. See in this regard Inge Marßolek, "Von Freiheitsgöttinnen, dem Riesen Proletariat, und dem Aufzug der Massen: Der 1. Mai im Spiegel der sozialdemokratischen Maizeitungen 1891 bis 1932," in idem (ed.), *100 Jahre Zukunft: Zur Geschichte des 1. Mai* (Frankfurt, 1990), 145ff. Many workers presumably recognized the mythical nature of the "working class," but public discussion of the problem remained taboo. I am grateful to

the mythologization of the "working class" to diminish one's ability to assess the balance of power and judge situations appropriately.

Both the general social construct of the "working class" and the particular mythology attached to it served primarily to lend meaning and purpose to experiences, conditions, and processes. However, the resulting conception of the "working class" was so standardized and homogenized that it excluded, overlooked, and depreciated many aspects of working people's lives,[21] especially in the cases of women, the unskilled, and ethnic minorities. "The positivity of the working class presumed the negativity of the others — and not just other classes but also other kinds of workers (for example, the unorganized, the rough and unrespectable, the criminal, the frivolous, the religiously devout, the ethnically different and of course the female), and of other elements of subjectivity — in effect all those aspects of identity that could not be disciplined into a highly centered notion of class-political agency."[22]

We attempt in this chapter to connect these theoretical considerations with empirical observations of the 1920s. In the first and second parts, we look at social and economic trends that were actually felt at the time. We concentrate first on those trends that tended to reinforce the social construct of the "working class" acting as a united whole. In the second part, we look at opposing trends that were actually felt and that eroded the cohesiveness of this class. Those who feel that the most important fact about the history of the labor movement in the 1920s was the failure of a united "working class" to emerge at key moments in the history of the Weimar Republic should be particularly interested in the everyday lives of workers and the reasons for the disagreements and splits within the labor movement. We do not intend to resort to deterministic explanations predicated on "objective" life experiences. The differing attitudes and behaviors of workers vis-à-vis society and the state were based much more on their differing interpretations of reality, which can only be outlined here. As Eduard P. Thompson said: "We can see a logic in the responses of similar occupational groups undergoing similar experiences, but we cannot predicate any law."[23]

In the third part, we look from a class-analysis perspective at the two workers' parties and the number of members and voters they were able to

---

Hartmann Wunderer for pointing this out. The mythologization of the working class in the historiography of the late 1960s and the 1970s would also be a good topic.

21. See in this regard the introduction in Dirks, Eley, and Ortner, *Culture/Power/ History*, 32.

22. Ibid., 32.

23. Eduard P. Thompson, introduction to *The Making of the English Working Class* (Harmondsworth, 1963).

attract. The fourth part examines social constructs of the state and the future, which greatly influenced the relationship between these two parties. The fifth part explores how politicians conceived of the "working class" and how their views contributed to the social construct of it. Finally, we look at a particular kind of social construct: myths.

Cohesive Forces

Who could fail to be impressed by the social and cultural networks that developed in working-class milieus, for instance in Hanover-Ricklingen or Berlin-Wedding?[24] Workers' dwellings, places of work, cultural associations, and cooperative stores usually lay cheek by jowl, as well as labor union offices and party offices. Communications were very intense in these milieus,[25] which proved quite resistant to National Socialism.[26]

Lösche and Walter studied the social and cultural influence of milieus like these during the Weimar Republic.[27] However, these researchers did not study them from the perspective of the "unity and solidarity of the

24. It was an article by Klaus-Michael Mallmann that revived the discussion about the cohesiveness of the "working class" in the Weimar Republic. Klaus-Michael Mallmann, "Milieu, Radikalismus, und lokale Gesellschaft: Zur Sozialgeschichte des Kommunismus in der Weimarer Republik," *Geschichte und Gesellschaft* 21, no. 1 (1995). Mallmann criticized the rather one-dimensional political histories of German communism written at the time — by which he meant dependence on the Soviet Union — and called for a sociocultural approach. See idem, *Kommunisten in der Weimarer Republik: Sozialgeschichte einer revolutionären Bewegung* (Darmstadt, 1996).

25. On the whole, three social spaces can be distinguished that together created a milieu that was all the more tightly knit the more interconnected they were: the factory and the union, the workers' cultural associations, and the working-class area in the city. Women who did not work outside their homes in working-class areas benefited from a rich social network stretching from neighbors to the people at the co-op. These milieus were important not least of all for the socialization they provided.

26. For basic information about the concept of milieus see M. Rainer Lepsius, "Parteiensystem und Sozialstruktur: Zum Problem der Demokratisierung der deutschen Gesellschaft," in Gerhard A. Ritter (ed.), *Die deutschen Parteien vor 1918* (Cologne, 1973); Karl Rohe, "Vom alten Revier zum heutigen Ruhrgebiet: Die Entwicklung einer regionalen politischen Gesellschaft im Spiegel der Wahlen," in Gerhard A. Ritter and Herbert Kühr (eds.), *Politik und Gesellschaft im Ruhrgebiet* (Königstein, 1979); Wolfgang Rudzio, "Wahlverhalten und kommunalpolitisches Personal in ausgewählten Oldenburger Gemeinden," in Wolfgang Günther (ed.), *Sozialer und politischer Wandel in Oldenburg* (Oldenburg, 1981); and Adelheid von Saldern, "Sozialmilieus und der Aufstieg des Nationalsozialismus in Norddeutschland (1930–1933)," in Frank Bajohr (ed.), *Norddeutschland im Nationalsozialismus* (Hamburg, 1993), 20–52.

27. Peter Lösche and Franz Walter, "Zur Organisationskultur der sozialdemokratischen Arbeiterbewegung in der Weimarer Republik: Niedergang der Klassenkultur oder solidargemeinschaftlicher Höhepunkt?" *Geschichte und Gesellschaft* 15, no. 4 (1989): 536.

'working class,'" preferring to concentrate solely on Social Democratic milieus and completely disregarding Communist ones. Lösche and Walter described the labor movement in the Weimar Republic as primarily a "Social Democratic solidarity community." Although their article seems intended to demonstrate how influential the Social Democrat milieus were, including from a quantitative point of view, the figures that the authors themselves provide at the end of the article go a long way toward qualifying this impression. Lösche and Walter suggested that workers sympathetic to the SPD should be divided into three basic categories: first, the great mass of such workers who voted SPD but were already heavily influenced by the popular culture impinging on them from outside their social milieus; second, the workers involved in the workers' cultural movement close to the SPD who may have been influenced by popular culture but still cultivated a particular ideological and philosophical standpoint of their own; and third, the very limited number of Social Democrats, estimated at about two hundred thousand, who are described as the "Social Democratic solidarity community" in the narrow sense.[28]

Hartmann Wunderer picked up on the last number to advance a view contrary to that of Lösche and Walter. Wunderer pointed from a purely quantitative perspective at the marginal nature of the "Social Democratic solidarity community," which probably did not include any more than 2 or 3 percent of SPD voters. He also highlighted the lack of political influence of the workers' cultural associations, for instance the freethinkers with their six hundred thousand members. They did not all vote SPD by any means and in many cases were more inclined to anarchistic syndicalism or the Communists.[29] In addition the Social Democratic milieus, like their Communist counterparts, excluded many people, despite all the overlap between them. The Social Democratic milieus therefore had mixed effects on "working-class unity": in some ways they mitigated the political split within the labor movement, and in others they aggravated it.

Regardless of how one feels about individual research results, the discussion has fostered greater awareness of the problems in this area. From a qualitative standpoint, there can be no doubt about the social and cultural importance of the Social Democratic milieus. However, we cannot ignore their limitations insofar as sheer numbers are concerned. Some groups of workers were hard to integrate into SPD-oriented milieus and apparently were also not much interested in mass rallies. Among them were youths (especially young women) and unskilled workers. These

---

28. Lösche and Walter, "Zur Organisationskultur," 536.
29. Further objections appear in Hartmann Wunderer, "Noch einmal: Niedergang der Klassenkultur oder solidargemeinschaftlicher Höhepunkt," *Mitteilungen aus der kulturwissenschaftlichen Forschung* 30 (1992): 277ff.

people were increasingly attracted to the new commercial culture with its cross-class appeal. The patrons of the new movie houses that were springing up were largely working-class people, especially those who were young, female, or unskilled, alongside office workers (especially women). Unskilled and semiskilled workers often moved in circles outside the traditional culture of the workers' associations and were therefore more easily attracted to the new, colorful, apparently classless world of popular culture.[30]

Although Social Democrats dominated certain social milieus and lent them their particular flavor, many non–Social Democrats could be found there too, including Communists. The same could be said about the numerous workers' cultural associations, where Communists and Social Democrats rubbed shoulders until the great split in the movement in 1928–29, even though the latter dominated with only a few exceptions. Communist social milieus had similar structurations,[31] only the other way around, with some Social Democratic families living in the area as well.[32] In addition, Communist and Social Democratic families often had personal ties. Members of the two parties frequently shared a common past: a study done in 1927 showed that 30.2 percent of KPD members had been in the Weimar SPD and 30.8 percent in the USPD (Independent Social Democratic Party of Germany).[33]

Another potential source of class-based political action was the

---

30. See in this regard Dietrich Mühlberg, "Modernisierungstendenzen in der proletarischen Lebensweise: Neuartige Ansprüche veränderter Menschen," *Mitteilungen aus der kulturwissenschaftlichen Forschungen* 30 (1992): 34–64; James Wickham, "Arbeiterpolitik und Arbeiterbewegung in den 1920er Jahren in einer Großstadt: Das Beispiel Frankfurt am Main," *SOWI* 13, no. 1 (1984): 22–29; Adelheid von Saldern, "Arbeiterkulturbewegung in Deutschland in der Zwischenkriegszeit," in Friedhelm Boll (ed.), *Arbeiterkulturen zwischen Alltag und Politik: Beiträge zum europäischen Vergleich in der Zwischenkriegszeit* (Vienna, 1986), 59; Detlev J. K. Peukert, *Jugend zwischen Krieg und Krise: Lebenswelten von Arbeiterjungen in der Weimarer Republik* (Cologne, 1987), 232.

31. See Anthony Giddens, *Social Theory and Modern Sociology* (Cambridge, 1986), 60ff. This term is intended to dispel the static quality associated with the word *structure*.

32. Cf. Mallmann, "Milieu," 17ff. Mallmann also mentions the kind of left-wing cultural milieu in which both political persuasions were quite strong and struggled with one another for preeminence, as in Steinheim am Neckar for instance. Ibid., 23. For an example of Communist dominance in a village see Hans-Joachim Althaus et al., *Da ist nirgends nichts gewesen außer hier: Das 'rote Mössingen' im Generalstreik gegen Hitler: Geschichte eines schwäbischen Arbeiterdorfes* (Berlin, 1982). It is a mistake to think that working-class milieus were only Social Democratic or Catholic. However, until the great split in 1929, most of the workers' cultural associations were dominated by Social Democrats. The non–Social Democratic, that is, Communist, milieus were concentrated around factories or in individual districts or parts of streets.

33. Mallmann, "Milieu," 12.

shared experience of alienated work. As a result of the rationalization and mechanization processes unleashed in the 1920s by Taylorism and Fordism, workers in different branches of the economy had more and more in common[34] as jobs were de-skilled and the labor force became more homogeneous. These processes sharpened the divide between management and workers in many respects, and the latter found that they had similar experiences.[35] Until the founding of the Communists' own labor unions in 1929, Social Democrats and Communists worked side by side in the unions, although the leadership was overwhelmingly Social Democratic. Mallmann speaks therefore of a "fund of common experiences of class society."[36]

Social Democrats and Communists had much in common as well on a philosophical and intellectual level. Working people were often anti-clerical, cultivated the myths of the proletariat, believed in progress, thought that history was rational, and had high hopes for the socialist future. They shared the same labor movement history and inheritance of Marxism, and they had many festivals and songs in common.[37]

The two parties occasionally undertook joint actions on the political and organizational levels. We could mention, for instance, the government coalitions in Saxony and Thuringia in 1923, the referendum regarding the expropriation of the princely houses in 1926,[38] the popular actions against Paragraph 218 toward the end of the Weimar Republic, and many strikes and demonstrations. Even during the Great Depression, when the hostility between the two workers' parties was at its height, instances of cooperation could be found on the local or regional levels.[39]

---

34. See for instance Eva Cornelia Schöck, *Arbeitslosigkeit und Rationalisierung: Die Lage der Arbeiter und die kommunistische Gewerkschaftspolitik 1920–28* (Frankfurt and New York, 1977), 172. However, rationalization was by no means as widespread as all the discussions about it would lead one to conclude. One sector that was already heavily rationalized was coal mining. See in this regard Uwe Burghardt, *Die Mechanisierung des Ruhrbergbaus 1890–1930* (Munich, 1995).

35. Stolle points out as well, however, the deterioration in communications. Ute Stolle, *Arbeiterpolitik im Betrieb: Frauen und Männer, Reformisten und Radikale, Fach- und Massenarbeiter bei Bayer, BASF, Bosch und in Solingen (1900–1933)* (Frankfurt, 1980), 251ff.

36. Mallmann, *Kommunisten*, 265.

37. Ibid., 266.

38. The referendum, called as a result of a KPD initiative, was to eliminate the payments to the princes who had ruled until 1918. A total of 14.4 million people supported this measure. In comparison, the SPD and KPD together managed to attract only 11 million votes in the previous election to the Reichstag in 1924.

39. For the relative independence of KPD members see Lore Heer-Kleinert, *Die Gewerkschaftspolitik der KPD in der Weimarer Republik* (Frankfurt and New York, 1983), 360ff.

For example, in the municipal government elections in Württemberg in December 1931, the KPD and SPD drew up joint lists of candidates in the face of the Nazi threat.[40]

Differences and Disagreements

There was much civil unrest between 1917 and 1923, in which many workers were involved, particularly the hunger disturbances and strikes of 1917–18, the revolutionary events of 1918–19, the struggle against the Factory Councils Act in 1920, the general strike against the Kapp Putsch in 1920, and the ensuing "Kämpfe in der Ruhr-Region," when the situation verged on civil war. In addition, there were the Mansfeld disturbances of 1921 and the Hamburg uprising of 1923. Each of these events unfolded in its own way and had its own history. In general, though, when outside pressures became sufficiently intense, the tensions within the working class tended to fade, especially when radical action seemed "legitimized by conflicts with the bourgeoisie that were interpreted in terms of the class struggle."[41] As shown by the example of Gotha, conflicts with the bourgeoisie (such as the Kapp Putsch) could strengthen the forces of unity in the working class, at least on the local level. However, such conflicts did not provide a long-term solution to the political fragmentation of the workers, and the internal differences came to the fore again, at the very least when the two parties found themselves competing for power and influence among the same workers.

The labor movement was destabilized and disoriented by the period of hyperinflation since this was an intangible class struggle in which all labor parties proved helpless. The mood among workers swung between radicalism and apathy. Labor organizations recovered only slowly after 1924 from the loss of confidence among their members. It is perhaps no coincidence that the KPD allowed itself to be "sovietized" at exactly this time and the SPD stagnated, at least on the national level.

The many and at times strong distinctions and disagreements among politically organized workers had sociocultural aspects as well. Society was modernizing by leaps and bounds in the 1920s, but not all workers were equally affected, and the resulting differences in their experiences and interpretations tended to increase. In areas where mod-

---

40. Mallmann, "Milieu," 21. Mallmann also mentions agreements between the local organizations of the two parties in Nuremberg, Hamburg, and Oberhausen.

41. For this and what follows, see for more details Helge Matthiesen, "Zwei Radikalisierungen: Bürgertum und Arbeiterschaft in Gotha 1918–1923," *Geschichte und Gesellschaft* 21, no. 1 (1995): 50.

ernization was most intense, it brought both advantages and disadvantages. Some workers saw their life prospects brighten, and they tended to view the world quite differently from those whose prospects dimmed.[42] Contrasting ideas of what future society would be like also had a major impact.

We will confine ourselves here to just a few indications of the asynchrony in the modernization process and the ambivalence of its overall effects. The industrial proletariat living in big cities comprised only a minority of working people,[43] and those who lived and worked in rural areas or small towns experienced very different conditions. In addition, factories differed enormously in size, and various branches of the economy mechanized to differing extents. Levels of rationalization were quite dissimilar. Furthermore, unemployment was not equally severe in all sectors of the economy and in factories of all sizes. Wages contrasted as sharply as the working conditions and jobs performed. Finally, job security and prospects for promotion also varied enormously.[44]

What experiences could a poorly paid typist or a restaurant employee or a shoe salesperson have in common with a lathe operator in an engineering works or a uniformed streetcar employee or a rural laborer? A major reason for the contrasting experiences was the increasing differentiation of society and work.[45] Workers' experiences and interpretations of these experiences grew more and more dissimilar. The differentiation of work also created many opportunities for small social advances, whether real or only apparent, which affected many people's hopes and plans for the future.

As society grew more diverse so did the socialization of the younger generation of workers. Some lived in quite stable families and took advantage of improving opportunities for education and training. Family life became more important for many workers, who had fewer children but devoted more attention to each one. Other young people had quite different experiences, if one is to judge by the many contemporary complaints about the moral decline of working-class youth,[46] the "wild

---

42. See in this regard the various works of Detlev J. K. Peukert, especially *Max Webers Diagnose der Moderne* (Göttingen, 1989); and David F. Crew's review of it, "The Pathologies of Modernity," *Social History* 17, no. 2 (1992): 319–28.

43. Jürgen W. Falter, *Hitlers Wähler* (Munich, 1991), 199ff.

44. The differences grew more marked in the period of relative stability after 1924. For an overview, see Detlev J. K. Peukert, *Die Weimarer Republik: Krisenjahre der klassischen Moderne* (Göttingen, 1987), 151; Heer-Kleinert, *Gewerkschaftspolitik*, 261ff.; Stolle, *Arbeiterpolitik*, 244ff.; Schöck, *Arbeitslosigkeit*, 153ff.

45. Schöck, *Arbeitslosigkeit*, 170ff.

46. Cf. for instance Bruno Theek, *SOS: Jugend am Kreuz: Notrufe aus der Großstadt-Unterwelt* (Hamburg-Bergedorf, 1929).

gangs" that were allegedly so hard to control,[47] the "conditions" prevailing in "red" neighborhoods,[48] and the consumption of commercialized, supposedly corrupting popular culture.[49] There were also some differences in generation-specific experiences. As Peukert remarked: "Although some tensions already existed between the older *Gründerzeit* generation, which had risen to positions of prominence in the Weimar Republic, and younger rivals from the 'front generation,' the generation from around the turn of the century had every reason to proclaim the 'rights of the young generation' against the gerontocracy. Young people felt unneeded and unwanted. Not only was the economy stagnant and labor markets crowded, but young people were commonly suspected of being 'depraved' by the experience of the war, while being too young to bask in the redeeming myth of the 'experience of the front.' This generation was especially hard hit by the job shortages of the Great Depression."[50] Some members of the "superfluous generation of 1900" proved particularly susceptible to the blandishments of political extremists, while others withdrew into an "apolitical" stance and cultivated their own subculture. This generation felt less connected than others to particular social milieus and was more likely to spend its spare time imbibing the new popular culture spanning the classes.

In addition to the contrasting socializations and experiences that members of various generations or even of a single generation could have, there were also gender differences. Karen Hagemann studied the milieu of female Social Democratic workers in Hamburg and noted the differences between their life experiences and those of the men in their lives.[51] The policies of the SPD and the labor unions were determined largely by men and often ignored the interests of women. Very few efforts were made to advance the cause of women, in particular in the areas of education, jobs, marriage, and the family. Although traditional concepts of the relations between the sexes were being called into question by dazzling images of the "new woman" and *Kamaradschaftsehen,* or marriages based on friendship, many working-class families still hewed to the traditional, patriarchic model. It is hardly surprising, there-

---

47. Cf. Peukert, *Jugend.*

48. See Eve Rosenhaft, *Beating the Fascists? The German Communists and Political Violence 1929–1933* (Cambridge, 1983).

49. See for example all the statements in the proceedings of the Reichstag and the Prussian Landtag; see also chapter 9 in this volume.

50. Peukert, *Weimarer Republik,* 30.

51. Karen Hagemann, *Frauenalltag und Männerpolitik: Alltagsleben und gesellschaftliches Handeln von Arbeiterfrauen in der Weimarer Republik* (Bonn, 1990).

fore, that women were not very attracted to either of the great working-class parties, which continued to be dominated by men.[52]

Despite the state subsidies for the construction of new housing estates, often on the outskirts of cities, only the middle classes or better-paid workers with few children could afford such modern dwellings. The broad masses of workers, many of whom worked only intermittently, had to make do with badly decaying housing, for instance in the Hanover Alstadt, poor districts in Hamburg, or Moabit in Berlin. "New living" was associated with the new image of humanity purveyed by the media, especially journals and newspapers. The new ideal emphasized health, good hygiene, cleanliness, and orderliness in rationalized, well-planned homes.[53] Those workers who could afford "modern" lives may well have felt culturally different from the majority living in "non-modern" conditions. There had certainly been differences among workers in earlier times in their housing and ways of life, but the differences now became much more systematic and fraught with social significance. The new housing estates and apartment buildings tended therefore to erode the social cohesion of the working class and draw higher-paid workers closer to lower- and midlevel white-collar employees, both literally and figuratively.[54]

Party Members and Voters

Social Democrats and Communists tended to have different living and working conditions and were therefore inclined to have different experiences and to interpret their experiences differently. The distinctions affected the kinds of people each party attracted. After 1929–30, the KPD became the party of the unemployed, and its membership tended to turn over quite quickly. It accordingly gained a public reputation for radical talk intended to win the support of the "antisocial" or young unemployed people. In comparison with the SPD, the KPD clearly appealed primarily to people who were especially disadvantaged or excluded and who felt

---

52. Women made up 23 percent of the SPD in 1930 and only 16.5 percent of the KPD in 1929. Weitz also points out that passivity of men toward housework was very seldom criticized in the Communist *Arbeiter-Illustrierte-Zeitung*. Eric D. Weitz, *Popular Communism: Political Strategies and Social Histories in the Formation of the German, French, and Italian Communist Parties 1919–1948* (Ithaca, 1992), 10.

53. Ulfert Herlyn, Adelheid von Saldern, and Wulf Tessin (eds.), *Neubausiedlungen der 20er und 60er Jahre: Ein historisch-soziologischer Vergleich* (Frankfurt and New York, 1987).

54. See in this regard Adelheid von Saldern, *Häuserleben: Zur Geschichte städtischen Arbeiterwohnens vom Kaiserreich bis heute* (Bonn, 1995), 153ff.

that their future prospects were dim.[55] Workers who had different experiences and views tended for the most part to ignore the KPD or at least did not feel very attracted by the Communists' policies and interpretation of society.[56] However, the KPD had not always been a party of "underdogs." As late as 1927, 39.9 percent of its members were skilled industrial workers, in comparison with 28.1 percent who were unskilled. Some 9.5 percent were tradesmen or people involved in commerce.[57] Although the KPD had already acquired its reputation as the party of underdogs by the time of the Great Depression,[58] it still had some "respectable" workers in its ranks, though their numbers were decreasing. KPD members were also not particularly young. Most were between twenty-five and forty years of age, which made the party similar in age structure to the prewar SPD.[59] The KPD was characterized as well by a relatively rapid turnover in members. This was due both to the inability of members who had become unemployed to afford the membership fee and to the fact that radical workers in the Weimar Republic did not necessarily become permanent members of the KPD. Many joined the syndicalist or left-Communist movements that arose in the early days of the republic.[60]

In contrast to the Communists, the Social Democrats spoke primarily for workers with "respectable" jobs. Most had skills and found that their hopes of getting ahead and building little careers for themselves were well received in the SPD. Relatively few unskilled workers joined the party. A representative survey of ninety-three local SPD associations in 1930 showed that although "workers" accounted for 59.4 percent of all members, only 5.3 percent of them were unskilled. On the other hand, the SPD was starting to make inroads into the middle classes. According to the same survey, 14.5 percent of the party members were office employees, public officials, and self-employed.[61] As Lösche and

---

55. Detlev J. K. Peukert, "Volksfront und Volksbewegungskonzept im kommunistischen Widerstand: Thesen," in Jürgen Schmädeke and Peter Steinbach (eds.), *Der Widerstand gegen den Nationalsozialismus: Die deutsche Gesellschaft und der Widerstand gegen Hitler* (Munich, 1985), 878.

56. Regional differences must also be considered however.

57. Mallmann, "Milieu," 11.

58. Ibid., 19.

59. Ibid., 12; cf. Hartmann Wunderer, *Arbeitervereine und Arbeiterparteien: Kultur- und Massenorganisationen in der Arbeiterbewegung (1890–1933)* (Frankfurt, 1980); cf. Ben Fowkes, *Communism in Germany under the Weimar Republic* (New York, 1984), 172ff.

60. Future research into the KPD should take a closer look at the relationships between the party and "worker radicalism."

61. Mallmann, "Milieu," 11.

Walter also point out, these figures indicate that the SPD was starting to develop in the direction of a *Volkspartei*. Although care should be taken, as we have seen, not to exaggerate the differences in the social strata to which the SPD and KPD appealed, analysis of their memberships does make it possible to draw some conclusions about the social-cultural diversification of the "working class," especially in the final years of the Weimar Republic.

Finally, we should not forget that many workers turned their backs on both great labor parties, either because these workers were apolitical, or were solidly anchored in the Catholic Center Party,[62] or sympathized with the German Nationals[63] or even the National Socialists.[64] These workers were always a minority, but since the working class itself was so large, they accounted for a considerable proportion of all voters. Attachment to the Catholic faith, in particular, created party loyalties that lasted for generations, especially when the workers also lived in Catholic social milieus.

About 16 million people, or half the active labor force, were "workers" in 1925.[65] According to the 1933 census, about 28 percent of the eligible voters were "workers." However, as electoral researcher Jürgen W. Falter has shown, when appropriate numbers of family members and retirees are added, it turns out that about 45 percent of eligible voters belonged to the working class.[66] Nevertheless, the KPD and SPD together usually received only about 30 percent of the total vote, including those people in the middle class, especially the lower middle class, who

---

62. For Catholic milieus see Cornelia Rauh-Kühne, *Katholisches Milieu und Kleinstadtgesellschaft: Ettlingen 1918–1939* (Sigmaringen, 1991), especially 127ff.; cf. Dieter Schott, *Die Konstanzer Gesellschaft 1918–1924: Der Kampf um die Hegemonie zwischen Novemberrevolution und Inflation* (Konstanz, 1989), especially 143ff.

63. See in this regard Amrei Stupperich, *Volksgemeinschaft oder Arbeitersolidarität: Studien zur Arbeitnehmerpolitik in der Deutschnationalen Volkspartei 1918–1933* (Göttingen and Zürich, 1982). According to its own figures, the Deutschnationale Arbeiterbund had 400,000 members who were workers in 1926.

64. On the other hand, the NSDAP often employed the tactic in its propaganda campaigns of appealing to various groups of workers separately and making concrete proposals about what should be changed to benefit them in particular. For instance, it promised rural workers higher wages, a concerted effort at mechanization, and new housing on small plots of land. Michael H. Kater, *The Nazi Party: A Social Profile of Members and Leaders 1919–1945* (Cambridge, MA, 1983), especially 52ff.

65. Dietmar Petzina et al., *Sozialgeschichtliches Arbeitsbuch* 3 (1978): 55. Among them were many workers married to women who did not work outside the home. Some 35.6 percent of women had outside jobs in 1925; ibid., 54.

66. Falter, *Hitlers Wähler,* 198. For the reasons why workers voted for the Nazis see Gunter Mai, "Arbeiterschaft zwischen Sozialismus, Nationalismus, und Nationalsozialismus," in Uwe Backes et al. (eds.), *Die Schatten der Vergangenheit: Impulse zur Historisierung der Vergangenheit* (Frankfurt and Berlin, 1990), 195ff.

supported them.[67] Timothy Mason deduced from these results already in the 1970s that a very large proportion of the wage-earning population never voted for the workers' parties and that, in the elections between 1930 and 1932, a maximum of half of all wage earners voted for them.[68] The number of people who voted for the workers' parties remained roughly steady, but these parties were unable to increase their vote as participation in elections increased.[69] Falter also calculated that about one in every four workers already voted National Socialist German Workers Party (NSDAP) in 1932 and that working-class households accounted for 40 percent of NSDAP votes that year.[70]

Even those researchers who are skeptical about Falter's calculations should feel compelled to look more closely at those groups of workers who were susceptible to National Socialism and therefore helped to demolish the myth that the "working class" was largely immune to Nazism. Nevertheless, workers were still heavily underrepresented among Nazi voters and even more so among party members. This is certainly not an insignificant fact.

Social Constructs of the State and the Future

The role of the state was quite different in the Weimar Republic from what it had been in the empire. Government intervened much more in society, and the welfare state expanded. Not all workers benefited directly by any means,[71] but the critical facto was not only improvements in concrete conditions for the socially disadvantaged but also basic be-

---

67. There were, however, substantial regional differences.
68. Cited in Annemarie Tröger, "Die Dolchstoßlegende der Linken: 'Frauen haben Hitler an die Macht gebracht,'" in *Frauen und Wissenschaft: Beiträge zur Berliner Sommeruniversität für Frauen* (Berlin, 1976), 355. This explosive charge was not addressed at the time by researchers into the labor movement.
69. Cf. Wickham, "Arbeiterpolitik."
70. Every sixth SPD voter switched to the NSDAP in 1932 according to Falter, *Hitlers Wähler,* 228. These were probably swing voters who were not firmly rooted in a workers' milieu. Jürgen W. Falter, "Warum die deutschen Arbeiter während des 'Dritten Reiches' zu Hitler standen: Einige Anmerkungen zu Gunther Mais Beitrag über die Unterstützung der nationalsozialistischen Herrschaft durch die Arbeiter," *Geschichte und Gesellschaft* 13, no. 2 (1987): 227ff. However, this conception has also been challenged recently. For more information, see Conan J. Fischer, "Gab es am Ende der Weimarer Republik einen marxistischen Wählerblock?" *Geschichte und Gesellschaft* 21, no. 1 (1995): 63ff.
71. Cf. Karen Hagemann, "'. . . wir werden alt vom Arbeiten.' Die soziale Situation alternder Arbeiterfrauen in der Weimarer Republik am Beispiel Hamburgs," *Archiv für Sozialgeschichte* 30 (1990): 247ff.

liefs about the state and its future possibilities.[72] There was, of course, a vast and contradictory range of personal experiences and interpretations of them, but for simplicity's sake, it might help to boil them all down to two opposing extremes. One view was that Germany had a constitutional government and a democratic, parliamentary system that was worth building on and that was able to provide modern social security, curb the excesses of capitalism, effect a social compromise, initiate mass social housing projects, and so forth. The other view was that the Weimar state was an instrument of suppression, a police state, which mirrored and administered class society. The state was just an arm of the monopoly financiers and large landowners. Its initiatives in the direction of a welfare state were a farce, and, since 1930 at least, it had become an organ of the fascists.

The German Communists took the young Soviet Union as the ideal they hoped to emulate. Their attachment to what they called the "mighty" Soviet Union and the fetish they developed around organizational discipline and loyalty to the party line served only to dissemble their own weakness. The ideologically meaningful exchanges between the German Communists and the Soviets turned, especially after 1924, into one-sided obeisance to decisions made in Moscow, which were accompanied by massive financial subsidies.[73] However, there was more to it than just this. As Eric D. Weitz has said: "In the voluntarism and the statist orientation of the KPD, many of these workers found an alternative — an alternative shaped not only by Comintern directives but also by the matrix of state interventionism and economic rationalization."[74]

The fundamental disagreements among workers about developments in the Weimar state and how it might function in the future affected their views of society as a whole. Diametrically opposed interpretations vied for supremacy in the labor movement. The split into the KPD and SPD and the enmity between the leaders of the two parties stemmed not only from differing experiences of the existing society but also from differing interpretations of what the future would hold. Consequently, the political strategies of the SPD and KPD drifted far apart.

---

72. Social constructs of the German state and society should actually be described in what follows in all their breadth and contradictoriness. This cannot be done, however, for reasons of space, and the various perceptions and interpretations are therefore summarized as types. The focus is not on the worlds of work and everyday life but on the state and concepts of what the future would hold.

73. This subjugation has often been too easily taken for reality in the literature, while the grass roots were virtually ignored. See the correction provided by Mallmann, "Milieu," 6; cf. Stolle, *Arbeiterpolitik;* Schöck, *Arbeitslosigkeit.*

74. Eric D. Weitz, "State Power, Class Fragmentation, and the Shaping of German Communist Politics, 1890–1933," *Journal of Modern History* 62 (June 1990): 297.

The KPD felt that a satisfactory outcome could be achieved only through revolution or at least a radical change in the power structure and the elites. It could therefore never be content for very long with mere reformism or obstructionism. The SPD, on the other hand, placed its hope in evolutionary change and paid less and less attention to the ultimate goal of "socialism."

The Social Democratic Party had already been torn under the empire between divergent concepts of how society would develop and divergent political strategies. For instance, the south-German wing was more inclined toward pragmatic reform, while Rosa Luxemburg and her political friends took the more radical path of advocating general strikes. In the Weimar Republic, the divergent concepts within the labor movement assumed greater importance and took on a life of their own because basic conditions had changed enormously and the great common enemy, the Wilhelminian political system, no longer existed. The SPD was theoretically opposed to capitalist society, and its relations with the Weimar state were therefore very conflicted. On the one hand, it had many opportunities to participate in government and society and did so; on the other, it felt helpless and impotent standing between the KPD and middle-class parties that were constantly drifting further to the right. This situation cast a cloud of uncertainty over its concepts of the future and the political directions it should adopt. How relatively simple things had been in prewar days, when the state could be roundly condemned as undemocratic and antirepublican, unjust and unfair! Under the Weimar Republic, policy was more complicated and resistant to simple interpretations. The guardians of the public order were no longer often conservative-minded former military officers, as had been the case before 1914, but in many cases civilians from the party's own ranks.

The Weimar state and society were developing many different faces, and the interplay among them was very complicated. As a result of the mounting complexity and differentiation of bourgeois society, labor organizations and their leaders could no longer judge it easily in its entirety and pass along their verdict to the grass roots in such a way that the "working class" could take united action. Different labor organizations focused on different aspects of society. This went so far that the two workers' parties, the KPD and SPD, could no longer hold a worthwhile, let alone effective, dialogue. The Social Democrats firmly distanced themselves from the Communists but still had to wrestle with all the problems created by an ambiguous, multidimensional society. The SPD was particularly torn between its roles as a governing party and the party of a particular class. The disavowal of its utopian beliefs of the past brought much heartache, but enough shreds of those beliefs remained to disrupt its attempts to pursue a purely pragmatic course, as could be seen in the party programs that were adopted, the concept of "economic democracy," and the sociocultural notion of the "new man." The party was left in an uncertain, equivocal position, rent by various factions. The leadership tried to resist the advances of both the right wing, the Hofgeismar Circle of young socialists, and the left wing, the Socialist Worker Youth (SAJ), whose slogan was *Republik das ist nicht viel; Sozialismus ist das Ziel* (A republic isn't much; socialism is the goal).[75]

The "Working Class" and the Social Constructs of Politicians

Paul Levi was a leading representative of the left wing of the SPD, who had returned to it by roundabout ways after being expelled from the Communist Party in September 1921. Discussing in retrospect in 1922 his astonishment over the split in the "working class" after the end of the First World War, he said: "The revolution that broke out divided German proletarians more than the outbreak of the war. . . . Many of us thought that the war of international capitalists against workers, which had just ended, would inevitably rebound into a war of workers against capitalists."[76] Instead the opposite occurred.

We will look subsequently at the interpretations of the "working class" in the discourses of various proletarian publics, which were themselves heavily influenced by politicians. We will examine in particular whether politicians discussed the forces driving workers together and pulling them apart. This includes the issue of united action and the concept of the "common front." The latter was understood to mean joint political activities and united action on the part of workers from different parties as well as unorganized workers who came together to serve the common cause and overcome the organizational and political divides among them. This concept was originally developed by the Communist International between its third and fourth world congresses. "The tactic of the common front is to make an offer to fight together with all workers in other parties or groups and with all workers who do not belong to any party in order to defend the most basic interests of the working class against the bourgeoisie."[77] The question of the possible formation of such a common front against the "fascist threat" became most pressing in the final years of the Weimar Republic. Some smaller groups, such as the

---

75. Cf. Mallmann, "Milieu," 15; cf. Lösche and Walter, *SPD*, 9ff.

76. Quoted in Klaus Schönhoven, *Reformismus und Radikalismus: Gespaltene Arbeiterbewegung im Weimarer Sozialstaat* (Munich, 1989), 208.

77. *Protokoll des Vierten Kongresses der Kommunistischen Internationale* (Hamburg, 1923), 2:1015.

Socialist Workers Party (SAP) and the Communist Party Opposition (KPO), attempted to bring about a rapprochement between the two large and mutually hostile workers' parties by providing a nucleus around which a new organization and ideology could crystallize but without success. In fact, the KPD and SPD began to smear and discredit each other toward the end of the Weimar Republic in ways that destroyed all remaining shreds of mutual political and cultural respect and devastated the activities that they still undertook together on the local level. The SPD agreed with the bourgeois parties in advocating the "red equals brown"[78] smear in conjunction with the theory of totalitarianism, while the KPD developed the even more damaging theory of "social fascism" under the influence of the Soviet Union.[79] The total incompatibility of these views illustrates the depth of the divide that had emerged over the ways in which reality was experienced and interpreted.[80] The concepts advanced by the KPD in response to the Nazi threat in particular did nothing to bring the parties closer together. Its proposals in connection with the "common front from below" would have led straight to the capitulation of the SPD or at least of its leadership. The KPD softened this rigid strategy to some extent through various offers of tactical alliances, especially after the SPD clearly joined the parliamentary opposition to the Papen government.

As mentioned previously, the Communists understood the "common front" as "the mass struggle of the German working class" against the Nazi threat. They were confident that there was a "will deep within the broadest masses for a common front to carry on the struggle. . . .

78. The "red equals brown" theory was based on the occasional cooperation of the KPD and NSDAP, for instance at the time of the Nazi–inspired referendum against the Social Democratic government in Prussia in August 1931 and the strike of workers in the Berlin transportation system in November 1932, when the Nazis allied themselves with Communists against the Social Democrats in the wage dispute. The "social fascism" theory claimed that the SPD was just a wing of the fascist movement and had to be combated first of all. The Communists were particularly upset over the SPD's policy of tolerating the Brüning cabinet beginning in the summer of 1930. At first, the social fascism theory was taken up only slowly and reluctantly by ordinary Communist supporters. However, "Bloody May" of 1929 and the memories it revived of "Bloodhound" Noske led to a certain degree of acceptance. See in this regard Mallmann, "Milieu," 17.

79. Wickham also sees 1929 and 1930 as decisive years when "the entire working-class movement was divided. Underneath the increased conflict between the KPD and SPD lay the disappearance of any common institutional arena within which activists of both parties could operate." James Wickham, "Social Fascism and the Division of the Working Class Movement: Workers and Political Parties in the Frankfurt Area 1929/30," *Capital and Class* 7 (spring 1979): 28.

80. Both workers' parties failed to seriously address the potential attractiveness of the NSDAP for some workers.

Joint meetings of Social Democratic, Communist and unaffiliated workers, common acts of resistance in factory departments, or strikes or any other active expressions of the joint will of workers — that is the reality of this common front. . . . To struggle against fascism means to struggle against the SPD. . . . There are only two camps, only two fronts: the front of the exploited, deprived German proletarians, without regard for party affiliation or sympathy, and the front of the smug and the well-fed from Ulrich to Borsig, from Breitscheid to Groener to Hitler."[81] The Communists thought that the common front would well up "from the depths of the working masses themselves" and sooner or later overwhelm the leadership of the SPD.[82] The KPD still clearly believed that "proletarians" thought as a single whole because they belonged to the same social class. Again and again the Communists invoked the "united working class," its "deep longing for unity," and awareness of "the main enemy, capitalism."[83] The political line adopted by the KPD supposedly reflected "the will of the working masses in factories, welfare offices, and working-class neighborhoods."[84] The Communists frequently repeated to workers sympathetic to the SPD that "as members of the same class, we can also find a common class language."[85] Although the Social Democrats dismissed the offer of a "common front" as a ruse and never had the slightest intention of taking it up, they began employing the term themselves. This leads one to conclude that either the Communists had not entirely appropriated the idea or the Social Democrats wanted to ensure that it did not become automatically associated with their great foe.

The Social Democratic leaders, for their part, looked forward to the collapse of the KPD. They too wanted to see the "working class" unite but on a Social Democratic footing. "Social Democracy must be able to enforce a policy of uniting the proletariat, even without or in opposition to the leaders of the KPD."[86] Friedrich Stampfer, the editor in chief of the central SPD newspaper *Vorwärts,* who was much more thoughtful

---

81. *Rote Fahne,* no. 210, November 18, 1931. This article addressed the suggestion of Rudolf Breitscheid, the Social Democratic leader in the Reichstag, to form a common front against Hitler.

82. Ibid. At times, however, the KPD was prepared to join alliances with the SPD.

83. For instance: Heinz Neumann in *Rote Fahne,* no. 178, supplement no. 1, September 15, 1931.

84. Letter from the KPD's district leaders in Berlin in *Rote Fahne,* no. 132, June 17, 1932.

85. *Rote Fahne,* no. 34, February 9, 1933.

86. Quoted in Reiner Tosstorff, "'Einheitsfront' und/oder 'Nichtangriffspakt' mit der KPD," in Wolfgang Luthard (ed.), *Sozialdemokratische Arbeiterbewegung und Weimarer Republik: Materialien zur gesellschaftlichen Entwicklung 1927–1933* (Frankfurt, 1978), 2:208.

and flexible than most party leaders in regard to the "common front," commented as follows: "A proletarian common front can emerge only if the Communists become Social Democrats or the Social Democrats become Communists; however, this will only be possible years or even decades from now, if at all. For the present, the common front means nothing but bitter struggle between the parties for the leadership of the proletariat, in other words, the very opposite of a common front. Nevertheless, the path to it will be much shorter under Social Democratic leadership than under KPD leadership." Stampfer backed his assertion by pointing to the larger membership of the SPD and then continued: "The common front of tomorrow is only possible if there is a will in the parties to create it." Stampfer analyzed what he believed to be the Communists' deeply flawed responses to political issues and concluded: "I have the general feeling that the bitterness over Communist actions of this kind is much greater among the Social Democratic masses than among the leadership. The Communists are deluding themselves if they think that the Social Democratic workers are on the verge of going over to them at any moment if only the nasty leaders did not prevent it through deceit and deception." Turning to the political fragmentation of workers, Stampfer described the situation as follows: "Formerly, there was only one pool on which the KPD could draw, namely the millions of SPD voters. . . . Nowadays, unfortunately, there are great masses of proletarians in the NSDAP as well, some of whom used to sympathize with the KPD." Stampfer concluded: "Where the battle against fascism is being waged with all one's strength, as we are doing, that is where the proletarian common front is arising!"[87] Struggle as the path to action as a united class — the KPD could have said that too, just under different leadership.

Social Democrats also still spoke about the "working class." Franz Künstler said for instance in a speech delivered in 1931: "It is the tragedy of the German working class that it is unable at this most ominous time to create a powerful whole."[88] In his view, a "call for unity in the struggle against fascism" was arising from "within the working masses," and the Communists were committing "class treason" by insisting on a fraternal war.[89] Künstler was paying the Communists back here for all that they regularly said about the Social Democrats. The reference to a "fraternal

87. *Vorwärts, Berliner Volksblatt: Zentralorgan der Sozialdemokratischen Partei Deutschlands*, no. 285, June 10, 1932. Stampfer overlooks the fact that even people who had previously voted for the SPD later voted for Hitler, as mentioned earlier. I would like to add by way of methodological self-criticism that the research into the social constructs of the "working class" should be much broader than could be provided here.

88. *Vorwärts*, no. 431, September 15, 1931.

89. *Vorwärts*, no. 541, November 18, 1931.

war" touched on a sore spot with both camps, especially when the honor of the other "brother" was assaulted ("sisters" were never mentioned). The labor unions affiliated with the SPD picked up on this point as well. They considered the united labor unions that prevailed until the Communists left in 1929 a potential "vehicle for the ideal of unity." As they stated in 1932, "The united front of political parties representing the German labor movement is only possible if everybody agrees voluntarily not to attack fellow comrades in demeaning ways." The main appeal was to organized workers, since they supposedly were in a position to show the way: "It is up to organized workers themselves to create the moral foundations needed for united action by the entire German labor movement."[90] However, these "moral foundations" never materialized. In response to the *Angriffspakt der Werktätigen* (attack pact of working people) proposed by the Communists, Stampfer finally suggested at least a *Nicht-angriffspakt* (nonaggression pact) between SPD and KPD just a few weeks before Hitler assumed power. This put a definitive end to the idea of united action or a common front. Stampfer apparently felt by this point that the SPD and KPD were able at most to fight the Nazis side by side and that, under the circumstances, this would be a desirable outcome.

Whenever the common front or united action was discussed, the underlying sociocultural concept of the "working class" was rarely seriously considered. In this regard as well, though, Friedrich Stampfer proved the exception and touched at least briefly in his comments on the common front on the divergent social worlds in which workers lived. Comparing the "KPD masses" with those of the SPD, he noted "the beginnings of a new social differentiation." He said that "in general, the relatively better-off strata show more understanding of the policies of Social Democracy and the worse-off are more inclined toward the Communist politics of emotion. Divides are beginning to appear here in the working class that are dangerous and must be closed. When deeply impoverished proletarians no longer feel that they belong to the same social class as skilled workers, the rift in the party acquires a social foundation. In this way the rift in the party and the concomitant weakening of it could be perpetuated." Stampfer then inquired why Communist workers continued to support the Communist leadership and failed to understand the policies of the SPD. He drew the conclusion that Social Democrats must try to fight "for the entire working class."[91]

It is striking that other sociocultural divides within the working

---

90. Quotations in Schönhoven, *Reformismus,* 226ff.
91. *Vorwärts,* no. 43, January 26, 1933.

class, notably gender differences, were not even mentioned. The question of why so few women joined political parties played no part at all in the discussions about the common front. It is no wonder that Social Democratic women themselves showed little interest in this issue and took a very sober view of the "unity" of the working class. They experienced daily the powerlessness of women in the party apparatus and labor unions; the traditional gendered division of work within labor movement organizations; the different amount of interest that men and women took in particular issues, especially abortion; the "competition between the sexes"[92] on labor markets; and wage discrimination against women. Social Democratic women certainly had similar views to men on a large number of issues related to politics and culture, the state and society, and women stuck with the party for this reason. Nevertheless, they were more likely than men to realize how little unified the "working class" really was because of their own marginalized position.[93] For the sake of appearances, they put the emphasis on party unity and what all Social Democrats had in common, as could be seen for instance when the chair of the women's conference, Marie Juchacz, announced: "We are first of all members of a great party. The [Social Democratic] women's movement is only one element in this great party." She described the women's conference modestly enough as a "women's study group" but complained tellingly that it did not have enough freedom of action within the party.[94] Among Communist women, there were no officially sanctioned women's action units, which would have contravened party principles. Even if women in both parties had wanted to form a common front of female workers, they would have been prevented from doing so by the men in their own parties.

In summary we can say that the political divide within the "working class" led to different social constructs of what that class really was. These constructs were influenced of course by divergent interests and interpretations of reality. Faced with the gathering Nazi threat, Friedrich Stampfer stated quite clearly that there was no chance of united action

92. *Sozialdemokratischer Parteitag in Magdeburg 1929 vom 26. bis 31. Mai in der Stadthalle: Protokoll mit dem Bericht der Frauenkonferenz* (Magdeburg, 1929; reprint, Glashütten, 1974), 226.

93. For more see Adelheid von Saldern, "Modernization as Challenge: Perceptions and Reactions of German Social Democratic Women," in Helmut Gruber and Pamela Graves (eds.), *Women and Socialism/Socialism and Women in Interwar Europe* (New York and Oxford, 1998), 95–135.

94. *Sozialdemokratischer Parteitag 1927 in Kiel: Protokoll mit dem Bericht der Frauenkonferenz* (1927; reprint, Glashütten, 1974), 302; *Sozialdemokratischer Parteitag 1925 in Heidelberg: Protokoll mit dem Bericht der Frauenkonferenz* (1925; reprint, Glashütten, 1974), 332.

by the SPD and KPD without an act of will by their respective leaderships. However, even Stampfer underestimated the extent of the sociocultural rifts in the labor movement and argued that the rifts in the "working class" could be closed. Paying little attention to "social reality" and "actual experience," the KPD still believed firmly in the unity of the "working class" and remained convinced that the SPD leaders' construct of that class was a "betrayal."

Myth Making

The great age of the mythologization of the "working class" was before the First World War. The myths grew up around labor movement organizations and were rooted in a broad alternate culture to Wilhelminian Germany. The period of the Anti-Socialist Laws was seen as the heroic age of Social Democracy, when its history began. The shared opposition to society and government authorities at the time constantly fueled the belief in the myth of the "working class." Visions of how the future would evolve or about the forthcoming revolution provided fertile soil for myths about the unique role of the proletariat in global history. An eclectic array of evocative symbols, such as rising suns, was adopted to embellish the working-class interpretation of history and utopian vision.

The great myths of the working class began to crumble during and after the First World War as a result of the split in the labor movement. Henceforth, there were at least two different views of the proletariat to mythologize. In addition, popular culture was beginning to offer proletarians some very different "myths," whose suggestive power both great workers' parties constantly underestimated, even though they attempted to incorporate some aspects of popular culture into their own cultures. In short, while Communist activists mythologized the impending revolution, many young workers were more interested in the myths of the movie world.

In the Communist myth of the "working class," there was a close relationship between the "working class" in Germany and the "revolutionary struggle of the world proletariat," which had achieved its first great victory in the founding of the Soviet Union. The myth of the German "working class" was therefore intimately related to the myth of the Soviet Union. The Communists argued that "for the first time in world history, we see in the Soviet Union a huge industry being built without capitalists, in opposition to capitalists. . . . There is no doubt that what is being accomplished in Russia for the first time represents the hopes and dreams of millions of Social Democratic workers around the world."[95] The Soviet Union and the Comintern became the Communist equivalent of the lost utopia, a beacon of strength and a source of confidence in ultimate victory. The fact that German Communists identified wholeheartedly with the "grand objective" was one of the major reasons why the party leadership submitted willingly to directives from Moscow, even when they did not seem to make much sense or were not very suited to conditions in Germany. The myth of the "Soviet Union" blinded German Communists to realities in their own country, especially after their hopes for a quick world revolution were dashed. They saw developments in Germany from a Soviet perspective, even though Germany was very different in many ways, from its economy to its political culture. Consequently, the German Communists failed to perceive the mounting fragmentation and differentiation of society and the effects on the "working class." In addition, Communist activists generally saw culture solely from a party angle and therefore never succeeded in establishing strong ties with the left wing of the avant-garde.

Meanwhile, the Social Democrats cultivated the great myths of their own history and the struggle for freedom before 1914. Their confidence in final victory, still very strong under the empire, had begun to fade however. Their May Day publications grew sparser, even though the old belief in a better future still flickered. The last verse of a May Day exhortation published in 1924 and written by Karl Bröger read as follows.

Schafft Raum, schafft Raum!	Make room, make room!
Brecht breite Bahn!	Clear a broad path!
Es ist kein Traum:	It is not a dream:
Der Mai rückt an.	May is coming.
In roten Rosen will er stehn	It wants to stand amid red roses
Und uns als Sieger sehn.	And see us as victors.[96]

The watchword of the day was "Let us translate our May Day vows into a willingness to help lead the working class forward too." The May Day newspapers of 1927 and 1928 published illustrations symbolizing hope and power, as if the party felt that it needed to resist the sense that utopia was slipping away. The title page of the 1927 May Day newspaper showed a naked male figure gazing out over a broad valley, and the 1928 paper bore the title "Power Is Ours" and depicted a heroic-looking proletarian standing before a bloodred sky and a landscape of factories.

95. Heinz Neumann, in *Rote Fahne,* no. 178, supplement no. 1, September 15, 1931.
96. Quoted in Marßolek, "Freiheitsgöttinnen," 156.

Fig. 1. *Workers' Strength.* **Cover picture from the May 1, 1928, issue. (From Inge Marßolek [ed.], *100 Jahre Zukunft: Zur Geschichte des 1. Mai,* 166 [Frankfurt, 1990].)**

The May Day article in 1931 bore the heading "May Day as a Symbol of the Will of the Masses."[97]

The Social Democrats developed a distinctive culture of mass festivals and demonstrations. As many as a thousand people participated actively in choruses of speech and movement. They created a ceremonial world of ritual and symbolism (*Weihespiele*) that gave workers a

97. Ibid., 159. Quoted also in Gottfried Korff, "Seht die Zeichen, die euch gelten: Fünf Bemerkungen zur Symbolgeschichte des 1. Mai," in Inge Marßolek (ed.), *100 Jahre Zukunft: Zur Geschichte des 1. Mai* (Frankfurt, 1990), 26. The term *masses* has a positive connotation here.

real break from the drudgery of their everyday lives and routines. The power and strength of the "working class" (at least its Social Democratic variant) was extolled in allegories, symbols, poetry, and songs, even as late as 1930.[98] Shows involving huge numbers of participants demonstrated the collective will and organizational abilities of the proletariat for all to see, regardless of the dangers posed by this pompous festival culture. Although this culture certainly enhanced the self-esteem of workers and their sense of community, it also suggested "a strength that was counter to reality."[99] The social constructs of the "working class" took on mythic proportions. Imitating Communist practices, the Social Democrats tended to limit their notion of the "working class" to their own supporters, or at least potential supporters, portraying them as the "true" representatives of the entire class. "The brunt of the struggle for liberty, without which there can be no socialism, falls entirely on our shoulders. We bear it on behalf of the entire working class."[100]

After Hitler assumed power, hopes rose among the working-class opponents of the Nazis that they would at last succeed in forming a common front. The social construct of the "working class" assumed greater urgency for party activists, who began thinking beyond mere tactical advantages.[101] Representatives of both parties viewed the "working class" as a historical subject, fully capable of practicing politics and taking united action. The common front concept did not begin to fade until the idea of forming a "popular front" emerged, a program was developed around 1936, and attention focused on the possibility that nonproletarians might join the Communists in the struggle against Nazism.[102]

The National Socialists also picked up on the myth of a united "working class," although they bent it to their purposes. Building on this myth, they developed the ideologically and racially driven concept of a

---

98. See in this regard William L. Guttsman, *Workers' Culture in Weimar Germany: Between Tradition and Commitment* (New York, 1990), 248ff.

99. Marßolek, "Von Freiheitsgöttinnen," 167.

100. Friedrich Stampfer, in *Vorwärts,* no. 43, January 26, 1933.

101. See in this regard Herbert Obenaus, "Arbeiterklasse und Einheitsfront als konzeptionelle Mythen? Zu den politischen Handlungsstrategien der Arbeiterbewegung im Dritten Reich und in der frühen Nachkriegszeit," in Adelheid von Saldern (ed.), *Mythen in Geschichte und Geschichtsschreibung aus polnischer und deutscher Sicht* (Münster, 1996), 228–47.

102. The compulsory formation of the Socialist Unity Party (SED) after the war should be seen in the context of the common front. The united action strategy of the 1920s thus ended in the formation of a united party. In both situations there was no doubt on the part of the Communists about the historical legitimacy of their hegemony.

united "German community" (*deutsche Volksgemeinschaft*) and cultivated a belief, rooted not least of all in cultural and aesthetic values, of
the "high-quality" German worker with a body "as hard as Krupp
steel."[103] Workers had already grown accustomed to a festival culture
drenched in ritual, allegory, and symbolism, in which the sun, strength,
and light figured prominently. It was therefore relatively easy for the
National Socialists to use the same symbols and allegories in order to
instill a feeling of recognition and belonging and create the impression
that "along with the symbols, proletarian objectives were also being
pursued."[104]

Summary

It would be only somewhat oversimplified to summarize as follows the
general condition of the "working class" in the Weimar Republic. One-
half of all workers were organized members of labor movement parties,
which proved unable, at decisive moments, to forge a common front or
take united action. The other half apparently did not interpret their
social condition as primarily a question of class, at least to the extent
that they would act on this basis and vote for one of the workers' parties
or even become a member. This reality poked gaping holes in the social
construct, not to mention the great myth, of a "working class" acting in
concert as a historical subject in the modern, highly industrialized society of the Weimar Republic. Nevertheless, the labor movement continued to cling to some extent to the social construct of a united "working
class" (in contrast to the period after the Second World War), even
though it was based on two very different models, the Communist and
Social Democratic.

It seems in retrospect that united action and even the creation of a
common front were certainly possible, especially in the dying days of the
Weimar Republic. There was clearly a desire at the grassroots level for
united action against the dangers of fascism. Workers still had many
experiences, interests, and aspirations in common in their everyday
lives, and the social construct of a united "working class" was not sheer

---

103. The Nazi myths certainly did help to shape reality, for instance the attempts to
exclude, delegitimize, and "eradicate" as well as the sense of identity and purpose instilled
by the increased esteem for the physical activity of male workers. See in this regard Alf
Lüdtke, *Eigen-Sinn: Fabrikalltag, Arbeitererfahrungen, und Politik vom Kaiserreich bis in
den Faschismus* (Hamburg, 1993), 283ff.

104. Horst Überhorst, "Feste, Fahnen, Feiern: Die Bedeutung politischer Symbole
und Rituale im Nationalsozialismus," in Rüdiger Voigt (ed.), *Symbole der Politik, Politik
der Symbole* (Opladen, 1989), 157.

fantasy.[105] However, united action between the two workers' parties for a limited period and a particular purpose would only have been possible if both sides had taken a rational, calculated view of what they had in common and decided that it was more important than all that divided them. Such an alliance would only have been feasible if understood by both parties as an act of will. Instead, many of their leaders relied on what they considered the objective unity of the "working class" and concluded that certain political actions, consistent with their respective social constructs, were virtually inevitable. The leaders of the two parties did not negotiate with one another as seriously as necessary, not least because they were both convinced that the "working class" would eventually act as a whole and drive events in the direction that they predicted. Here we see the social constructs of the "working class" imbued by the mythology of an enormously powerful entity that would eventually act in what each party considered the "right" way.

The upper-middle-class *Deutsche Allgemeine Zeitung* noted quite correctly in its edition of September 15, 1931: "From the standpoint of middle-class politics, it is gratifying to see the two red brothers at each other's throats because this battle within socialism has been very good for the middle classes since 1918." The editor neglected to mention that the middle classes too had proved unable to unite politically and overcome the fragmentation of their parties.[106] It was therefore hardly surprising that all attempts to rally the non-Nazi middle classes in the final days of the Weimar Republic failed miserably and the door was left open for Hitler.

From a more long-term perspective, the Weimar Republic can be seen as a transitional phase in German history. On the one hand, society was sufficiently differentiated by now that the "working class" was unable to function politically as a unified whole. On the other hand, the emergence of a system of *Volksparteien* operating on the basis of a

---

105. Mallmann comes to a somewhat different general conclusion. He places greater emphasis than I on the proletarian "camp" and the line between the classes. He notes the rivalry between the Social Democrats and Communists "but on the basis of identical interests, a shared tradition, and the same idea of the enemies." Mallmann, *Kommunisten,* 383.

106. At this point we should actually discuss "the" bourgeoisie or "entrepreneurs" because the idea that there was a "working class" rested, as Eduard P. Thompson pointed out, on the relations between the classes and the interpretations given to them. As Thompson himself said: "And class happens, when some men, as a result of common experiences (inherited or shared), feel and articulate the identity of their interests as between themselves, and as against other men whose interests are different from (and usually opposed to) theirs." Thompson, *Making of the English Working Class,* introduction. However, we cannot even begin here to delve into this question.

democratic consensus, welfare capitalism, and participatory industrial relations was meeting with strong resistance. The old elites and much of the bourgeoisie, even the petite bourgeoisie, still opposed such a political change and were even prepared to fight against it.[107] It is hardly surprising, therefore, that the mentalities and actions of most labor movement politicians still reflected the mythologies, social constructs, and empirical experiences of class and class society. They did not speak, therefore, of building a broadly based party but of the "battle to liberate workers," as could be seen in the SPD's Heidelberg Program of 1925.

---

107. Here the particular development of the German bourgeoisie comes into play. See in this regard David Blackbourn and Geoff Eley, *The Peculiarities of German History: Bourgeois Society and Politics in Nineteenth-Century Germany* (Oxford and New York, 1984). The connection between social development and the labor movement is also addressed by Molly Nolan, "Workers and Politics in Wilhelminian and Weimar Germany," *International Labor and Working-Class History* 33 (spring 1988).

Social Rationalization
and Gender

"Instead of Cathedrals, Dwelling Machines": The Paradoxes of Rationalization under the Banner of Modernity

(In memory of Detlev J. K. Peukert)

Introduction

"We want and can do only what is most real," said Bauhaus artist Oskar Schlemmer, before going on to argue that cathedrals should be replaced by "dwelling machines" (*Wohnmaschinen*).[1] Only someone who placed all of his or her hopes for human emancipation in modernity could say such a thing.[2] Speaking about the "standard needs" of "the average person," Le Corbusier stated that "they want machines to live in — machines that are worthy of a human being," thus bringing the paradoxes to a head, even though they were not seen as such at the time.[3]

It is unlikely that anyone still believes in "modernity" in the same way that Oskar Schlemmer and many other artists, academics, and scientists did in their day. "The susceptibility of modern industrial society to disaster"[4] has been all too apparent. One could mention in this regard

---

1. Oskar Schlemmer (1922), quoted in Detlev J. K. Peukert, *Max Webers Diagnose der Moderne* (Göttingen, 1989), 73. This concept is better known from the writings of Le Corbusier; cf. Klaus Lesemann, *Sanieren und Herrschen: Zur Gewaltstruktur gebauter Räume* (Giessen, 1982), 127.

2. For the term *modernity* see the introduction to this volume.

3. Quoted in Thilo Hilpert, *Die funktionelle Stadt: Le Corbusiers Stadtvision* (Braunschweig, 1978), 22.

4. Detlev J. K. Peukert, *Die Weimarer Republik: Krisenjahre de klassischen Moderne* (Göttingen, 1987), 11.

"postmodernism," which at least in some quarters is "fully aware of the limitations and political failures of classical modernism."[5] In the Federal Republic of Germany, Detlev J. K. Peukert in particular devoted the last years of his life to exploring the multifarious, conflicting potentialities of modernity. It has both positive and negative sides, he wrote, that cannot be separated, like the two sides of a coin.[6] The essence of the historical analysis of various states and societies lies therefore in the study of their very different approaches to all the potentialities of modernity (comparing phases and nations). These potentialities were generated mostly by the constant growth of the forces of production but also by the ever-increasing bureaucratization, professionalization, and "scientification" of social relations and the world order, which continually grow more complex.[7]

Peukert's approach was out of step with previous understandings of the Third Reich, at least insofar as modernization and antimoderniza-tion were concerned. The literature tended to be dominated by opposites:[8] that is, Hitler's methods and strategies were "modern," but his goals and National Socialist ideology were "antimodern," and many of the measures he adopted were contemptuous of the standards of modern society.[9] Peukert, on the other hand, avoided terms such as *anti-modernism* and *antimodernity* and searched instead for forms of modernity that were peculiar to fascism: "Whatever happened after the 1930s, the results of modernity could no longer be reversed; you could try at most to coexist with it or rise above it."[10] Elsewhere he said: "Neither in its methods nor its goals did National Socialism try to reverse the results of modernization. It represented instead an attempt to change course by reinforcing some tendencies in modernization and rationalization and

---

5. Andreas Huyssen, "Postmoderne: Eine amerikanische Internationale?" in Andreas Huyssen and Klaus R. Scherpe (eds.), *Postmoderne: Zeichen eines kulturellen Wandels* (Reinbek, 1989), 34.

6. This does not mean that he advocated any sort of determinism. The conviction that modernity had a multifarious potential means that there were various possible ways of acting upon it.

7. It is therefore no coincidence that Peukert often refers to Max Weber.

8. This is all the more surprising in that doubt was already frequently cast on the dichotomy between "traditional" and "modern" in the 1970s. Cf. Hans-Ulrich Wehler, *Modernisierungstheorie und Geschichte* (Göttingen, 1972), 14ff.

9. See in this regard, for instance, Jeremy Noakes, "Nazism and Revolution," in Noel O'Sullivan (ed.), *Revolutionary Theory and Political Reality* (Brighton, 1983). The discussion about whether the term *revolution* is applicable to the Third Reich should be dropped because it is artificial and only makes it more difficult to analyze problems and assess the Nazi system. For recent publications on the issue of modernity and the Third Reich, see also the introduction to this volume.

10. Peukert, *Max Webers Diagnose*, 66.

suppressing others. National Socialism was therefore one of the many directions that modernity could take, albeit the most awful."[11]

Peukert felt that the descent into barbarism was always a possible, though not inevitable, path that modernity could follow and that it represented an "antiliberal variant in the modernization process, the heir to a dehumanized variant in the rationalization movement."[12] He thereby reoperationalized for the empirical study of history what Adorno and Horkheimer called the "dialectic of the Enlightenment." The divergence from the long-term constructs of modernization theory[13] thereby becomes fully apparent, as well as the contrast with those schools of thought that ascribe primary responsibility for the catastrophe of 1933 or 1939 to the "premodern" and "antimodern" elements in German history.

Peukert's view of modernity and of the diverse possibilities it harbored also invites a reinterpretation of the history of the German Empire. Most professional historians have long endorsed the theory of a German Sonderweg, a view initially advanced in the 1960s and 1970s with an eye to liberating the study of history from the conservative view of the history of the day. The theory of a German Sonderweg was based largely on an overly neat division of the various strands of development into what were deemed to be "modern," "premodern," and "antimodern" strands, according to relatively rigid criteria and norms.[14] The result of all this work, as we know, was the discovery that "premodern" and "antimodern" strands were particularly abundant in the empire (in comparison with what was considered the "normal" situation in the countries of western Europe). It was therefore necessary to speak of a German Sonderweg, which culminated ultimately in the Third Reich and was eliminated only by force of arms after 1945. This approach tended implicitly (and at times explicitly) to cast a positive light on "modernization" and "modernity" and a negative light on all that was "premodern" or "antimodern." The more that everything negative was associated with "premodern" or "antimodern" elites and social groups, especially the large landowning nobility

---

11. Ibid., 82.

12. Ibid., 82. Roland Smelser takes a similar view when he too emphasizes the modern aspects of the Nazi system and says that the political system "was a very 'modern' form of tyranny." Roland Smelser, "How Modern Were the Nazis? DAF Soul Planning and the Modernisation Question," *German Studies Association* 13, no. 2 (May 1990): 299.

13. See in this regard Horst Matzerath and Heinrich Volkmann, "Modernisierungstheorie und Nationalsozialismus," *Geschichte und Gesellschaft,* special edition 3 (1977): 87ff. For recent literature, see as well the introduction to this volume.

14. The most concise study of the German Sonderweg is considered to be Hans-Ulrich Wehler, *Das Deutsche Kaiserreich* (Göttingen, 1973). In the meantime, the theory of a German Sonderweg has lost much of its heuristic value. See also, in this regard, the introduction to this volume.

in the eastern parts of Prussia, the Junkers, the easier it became to sympathize with modern industrial capitalism. Peukert, however, took an opposing view: what happened in Germany was not due primarily to "premodernity" or "antimodernity" but to the potentialities inherent in modernity itself, that is, in industrial capitalism, in modern bureaucratization,[15] in strategies to engineer greater social integration, in the hegemonic claims of science and technology to have discovered allegedly inherent necessities, and in the related attempts to rationalize daily life and therefore reeducate people and forcibly rearrange their lives in accordance with preconceived and in some cases "well-intentioned" ideas. We will attempt in this chapter to clarify this general overview by providing concrete examples of rationalization efforts.

The Reconstruction of Society: Remodeling the Spaces of Everyday Life

Modernity and its apparently limitless potentialities elicited in contemporaries a sense of uncertainty and crisis as well as an eagerness to rise to the challenge, that is, "to systematize the New and attitudes toward it, to examine it and draw the most radical of theoretical or practical conclusions, and to elaborate in this way plans for the future whose excessiveness and one-sidedness had the advantage of insinuating that there was no room for doubt and of instilling great self-assurance."[16] Thus the temptation grew to try to break people of recalcitrant behaviors so that they would fit more easily into the "modern, rational" system. Science and the bureaucracy were the guarantors of rational social planning and the rational management of everyday life.

Peukert pointed quite rightly to "rationalization" as one of the key concepts of modernity.[17] In the 1920s, it was considered a principal feature of modern culture.[18] The discourses about rationalization and the attempts to put it into effect focused primarily on large factories (Taylorism), social programs, urban planning, housing and construction, and the ways in which people lived. Rationalism and rationalization were the foundations of the modern utopia and of all that could be

---

15. The heavy layers of bureaucracy, the powerful government apparatus with its broad array of functions, and the tendency of the people to do what they were told and trust in the state were certainly particularly German.

16. Peukert, *Max Webers Diagnose,* 66.

17. Ibid., especially the chapter "'Rationalisierung' zwischen utopischem Entwurf und krisenhafter Zurücknahme," 70ff.

18. Cf., for instance, the telling title of Bruno Rauecker's contemporary work *Rationalisierung als Kulturfaktor* (Berlin, 1928).

achieved, it was thought, through urban planning and the construction of housing. The solution to any problems that arose seemed to lie in *planende Gestaltung,* or planning and shaping in accordance with the principles of modern science and an aesthetic predicated on it.

The goal at first was nothing less than to reconfigure all of society. Artists and architects were swept up in the enthusiasm for the new age after the First World War, and many did what they could to support the revolution (especially on the Workers' Council for the Arts). They drew inspiration from what they saw as the liberating belief and claim that art and the people must be one.[19] They wanted to recast all of society, or at least urban society, in the image of modernity, which they saw as a great emancipatory force. The individual and the community would mesh and interact in new ways thanks to creative planning based on pure reason. It was no accident that the Hall of the People in Taut's urban plan was reminiscent of medieval cathedrals, for it would now be the hub of the community, giving it focus and meaning.[20] "Dwelling machines" had not yet been imagined.

The architect and urban planner Le Corbusier was also thinking at the time in terms of society as a whole, going so far in 1920–21 as to describe architecture as an alternative to revolution: "The social machinery has been badly shaken and hangs between progress of historic dimensions and catastrophe. The deepest instinct of all living beings is to create ideal images. The active classes in society no longer have suitable ideal images, whether the workers or the intellectuals. The key to restoring the lost balance is now the art of building: architecture or revolution."[21] Revolution was evidently equated here with chaos, from which architecture would be the savior; good design was inflated into a kind of social panacea. The ability of architecture and urban renewal to bring about social change was certainly vastly exaggerated, and there was no hint of any suspicion that such extravagant plans for all of society could ultimately have very ambivalent effects.

The end of the revolution in Germany dampened the enthusiasm

19. See Ulrich Conrads, *Programme und Manifeste zur Architektur des 20. Jahrhunderts* (Braunschweig, 1981), 42; see also from this point of view the contemporary urban designs of Bruno Taut; ibid., 38ff.

20. Mechtild Schumpp, *Stadtbau-Utopien und Gesellschaft: Der Bedeutungswandel utopischer Stadtmodelle unter sozialem Aspekt* (Gütersloh, 1972); Uwe M. Schneede (ed.), *Künstlerschriften der 20er Jahre,* 3d enl. ed. (Cologne, 1986). We should point as well in this connection to Ebenezer Howard's plans for a garden city around the turn of the century.

21. Quoted in Julius Posener, "Tendenzen der modernen Bewegung in Deutschland," *Arch+* 11 (1979): 63.

for a new age and changed the kind of utopias that modernity might bring. There was little interest henceforth in exorbitant plans to reconfigure all of society, with architecture playing a central role. The socially committed avant-garde had to lower its sights and come to terms with the true potential of the newly established Weimar Republic. This is exactly what it did, as can be seen in the foundation and mode of operations of the Bauhaus. When the new republic began building heavily subsidized housing for the people after 1924, architects and builders saw an unparalleled opportunity to put their theories of functionalism and rational planning into effect and gain broad influence. The strategies for reforming society inevitably mutated and were adapted to the new opportunity to play an active role. Since it was henceforth impossible to remodel society all at once, change would have to be carried out from various islands of opportunity, such as housing. The passage from "cathedrals" to "dwelling machines" was not inevitable but one of a number of possibilities. The more architects, urban planners, and reformers thought about housing, the more they came to recognize how vital it was because private lives were involved, which were otherwise very difficult to influence. There was certainly no doubt in their minds that private lives also needed reforming and modernizing. A utopian streak still existed in many architects and urban planners, who were convinced that they could emancipate the people and solve social problems. The magic word was *rationalization* — one could even speak of a rationalization utopia.

"Planning on a Grand Scale": Architects as the Remodelers of Humankind

Most of the well-known functionalist architects and directors of municipal construction, such as Ernst May and Walter Gropius, were in the vanguard of the reform movement, one of whose aims was to rationalize private lives. They would have preferred to build only furnished housing so that the occupants would make as few mistakes as possible and could be trained most easily in a rationalized way of life. As the architect Gustav Wolf once said: "[O]ur plans do not have empty rooms, just furnished ones."[22] However, this "simple solution" could not be adopted, with the exception of a few models, not least of all because the new housing was too expensive for much of the working class and would only have been made dearer.[23] Gropius continued to insist, though, that people had to be

---

22. *Die Wohnung: Zeitschrift für Bau- und Wohnungswesen* 6 (1931): 41ff.

23. Despite relatively generous subsidies for the construction of housing, the minimum economic rent could usually not be driven low enough for large numbers of workers to

taught "proper living" and was convinced that "systematic use should be made of housing advisers."[24] A conscious attempt to educate and inform could create the "new man," living in modern, rationalized conditions. According to a declaration of the Congrès Internationaux d'Architecture Moderne, founded in 1928, "the new principles of housing and domestic life could be effectively inculcated through instruction in our educational institutions: insistence on cleanliness, the effects of light, air and sun, basic hygiene, and the practical use of home appliances."[25]

Architects remained intensely interested in social issues throughout the Weimar Republic. They considered themselves not just architects in the narrow sense but artists as well, as could be seen in the entire concept behind the Bauhaus. They felt that architects deserved to be in the first rank of the remodelers of society as a whole, comparable to such other modern or modernized professions as physicians, "race hygienists," social workers, youth workers, and technicians. However, architects and urban planners seemed particularly prone to towering hubris. The give-and-take among architects, people, and society was all too easily overtaken by a claim to hegemony. The seductive potential of modernity was having its effect.

The architectural avant-garde often seemed euphoric over all that could be devised and done in the modern age, and rational planning played a central role in its claim to hegemony. As Walter Gropius stated in 1924: "Generally applicable solutions truly in keeping with modern times have not yet emerged because the question of how to construct housing has never been grasped in terms of all its sociological, economic, technical and formal ramifications and systematically solved in a sweeping way from the ground up. . . . However, once the full extent of the intellectual challenges involved in building housing is clearly understood and defined, tactical execution will only be a matter of methods and planning on a grand scale."[26] Gropius was not the only person harboring such thoughts. The director of municipal construction in Berlin, Martin Wagner (who was actually quite close to the labor movement), felt that the primary task of modern management was to provide "central control over the formal development of the city, fully in the tradition of Prussian

afford the new apartments. See in this regard Adelheid von Saldern, "Die Neubausiedlungen der Zwanziger Jahre," in Ulfert Herlyn, Adelheid von Saldern, and Wulf Tessin (eds.), *Neubausiedlungen der 20er und 60er Jahre: Ein historisch-sociologischer Vergleich* (Frankfurt and New York, 1987), 33ff.

24. Technical conference of the Imperial Society for Research, *Die Wohnung*, no. 1 (1929): 31.

25. Quoted in Conrads, *Programme*, 105.

26. Walter Gropius, *Architektur: Wege zur einer optischen Kultur* (1924; reprint, Frankfurt, 1982), 153.

absolutism."[27] Wagner's reference to Prussian absolutism was not intended to express any opposition to modernity; in fact, he wanted to use the enormous power that the Prussian civil service had amassed since the days of absolutism to help bring about the triumph of modern rationalism.

Some people warned about the consequences of these ideas, one of whom was Adolf Behne. With only some exaggeration, he described the new "dwelling machines" as follows: "At least among those architects who are consistent, people are supposed to face east when they go to bed and west when they eat or answer letters from their mother, and the housing will be designed in such a way that it is practically impossible to do otherwise. . . . Here in Dammerstock, human beings are becoming abstract housing creatures, who may well end up moaning 'Help . . . I have to live!' over all the well-intentioned orders from architects."[28] Adolf Behne considered himself a modern man, and he was not generally opposed to the principles of "light, air, and sun" or even to "ribbon development" (development along a highway). He was simply clear sighted enough to warn against the "untimely calcification of the new architecture into dogma."[29] He apparently recognized the ambivalence of modernity in architecture and housing.

Gropius argued in turn that rationalization did not necessarily mean uniformity. What was wanted, he said, was actually "a combination of the greatest possible standardization with the greatest possible variety."[30] Was this an attempt to square the circle? Not necessarily, because variety could be achieved through serial standardization. What was meant was a basic type that would be made variable by "the construction of alternate extensions and tops."[31] Gropius's avowal of the importance of "variety" put a conceptual brake on thorough rationalization, although in actual practice the trend toward uniformity was already apparent in Weimar times. One could point, for instance, to the huge housing estates of Frankfurt-Westhausen or Karlsruhe-Dammerstock, where the transition from a serial aesthetic to hyperrational uniformity was already becoming evident.[32]

---

27. In Ludvica Scarpa, *Martin Wagner und Berlin* (Braunschweig and Wiesbaden, 1986), 9.

28. Adolf Behne, "Dammerstock," *Die Form*, no. 6 (1930): 170.

29. In Lieselotte Ungers, *Die Suche nach einer neuen Wohnform: Siedlungen der 20er Jahre damals und heute* (Stuttgart, 1983), 132.

30. Siegfried Gideon, *Walter Gropius: Mensch und Werk* (Stuttgart, 1954), 69.

31. Ibid.

32. The variations grew more and more infrequent, and there was a danger of falling into uniform, dull rationalism. This did not really occur until the construction of the large apartment buildings in the 1960s and 1970s. Cf. Herlyn, von Saldern, and Tessin, *Neubausiedlungen*.

ZWOFA 3.40|3.42

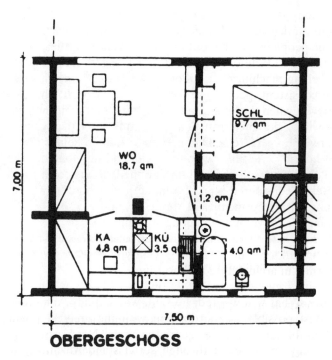

OBERGESCHOSS

Fig. 2. Floor plan of one of the Westhausen flats (52.5 square meters). (From *50 Jahre Westhausen: Einwohner zeigen ihre Siedlung im Wandel von fünf Jahrzehnten*, 11 [brochure].)

The strongest impulses in the direction of excessive rationalization came from the prevailing view of humankind. The masses were seen solely as objects in need of assistance. What modern science demonstrated to be right had to be good for them. Once this attitude became widespread, there was no reason for any discourse about whether certain traditional aspects of everyday culture might be worth preserving. Instead, people would be educated and trained for the modern world through the reconfiguration of their environment. The logic was clear, and there was no reason for the objects of the campaign to have anything to say. The space allowed for their own creative impulses would be reduced to a minimum or eliminated if possible, in accordance with the insights of classical Taylorism. Fritz Wichert was especially proud that "these houses, which appear so trifling and inconsequential, actually

Fig. 3. A model for the modern housing estates, Frankfurt-Westhausen.
(From *50 Jahre Westhausen: Einwohner zeigen ihre Siedlung im Wandel von fünf Jahrzehnten,* cover picture [brochure].)

inculcate a whole new spirit. They are designed to tap the purest, most healthful founts of life but nevertheless require a certain asceticism and renunciation of mindless comfort and a certain subjugation to the surrounding society."[33] The views of Ernst May, the director of municipal construction in Frankfurt, are also instructive in this regard. He compared the inhabitants of housing estates to worker bees returning to their honeycombs in the evening when their labors were done[34] and was concerned for the most part with keeping "the *Volk* content and hardworking."[35] Le Corbusier said that one of the purposes of modern housing estates was to keep a tight rein on "millions of individuals."[36] Their apartments were compared to honeycombs — uniform, highly functional, and fitted together in a way that seemed to evince a rational inner order. Mathematics, the most logical of the sciences, gained untoward influence over the dimensions of the housing and the floor

33. Quoted in Heinz Hirdina, *Neues Bauen, Neues Gestalten: Das neue Frankfurt/die neue Stadt: Eine Zeitschrift zwischen 1926 und 1933* (Berlin, 1984), 277.

34. In Gert Kähler, *Wohnung und Stadt: Hamburg, Frankfurt, Wien: Modelle sozialen Wohnens in den zwanziger Jahren* (Braunschweig and Wiesbaden, 1985), 205.

35. In ibid., 204.

36. In Thilo Hilpert, *Hufeisensiedlung Britz 1926–1980: Ein alternativer Siedlungsbau der 20er Jahre als Studienobjekt* (TU Berlin, Dokumente aus Forschung und Lehre, no. 1, Berlin, 1980), 20.

plans. The most efficient spaces for sleeping, living, and doing chores were reduced to mathematical formulas for the purpose of making the homes smaller.[37]

However, statements like these did not go unchallenged. Bruno Taut suggested that "this idea is predicated on a basic mistake in logic, first of all because of the comparison with mathematics. Mathematics is pure logic and therefore a totally abstract discipline. Architecture is the complete opposite, concrete in every way and not in the least abstract."[38] Lifestyles could not be determined "by mathematical means": "They are much more a product of custom and desire and one's social circles in various parts of the country. A host of imponderables interact and cannot be reduced to some universally applicable formula—thank heavens."[39]

The sort of affiliations that modernity was potentially capable of entering can be seen in an example from 1933. The final edition of *Neue Stadt,* published abroad in Zurich in July of that year because of the Nazi takeover, contained a letter from a young architect named Max Cetto to the new minister of propaganda and popular enlightenment, Joseph Goebbels. Cetto tried to persuade him that strictly functional architecture could be politically useful to the Nazis: "What is certain is that radical architecture . . . could be capable of raising stone monuments for the ages to daring German statesmanship by virtue of its practicality, which is inimical to individual idylls, its constructive fervor, and most of all, its relentlessness while preserving a will to impose form."[40] Nothing militated in principle against a marriage between functionalism and fascism, as could be seen in Italy.

The National Socialists in Germany chose another path, driving avant-garde architects into exile and encouraging traditional regional facades for private homes (though not industrial complexes), under which the modern achievements lay hidden.[41] The avant-garde had waged a relentless campaign against the cultural values of Wilhelminian times and tended to decry all of their opponents as antimodern. However, this assessment is much too simple. It was not a question of categorical antimodernism but of how to deal with modernism and its potentiali-

37. Cf. *Zentralblatt der Bauverwaltung,* no. 34 (1928): 545.

38. Bruno Taut, "Die Grundrißfrage," *Wohnungswirtschaft,* no. 21–22 (1928): 313ff.

39. Ibid.

40. Quoted in Christian Borngräber, "Der soziale Anspruch des Neuen Bauens ist im Neuen Frankfurt gescheitert," in *Paris-Berlin 1900–1933* (Munich, 1979), 378ff.

41.Winfried Nerdinger (ed.), *Bauhaus-Moderne im Nationalsozialismus: Zwischen Anbiederung und Verfolgung* (Munich, 1993); see also Barbara Miller Lane, *Architecture and Politics in Germany, 1918–1945* (Cambridge, MA, 1968).

ties. Even conservative architects were not totally opposed to modern ways of rationalizing the construction of housing. They opposed *radical* rationalization and wanted to reflect the (asynchronous) mentalities they found on all sides. For this reason, they resisted what they saw as the hubris of their radically functionalist colleagues. The author of a polemical article from conservative circles states: "The elimination of soul from architecture is . . . a precondition for the industrialization of it, just as the creation of a new kind of man is a precondition for the consumption of these soulless products."[42] Conservative architects also felt that rationalization should not be pushed too far in difficult economic times and that it was better to keep local artisans employed than manufacture structural elements in factories. Although flat roofs seemed more functional and rational, conservative architects continued therefore to favor steep or hipped roofs. This more traditional aesthetic fueled controversy and was considered emblematic of the resistance to all-out rationalization.

The conservative approach to modernity was also no guarantee against "the descent into barbarism." Although it avoided the utopian belief of the functionalists that everything could and should be rationally planned and implemented, it culminated in a belief at least as fatal in *eine heile Moderne* (safe and sound modernity), or a modernity in and through which conservative and even reactionary ideas about humankind, society, and the state could be realized. Under the influence of the celebrated conservative architect Schultze-Naumburg, the discussion about the "right architecture" took a racist and nationalistic turn that carried it in the direction of National Socialism.

Everyday Spaces

Many people spend their everyday lives in three kinds of spaces: at work, in public areas, and in the privacy of their own homes and apartments. As modern rationalization took hold, all three of these spaces were reconfigured in far-reaching ways. Rationalized companies were widely seen as providing a prime example of spaces designed in accordance with consistent principles. Rationalization and mechanization changed the spatial configuration of factories and increased control over production and output to a previously unimaginable extent. Even though maximum rationalization, as advocated by Taylor, was often not so thoroughly implemented in Germany as could be seen in the Fordism adopted in the United States, factory owners and managers still ensured that working

---

42. "Der angebliche neue Menschentyp für den Baukubismus," *Deutsche Bauhütte*, no. 26 (1930): 422.

people did what was needed to take advantage of modernity's potential for producing goods and profits.[43] The changes in the organization of work necessitated changes in the spaces in which it was done. A contemporary observer described the introduction of "assembly line" production as follows: "The entire factory has a new look. The individual machines no longer stand apart in various rooms but are located beside or behind one another, for instance the smelting furnace is beside the lathe, which is beside the acetylene welding stand near metalworking."[44] Le Corbusier gushed: "Big companies have developed new moral values. Nowadays, big companies are healthy, moral organisms."[45] He found it fascinating to see how human activity could be dictated by the plan of a room: "Within workshops and factory halls, a marvelous order reigns. It prescribes the structure of the machines, affects how they operate, and determines every gesture of the workers."[46]

It is hardly surprising that avant-garde architects considered homes and public spaces in cities to be chaotic, wasteful, and lacking in good planning in comparison with rationalized factories. Taylorism seemed like the antidote to this "irrational chaos," a social and technical system for structuring cities as well. Like factories, cities too could be divided into areas with particular functions, which would be connected with one another by transportation corridors. In this way, the complex urban maze would be straightened out and made easier to control and regulate, if still necessary. The idea of dividing cities into areas determined by function (living, shopping, transportation, recreation) had been accepted as an unwritten law long before the Charter of Athens (1933) but with only some success. The ability to force activities into particular areas through design and layout alone was quite limited. The unfortunate result, according to the avant-garde, was that police and other authorities would still be needed to maintain "peace and order" on public streets and squares.

While the appropriate authorities kept factories and public areas under firm control (in theory if not always in practice), no one was really responsible for domestic spaces. Building regulations and zoning provided a loose framework, but life in the home generally remained a

43. See in this regard Mary Nolan, *Visions of Modernity: American Business and the Modernization of Germany* (New York and Oxford, 1994).

44. Elisabeth Schalldach, *Rationalisierungsmaßnahmen der Nachinflationszeit im Urteil der deutschen freien Gewerkschaften* (Jena, 1930), 62ff. For contemporary discussions of the rationalization of industry, see Gunnar Stollberg, *Die Rationalisierungsdebatte 1908–1933: Freie Gewerkschaften zwischen Mitwirkung und Gegenwehr* (Frankfurt, 1981); Nolan, *Visions of Modernity.*

45. Quoted in Hilpert, *Funktionelle Stadt,* 21.

46. Quoted in ibid., 42.

private matter. This state of affairs was not easily changed, since the sanctity of one's home was one of the most important achievements of the liberal, constitutional state. In order for the authorities to enter, a search warrant was usually needed from a judge. Such a warrant was easily obtained in the case of lawbreakers, of course, and of people belonging to certain, largely political groups when a state of emergency was declared. However, this was hardly the way to remodel the private living spaces of the masses in a modern, rational fashion.

Other approaches were called for. If we look back to the nineteenth century, we see that as industrialization and urbanization progressed, activist reformers showered the masses, and women in particular, with advice and exhortations.[47] They should keep their homes clean so that their families would be less susceptible to communicable diseases; little brothers and sisters should not sleep together in one room; having boarders should be discouraged because they detracted from the ideal nuclear family in its own little abode; and parlors should be used more often and better because they were all too obvious evidence of everyday irrationalism in the home. Housewives were urged to be clean, thrifty, and industrious and to devote any free time to the emotional needs of their husbands and children. A movement to reform taste arose that provided instruction in aesthetic matters, finally culminating in the foundation of the Deutscher Werkbund in 1907. Many more examples of well-intentioned efforts to provide advice could be added, but these sorts of undertakings did not influence most working people very much or at least not fast enough to suit the reformers. Mentalities are not easily changed.

Middle-class reformers in Wilhelminian times therefore sought other ways of penetrating the private realm of the home. Housing inspectors were appointed and assigned a variety of tasks.[48] They alerted the public to the deplorable living conditions of the lower classes by carrying out investigations and writing reports and also pressured irresponsible landlords into performing urgently needed repairs. In addition, they provided a window for reformers onto the living conditions of the lower classes. What was usually observed could only horrify anyone who had grown up in the lap of the middle class. Many photographs and written

---

47. We do not look here at preindustrial attempts to instruct and enlighten the population because they were still carried out in the social context of feudal estates and cannot be compared very well with the instruction provided in modern times or for modern times.

48. Cf. Peter R. Gleichmann, "Wandlungen im Verwalten von Wohnhäusern," in Lutz Niethammer (ed.), *Wohnen im Wandel: Beiträge zur Geschichte des Alltags in der bürgerlichen Gesellschaft* (Wuppertal, 1979), 65ff.

descriptions have survived of the terrible housing shortages and wretched conditions, although not all strata of the working class lived so miserably. The crucial question for reformers was how to modernize and upgrade the lives of the lower strata of the working class when the living conditions were so poor. Various cholera epidemics had heightened awareness of the connection between the spread of disease and poor hygiene in the home.[49] Under the influence of behaviorism and social ecology, a firm belief had also arisen in the effect of the environment on behavior: if people could only be placed in a different milieu, they could and would change. Massive new housing developments were clearly needed.

Government and society were not yet prepared, though, to bear any of the expense of rebuilding the private homes of the disadvantaged. Middle-class parties, municipal authorities, and government institutions refused to extend social interventionism so far that it included the construction of housing. Many reform movement organizations and even state insurance institutions did much to support the construction of housing, but there was no great breakthrough prior to 1914.[50] Enlightenment of the people through better living spaces therefore remained an impossible dream. Only in the wake of the war and revolution did conditions change. The new Weimar Republic set itself the task of "ensuring that every German has a healthy home."[51] After the difficulties caused by the hyperinflation were overcome, the mass construction of social housing began in earnest with the institution of the tax on houses in 1924. Social housing was built not only in Germany but in other European countries as well.[52]

Middle-class reformers hoped that the new housing estates would also model and encourage a modern way of life. There had not been any experience at the time with this kind of attempt to influence public attitudes, and architects threw themselves in all good faith into an effort to reform private lives through the spaces in which these lives were lived, especially through rationalized floor plans. The main idea was to rationalize the total amount of room needed and thereby minimize it. Life in the home was reduced to the individual functions performed in each room, which were carefully analyzed and calculated, along with the

49. Cf. Richard J. Evans, *Death in Hamburg: Society and Politics in the Cholera Years 1830–1910* (Oxford, 1987).

50. For initial efforts to reform housing before 1914 see Thomas Hafner, *Kollektive Wohnreformen im Deutschen Kaiserreich 1871–1918* (Stuttgart, 1988).

51. See Article 155 of the Weimar constitution in Ernst Huber (ed.), *Dokumente zur Deutschen Verfassungsgeschichte* (Stuttgart, 1966), 3:151.

52. Only in the United States did they still believe in the superiority of free market forces in this area at that time.

necessary passageways between rooms. The regular movements of the inhabitants, especially women, were studied in great depth, and calculations were made to optimize them. From these efforts sprang the notion that "from a biological point of view, only a small amount of living space is really needed, especially when the operations are properly organized."[53] Architects hoped that rationalized floor plans would induce or subtly compel families to rationalize their own behaviors. All rooms had to open onto the hallway, and war was declared on the use of kitchens as living rooms, because this was considered unhygienic. The new kitchens were often made so small (the so-called Frankfurt kitchen [*Frankfurter Küche*])[54] that they could not possible be used as anything but a work space, usually for women.[55]

Even procreation did not escape the attention of the rationalizers. Although demographers said that the average family needed to have three children if the German people were to survive and grow,[56] housing activists decried families with more than two as irresponsible unless they were prosperous enough to raise the children without running into any space problems or financial difficulties. Regardless of how modest, apartments were built with two rooms for the children, if at all possible, even if the rooms were only tiny. This was to encourage rational procreation by the very floor plan and promote the idea (also advanced by nineteenth-century reformers, as mentioned earlier) that little brothers and sisters should not sleep in the same room.[57]

The usual attempts to educate and enlighten the people continued alongside "education through space." For instance, exhibitions were held of model goods, and these goods were offered for sale in an attempt to improve the taste of the general population. The managers of large housing estates published their own magazines in which they tried to influence the way in which the inhabitants lived and guide them in the "right direction." Property managers also issued rules and regulations for apartments and the surrounding grounds that may have seemed rigid

---

53. Walter Gropius, quoted in Hilpert, *Funktionelle Stadt,* 104.

54. Grete Schütte-Lihotzky, the female inventor of the Frankfurt kitchen, wanted it primarily to reduce the work of housewives.

55. The separation of functions applied to sanitation as well. Earlier water was often only available in the kitchen, while the toilets were on the half-stair.

56. See Alfred Grotjahn, *Die Hygiene der menschlichen Fortpflanzung,* 127–28 (Berlin and Vienna, 1926); Cornelia Usborne, *The Politics of the Body in Weimar Germany: Women's Reproductive Rights and Duties* (Ann Arbor and London, 1992).

57. For the rationalization of reproduction, see the work of Karen Hagemann, *Frauenalltag und Männerpolitik: Alltagsleben und gesellschaftliches Handeln von Arbeiterfrauen in der Weimarer Republik* (Bonn, 1990); and Atina Grossmann, *Reforming Sex: The German Movement for Birth Control* (Oxford, 1995).

but were certainly very rational. People were also encouraged to look down on older ways of life as "outdated." The future belonged to modernity alone.[58]

The rationalization of housekeeping is a subject of its own. Here too, architects and reformers followed the principles of Taylorism, studying the movements involved in particular household tasks and attempting to systematize them in order to determine particular room sizes and uses. The work of the housewife was to be planned and rationalized. Parallels were drawn between it and factory labor, and promises were made that housework could be considerably alleviated, especially if appliances were used. As a result of all this, women could continue to assume sole responsibility for housekeeping. The division of labor by gender was legitimized once again in the most modern possible way. "The social canon of mothers and housewives who were orderly, clean, and good was extended to include rational and efficient."[59]

The rational, well-planned program to construct housing seemed to obviate the need for the old apartment inspections carried out under the empire. In any case, there was a less conspicuous way to "assist" those tenants who did not abide by the principles of modern living: apartment managers. As a result of the huge housing developments of the 1920s, large numbers of leases and rental conditions were essentially the same for the first time in history and could be handled in a professional, rationalized manner. The managers of the large housing estates enjoyed considerable authority. Usually they could select suitable tenants from lists drawn up by the municipality of people entitled to apartments. They could terminate the leases as well because only older buildings were covered by the extensive legal protections against termination. A further advantage enjoyed by management was the fact that it retained control over the apartments as its private property from a legal point of view. Under the leases, management often had the right to enter apartments unannounced at any time. Usually this right was not exercised, but the possibility that management might appear at the door normally sufficed to make tenants careful. Management often visited "only" to hunt for vermin. Although few apartments in the new buildings became infested, management did not hesitate to complain about dirty conditions and

---

58. Further examples in Adelheid von Saldern, "The Workers' Movement and Cultural Patterns on Urban Housing Estates and in Rural Settlements in Germany and Austria during the 1920s," *Social History* 15, no. 3 (1990): 346ff.

59. Cf. in this regard Barbara Orland, "Effizienz im Heim: Die Rationalisierungsdebatte zur Reform der Hausarbeit in der Weimarer Republik," *Kultur und Technik* 7, no. 4 (1983): 221ff.; and Hagemann, *Frauenalltag*, 99ff.

continued its efforts to enlighten its tenants through estate magazines and newsletters, usually without mentioning any names.[60]

Alongside the efforts of the building managers, there were so-called Wohnungspflegerinnen, or female housing advisers, who helped to educate housewives about modern living using especially gentle coercion. They appeared at the door to offer advice and acquaint one with all the wonders of modernity, explaining for instance how housekeeping could be rationalized, what appliances should reasonably be purchased, what furniture suited small rooms, how to make new furniture from old, and how to eliminate kitsch. If one was not fortunate enough to be visited, similar advice was always available in the estate magazines and newsletters.[61] The idea was to align education and the modern aesthetic seen in goods.[62]

From Cleaning up Slums to Cleaning up the Race:
Old Working-Class Areas and the Mania to Clean Up

The welfare state instituted under the Weimar Republic had only limited ability to meet the needs of the population. This became very apparent in the realm of housing as well as elsewhere by the time of the Great Depression at the very latest. An impressive amount of housing had been built (about 2 million units over the short period between 1924 and 1930–31), but the shortages remained acute. It was increasingly obvious that social housing could not meet the needs of most of the working class because the rents were still too high, especially after the onset of the Great Depression. The great project of "modern urban redevelopment" was therefore increasingly approached from another angle. Plans had been made as far back as the empire to clean up the old part of cities, especially in Hamburg, but these plans had been largely shelved during the 1920s because of the boom in new construction. Now, however, they were dusted off and became a subject of public discussion and planning. Advocates of slum clearance could stand on the modern principle of rationalization because nothing could be more rational than to raze old areas where the buildings were decaying and crammed together in ways that certainly did not meet the test of logic. Who could oppose building

---

60. This is especially true of the large estates in Frankfurt.

61. However, the extent of the activities of the housing advisers should not be exaggerated.

62. How people reacted to this and the ways in which they appropriated their own apartments are not addressed in this chapter, which focuses on concepts and models. Some of the research results are reproduced in Herlyn, von Saldern, and Tessin, *Neubausied-lungen;* see also the following chapters in this volume.

something "up-to-date" and "better" in areas that failed to meet modern hygiene and design standards and that the police often found difficult to control? The people living in these areas were often resistant to a modern, rationalized lifestyle[63] but were dismissed as having antiquated mentalities and would obviously have to find shelter elsewhere. No one knew exactly where, but that was only a minor problem in the eyes of the architects and urban planners. If old-fashioned people were scattered and prevented from creating another tightly knit quarter in the city, they could probably be induced to conform to modern ways, and at least they would no longer be visible.

The drive to clean up the slums reached its historic pinnacle during the Third Reich. The argument is often heard in similar situations that the plans had already been laid before the Nazis came to power and therefore had nothing in particular to do with them. However, the heuristic value of this argument is small[64] for it implies that a self-fulfilling principle was at work (a so-called secular trend), which fails to explain the decision of the Nazis to give slum clearance a high priority.[65] On the other hand, it is also misleading to brand slum clearance as a typically fascist policy. It was adopted outside Germany as well in the 1930s, for instance in England and the United States, where it was lauded as progressive, reasonable, and essential for modernization. The Federal Republic's own history of razing and rebuilding particular urban areas shows that political systems neither were nor are a major factor in slum clearance. It has more to do with a particular understanding of modernity, like the belief of a surgeon who thinks that "what is bad has to be eliminated."

Initially, therefore, Nazi Germany did not seem out of step with other nations in respect to slum clearance. Can one say accordingly that Nazi Germany behaved like a modern, rational "Normative State" (Ernst Fraenkel's term) insofar as slum clearance was concerned? It was certainly modern and rational in some ways but with a specifically fascist twist. It is helpful to draw on some concepts advanced by Fraenkel in order to compare behaviors typical of capitalist societies predicated on

---

63. See, for instance, Michael Grüttner, "Soziale Hygiene und soziale Kontrolle: Die Sanierung der Hamburger Gängeviertel 1892 bis 1936," in Arno Herzig, Dieter Langewiesche, and Arnold Sywottek (eds.), *Arbeiter in Hamburg* (Hamburg, 1983); Eve Rosenhaft, *Beating the Fascists? The German Communists and Political Violence 1929–1933* (Cambridge, 1983).

64. This argument was advanced by Winkler, for example, at the time of the debate about National Socialist policies toward the middle class. Hans Heinrich Winkler, "Der entbehrliche Stand: Zur Mittelstandspolitik im 'Dritten Reich'," *Archiv für Sozialgeschichte* 17 (1977): 7.

65. In general see Adelheid von Saldern, *Häuserleben: Zur Geschichte städtischen Arbeiterwohnens vom Kaiserreich bis heute* (Bonn, 1995), 194ff.

an elaborate system of norms and rules with behaviors typical of fascist dictatorships predicated on dictatorial prerogative and free of any legal constraints. According to Fraenkel, the "Normative State" and "Prerogative State" did not function as two separate entities but were combined in a "Dual State," in which the "Prerogative State" held the upper hand.[66]

As in other areas of life, the specifically fascist aspect of the movement to clean up the old areas of cities was easy to see. Slum clearance was generally a matter for the Normative State, but the Prerogative State added a racist component by incorporating into the apparently modern, rational attempt to clean up the cities an effort to clean up the *Volk* as well. Many demographers and specialists in social and race "hygiene" considered the latter aspect of slum clearance just as "modern" and "rational" as the rest, except that it was the people who were being cleaned up instead of the buildings. The differences between the two and the qualitative leap in logic were easy to overlook because the categories and habits of thought were the same. Cleansing was strongly associated with the world of medicine and good health. For the first time, raising a healthy (Aryan) race was not only conceivable but feasible under a dictatorship. The effort to clean up cities and the race naturally assumed a "scientific" air, and professionals were called in. A social geographer named Walther drew up a map of the city of Hamburg on the basis of verifiable scientific criteria showing the degree of *Gemeinschädlichkeit* (harmfulness to the community) of the local inhabitants, meaning above all those who were Communist or "asocial."[67] The connection between this map and urban redevelopment was discussed at an international conference in 1935 by the director of construction for the city of Hamburg, a man named Köster: "The population of areas to be cleaned up, especially the asocial elements, cannot be forced to accept particular new apartments. . . . Making a healthy city therefore requires not only 'curative plans' for individual apartment buildings, streets or areas but a curative plan for the entire city, which, in a broader sense, should also be a

---

66. Ernst Fraenkel, *The Dual State: A Contribution to the Theory of Dictatorship* (New York, 1941). Fraenkel emphasized that a "political authority" and a "political sphere" (without any guaranteed rights) had virtually detached themselves from the prevailing legal system and provided the basis for the so-called Prerogative State. Under it, all laws were subordinate to political considerations, and all legislation or legally binding agreements were disregarded in the exercise of supreme authority. No realm of social or economic life was beyond the reach of the Prerogative State.

67. See in this regard Dirk Schubert, "Gesundung der Städte: Stadtsanierung in Hamburg 1933–1945," in Michael Bose et al., *". . . ein neues Hamburg entsteht . . ." Planen und Bauen von 1933 bis 1945* (Hamburg, 1986), 74ff.

resettlement plan."[68] In uttering these words, Köster hardly caused any international eyebrows to rise because other countries also had population policies that played an increasingly important role in slum clearance.

The difference in Germany can only be fully understood when the Nazi "Prerogative State" operating outside all norms and rules is taken sufficiently into account. The "Prerogative State" used its hegemony over the "Normative State" in two ways in particular: "incorrigibly asocial" people (an administrative category that had already existed under the Weimar Republic) were sometimes forcibly sterilized, especially when they were women,[69] and under some circumstances were even jailed or sent to work camps or concentration camps.[70] In addition, the campaign to clean up German cities and make them healthy included "cleansing" various areas of political enemies, especially Communists, who were deemed sick and injurious to the community, in short *gemeinschädigende Personen.*[71] Walther wrote in 1936: "For the sake of the future of the *Volk,* he [the Führer] is determined that elements harmful to it will no longer be weakly tolerated but will be controlled and rendered harmless. This means an entirely new approach to cleaning up our big cities. Curing society has become a priority in urban planning."[72]

This was not premodern or antimodern; it was modernity itself but the other side of the coin, the side of inhumanity and barbarism. At one time, the main task of city and housing hygienists had been to rid housing of pests and vermin; now it was to rid the *Volk* of harmful elements. At one time, the goal had been to create "dwelling machines," that is, to introduce Taylorism into the home by dividing household tasks and recombining them in new ways,[73] and to put an end to the chaos that reigned in the cities by creating new structures that could be connected and controlled. Now German fascism crossed the Rubicon to the application of the same modern, rational principles of division and controlled recombination to people themselves, eliminating those deemed harmful or inferior. Rationalization of work, rationalization of the home, and

---

68. In ibid., 79.

69. Gisela Bock, *Zwangssterilisation im Nationalsozialismus: Studien zur Rassenpolitik und Frauenpolitik* (Opladen, 1986). However, I cannot support her generalizations and parallels.

70. Voigt describes one of the Nazis' modern work camps in Bremen to which "antisocial families" were sent. Wolfgang Voigt, "Wohnhaft: Die Siedlung als panoptisches Gefängnis," in *Arch+* 16, no. 75–76 (1984): 82–89.

71. For "electoral behavior" as a criterion for slum clearance, see Harald Bodenschatz, *Platz frei für das neue Berlin! Geschichte der Stadterneuerung in der "größten Mietskasernenstadt der Welt" seit 1871* (Berlin, 1987), 128.

72. Quoted in Bose et al., *Neues Hamburg,* 78ff.

73. Lesemann, *Sanieren,* 129.

rationalization of everyday human behavior were parts of a continuum to which the Nazis, in apparently logical progression, added the biggest part of all: rationalization of the entire German people.

The route that the Nazis took was not direct and certainly not predetermined. There were many ways of exploiting the intrinsic potential of modernity. However, it was modernity itself, and especially the arrogant, deep-seated belief that everything was possible and everything could be controlled, that posed an enormous temptation not only to National Socialists but also to many others who considered themselves apolitical experts — a temptation that they could not resist and to which millions eventually fell victim. Modernity revealed its destructive potential while political and ideological dictatorship reduced all countervailing forces to impotence. Nazi social policy must therefore be seen, in Peukert's words, "as an antiliberal variant in the modernization process and the heir to a dehumanized variant in the rationalization movement."[74]

And nowadays? The multifarious (including destructive) potential of modernity has only increased, and the danger of hubris remains. To the extent that the people responsible for scientific developments have any sense of social responsibility, it is largely subject to a worldwide capitalist logic and single-minded pursuit of success and achievement. However, the situation has changed in some ways since the period between the wars. The fervent belief in "progress" so typical of that time and so apparent in the desire to rationalize everything has waned among large parts of the population. There is more awareness now of the dangers of modernity and of the perpetual temptation to go too far, see things in terms of absolutes, and strive for total command and control. There is greater alertness to the destructive, barbaric side of modernity, and historians too have gained more insight.

---

74. Peukert, *Max Webers Diagnose,* 82.

CHAPTER 4

"How Should Linoleum Floors Be Cleaned?": A Contribution to Alltagsgeschichte and the Social History of the 1920s

Introduction

In response to a housewife's question in 1929 about how to clean linoleum floors, the following appeared in *Die Siedlung,* the magazine of reform movement housing in Frankfurt. "Linoleum floors are best cleaned every four to six weeks with a linoleum cleaning mixture or soapy water that does not contain any sodium, then rubbed down with turpentine linoleum wax, and polished. Between times, do not put hot water on it. Just wipe with a damp towel and polish with a cloth or floor polisher."[1] Much of this kind of harmless advice about how to keep things clean was dispensed in the 1920s. Many materials, like linoleum, were still quite new, and what housewife would not be interested in learning how to care for them properly?

Cleaning one's home is part of the perpetual everyday struggle between humans and nature: housewives dust or clean up, new dust or dirt is deposited in a few hours, and the whole process is repeated. If things are not cleaned for too long, nature begins to take over. Homes

---

1. *Die Siedlung: Monatsschrift für gemeinnützige Siedlungs- und Wohnungswirtschaft* 1, no. 3 (1929): 5. This and various other magazines, which were published as management expanded to handle the larger reform housing estates in the 1920s, are valuable sources on the history of everyday life, although they are difficult to find. These magazines should certainly not be considered representative, but they do provide us with an idea of how "modern living" was applied to everyday life. How people actually lived can usually only be indirectly deduced by reading these magazines "against the grain."

and their inhabitants grow dirty, and vermin begin to spread. No one would want that, and so the cleaning continues. Beginning in the late nineteenth century but especially in the twentieth, reliance on chemicals increased. Even they, though, could not bring permanent victory. Any triumph over dust and dirt was short lived, even if the ecological side effects of chemicals were disregarded.[2]

Linoleum was considered a "hygienic material"[3] that was especially easy to keep clean, but even it needed some care. At first, the product directions were nothing more than well-intentioned advice, but eventually they were incorporated in full detail into the house rules of reform movement housing in Frankfurt. Advice hardened into instructions, legitimized by prior "discussion in expert circles and the understanding shown by our readers." Since reform housing had similarly worded mass leases, the proper cleaning of linoleum floors became a duty imposed on large numbers of people, with the monthly *Die Siedlung* (circulation of fifteen thousand) functioning as the "Bulletin of the Building Cooperatives and Societies of Greater Frankfurt am Main."[4] The efforts of the social reform movement to improve housing were particularly pronounced, it must be admitted, in the Frankfurt of Ernst May, the functionally minded director of municipal construction; however, similar trends could also be seen in the "Einfa" housing administration that oversaw the reform buildings of the trade unions in Berlin.[5]

A Contribution to Social History and Alltagsgeschichte

The cleaning of linoleum floors as an example of the cleaning of homes as an example of Alltagsgeschichte — can this be serious? Or is it just "historical or historiographical girl talk"? Or the history of pointless trivialities?

---

2. Any further discussion of the technical details is omitted for lack of space. We might mention in passing, though, that the kind of advice that does not shed much light on the technical realities is typical of "consumer advice" in the twentieth century.

3. *Brockhaus,* 1932.

4. *Die Siedlung* 2, no. 5 (1930): 54. This magazine was distributed to all families renting housing from the amalgamated building cooperatives and cooperative building societies. Its circulation of fifteen thousand must therefore have been roughly equivalent to the number of households. If there were generally two or three people per family, one can conclude that between thirty thousand and forty-five thousand people were reached in this way.

5. Here too advice about proper modern living easily turned into moral pressure to follow the advice; see in this regard various articles in *Einfa,* the magazine named after the eponymous apartment management company owned by the trade unions.

Just as homes and housing are part of everyday life, so the historical analysis of them is part of the history of everyday life. The topic of homes and housing encompasses many different activities, such as eating, sleeping, working, and playing, carried out in rooms that have generally been furnished and decorated according to the tastes and financial means of the occupants. We therefore see in this realm people who are actively engaged with their environment. The appropriation process can be witnessed on the emotional, cognitive, and aesthetic levels.[6] There is some connection, of course, between people's homes and society in general, and social developments are often reflected in the home. In addition, outside attempts to influence how people live and what they do in their homes are not unusual. These attempts can be seen primarily in a variety of discourses advancing ideas for social reform and exploring their relevance to the home.[7]

Alltagsgeschichte portrays people as historical subjects, and it needs therefore to be placed in a broader social context, as the example of housing and domestic life makes clear. On the other hand, social history that ignores everyday life eventually grows arid, especially in respect to housing and domestic life. This chapter attempts to show therefore how housing and domestic life can make a contribution to the debates surrounding social history and Alltagsgeschichte by analyzing a central topic, primarily reform movement housing in the 1920s. It is necessary to focus on particular areas of study because it would be impossible to investigate housing and domestic life per se. One describes either the buildings and furnishings or else individual activities and the discourses about them. Discourses certainly affect everyday life too and are therefore very much a part of Alltagsgeschichte. The remainder of this chapter concentrates primarily on reconstructing the discourse surrounding cleanliness in the home. In this we are selecting a central theme of everyday life since cleanliness was seen at the time as essential for pleasant, comfortable living, which was considered synonymous with high living standards. The frequent references to the reform movement and

---

6. Cf. Michael Andritzky and Gert Selle, *Lernbereich Wohnen*, vol. 2 (Reinbek, 1979); Paul-Henry Chombart de Lauwe, "Aneignung, Eigentum, Enteignung," *Arch+* 9, no. 34 (1977): 2–6.

7. The analysis of contemporary discourses is growing more and more important as historians realize that discourses can reveal how things were understood and interpreted at the time and that they affected people's lives and mentalities. Nevertheless, this methodology should not be pushed too far and certainly cannot replace the usual methods for studying social history and the history of everyday life. For an introduction to this kind of analysis, see Jürgen Fohrmann and Harro Müller, *Diskurstheorien und Literaturwissenschaft* (Frankfurt, 1988).

the housing built at its prompting in the 1920s spring from the widespread impression among contemporaries that it exemplified and sought to instill cleanliness.[8]

"The Spirit of Cleanliness" and Reform Movement Housing

In the 1920s, cultural conservatives wanted primarily to compensate for the loss of what they felt was the safe, orderly world of the German Empire, which had been destroyed by war, revolution, and the new republic. Sentiments of this kind were present throughout the life of the republic. Clean, orderly homes were all the more desirable because they lent a feeling of security and stability in unsettled times.

Reform circles close to the labor unions had similar feelings, although in a different social and political context. Voices within Einfa lamented the storm that "is now shaking all peoples, lifting the foundations of the economy, and overthrowing entire *Weltanschauungen*. . . . In the screeching dissonance of the worldwide tumult, we find refuge in our homes, like peaceful cloisters. Regardless of how small or humble, our homes assume greater importance, become our bastions against the storm. The goodly spirits of the home, the spirits of cleanliness, quiet and joy, gain ascendancy over us as we, in an attempt to be frugal, no longer seek outside amusement in movie houses and pubs or on the streets. Cleanliness is the very foundation of all cultivated living. It is essential for hygiene and a sense of order. Clean, simple things foster purity of the spirit; orderly objects stabilize the soul."[9] This statement seems to flow smoothly from one element to the next. Clean, orderly homes and the purity of spirit that they foster are bulwarks against the storms of life. Even amusements outside the home, which expanded greatly in the 1920s with the breakthrough of commercialized popular culture, pose a threat.

Governing elites, company owners, and bourgeois reformers had always attempted to influence the lifestyles and living conditions of the people, especially the lower classes. However, the opportunities to do so in the 1920s were unprecedented, thanks to the construction of state-subsidized housing for the masses. Urban planners, architects, physicians, social reformers, building cooperatives, and housing management firms all tried in their own ways and in quite different situations to modernize everyday life in the home in accordance with their own ide-

---

8. This is especially true of the Bauhaus style, which in the eyes of its advocates represented the clearest, cleanest solution to the existing problems.

9. In *Einfa: Nachrichtenblatt der Einfa* 3, no. 6 (1932): 2.

als. One thing that was common to all of them was insistence on the greatest possible cleanliness.[10]

The discourse around hygiene was part of a broad civilizing process and one of the driving forces behind it.[11] The need for good hygiene had been one of the central topics in society ever since the late nineteenth century, and the degree to which it had already become the social norm can be seen in the *Handbuch der Hygiene* (Handbook of hygiene), which went through a second edition as early as 1912.[12] When the *Handwörterbuch des Wohnungswesens* (Pocket dictionary of housing), commissioned by the German Association for Housing Reform, was published in 1930,[13] it had little to add. The article entitled "Hygiene of Urban Development and the Construction of Housing" contained the following subtopics: (1) General Information, (2) Air, (3) Light (including lack of cleanliness in the home), (4) Communicable Diseases, Vermin, and the Effects of Overcrowding and of Dense Buildings and Housing, Germ Carriers, and Tenement Buildings, (5) Effects of Housing on the Psyche and Morals, Alcoholism, Sexually Transmitted Diseases, Declining Birthrates, and (6) Basic Requirements. Dirtiness was repeatedly

---

10. The cleanliness problem grew more acute in the second half of the nineteenth century in the wake of urbanization and cholera epidemics. Advances in medical knowledge prompted ever more reform-minded people to take up the cry. People were certainly aware that good hygiene — the scientific word for cleanliness — depended on living conditions, and they generally felt that people could influence how good their conditions were. In *An Enemy of the People,* Ibsen puts the following words in the mouth of Doctor Stockmann: "In a house which does not get aired and swept every day — my wife Katherine maintains that the floor ought to be scrubbed as well, but that is a debatable question — in such a house, let me tell you, people will lose within two or three years the power of thinking or acting in a moral way. The lack of oxygen weakens the conscience." Quoted in Hugo Hillig, *Die Hygiene der Arbeiterwohnung* (Berlin, 1910), 81.

11. See in this regard in general Norbert Elias, *Der Prozeß der Zivilisation,* vol. 2, (Frankfurt, 1976); Peter Gleichmann, "Die Verhäuslichung körperlicher Verrichtungen," in Peter Gleichmann (ed.), *Materialien zur Norbert Elias Zivilisationstheorie* (Frankfurt, 1977); Marianne Rodenstein and Stefan Böhm-Ott, "Gesunde Wohnungen und Wohnungen für gesunde Deutsche: Der Einfluß der Hygiene auf Wohnungs- und Städtebau in der Weimarer Republik und im 'Dritten Reich,'" in Gert Kähler (ed.), *Geschichte des Wohnens, 1918–1945: Reform, Reaktion, Zerstörung* (Stuttgart, 1966), 4:453ff.

12. See in this regard Klaus Mönkemeyer, "Schmutz und Sauberkeit: Figurationen eines Diskurses im Deutschen Kaiserreich," in Imbke Behnken (ed.), *Stadtgesellschaft und Kindheit im Prozeß der Zivilisation: Konfigurationen städtischer Lebensweise zu Beginn des 20. Jahrhunderts* (Opladen, 1990), 74; cf. also Beatrix Mesmer, "Reinheit und Reinlichkeit: Bemerkungen zur Durchsetzung der häuslichen Hygiene in der Schweiz," in Nicolai Bernard and Quirinus Reichen (eds.), *Gesellschaft und Gesellschaften* (Bern, 1982), 485; in general Geneviève Heller, *"Propre en ordre": Habitation et vie domestique 1850–1930: L'example vaudois* (Lausanne, 1979).

13. Gerhard Albert et al. (eds.), *Handwörterbuch des Wohnungswesens* (Pocket dictionary of housing) (Jena, 1930), 374ff.

associated with a lack of light. Dust and dirt could supposedly not be seen in poorly lit rooms or were ignored because of a lack of pleasure in life, which was itself a consequence of poor lighting.

Conclusions of another kind were then drawn: "Uncomfortable, dirty, unkempt, overstuffed homes almost inevitably drive [male] house-holders into pubs and places of dubious entertainment and therefore into the arms of alcohol and fornication." There was always an implication that this "flight from the home" was a great "loss for the family as a pillar of the nation and for the *Volk* community."[14] Various inferences can be drawn from these passages. Although they concentrate primarily on the need for a general improvement in living conditions, certain people are targeted. Women are not explicitly said to be in charge of dust and dirt, but it is clearly they who are meant because the person leaving home to go to pubs and movie houses is the *Inhaber,* or male householder. Other inferences can be drawn. Activities beyond the scope of home and the family are considered damaging to the pillars of the nation and the *Volk* community, whatever is meant by that. It would be only somewhat exaggerated to say that clean homes are inflated, through the ideology of the family, into a matter of grave national concern.

The new homes that were built gained a reputation as models of modern housing and domestic life, thanks not least of all to the efforts of the weekend supplements to daily newspapers. By 1930, about every seventh dwelling in Germany was newly constructed,[15] and the modeling effect of these dwellings must have been quite substantial, especially as the directors of municipal construction, who often sympathized with the reform movement, were able to bring their influence to bear in many different ways on the types of construction that were used and the character of the housing, even when private funds were involved.[16] Although

---

14. Ibid., 378.

15. *Blätter für Wohnungswesen* 10, no. 8 (1930): 12. This magazine was the organ of the Solingen Savings and Building Association. The vast majority of new housing received public subsidies, with the proportion varying between 77 and 93 percent during the so-called rent tax era from 1924 to 1931. This housing therefore had to comply to some extent with the reform ideas of the municipal building administrations that were in charge of distributing the subsidies. The percentages that are provided are taken from Peter Christian Witt, "Inflation, Wohnungszwangswirtschaft, und Hauszinssteuer: Zur Regelung von Wohnungsbau und Wohnungsmarkt in der Weimarer Republik," in Lutz Niethammer (ed.), *Wohnen im Wandel: Beiträge zur Geschichte des Alltags in der bürgerlichen Gesellschaft* (Wuppertal, 1979), 403.

16. Reif too assumes this modeling effect. Heinz Reif, "Stadtentwicklung und Viertelbildung im Ruhrgebiet: Oberhausen 1850 bis 1929," in Wolfgang Hardtwig and Klaus Tenfelde (eds.), *Soziale Räume in der Urbanisierung: Zur Studien zur Geschichte Münchens im Vergleich 1850 bis 1933* (Munich, 1990), 174.

modern living was epitomized in the eyes of the media and in public statements by the large urban housing estates, all new housing could exemplify it. Even old-fashioned homes and domestic lives could be updated, as shown by the following quotation: "So long as people do not change their mentality within their existing homes, the new kind of construction will not lead any further. People whose mentalities have not changed will necessarily build in the old spirit, or if the new spirit is forced upon them, they will ruin it through compromises and half-measures. Almost all the housing estates built so far are convincing proof of that. The transition must therefore be made within the old housing. It would be unjust to write off the hundreds of thousands of existing tenements and abandon those people to their fate."[17]

With all the public funds at the disposal of reform housing construction, this provided an unprecedented opportunity to influence private lives, a sphere that was generally quite resistant to outside control. The housing reformer Hildegard Margis proclaimed in 1928 that women must strive "to create homes that are clean and comfortable."[18] All housewives had a duty to use modern appliances and keep their new housing good and clean.[19] Cleanliness standards had risen enormously, however, in the age of modern hygiene, and the pressure on housewives increased accordingly. Since good hygiene was widely equated with disease prevention, housewives neither could nor wanted to resist. Many of them, especially in the conservative Housewives' League, were strong supporters of the new trend.

The traditional combined kitchen and living room fell under the well-founded suspicion, because of all its uses, of failing to meet or of just barely meeting the new cleanliness standards. The modern alternative was the "working kitchen," which, like the famous *Frankfurter Küche* (Frankfurt kitchen) totaling about five or six square meters in area, was so tiny that nothing could possibly be done there except cook and wash dishes. The reformers thought that tiny kitchens would also force the inhabitants to be extremely neat, an important prerequisite for cleanliness.

17. Bruno Taut, *Die neue Wohnung: Die Frau als Schöpferin* (Leipzig, 1924), 58.

18. Hildegard Margis, "Die Frau als Heimgestalterin," in H. Ritter (ed.), *Wohnung, Wirtschaft, Gesellschaft* (Berlin, 1928), 78.

19. At the time, modern amenities were understood to mean primarily a toilet and a bath or shower in the apartment. To them were often added a gas stove, instead of the old coal stove; electric lights; running water in the kitchen; and sometimes a balcony. Much work needed to be done in order to keep the new apartments clean. They were bright and light, showing every speck of dust, which was considered a health risk. The invention and marketing of the vacuum cleaner came at just the right moment, although vacuum cleaners were still expensive and could only be afforded by the well-to-do families of the middle class.

Good Taste as a Matter of Good Hygiene

The logic of rationalization and good hygiene penetrated every aspect of everyday life. The cluttered, ornate furniture of Wilhelminian times was rejected not so much as a matter of taste as from pure reason.[20] People who could not afford new furniture were urged to modernize the old in order to make it more hygienic by smoothing the outer surfaces and cutting away any unnecessary embellishments. If the war on dust was to be properly rationalized, furnishings had to be spare and designed in such a way that they would not trap dust. Bruno Taut published instructions for "renovations to middle-class living rooms," adding the apparently resigned comment "still too much furniture, but housewives consider it indispensable."[21] Taut was referring to the insistence of many housewives on doing things their own way and only partly following the advice of architects. Photographs or pictures on the walls were also decried as dust traps. Such souvenirs of one's life were to be sacrificed on the altar of reason and utilitarianism. The "new man" was supposed to be uncompromisingly modern, whether on the job or in the home. As the magazine published by a union-owned housing estate succinctly stated: "If I am a man of today, the rooms in which I live should not reek of a bygone era."[22]

No allowance was made for any asynchronousness in human needs and tastes or for the occasionally clumsy attempts of people to ease their feelings of alienation through old knickknacks and other mementos. Such thoughts would have been contrary to the belief in progress. However, the ideas of the Werkbund and the Bauhaus for a differentiated but thoroughly modern taste in housing predicated on functionalism and practicality often foundered on the mentality of the people who lived in it. "An architecture that seeks commitment to a standard contemporary style encompassing every aspect of life, housing and work underestimates the opposition and resistance of people to innovation and change for the better. Unfulfilled lives internalize their suppression in the field of housing as well, and even especially here. No architecture can eliminate this response simply by providing aesthetic, rational, reasonable models. An additional lever is needed that will begin to emancipate needs from their current reified state."[23] Alltagsgeschichte studies resistance to change for

---

20. The transformation of taste was, however, not only a question of cleanliness, although this subject cannot be explored any further here.

21. Taut, *neue Wohnung,* 56.

22. *Einfa* 2, no. 10 (1931): 2.

23. Peter Gorsen, "Zur Dialektik des Funktionalismus heute: Das Beispiel des kommunalen Wohnungsbaus im Wien der zwanziger Jahre," in Jürgen Habermas (ed.), *Stichworte zur "geistigen Situation der Zeit"* (Frankfurt, 1979), 2:692ff.

the better in particular historical circumstances when it looks at the social logic of individuals.

The Propagation of the Discourses about Cleanliness

Concepts of cleanliness became widely accepted and greatly affected everyday life in the home. They did not stand in isolation, though, and played an increasingly prominent role in a variety of discourses, including not only discourses about medicine and health care but also about popular culture, population policies, and eugenics. "Cleanliness" became the common denominator in the discourses, for instance in the discussions about the revolution, morality, and commercialized popular culture. The latter was frequently described as "filthy," and a "clean" culture was said to be necessary to protect the youth from the flood of smut.[24] According to cultural conservatives, a widespread decline in morality was much to blame for the problem. What they reproved, on an explicit level, was at first only the alleged frequency of "dirt and trash" in films and pulp magazines, especially after the censorship laws were briefly lifted in 1918. However, the views of cultural conservatives on smut remained ambiguous, and sometimes the events of the revolution seemed to be included. Since smut is soft, dirty, and lacking in contour, it also became associated with a negative view of women. Eventually, attempts were made to use the campaign against "dirt and trash" to discredit the revolution of 1918–19. Anyone who "loves morality," it was said, must take action against "dirt and trash." "Otherwise, the poison creeps along, seeping into the *Volk* and leaving the nation ripe for destruction." A "dam" had to be erected against the "flood of smut" and "dirty goings-on." There was much talk about the "moral collapse of the German people" and "moral degeneracy," and people allegedly needed to be "cleansed of impurities." "A spiritual cleansing" was necessary to produce "pure souls," and cultural policy should be guided by the "feelings of the healthy-thinking population" and the "spiritual health of the *Volk*."[25]

Whores, women who seemed too manly, and the girls who paraded about in shows[26] were decried as dirty and immoral, while mothers and

---

24. Klaus Theweleit illuminates some of the psychoanalytical aspects. Klaus Theweleit, *Männerphantasien: Frauen, Fluten, Körper, Geschichte* (Reinbek, 1980), 1:401ff.

25. For other sources see chapter 9 in this volume. For the connection between cleanliness and citizenship see Mesmer, *Reinheit*, 485.

26. For these shows, see Sigrun Anselm, "Emanzipation und Tradition in den 20er Jahren," in Sigrun Anselm and Barbara Beck (eds.), *Triumph und Scheitern in der Metropole: Zur Rolle der Weiblichkeit in der Geschichte Berlins* (Berlin, 1987), 267ff.

housewives epitomized all that was wholesome and clean, especially if they were German. It was no accident that housewives were advised always to present a neat, clean appearance to the outside world. They allegedly could easily win the never-ending war on dirt with the help of modern technology. White underclothing and bleaching detergents like Persil were used in marketing strategies because of their strong symbolic value.[27] An advertisement for Persil from 1925 illustrates the link between the discourses about motherhood and cleanliness. The illustration is of a woman dressed in white leading her two daughters, also dressed in white, by the hands. The "white lady" is the incarnation of the pure mother.[28]

"Valuable Public Property"—Enforcing Cleanliness

Problems arose when individual households or families paid no attention to the socially acceptable limits and gained a reputation for being dirty and unkempt. As early as 1908, reform circles advocated the mandatory cleaning of apartments, as practiced in Japan, where compulsory cleaning days were reputedly held once or twice a year and the results inspected by the authorities.[29] Some German cities had sent around housing inspectors in Wilhelminian times, although they were less concerned with cleanliness than with discovering totally decayed housing, that is, with revealing abuses on the part of property owners. Like their Japanese counterparts, though, these inspectors had to be allowed entry.[30]

In the 1920s, there were more social workers with expanded duties visiting apartments, and the housing advisers were marginalized. There were still other ways, though, of monitoring the cleanliness of apartments. In the reform housing estates in Frankfurt, management representatives would occasionally appear at the door and demand to be admitted in order to search for any pests that had gained a foothold. (Pests really were a problem, apparently, in some of the buildings in the new Frankfurt housing estates, especially moths and cockroaches.)[31] In parts of the Altstadt that were ripe for slum clearance and where unemployment was especially high, social workers would come to inspect the

---

27. For an overview see Barbara Orland, *Wäsche waschen* (Reinbek, 1991).
28. Cf. Ute Daniel, "Der unaufhaltsame Aufstieg des sauberen Individuums: Seifen- und Waschmittelwerbung im historischen Kontext," in Imbke Behnken (ed.), *Stadtgesellschaft und Kindheit im Prozeß der Zivilisation: Konfigurationen städtischer Lebensweise zu Beginn des 20. Jahrhunderts* (Opladen, 1990), 43ff., picture on 52.
29. *Reformblätter* 11, no. 7 (1908): 162.
30. *Reformblätter* 11, no. 8 (1908); see also 7, no. 3 (1904): 66.
31. *Die Siedlung* 1, no. 4 (1929): 13.

living conditions, often with drastic effects on the amount of municipal welfare payments.

The efforts to exert social controls generally intensified in the final phase of the Weimar Republic.[32] The example provided by reform housing was not as successful at inducing people to change their ways as had been hoped a few years earlier. The housing advisers (*Wohnungsfürsorgerinnen* or *Wohnungspflegerinnen*) were consequently assigned responsibility for "overseeing the layout and use of all living and sleeping quarters from a health point of view." Visits were arranged for all apartments, even in new buildings.[33] No law was passed, but a directive from the Prussian welfare ministry in 1929 underlined the importance of regular monitoring.[34] Even older housing was "valuable public property," whose preservation was essential in view of the housing shortage. There was all the more reason, therefore, to monitor the treatment of the newly constructed housing in order to ensure that any abuses were promptly corrected. According to the directive, it was not sufficient for the authorities to intervene only upon receipt of complaints or accusations. Instead, there should be planned, regularly scheduled inspections. In areas where there were no housing offices, attempts should be made to hire knowledgeable inspectors. If funds were not available to hire a sufficient number of paid officials, according to the directive, people should be asked to serve in an honorary capacity.

The line between advice and coercion became increasingly blurred. Tenants of reform housing estates in Frankfurt in particular were required "to take advice willingly and not consider well-intentioned instructions as an infringement on their personal rights."[35] This requirement was based on observations in some of the newly constructed estates, which, though they may have been extreme cases, still lead one to conclude that tenants could not be steered in the right direction quite as easily as the authorities wished. According to reports, "many tenants" felt that it was "absurd" to treat new housing with special care. Furthermore, "the most unbelievable junk can often be found in the apartments, furniture that is inappropriate and unnecessary. The same holds true of the decorations on the walls. Very often, the kinds of curtains severely impede air circulation. Such impractical furnishings are also dreadful dust traps."[36] Once again, dust

---

32. See in general in this regard Detlev J. K. Peukert, *Grenzen der Sozialdisziplinierung: Aufstieg und Krise der deutschen Jugendfürsorge 1878 bis 1932* (Cologne, 1986).

33. *Blätter für Wohnungswesen* 10, no. 3 (1929): 6.

34. Directive II B 226 of January 24, 1929, mentioned in *Die Siedlung* 1, no. 6 (1929): 11.

35. *Die Siedlung* 3, no. 6 (1931): 88.

36. Ibid., 89.

Fig. 4.   Before (*above*) and afterward (*facing page*). Proposal for an alteration
of a worker's living room in the context of modernity. (From Bruno Taut, *Die
neue Wohnung: Die Frau als Schöpferin,* 57 [Leipzig, 1924].)

and dirt were offered as the reasons why people should make the desired
changes to their furniture.

". . . and get them back to the home": The Role of Women in the Light of the Cleanliness Standards

The emergence of new social standards, especially in regard to cleanliness and neatness, had contradictory effects on the roles of the sexes.
Almost all the ideas and measures of the reformers were oriented toward the ideal of the private, single-family household, for which the wife
bore most of the responsibility. Most wives and husbands pursued this
ideal as well,[37] since the ability to maintain a household of one's own had
long been considered a sign that one was fully of age and ready for
marriage and a family. On the surface, very little changed in the everyday lives of women, who continued to tend the home and mind the

37. See in this regard Karen Hagemann, *Frauenalltag und Männerpolitik: Alltagsleben und gesellschaftliches Handeln von Arbeiterfrauen in der Weimarer Republik* (Bonn,
1990); Günther Uhlig, *Kollektivmodell "Einküchenhaus": Wohnreform und Architek-
turdebatte zwischen Frauenbewegung und Funktionalismus 1900–1933* (Gießen, 1981).

children, as they had always done.[38] Upon closer examination, though, changes can be seen, because housework was deeply affected by the new cleanliness standards and the trend toward rationalization and professionalization. Housework was urged on women as a thoroughly modern activity. Cultural conservatives perceived a threat to the traditional roles of the sexes since as many middle-class families were releasing their servant girls for economic reasons, more girls and women than ever before were in the labor force, at least prior to marriage, and the fashionable "new woman" showed more interest in pursuing modern pleasures than in fulfilling the old duties. Even the Munich trade unionist Heinz Potthoff appeared prone to such fears when he declared that a "primary objective of social policy is precisely to get wives and mothers away from factories and offices and get them back to the home."[39] In an attempt to make life in the home more attractive for women, Potthoff suggested allowing them a greater say in the design and finishing of dwellings, an

---

38. In her study, Heidi Rosenbaum warns however against exaggerating the division of labor by sex, at least insofar as the raising of children was concerned. Heidi Rosenbaum, *Proletarische Familien: Arbeiterfamilien und Arbeiterväter im frühen 20. Jahrhundert zwischen traditioneller, sozialdemokratischer, und kleinbürgerlicher Orientierung* (Frankfurt, 1992).

39. *Blätter für Wohnungswesen* 5, no. 12 (1925): 6.

idea that was shared by reform-minded architects. Potthoff's ultimate goal was to create and preserve "clean, comfortable homes"[40] (once again "clean" and "comfortable" are closely identified).

Clean Homes, Modernization, and Happy Marriages

"Can you tell me what I should do to be a good wife?" asked a tenant of one of the new Frankfurt housing estates in the "Tenants Ask — Tenants Answer" column in *Die Siedlung*. Answer 56 was carried in the January 1, 1933, edition: "An exhaustive reply to this question cannot be given here, but start by providing your husband with a comfortable home and good food, so far as possible under current economic conditions. You have a fine opportunity to provide the first of these in our well-tended housing estates, especially if you equate comfort with cleanliness as well. The second can be provided, even if your housekeeping funds are limited, by attending if necessary the numerous free courses offered by the Frankfurt Bund für Volksernährung. Always remember that your husband has entrusted his stomach, nerves, mind and spirit to your care. Never receive him sullenly or with complaints. Your husband will gladly go out to work if, thanks to your care, he enjoys a convivial home life. However, even the strongest nerves and the best disposition cannot long endure incessant quarreling, arguments and complaints. Your husband will also be in such a bad mood that he will not have the strength to do his job well. Nowadays, this can easily have disastrous consequences for both him and his family, that is to say, for you too. Show an interest in his work. Try repeatedly to win your husband over anew. Clean, pretty clothing, regardless of how inexpensive, and a friendly smile are as captivating now as before your wedding. Do not bother him with tasks and matters related to the children, who are your responsibility, unless you happen to be sick. If you are, he will certainly be glad to help out. Be friendly to him in all ways: what comes from the heart, goes to the heart. He will be grateful to you, for no man can long resist noble femininity, least of all that of his own wife."[41]

In reading this passage, one feels at first transported into the early nineteenth century. Women are defined through their husbands, and housework is their responsibility, unless they are sick. Upon closer examination, though, the typical discourse of more contemporary times becomes evident. Comfort is associated with cleanliness, and the Frankfurt Bund für Volksernährung disseminates modern nutritional information and professionalizes the art of cooking, making it more of a science.

---

40. Ibid.
41. *Die Siedlung* 5, no. 1 (1933): 8.

Finally, the new housing estates are portrayed as models of clean, comfortable living. The short answer to the question about how to achieve a happy marriage would be to combine the same old gendered roles with the necessary modernization of domestic life. Although the answer quoted here did not mention the crucial elements of rationalization and mechanization, other articles did, for instance one from October 1932: "Rationalization! that is the motto. If it is especially needed anywhere, then in the home. Not only does it liberate housewives from heavy labor but it saves them a considerable amount of money and makes more time available for the important tasks of raising children and pursuing cultural interests and health. . . . Our technology has now produced a potato slicer of ingeniously simple construction, with which you can cut more in five minutes than with a knife in half an hour, and more cleanly and evenly. Lack of space prevents us from describing many other kinds of cooking, frying and baking wonders that will enable you, dear housewife, to preserve the love of your husband — for the way to a man's heart is through his stomach. Modern housing in an estate, modern housekeeping and soon, an end to the hard times — then you will reign once again with grace and beauty over the realm of the housewife."[42]

Here we see the same pattern as before: modern housekeeping, this time in the form of rationalization and mechanization, combined with further entrenchment of traditional gender roles. These comments, like many others, quickly provide a use for any time saved thanks to rationalization: it should be devoted to raising children and to one's own health and further education. Encouraging housewives to continue their education might seem meant to benefit women themselves, but this advice could also be interpreted differently: love requires not only a full stomach but a wife who shows understanding. As life grew more complicated, a certain amount of education was needed in order for women to demonstrate this understanding very convincingly. By no means, though, should the time saved thanks to rationalized home life be devoted to the modern pleasures of movies; "shallow" popular music on the radio; or even the new magazines and cheap, trashy literature. We should note in conclusion that even the electric potato slicer was described as "clean." Mechanization apparently was closely linked to cleanliness.

Graffiti, Flags, and the Plague of Cats

As has been pointed out, "cleanliness" was associated with certain concepts of society. As life grew increasingly politicized in the Great

---

42. *Die Siedlung* 4, no. 1 (1932): 130.

Depression and the final years of the Weimar Republic, management of the reform housing estates in Frankfurt attached even greater significance to cleanliness. Since the reality fell somewhat short of the ideal, there was no shortage of complaints. Children, teenagers, and adults were said to be "defacing any fixed property they can reach with a surfeit of political signs and symbols, regardless of which persuasion." Furthermore, "among the thousands of clubs in Germany, the only one still missing is the 'Association to Combat the Defacing of Houses, Doors, Walls, etc.' Do we really want to let things deteriorate so far that it becomes necessary? Let's try to avoid it. Our cry is for 'peace and quiet in the estates,' so let our motto be 'cleanliness in the estates.'"[43]

It is not surprising, under the circumstances, that all flags were forbidden, in contrast to the decision made for instance by the Solingen Savings and Building Association. The executive of this cooperative made a point of the fact that its tenants could raise flags whenever and however they wanted.[44] The self-management boards of the cooperative reform estates, like those in Solingen, limited the expanded demands for cleanliness, in contrast to the huge estate managements in Frankfurt.

Not only graffiti fell victim to the cleanliness campaign in the Frankfurt estates but cats as well. The building managers spoke of a "plague of cats" on the well-known Westhausen estate, built by Ernst May in a functionalist spirit. Even these rather clean creatures were seen as somehow dysfunctional. Since the tenant leases forbade domestic animals, tenants were "urged to remove the cats immediately. Any permissions that may have been issued earlier to keep cats are hereby revoked." Nothing was said about how these cats were supposed to be not only "removed" but "immediately" so. No reasons were given for this harsh prohibition, apart from vague intimations about tenant complaints concerning the "rampant plague of cats" and about the "nature of the Westhausen estate as a garden city." What garden cities had to do with cats was never explained.

Physicians as Experts in Cleanliness and Other Problems of Everyday Life

The magazine of the Frankfurt housing estates published a simulated conversation between a housewife and her physician, written by the city's medical officer of health, Dr. W. Hagen, under the heading "Hygienic Directions for New Apartments." Various topics were addressed, includ-

---

43. *Die Siedlung* 4, no. 6 (1932): 73.
44. For Solingen, see *Blätter für Wohnungswesen* 12, no. 7 (1932): 8.

ing how to clean stone floors, the "lowest comfortable temperature" (20°C, or about 68°F, was deemed "clearly too high"), food storage, showers in the bathtub, the removal of washbasins from bedrooms, the drawbacks of glass verandas, sleeping by open windows, and so forth. Read against the grain, this source is very informative about the everyday life of this supposed middle-class housewife and customs that were still widespread. It is hardly surprising by now to see the doctor decry silk lampshades as "dust traps" and laud the housewife for having "amputated a few legs from her old Renaissance furniture, lowered the tables and chairs, and removed knickknacks."[45] He then urged her to ensure above all that the bedroom was kept "spick and span."[46] This advice was dispensed under the cloud created by the epidemics of tuberculosis and other illnesses, which were blamed quite rightly on poor living conditions and lack of hygiene in the home. The physician played the role in the "conversation" of the scientific authority who always knew best and wanted to make living conditions practical, rational, and hygienic, in keeping with the latest scientific knowledge.

The Social Rationale for Cleanliness

"Cleanliness" was defined and standards were set through various social discourses, one of which was the discourse about the need for better hygiene in the home. Over time, mentalities clearly changed. The new standards were gradually internalized, including elements that had been added mostly to tighten social discipline, and domestic culture evolved in the course of the twentieth century.[47]

A history of everyday life can hardly be fully content, however, with such a conclusion. It is also important to understand the inhabitants of modern housing as historical subjects and not just objects of social discourses or strategies to increase social discipline. The people at whom all the advice in the newspapers, estate magazines, and other media was directed usually considered it well intentioned and, in any case, not compulsory. People felt for the most part that the recommendations were meant to improve their health and well-being.

---

45. *Die Siedlung* 1, no. 2 (1929): 2.

46. Ibid.

47. The compulsive "anal character" made famous by Freud must be seen in the context of the civilizing process in the late nineteenth and the twentieth centuries. See in general in this regard Elias, *Prozeß der Zivilisation;* Michael Erbe, "Mentalitätsgeschichte: Zur Erforschung des Einwirkens von Erfahrungsmustern auf die Wirklichkeit," in Gerhard Brunn and Jürgen Reulecke (eds.), *Berlin . . . : Blicke auf die deutsche Metropole* (Essen, 1989), 13ff.

There was also a certain social rationale for good hygiene because it enhanced the prestige of the entire family: the children at school; the husband at work; and most of all, the housewife and mother at home among her neighbors and the friends and acquaintances who visited. People liked clean homes, as interviews have showed. One man, looking back on his reform housing, described it as his "heaven."[48] A clean home and a neat, nicely dressed housewife came to symbolize professionalized, rationalized living, which alone could make it possible to maintain such high standards while "smiling all the way," that is, without expending too much energy. Modern housekeeping was not supposed to be hard work. High cleanliness standards increased respect for housework and, with it, respect for housewives. The advice that was dispensed did not have to be followed slavishly, and a certain amount of latitude always remained to make one's own decisions and do what one wanted, a latitude that was used to individualize homes and make them one's own.

On the whole, the discourse about cleanliness was viewed quite positively by the people at whom it was directed, as shown in discussions of their memories and in contemporary sources. Reconstructing these subjective impressions and reactions falls within the compass of Alltagsgeschichte, although there are clear connections with social history as well. The correlation in our example is on the level of discourse.

Conclusions

We have intentionally not yet mentioned the concepts of cleanliness advocated by the Nazis after 1933 — neither their ideological and political reasons for concentrating on cleaning up the old parts of town nor the ways in which they legitimized political and racial "cleansing."[49] "Filth," "vermin," and "degeneracy" were met with "cleanliness," "purity," and "eradication." The agents of the Holocaust were tough but "clean." It would not be historically accurate, however, to portray the discourse surrounding cleanliness and good hygiene in the 1920s as leading straight to the Third Reich. This conclusion is unacceptable not least because of the international nature of the discussion.

The "break with the past in 1933" can be summarized very suc-

---

48. See Adelheid von Saldern, *Neues Wohnen: Wohnungspolitik und Wohnkultur im Hannover der Zwanziger Jahre* (Hanover, 1993).

49. See Peter Weingart, Jürgen Kroll, and Kurt Bayertz, *Rasse, Blut, und Gene: Geschichte der Eugenik und Rassenhygiene in Deutschland* (Frankfurt, 1988). The various contexts of eugenics are shown in particular by Michael Schwartz, "Sozialismus und Eugenik: Zur fälligen Revision eines Geschichtsbildes," *IWK* 26, no. 4 (1989): 465–89. For a basic discussion: Detlev J. K. Peukert, *Max Webers Diagnose der Moderne* (Göttingen, 1989).

cinctly as follows: the discourse about cleanliness became radicalized and moved outside the rule of law; there was an emphasis on preserving the purity of the German race; and the creation of ideals was monopolized through rigorous suppression of any opposing voices. Although 1933 marked a profound break with the past, there were some continuities of course between the periods before and after the Nazi seizure of power. Regardless of how justified many of the individual recommendations about cleanliness may have been, they already tended in the two decades before 1933 to reinforce concepts of social and racial "hygiene." The discourse about cleanliness encouraged a utilitarian frame of mind that proved favorable to goal-oriented arguments in favor of racial "cleansing" after 1933. These arguments were supported by the belief in a "utopia" where "society and health could be planned"[50] and society thoroughly cleansed. The mania for cleanliness was fixated both on alleged "pollution" of the Germans by Jews and on pollution by "vermin" or "inferior" people, whether they were sick, feeble minded, homosexual, asocial, or Communist.

No one would deny the need to keep homes clean or would want to glamorize the poor living conditions of earlier times. Questions about how to clean linoleum floors were and are justified. Technology was already developing so rapidly that advice from experts was needed. It was requested by people for their everyday lives and was by no means forced upon them. However, when the need for good hygiene became so exaggerated that anything and everything was potentially in need of cleansing, it is clear that there was a close connection of some kind between an everyday event like cleaning linoleum floors and the overall condition of society, that is, social history. In conclusion, I would like to recall the piece of everyday wisdom that you are most likely to slip and hurt yourself when the floors have just been cleaned.

---

50. Mönkemeyer, "Schmutz und Sauberkeit," 73.

CHAPTER 5

The Social Rationalization of Domestic Life and Housework in Germany and the United States in the 1920s

Introduction

This chapter deals with concepts related to the social rationalization of domestic life and housework and does not investigate how people resisted or adapted to it or how they really lived. Many aspects of everyday life in working-class neighborhoods in both Germany and the United States, as well as in immigrant neighborhoods in the United States, were certainly not rationalized. Despite the limitations on its influence, however, rationalization was by no means without major long-term effects on the norms and values of U.S. and German society in both the public and private spheres.

Mentalities are very deep-seated and have a time structure of their own. In other words, they change slowly, but they do change, as shown for instance by Norbert Elias in his graphic descriptions of earlier centuries. His study of the civilization process should be continued for the twentieth century. Cleanliness is one area in which large acculturation processes have been at work over the last century. Families change their behaviors not just in response to technological inventions and new discoveries about health and cleanliness but also in response to new norms

I am very grateful for the criticism and advice received as a result of an earlier draft of this chapter presented to U.S. universities in 1989–90 and 1994, especially at the University of Chicago and Rutgers University, and at two conferences on social rationalization in a historical perspective, one at Columbia University in New York in 1994 and the other at the Werner Reimers Stiftung in Bad Homburg in 1995. I also wish to thank the German Marshall Fund for funding the research. Many thanks also to Gisela Johnson, who helped with my English.

that take root through public discourse, education, and socialization over a period of decades. This should not be understood, of course, as a unidirectional process from above to below. Here also the complex dynamics of appropriation, as well as the duality of norms and practices, must be included in the analysis. The outcome, however, is unambiguous: standard behaviors toward cleanliness have changed substantially over the decades.

There were considerable similarities between Germany and the United States. Compared with Great Britain, both were relative newcomers to industrialization and urbanization in the second half of the nineteenth century. In the United States, cultural values and dreams were increasingly influenced by urbanized consumer society, although working-class people, except for well-paid skilled workers, could scarcely participate in it.[1] The new era was perhaps best symbolized by the automobile, Fordism, the so-called new woman, and movies. The new "servantless home"[2] began to be filled with electric appliances and brand-name products: the "consumer home" spread,[3] driven by industry and the authority of modern science. In Germany, too, the first signs of the consumer society were beginning to appear, despite all the turmoil of the lost war, the revolution, and the major economic and social crises that ensued. For most people, the consumer society was more a desire or a hope than a reality, but it was still strong enough to be seen as a major cultural movement of the future that would affect both the public and private sectors.[4]

The term *social rationalization* emerged in recognition of the fact

---

1. In future research, the exact determination of "consumer society" in reality and in the images projected for various strata of the population in the 1920s must be investigated more intensively. For many people, especially working-class people and even in the United States, the consumer society spread "only gradually, starting in the late 1920s." Elizabeth Cohen, *Making a New Deal: Industrial Workers in Chicago, 1919–1939* (Cambridge, 1990), 119. The concept of the consumer society emerged first in pictures, images, models, and visions and then in the hopes and expectations people expressed in their own terms for their children. The "necessity" of using the "wide-ranging consumer market in style," especially by immigrants, has been stressed by Stuart Ewen, *All Consuming Images: The Politics of Style in Contemporary Culture* (New York, 1988), 76. Other scholars take the critical view that the consumer society was supposed to legitimize the oppression of workers by the state. As another consequence the unions lost their "ability to imagine a fundamentally different social and economic order." Dana Frank, *Purchasing Power: Consumer Organizing, Gender, and the Seattle Labor Movement 1919–1929* (Cambridge, 1994), 248.

2. A connection was often drawn in advertising between electricity and the servantless home. In Germany, the 1920s witnessed a drop in the number of domestic servants.

3. Glenna Matthews, *'Just a Housewife': The Rise and Fall of Domesticity in America* (New York and Oxford, 1987), 176.

4. See in general Detlev J. K. Peukert, *Die Weimarer Republik: Krisenjahre der klassischen Moderne* (Göttingen, 1987).

that not only the economy could be rationalized but every aspect of life and society, including the domestic sphere. It conveys the idea that every nook and cranny of society, as well as the individuals themselves, could be planned and organized according to rational principles, just like an optimally functioning machine shop.[5] Social rationalization was considered synonymous with progress and the modernization of society. In the United States, Fordism seemed the epitome of rationalization and played an important role in the new confidence in the nation's future and in its economic and cultural place in the world.[6] In Germany, the concept of a "Germanized Fordism" was based on the hope that rationalization could be combined with German culture and traditions. Domestic life was also thought to need rationalization since it, in contrast to the public sphere and the workplace, was normally free from control and regulation by the police or employers. Many reformers felt, therefore, that it was imperative to foster self-discipline in the general population. The question that arises is what kind of educational efforts were made during the era of the great breakthrough of modernity in the 1920s. As we know, attempts to educate people about taste and morality were far from new. In the decades before the First World War, reformers had tried to "refine" the domestic culture of the working class, aiming their efforts primarily at women.[7] The rationalization movement of the 1920s lacked the innovative aspects of the Progressive Era, as a movement of and for women, and instead "complemented the goals of American industry."[8]

Social Rationalization in the Context of Housing Policy and Suburbanization

Faced with a great housing shortage after the First World War, Germany instituted a huge subsidized housing program, particularly in the years

---

5. For more details on the concept of social rationalization see the next section of this chapter.

6. See for example George E. G. Catlin, "American under Fire: A European Defense of our Civilization," *Harper's Magazine* 155 (July 1927): 224ff.

7. For the United States see for example Richard L. Bushman, *The Refinement of America: Persons, Houses, Cities* (New York, 1992); in respect to Catherine Beecher and Harriet Beecher Stowe see 444ff. of the Bushman work.

8. Jean Gordon and Jan McArthur, "American Women and Domestic Consumption, 1800–1920: Four Interpretive Themes," *Journal of American Culture* 8, no. 3 (fall 1985): 42. The authors refer to Catherine Beecher and some other reformers. See also Ruth Schwartz Cowan, "The Industrial Revolution in the Home: Household Technology and Social Change in the Twentieth Century," in Nancy F. Cott (ed.), *Domestic Ideology and Domestic Work*, Pt. 2 (New Haven, 1992), 375ff., 427ff.

between 1924 and 1930–31. For the first time in history, housing policy became an important aspect of the German welfare state. Relatively large and well-equipped housing estates were constructed, usually consisting of two-, three-, or four-story multiple-family dwellings. The attempts to rationalize domestic culture focused largely on the tenants of these buildings, who were mostly low-ranking civil servants and office employees as well as some skilled workers. These tenants were considered representative of the entire urban society,[9] although they were far from that.[10]

The United States, by contrast, did not institute a large state subsidized housing program in the 1920s. Instead, the construction of housing generally remained a matter of private enterprise and the generation of profit. Speculation on housing markets flourished because of tax considerations,[11] although only a few wealthy people were willing to invest their money in housing, especially low-cost housing. Investment in the construction of housing was considered relatively uncertain and unprofitable in comparison with other opportunities. Only in the 1930s did housing policy change in the framework of the New Deal. Slums were cleared, and subsidized housing was built for slum dwellers and other low-income groups. The new public housing program was very limited, however,[12] and the reputation of the housing built in the 1930s was often not very good, in contrast to that of the subsidized housing built in Germany in the 1920s. This difference was largely a consequence of the different social strata that moved into the subsidized housing: middle-class and upper-working-class people in Germany versus former slum dwellers, that is, very-low-income groups, in the United States.

In the United States, housing policy between the wars was conducted in a context of increasing suburbanization. The suburbs became

9. Neither the upper classes nor the lower working classes moved into these apartments. The former were not interested, and the latter could not afford to do so despite the subsidies.

10. Housing policy in Germany and the modernization of domestic culture in the 1920s were part of an interdisciplinary project in the late 1980s that was sponsored by the Volkswagen Stiftung. See Ulfert Herlyn, Adelheid von Saldern, and Wulf Tessin (eds.), *Neubausiedlungen der 20er und 60er Jahr: Ein historisch-soziologischer Vergleich* (Frankfurt and New York, 1987); see also Adelheid von Saldern, *Häuserleben: Zur Geschichte städtischen Arbeiterwohnens vom Kaiserreich bis heute* (Bonn, 1995); Mary Nolan, *Visions of Modernity: American Business and the Modernization of Germany* (New York and Oxford, 1994), especially 206ff.

11. See for example Nathan Straus, *The Seven Myths of Housing* (1945; reprint, New York, 1974). Speculation was also found in areas that were in decline.

12. Joan C. Teaford, *The Twentieth-Century American City: Problem, Promise, and Reality* (Baltimore and London, 1986), 87ff. There was no agreement on whether public housing for lower-class tenants was to be of low- or middle-class quality.

attractive in the 1920s thanks to the rise of the automobile,[13] and millions of Americans began to dream of a home there.[14] Privately planned and built housing resulted in the development of many new suburbs for white, middle-class Americans (and some ethnic groups). The 1920s saw the growth of decent suburban housing in the form of single-family or terraced houses, and by the end of the decade, 5,176,000 people had moved to the suburbs.[15] In suburban Cleveland, the population of Shaker Heights increased 1,000 percent between 1920 and 1930.[16] The various classes and ethnic groups were carefully separated in the suburbs through price as well as through the relatively new zoning regulations.[17]

In Germany, much of the new housing was located on the edges of cities. The social profile of these "suburbs" differed substantially from the profile of those in the United States because of their relatively high density. There were other differences as well. The new housing estates in Germany were served by public transportation systems, which enabled people without cars to move there. In addition, since the estates were government subsidized and their architecture had to meet the approval of the local authorities, the estates and the domestic culture that they encouraged became a matter of local public concern.

---

13. See for example Teaford, *American City,* 67. In the rise of the suburbs, continuity with past patterns was strong. See Richard A. Walker, "The Transformation of Urban Structure in the Nineteenth Century and the Beginnings of Suburbanization," in Kevin Cox (ed.), *Urbanization and Conflict in Market Societies* (London, 1978), 165–213.

14. Perin has shown the link between land use and the social order of that period. Constance Perin, *Everything in Its Place: Social Order and Land Use in America* (Princeton, 1977). Cf. also Robert B. Fairbanks, *Making Better Citizens: Housing Reform and the Community Development Strategy in Cincinnati, 1890–1960* (University of Illinois, 1988), 60. Some planners and architects, for instance Clarence Stein and Henry Wright, hoped to create a utopia in suburban model communities such as Radburn in New Jersey. Teaford, *American City,* 68. The beginning of catalog-order houses and of the rationalizations during the U.S. prewar period have been described by Marta Banta, *Taylored Lives: Narrative Productions in the Age of Taylor, Veblen, and Ford* (Chicago and London, 1993), especially 205ff.

15. Joseph L. Arnold, *The New Deal in the Suburbs: A History of the Greenbelt Town Program, 1935–1954* (Columbus, 1971), 10.

16. Teaford, *American Cities,* 69.

17. Ibid., 70ff. Although zoning was relatively new in the United States, there were continuities between the zoning and planning movements of the Progressive Era and the 1920s. See Arthur S. Link, "What Happened to the Progressive Movement in the 1920s?" in Barton J. Bernstein and Allen J. Matusow (eds.), *Twentieth-Century America: Recent Interpretations,* 2d ed., (New York, 1972), 133. For an example of a contemporary statement on segregation, see Greta Grey, *House and Home: A Manual and Text-Book of Practical House Planning,* 2d ed. (Philadelphia, 1927), 312. In 1920, 46 percent of all American families owned their home. Gwendolyn Wright, *Building the Dream: A Social History of Housing in America* (Cambridge, 1985), 195.

The attempts at social rationalization in both countries were not much affected at first by the differences in housing policy and in the nature of the suburbs and of the newly constructed housing because the rationalization movement concentrated largely on model dwellings for nuclear families. These dwellings included both modern (subsidized) multifamily apartment buildings and single-family houses in the suburbs. The main difference lay in the importance of these models in both countries and, consequently, the conditions faced by the social reformers. "Changes in the imaging of modernity after 1930 are so marked that they seem to constitute a major shift from the structures of the 1920s."[18] In Germany, this major shift was marked by reactionary, fascist patterns.[19]

Social Reformers and the Importance of Rationalization Models

In both countries, the social reform movement started back in the nineteenth century. Frank Lloyd Wright designed "rational, functional, and breathtakingly sophisticated homes in the 'prairie-style'" and pondered how to bring "sane living to the general public."[20] The cultural slogan was back to scientifically executed simplicity, and this idea was taken up by Richard Neutra and other architects.[21] Beginning in the nineteenth century, the philanthropic tenement movement in the United States[22] had relied on established models and the concept of enlightened capitalism to solve housing problems. The tenement movement failed, however, because of the scarcity of enlightened entrepreneurs willing to limit profits as a condition of investment.[23] Throughout the United States, only about twenty thousand dwellings were erected on a nonspeculative basis,[24] including both philanthropic efforts and those of labor unions and Jewish organizations.

18. Terry E. Smith, *Making the Modern: Industry, Art, and Design in America* (Chicago, 1993), 159.

19. Only in the 1930s during the Third Reich were new, privately financed, middle-class suburbs with small houses erected. While in general U.S. housing policy in the 1930s took up some of the principles of German housing policy in the 1920s, German housing policy in the 1930s shifted in part to U.S. housing policy in the 1920s, although there were big differences because of the general context created by racist National Socialism.

20. Banta, *Taylored Lives,* 229.

21. Cf. ibid., 229. The Arts and Crafts movement also pursued the path of simplicity and honesty.

22. Cf. Ronald Lawson (ed.), *The Tenement Movement in New York City, 1904–1984* (New Brunswick, NJ, 1986); Louis H. Pink, *The New Day in Housing* (New York, 1928).

23. Michael Lipsky, *Protest in City Politics: Rent Strikes, Housing, and the Power of the Poor* (Chicago, 1970), 41ff.

24. Catherina Bauer, *Modern Housing* (Boston and New York, 1934), 240.

A chief characteristic of the U.S. housing model was "the basic denial of politics, power, and the diversity of the public domain."[25] The development of models was considered a "sign of hope" in a society in which social reformers could not or did not want to reform housing through political parties or local authorities. Reformers may have experimented with a housing movement but ultimately were not interested in it. Few U.S. reformers were willing "to attack directly the causes of the problems they saw around them, whether the issue was social inequality, class antagonism, family instability, women's rights or working conditions. Instead they tended to propose ideal social and architectural models that would, in their theories, bring about a situation where the problem would no longer exist."[26]

Consequently and in contrast to Germany, housing did not become a major public issue until the time of the New Deal — not even for labor unions.[27] Even those U.S. reformers who developed their own organizations and networks had little influence on the political parties. This situation led to the construction of philanthropic nonprofit model housing by limited-dividend companies, which at that time could be seen as "something peculiarly American."[28] By 1938, there were twenty-three such models in the United States. Some were partially successful and survived for a time, while others failed quickly.[29] One of these models built by a philanthropist was the Lavanburg Homes on the lower East Side of New York, built in 1927 for about five hundred people. The manager, Abraham Goldfeld, carefully selected the people who were allowed to move in. They were supposed to have low incomes and to have children. Goldfeld checked the homes where these people lived at the time of their application to ensure that they met the "standards of cleanliness and decency."[30] Later, he experimented successfully with accepting people (up to 10 percent) from substandard homes and noticed that most of them changed their habits after a while and kept their new homes clean.[31]

In Germany, some model reform housing was also built in cities but mostly before 1914. Some was constructed by nonprofit cooperative building societies and a little by local authorities and the state.

25. Wright, *Building the Dream*, 293.

26. Ibid., 293.

27. Bauer, *Modern Housing*, 254.

28. Wright, *Building the Dream*, 293. For instance, Chatham Village in Pittsburgh or the Rosenwald apartments in Chicago.

29. Langdon W. Post, *The Challenge of Housing* (New York and Toronto, 1938), 120.

30. Abraham Goldfeld, *The Diary of a Housing Manager* (reprint, Chicago, 1940).

31. Goldfeld, *Diary*, 2.

There were also the so-called garden cities, such as Staaken near Berlin and Rüppurr near Karlsruhe.[32] In contrast to the United States, the situation in Germany changed rapidly after the First World War. German reformers also worked with model housing, but after 1918 these models could be built on a much vaster scale than in the United States. About 2.5 million government-subsidized apartments were built for some 7 to 9 million people (out of a total population of 60 million), demonstrating how people would live in the future.[33] The models of social rationalization became "mass models." The impact of the new mass models on people who could not afford such apartments was far greater than the impact of the older type of individual philanthropic models in the United States and prewar Germany. In contrast to the U.S. suburbs, the housing estates in Germany were very much a part of the public sphere and the discourse about social rationalization because they were government subsidized and therefore of public concern. This was a major difference between the new kinds of housing in the two countries.

In both countries, there were many social reformers among city planners, architects, builders, governmental officials, philanthropists, sociologists, interior decorators, housewives, labor union members, publishers, and so on. Reformers in both countries were also convinced that people would change their habits if their living conditions improved. There was a strong belief at the time, especially in the United States, in a direct relationship between space and human behavior, as described by sociologists of the Chicago school and behaviorists such as Watson. Hopes in both countries focused on "the home as a locus of moral reform."[34] Many reformers also linked their educational efforts to the notion that people should be regarded as "human capital" and treated in the same carefully rationalizing way as other sorts of capital (*Menschenökonomie*).

There are also some differences, however, between the social reform movement in the United States and the reform movement in Germany. The connections among the various groups of reformers were closer in Germany than in the United States, as were the connections between the reformers and the local authorities, which in Germany were

---

32. Garden cities were meant to follow Ebenezer Howard's concept, but in practice they were more similar to green suburban settlements.

33. Peter Christian Witt, "Inflation, Wohnungszwangswirtschaft, und Hauszinssteuer: Zur Regelung von Wohnungsbau und Wohnungsmarkt in der Weimarer Republik," in Lutz Niethammer (ed.), *Wohnen im Wandel: Beiträge zur Geschichte des Alltags in der bürgerlichen Gesellschaft* (Wuppertal, 1979), 385–408.

34. For the United States see Wright, *Building the Dream,* 292. The opposite of "the locus of moral reform" was seen in slum areas.

the "centers" that made the main housing decisions. Some German reformers, especially in circles committed to the Bauhaus, were extremely interested in using the unique opportunity afforded by the public mass housing program in order to educate people "through the modeling of space and architecture."[35] The Bauhaus group cultivated a radical functionalism and "new objectivity" in architecture as well as domestic life and in this way distanced itself from the cultural norms of the Wilhelminian period. It decried Wilhelminan culture as overdone and dishonest in the sense of artificial. The new attempts to rationalize personal taste resulted in the categorical rejection of decorations and ornaments, regardless of whether they were art nouveau or prewar neohistorical in style.[36] Carried away by its own ideas for reform, the Bauhaus circle thought and acted like a "cultural pope." Unlike North American planners, the Bauhaus circle felt that it did not need to consider the tastes and desires of the population, acting thereby in the same way as "German officials who thought of themselves as well-trained professionals who knew what was best for the people."[37]

In Germany as well, the labor unions, the influential Social Democratic Party, and the cooperatives were all involved in the "program" of social rationalization, in contrast to the situation in the United States. The Bauhaus's radical rejection of Wilhelminian culture seemed to be in step with the radical rejection by the SPD and union leaders of the political system and the class society of the empire. Leading groups in the labor movement, especially in Berlin, were therefore inclined to feel that the Bauhaus had much in common with them.[38] They were fascinated by the notion of a modern, rationalized way of life, as represented by the Bauhaus and other reformers. As a result, they too tended to dismiss the traditional interior of workers' homes with its ornamental furniture and kitchen-cum-living room as old fashioned, unhealthy, and worthless. The aim of these leading groups was to upgrade the everyday life of workers in order to demonstrate the cultural capacity of the people within the existing bourgeois society and create, as the Social Democrats put it, the "new man" (*neuer Mensch*). They would nurture a "cultural socialism" (*Kultursozialismus*), which they saw as an important stepping-stone to-

---

35. See also chapter 3 in this volume.

36. There was also a conservative, German-nationalist variety of modern living. The differences between the functionalist reformers and the conservatives did not affect the general contents of the educational efforts, apart from issues of taste and style.

37. John R. Mullin, "City Planning in Frankfurt, Germany, 1925–1932, *Journal of Urban History* 4, no. 1 (1977): 6.

38. Martin Wagner in Berlin was committed to strengthening the ties between the unions and the Bauhaus.

ward the socialist society of the future. Viewed in retrospect, their enthusiasm for social rationalization and modern living as supposed liberation from the working-class life of earlier times shows how lacking they were in a critical eye for the ambiguous nature of modernity in general and social rationalization in particular.

In the United States, there was also a network of architects, urban planners, and housing reformers, as noted for example by Robert Fairbanks in Cincinnati. However, this network was not as dense as in Germany and was not associated with a comprehensive political and cultural ideology — as could be seen in the connections drawn in Germany among cultural socialism, eugenics, and the "new man." Furthermore, the U.S. network had fewer ties to local authorities and was less driven by a commitment to social reform. Instead, it was more market oriented. As the Cincinnati example shows, planners often lacked even the social consciousness generally characteristic of the socially minded housing reformers.[39] In further contrast with Germany, there were not any institutions in the United States, such as the Bauhaus, that were trying to establish their hegemony over architecture and domestic culture. In the United States, pluralism in taste, including many eclectic elements in architecture and domestic arrangements, was more accepted and less controversial.[40] The effort to promote social rationalization was not as strongly connected with architecture and urban planning as in those areas of German housing policy influenced by the Bauhaus.

Home Interiors as a Symbol of Social Rationalization

Behaving like missionaries without respect for alternative cultures, the German avant-garde architects sought to introduce the principles of social rationalization not only into the architecture but also into the interiors of apartments. In the eyes of the avant-garde, tenants (and especially women) were nothing more than objects to be educated in the rationalization of behavior and taste. Bruno Taut, for example, explained to housewives: "When after a rigorous and ruthless choice, you get rid of everything in the apartment — and I mean everything — that is not essential for living, not only does your work become easier but a new kind of beauty will automatically emerge."[41]

The radical cultural views of the avant-garde architects met with the

---

39. Fairbanks, *Better Citizens,* 3.

40. Wright, *Building the Dream,* 202ff.

41. Bruno Taut, *Die neue Wohnung: Die Frau als Schöpferin* (Leipzig, 1924), 31ff. In this light, it was no coincidence that the Bauhaus was committed to designing items of domestic culture.

approval of the other reformers since sparse, functionally furnished rooms helped to maintain the cleanliness and orderliness required under the new standards of hygiene. Many reformers attempted to generate new standards and norms to which individuals were supposed to adapt. For instance, the kinds of parlors with decorated furniture to which the better-paid workers had grown accustomed were decried as an offense against modern, rational humanity. Whenever architects had an opportunity to do so, they supplied the furniture for the entire apartment as a model and in order to prevent the tenants from furnishing it in their own "ugly and irrational" way. Once the "correct conceptual solution" had been found, it was incumbent upon the tenants, especially women, to adapt to it. When the rigidly modernist Bauhaus concept of social rationalization failed to make many inroads with tenants, methods such as advertisements, newspaper supplements, magazines, and shop windows were used to transmit the same message, although presumably not as much as in the United States.[42]

In the United States, professional interior decorators considered themselves essential if people were to cope with the modernization and rationalization of domestic culture.[43] In contrast to the Bauhaus architects, most U.S. architects were interested primarily in the exterior appearance of homes and only secondarily in interior design and furniture.[44] Modernist reformers were more concerned about kitchens and bathrooms than about living rooms or bedrooms, which often remained traditional. Architects, designers, and merchants who promoted prefabricated houses and furniture for a wide range of customers generally had no use for the U.S. Arts and Crafts movement, which demanded "an intricate simplicity only the affluent could afford to buy for their intricately simple and expensive houses. . . . They were scathing in their critiques of the 'appalling waste' that comes from 'slow, inefficient hand labor' in contrast to the 'fast, accurate machines' used to manufacture their house models." The Arts and Crafts movement was considered "anathema to the goals of scientific management."[45]

There was therefore a trend in the United States as well toward the rationalization and reorganization of domestic life. American decorators implied that only they knew what correct furniture was. They even

42. The supplements of newspapers were used in chapters 4 and 5 in Adelheid von Saldern, *Neues Wohnen: Wohnungspolitik und Wohnkultur im Hannover der Zwanziger Jahre* (Hanover, 1993).

43. Wright, *Building the Dream,* 208.

44. Compare Witold Rybczynski, *Home: A Short History of an Idea* (New York, 1986), 186.

45. Banta, *Taylored Lives,* 375.

developed a way of differentiating male rooms from female rooms.[46] "Emily Post and other decorators parlayed Sigmund Freud and Havelock Ellis into a formula of 'sex psychology' for decorating and architecture. 'The kind of room a man likes' had dark colors, substantial furniture, and bold, rugged materials. . . . 'The lady's touch' was more pervasive, exemplified in chintzes and floral patterns, delicate furniture, and lacy curtains, though the adventurous woman could also express her femininity in colonial antiques or in modern Art Deco 'skyscraper furniture.'"[47] Advertisements informed Americans that they should no longer have the "wrong" furniture. Social acceptance, it was said, "depended on modern bathroom fixtures and fashionable décor,"[48] and advertisers tried to exploit people's fear of being looked down upon as old fashioned. In contrast to Germany, all these attempts to modernize taste were closely connected to the flourishing consumer market. Fake, mass-produced art deco furniture was in style and was supposed to exhibit the principles of social rationalization more than the genuine article. While authentic art deco was not for the masses and in some ways was out of step with modernity, "ordinary" art deco "became a coarsened and sanitized version of its original risqué self."[49]

The *Ladies' Home Journal* became a leading arbiter of taste in the United States, where it was read by 1.75 million people a month in the 1920s. It served as a model and a source of advice. The consumer market was stratified and fragmented according to various tastes (Victorian, art deco, colonial revival), and the stated aim of the *Ladies' Home Journal,* as a supplement to the consumer market, was to help people find solutions suited to their "individual needs" and create their own glamorous, smart "personalized homes."[50] In an era of Freudianism and, in Germany at least, reform pedagogy, limited individualism was part of the successful strategy for social rationalization. Modern homes in both countries were "allowed" or even "obliged" in some ways to look different from one another.[51] Taste was a means of social distinction.

46. Wright, *Building the Dream,* 209. For the discussion of continuities in a gendered view of domestic space see Eileen Boris, "Crossing Boundaries: The Gendered Meaning of the Arts and Crafts," in Janet Kardon (ed.), *The Ideal Home 1900–1920: The History of Twentieth Century American Craft* (New York, 1993), 32ff.

47. Wright, *Building the Dream,* 209.

48. Ibid., 208.

49. Rybczynski, *Home,* 201. The "unglamorous warehouse cube style" was especially suited to postdepression sobriety. Ibid. See also Smith, *Making the Modern,* 368.

50. Wright, *Building the Dream,* 208; Jean Gordon and Jan McArthur, "Popular Culture, Magazines, and American Domestic Interiors, 1898–1940," *Journal of Popular Culture* 8, no. 3 (fall 1985): 48ff.

51. Rybczynski, *Home,* 191ff.

Although the differences were often superficial and mere variations of fundamentally similar patterns or elements of prefabricated construction and design, "small differences" (Bourdieu's term) took on new importance as cultural indicators of taste and values.

In sum, there were considerable similarities between Germany and the United States in regard to the efforts to alter taste. The anxiety felt by many people about being old fashioned was exploited in both countries. Taste was pictured as a reflection of one's sociocultural status. Reformers thought that by emphasizing the light that furniture cast on people, especially housewives, they could succeed in inducing people to change their furniture "voluntarily," even if it was still usable or if the new furniture was beyond the means of the people purchasing it.[52] The reformers' interest in prompting people to buy modern furniture meshed with the interests of the furniture industry, although the industry was more influenced by taste than the reformers were.

The efforts to rationalize and refine taste were more politicized in Germany than in the United States (because of the avant-garde architects in the former) and more connected to a particular view of society and culture in general (a Weltanschauung). Reform efforts in the United States, on the other hand, were usually more related to the marketing process, in which magazines and advertising played major parts.

The Social Rationalization of Housework

In the eyes of reformers in both countries, the general population needed to change its everyday behaviors and adopt more clean, orderly ways. The main task was to get rid of all the dirt allegedly found in many older homes and keep new housing clean and neat.[53] The efforts to improve cleanliness were backed in both countries by scientists, who said that dust was unsanitary and a source of germs and illness. Household appliances not only alleviated the work of housewives but also raised standards of cleanliness and orderliness. The long-term goal, first in the United States and then in Germany, was to develop "home engineers," who performed jobs considered peculiarly female. The U.S.

---

52. An example of this "voluntary" change can be found in Adelheid von Saldern, "Reformwohnungsbau und Familie: Einige Aspekte aus dem Hannover der Weimarer Republik," in Jürgen Schlumbohm (ed.), *Familie und Familienlosigkeit: Fallstudien aus Niedersachsen und Bremen vom 15. bis 20. Jahrhundert* (Hanover, 1993), 256ff.

53. Contemporary inquiries showed, though, that while tenement buildings often had a dirty outward appearance, the apartments inside were clean. See for example Elizabeth Ewen, *Immigrant Women in the Land of Dollars: Life and Culture on the Lower East Side, 1890–1925* (New York, 1985), 156. For the topic of cleanliness, see also chapter 4 in this volume.

home economist Helen Campbell wrote: "To keep the world clean, this is the great task for women."[54] Contemporary studies showed that housewives were spending more time cleaning their homes,[55] while the time they spent on preparing meals, making clothes, and preserving and canning food had declined from six hours a day to one.[56] Housekeeping in the narrow sense (apart from raising children) was a nine-hour-a-day job at a minimum, according to home economist Christine Frederick in 1920.[57]

The second task was to mechanize, rationalize, and professionalize housekeeping.[58] Regardless of the level of mechanization achieved, housewives in both countries were regarded as ultimately responsible for the home. This conviction was in keeping with traditional notions of the gender division of labor, but the justification for it changed as traditional views were updated with more modern concepts of the household and everyday life. In other words, what changed were the rationales and contexts, not the view of gender itself. A "regendering" process took place to reflect modernized households. Among the symbols of modernity was electricity, which enabled the "modern woman" to alleviate household chores. She had a modern servant of her own in electricity.[59] Thus, the gender division of labor was not renounced, nor did it remain truly traditional; instead it was reconstructed and renewed, that is, "regendered" on the basis of modern social rationalization.[60]

The rationalization of housekeeping also meant the rationalization of housewives' work and in some ways the rationalization of housewives

54. Quoted in Steven Mintz and Susan Kellogg, *Domestic Revolution: A Social History of American Family Life* (London, 1988), 125.

55. Ibid., 125. Moreover, the time spent on driving, shopping, and waiting increased. Ruth Schwartz Cowan, "Twentieth-Century Changes in Household Technology," in Arlene S. Skolnick and Jerome H. Skolnick (eds.), *Rethinking Marriage, Sexuality, Child Rearing, and Family Organization* (Boston and Toronto, 1986), 69. The task of transporting children by car became a new duty for women, in addition to shopping. Schwartz Cowan, *Changes,* 63ff.

56. Mintz and Kellogg, *Domestic Revolution,* 125.

57. Daniel T. Rodgers, *The Work Ethic in Industrial America 1850–1920* (Chicago and London, 1978), 203.

58. For Germany see Carola Sachse, "Anfänge der Rationalisierung der Hausarbeit in der Weimarer Republik: 'The One Best Way of Doing Anything'" in Barbara Orland (ed.), *Haushalts(t)räume: Ein Jahrhundert Rationalisierung und Technisierung im Haushalt* (Königstein, 1990), 49–61.

59. Dolores Hayden, *Redesigning the American Dream: The Future of Housing, Work, and Family Life* (New York and London, 1984), 105.

60. For the United States see Mintz and Kellogg, *Domestic Revolution,* 112. It should be mentioned, however, that home economists, such as Lillian Gilbreth, insisted that gender differences were irrelevant to the efficiency of work in the household.

themselves. The typical movements of housewives were measured and evaluated (Taylorism), and this concept was passed along to Germany.[61] The reform studies were based on efficiency tests devised in industry. The peculiarities of housework and the habits of many "mere" housewives were ignored in these studies, for instance the special difficulties that arose when rationalized housework was combined with caring for children or the desire of housewives to demonstrate that their work really was work or to do it in ways that met their own special needs.

In both countries, the professionalization of housework became an important goal of all housewives' associations. Women were supposed to derive sufficient satisfaction in life from doing rationalized housework in a scientific way while listening to the radio.[62] This would keep them happy at home. There were some ambiguous aspects to the "professionalization" of housework. The purpose was to raise public regard for housework, but at the same time it was not paid, quite contrary to the general meaning of the word *professionalization*. The rationalization and professionalization of housework put the gender division of labor[63] on a more modern footing. This can be seen as a "regendering" process.

Advertisements and magazines can be seen as "social tableaux" showing the cultural image of women and the changes to it as a result of the professionalization of housework. Advertisements and magazines projected both polarized gender spheres and the work of modern women. A woman's modernity could supposedly be seen in her adaptation to consumer culture and her professional efficiency in the home. In other words, the modern homemaker was portrayed as the female counterpart of the male business executive. Women were shown as rational decision makers in the realm of consumption, although their ultimate subordination to their husbands remained unchallenged.[64]

While paying lip service to the goal of professionalization, modern

61. For German efforts at social rationalization see for instance Mary Nolan, "'Housework Made Easy': The Taylorized Houswife in Weimar Germany's Rationalized Economy," *Feminist Studies* 16, no. 3 (1990): 549–78. The U.S. influence on Germany in the area of modern housekeeping is a special topic that cannot be discussed here.

62. Gert Raeithel, *Geschichte der nordamerikanischen Kultur* (Weinheim and Berlin, 1988), 2:346; Nancy Reagin, "Die Werkstatt der Frau: Bürgerliche Frauenbewegung und Wohnungspolitik im Hannover der Zwanziger Jahre," in Sid Auffarth and Adelheid von Saldern (eds.), *Altes und neues Wohnen: Linden und Hannover im frühen 20. Jahrhundert* (Seelze-Velber, 1992), 156–65.

63. Matthews, *Housewife*, 162.

64. Roland Marchand, *Advertising the American Dream: Making Way for Modernity* (Berkeley, 1985), 168ff. Ultimate subordination evidently did not pose too much of a hindrance to the search for more democracy within family patterns. See especially Paula S. Fass, *The Damned and the Beautiful: American Youth in the 1920's* (Oxford, 1979), 71ff.

consumer culture also had a "de-skilling" aspect that devalued the work of housewives[65] since they usually no longer had to know how to bake bread, preserve fruit and vegetables, and so on. However, this aspect remained hidden in the supposed upgrading and professionalization of housework through mechanization and electricity. It was true, of course, that women had to become more knowledgeable in some ways. As the norms and content of housework changed and it expanded rapidly, women's knowledge had to change. Those "mere" housewives who were committed to modern housekeeping could find their lives enriched. However, housewives had to become familiar only with the manipulation of machines and not with their technology or how to repair them. As a result, the disparity in technological knowledge between men and women increased rather than decreased.

The new, "servantless," middle-class housewife was professionalized through social pressure not to appear old fashioned, ignorant, and odd. Women assumed the new task of remaining well informed about consumer products. Part of the effort to professionalize housework revolved, therefore, around the supply of these products. The *Ladies' Home Journal* therefore contained articles on the use of new food substitutes and electric appliances. Women who resisted change were pictured as clinging to the past. Coping with consumer society in the "right way" was part of social rationalization. Christine Frederick emphasized that housewives spent money and therefore had to learn about the market so that they could make decisions in keeping with their particular family income and needs.[66] In both Germany and the United States, social rationalization was an important part of the special type of "new woman" held up as a model to emulate.[67]

In Germany, the effort to rationalize housework often led, as mentioned earlier, to disdain for the combined kitchen and living room traditionally favored by workers. Instead the *Frankfurter Küche* (Frankfurt kitchen) was encouraged, and in some ways it became a symbol of Americanization and social rationalization. This kitchen had built-in furnishings and was only five or six square meters in size. Only one

---

65. Matthews, *Housewife*, 195.

66. Cited in Susanne Strasser, *Never Done* (New York, 1982), 247.

67. See for instance for Germany Atina Grossmann, "Girlkultur or Thoroughly Rationalized Female: A New Woman in Weimar Germany?" in Judith Friedlander et al. (eds.), *Women in Culture and Politics: A Century of Change* (Bloomington, 1986), 62–80. One should bear in mind the fact that the model "new woman" had many aspects and that women from the women's movement or from the housewives' organizations were far from accepting every aspect of this model or even preferred a new combination of the aspects. Social rationalization was supposed to be equivalent to a "new culture of love" between husband and wife.

person ("naturally" the housewife) could work there, in relative isolation from the rest of the family. The height of the kitchen furnishings was determined precisely by the height of the average woman, who was naturally shorter than the average male. Thus production continued to follow the traditional division of labor between the sexes, which was newly legitimized as rational and modern.

The goal of clean, mechanized, rationalized, professionalized households was not controversial in either country, in contrast to taste and architecture. However, people differed in regard to the intensity and pace of the change that they advocated, and the possibilities of realizing their ideas differed as well.

Social Rationalization by Special Organizations and "Professionals"

In both Germany and the United States, special associations and magazines were founded to instruct housewives. The *Ladies' Home Journal* is a good example of a conduit of information from industry to housewives.[68] In Germany, there were no similar magazines in the 1920s, and instructions and advice were dispensed by periodicals published for tenants of the big housing estates or for experts and reformers. The information in publications such as *Wohnungswirtschaft, Soziale Bauwirtschaft,* and *Die Form* was conveyed to tenants by *Wohnungsberaterinnen* (advisers on apartment living) or in supplements to newspapers and magazines or at exhibitions.

The American Home Economics Association, which had been founded in 1908 and was quite well known in the United States by the 1920s, published the *Journal of Home Economics,* and in July 1923, the federal government established the Bureau of Home Economics as a part of the Department of Agriculture. The bureau furthered the interest of housewives as modern consumers as well as the interests of agricultural producers.[69] The home economists also had ties to other reform circles.[70] In 1922 a so-called Better Home Movement, supported by many locally and even nationally prominent people, assumed the task of providing education on a nationwide level.[71]

In Germany, the Reichsforschungsgesellschaft (National Research

---

68. See for example the *Ladies' Home Journal,* November 1928, May 1929, June 1929, and December 1929.
69. Matthews, *Housewife,* 158ff.
70. Ibid., 160.
71. Irene M. Witte, *Heim und Technik in Amerika* (Berlin, 1928), 74ff.

Society) and the politically conservative Hausfrauen-Verein (House-wives' League) were very active in the promotion of modernized, ratio-nalized, professionalized households. Rationalized housework was in-troduced as a regular subject in school under the heading of home economics.[72] American pupils also studied home economics. The social rationalization movement in the United States was closely associated with the breakthrough of middle-class suburbs and such indirect influ-ences as movies, magazines, and, most of all, the "culture of advertis-ing." The same processes were at work in German cities but to a lesser extent.

Apartment owners had *Hausmeister,* or caretakers, who ensured that multifamily dwellings preserved their good reputations and the properties did not lose value because of tenant misbehavior. In some of the new housing estates, professional administrators had the right to check the apartments at any time, and this was in the forefront of ten-ants' minds, even if not exercised very often. Tenants were required, for example, to keep radios turned down and to refrain from walking on lawns or hanging up their laundry to dry on Sundays. Rigorous house rules and inspections by the management of the huge apartment build-ings were supported by reformers in general and architects in particular as a way of inculcating greater discipline. While the inspections by estate management were new, the old local housing inspections of Wilhel-minian times virtually ceased, although in the late Weimar Republic they were supposed to be revived. They were replaced to some extent by visits from social workers, who inspected the housing of the very poor in order to determine the amount of local welfare payments.

In the United States, informal, market-related "controls" were ap-plied only to middle-class suburbanites and not to lower-class tenants, who were instructed and controlled in a direct and organized way.[73] A key part of the Octavia Hill Association's work, for example, was the "friendly rent collector," who was to ensure "regular payments, inspect the premises, and instruct the tenants in cleanliness, sanitation and good housekeeping."[74] The City and Suburban Homes Company found that

---

72. Compare Karen Hagemann, "Erziehung für den 'weiblichen Hauptberuf': Der Hauswirtschaftsunterricht für Mädchen an Hamburgs Volks- und Berufsschulen," in Hans-Peter de Lorent and Volker Ullrich (eds.), *Der Traum von der Freien Schule: Schule und Schulpolitik in der Weimarer Republik* (Hamburg, 1988). An introduction to rationalized housework was also taught in U.S. schools.

73. In both countries, churches were also important in educating people in matters of home and family life. This subject still lacks any research.

74. Fairbanks, *Better Citizens,* 63.

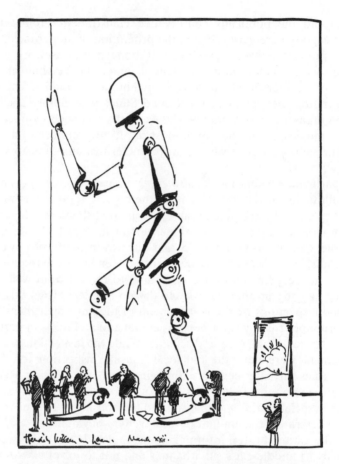

Fig. 5.   *Homo Economicus.* **In the economic laboratory "Theoretically we have made the creature perfect; and yet it won't work."**
(From *Survey,* **April 22, 1922.)**

rent collectors could have a great influence on tenants. By dealing sym-
pathetically with the problems and desires of the inhabitants, "the company has adopted a policy which has rewarded it with appreciative tenants of a better class than is normally found in low-rent apartments."[75] A
philanthropically minded U.S. corporation declared that orderliness was
an important ingredient (alongside decency, comfort, and attractiveness) in preserving "the self-respect of the tenants."[76] Rent collectors

75. Federal Housing Administration (ed.), *Four Decades of Housing with a Limited
Dividend Corporation,* (Washington, DC, 1939), 65ff.
    76. *Four Decades,* 66.

and housing administrators habitually combined education with social control. In the philanthropic model housing in New York called Lavanburg, the tenants received constant instruction in how to use modern appliances such as burglar locks, lawn mowers, and dumbwaiters. These conveniences were previously unknown to most of them and "first gave much trouble."[77] Toilets often became clogged because of tenant carelessness. Some tenants persistently threw garbage down the dumbwaiter shafts.[78] Housing reformers tried to cope with other people who were used to throwing garbage out the window. But after the city street cleaners left, "garbage was scattered over the pavement again."[79] As we know from the experience of Cincinnati, housekeepers taught poor people how to "make the best of bad living conditions."[80] Housekeeping centers were erected for this purpose in "dirty urban neighborhoods," although it is not clear how many such centers were established.

Disorderliness was associated not only with the poor but with immigrants as well, especially before the First World War but afterward to some extent also. According to housing reformers, "the disorder is due to the widely varying customs of our immigrant population."[81] Immigrants must "be taught to maintain sanitary standards." The ways in which they deviated from U.S. norms were emphasized: "[T]o the tidy American housekeeper, Orchard or Hester Street seem picturesque, but repulsively dirty." The crucial task was that "of educating our citizens, native and foreign, to assume their responsibilities . . . to care for the facilities provided, and to cooperate in the city housekeeping instead of acting like careless children." In this respect, the "far-famed German cities" were considered models of "clean dwellings."[82] This reaction was a response to the high number of immigrants in the United States.[83] Middle-class Americans reacted to the immigrants "with a complicated mixture of alarm, disdain, and a certain compassion. What was rarely present was any kind of cultural relativism."[84]

---

77. Goldfeld, *Diary*, 20.

78. Ibid., 34, 87.

79. Ibid., 11ff., 35. When slum clearance was undertaken in the 1930s, social control and education of the tenants in the new buildings were continued and presumably intensified.

80. Fairbanks, *Better Citizens*, 65.

81. *Housing Reform in New York City: A Report of the Tenement House Committee of the Charity Organization Society of the City of New York, 1911, 1912, 1913* (New York, 1914), 1.

82. Ibid., 2.

83. The law of 1924 placed a limit on the number of new immigrants.

84. Matthews, *Housewife*, 163. Sometimes there was even a tradition of a eugenic interest in improving the Anglo-Saxon race. Eugenic topics were also taught as a new discipline by home economists such as Ellen Richard. Ibid., 163.

As Fairbanks found in Cincinnati after the 1920s, tenant education became more emphatic.[85] The "Better Housing League" used its house-keepers to initiate "a systematic educational program that would inform the tenants of their rights and responsibilities as well as instruct them in the fundamentals of good housekeeping."[86] The visiting housekeeper staff consisted of six and later fifteen people. Between 1917 and 1927, the housekeepers made 57,123 visits. They oversaw repairs and helped to "improve" housekeeping practices. They also provided housekeeping lessons — 2,781 in 1929 alone.[87] In general, these efforts met with public approval.[88] The Better Housing League in Cincinnati also converted a typical three-room tenement into a model apartment, where from 1920 onward it conducted classes in housekeeping, sewing, and cooking. To-gether with other committees and clubs, the league taught new immi-grants "both American and urban ways of living."[89]

One of the housekeeping centers in a "dirty neighborhood" was depicted by Virginia Campbell in a periodical called the *Survey.* The first instructions to the families who came there were as follows: "Keep neat and clean. Do the work given you the best you can. Scald dishes thor-oughly. Wash out dishtowels when dirty. Measure carefully when cook-ing. If you spill anything, clean it up at once. Straighten beds after rest hour. Cut pictures in dining room only. Keep back screen hooked. Be happy and make others happy. Be fair, honest and industrious. Be cour-teous to company by entertaining them. Talk in a low voice. Always remove the bed spread when you lie down." Five "don'ts" then fol-lowed: "Don't lie on beds except during the rest hours. Don't lay things down. Put them back where you got them. Don't waste time. Don't throw anything around the house. Don't leave the bath tub dirty." Fi-nally a daily schedule was worked out: "Rise at 6:30. Throw back covers to air. Drink at least a glass of water. Wash and comb. Brush teeth. Prepare breakfast. Eat, and wash dishes at once. Make beds. Clean up house and porches. Prepare dinner 11–12. Wash dishes and clean up kitchen and dining room. Rest hour 1:30–2:30. Bathe and clean up. Sew, mend, notebooks, etc. Prepare supper 5:30–6:00. Wash dishes. Recreation. Bed at 9 o'clock."[90]

As this behavior model and daily schedule suggest, traditional norms and values were stressed, for example, the injunction to be fair, honest,

85. Fairbanks, *Better Citizens,* 55.
86. Ibid., 52.
87. Fairbanks, *Better Citizens,* 82, 68.
88. Ibid., 63.
89. Ibid.
90. *Survey,* March 15, 1925, 765.

and industrious. It is interesting to note the ways in which the home engineering program changed when aimed at different social groups. In the case of lower-class people, as in this example, the focus was on cleanliness as a key attitude. The extent to which the advice concerned very personal matters is also striking. It shows very clearly that social rationalization applied not only to housekeeping and house engineering but to the entire individual as well. The Housekeeping Center also provided advice for poor people on how to cope with the new consumer society. The advice was general, but some points were targeted at poor people in particular: "Plan what you want before going to market. Always ask the price. Do not get large amounts of perishable foods. Choose from food. Don't just read the order. Buy things in season. They are cheaper and have better flavor. If the prices are higher than you can afford to pay — get something in its place. Buy medium sized fruit and vegetables. Always check your bill and count your change. Don't buy a thing just because it is cheap — be sure you need it. Remember the good brands. Buy where you can get things at the cheapest price."[91]

In conclusion, it is difficult to determine whether direct control over homes was more intensive and widespread in Germany or in the United States. For those familiar with Germany's reputation for social discipline, it is striking that there was so much effort to control homes in the United States, especially the homes of the poor and the impoverished immigrants. In any case, the examples suggest that the United States' reputation as a culturally liberal, purely market-driven society is not very accurate.

Social Rationalization for a "Better Family"

Although married women were an integral part of the workforce, despite persistent job discrimination,[92] and although home economists said that women who were gainfully employed were even more dependent on rationalized housework than those who were not, reformers did not concentrate their efforts on wage-earning mothers in either Germany or the United States. Instead, the new ideal of rationalized domestic life was simply added to the traditional ideal of the "mere" housewife and mother.[93] Women were supposed to find self-fulfillment in

91. Ibid.

92. Alice Kessler-Harris, "Independence and Virtue in the Lives of Wage-Earning Women: The United States, 1870–1930," in Judith Friedlander et al. (eds.), *Women in Culture and Politics: A Century of Change* (Bloomington, 1986), 3–17.

93. Cf. for instance Leslie Woodcock Tentler, *Wage-Earning Women: Industrial Work and Family Life in the United States, 1900–1930* (New York and Oxford, 1979), especially 182ff.

emotional fulfillment, especially through modern child rearing[94] and, particularly in the United States, the "culture of consumption." These "therapeutic imperatives helped to domesticate the drive towards female emancipation . . . and many women accepted this new version of male hegemony."[95] Life as the mother in a family was highly valued and recognized as "a fine art," and a major department in modern education was devoted to it.[96] The home economics curriculum had broadened steadily since its early days, when it had consisted largely of training in domestic skills such as sewing, cooking, and laundry. As Miss Whitcomb of the U.S. Bureau of Education said, the new curriculum "should aim definitely at the improvement of human living and behavior for all persons."[97] Courses were established, therefore, to educate people about social and family relationships.[98] Over a thousand home economists attended the annual conference of the American Home Economics Association in 1924, at which the "program indicated an increasing shift away from the technical aspects of sewing and cooking toward a broader teaching, covering more truly the profession of 'homemaking.'"[99] Although this comment was addressed to American housewives, it applied to Germans as well.

One of the main prerequisites for a "better family" was thought to be the social rationalization of sexual behavior and fewer children. In both countries, nuclear families with two children were encouraged in the expectation that they would provide more intensive care for each child. It was no coincidence that families with four or more children began to feel like social outcasts in the Weimar Republic and therefore became organized. They were supported by demographers and—at least insofar as "healthy" families were concerned—by eugenicists. The Reichsbund kinderreicher Familien (Organization of Families with Many Children) demanded larger and often subsidized apartments. In general, though, the new housing was built primarily for small, rationalized families.[100]

---

94. Fass, *Damned,* 97; see also Judith Walzer Leavitt (ed.), *Brought to Bed: Childbearing in America, 1750 to 1950* (New York and Oxford, 1986).

95. T. J. Jackson Lears, "From Salvation to Self-Realization: Advertising and the Therapeutic Roots of the Consumer Culture, 1880–1930," in Richard Wightman Fox and T. J. Jackson Lears (eds.), *The Culture of Consumption: Critical Essays in American History 1880–1980* (New York, 1983), 27. Although this statement was aimed only at American housewives, it could be applied to Germans too.

96. *Survey,* December 15, 1929, 350.

97. Quoted in *Survey,* December 15, 1929, 351.

98. *Survey,* December 15, 1929, 351.

99. *Survey,* July 15, 1927, 425.

100. For more see von Saldern, "Reformwohnungsbau," 245ff.

Fig. 6. Advertisement. Conventional gender roles in a modern setting. (From Gwendolyn Wright, *Building the Dream: A Social History of Housing in America*, 211 [Cambridge, MA, 1981].)

Social rationalization and housekeeping technology were supposed to free up more time for women to devote to children and their activities. This was part of the emotional role that the home had gained by the nineteenth century and that became even more important in the early twentieth century.[101] Men and women were supposed to see clearly each day the importance of the proper care, training, and education of children. Mothers should seize the opportunity afforded by the alleviation of housework to tend more carefully to their children and improve themselves so that they would be better mothers.

The efforts to reform domestic culture under the banner of modernity and social rationalization extended as well to the outward appearance of housewives and mothers. Women were supposed to lend expression to the changes in their everyday lives through corresponding changes in the style of their clothes. The *Ladies' Home Journal* recommended simple, "sensible," and above all clean dress because,[102] as a U.S. advertisement of 1928 stated, "people have a way of associating unclean clothes with other questionable characteristics."[103] In Germany, modern housewives were supposed to wear a smock while doing housework so that when they finished they still looked *adrett,* or smart and proper.[104] Their appearance should not betray any sign of work. Housework was now considered just a part-time activity, and housewives were supposed to spend the rest of their day interacting with their families or educating themselves.[105]

The rationalization and professionalization of domestic life and housework was aimed at private, single-family households. The many utopian and alternative ideas developed in earlier decades about the organization of family life dwindled away. These ideas included, for example, cooperative communities in the tradition of the early socialists, such as Fourier, and of August Bebel's *Frau und Sozialismus.* The attempts in Berlin before the First World War and in "Red Vienna" after the war to develop community kitchens were not intensively discussed and did not have much political and cultural influence in the 1920s. In

---

101. Matthews, *Housewife,* 181.

102. In Christopher P. Wilson, "The Rhetoric of Consumption: Mass-Market Magazines and the Demise of the Gentle Reader, 1880–1920," in Richard Wightman Fox and T. J. Jackson Lears (eds.), *The Culture of Consumption: Critical Essays in American History 1880–1980* (New York, 1983), 54. Wilson's article is a convincing interpretation of the *Ladies' Home Journal.*

103. In *Ladies' Home Journal,* 1928, cited in Wright, *Building the Dream,* 211.

104. *Einfa* 3, no. 5 (1932); 3, no. 10 (1932); 3, no. 11 (1932); 4, no. 2 (1933).

105. Housekeeping, according to an article in the *Survey,* was not expected in the future to become a leisure-time job as long as homemakers, assumed to be female, prepared the meals and did the laundry. *Survey,* June 1, 1929, 301, 333, 336.

the United States, community kitchens and community dining clubs[106] also faded as objects of serious discussion. Women in Germany (except for some young Social Democrats) saw in these ideas the beginnings of the decline of the family and—with a view to the Soviet Union—the specter of Communism. So long as women were employed in inferior jobs, they saw their own individual households as the place where they could display their talents. The concept of individual households was therefore never seriously questioned in either Germany or the United States. Industry in both countries also "naturally" had an interest in individual households as individual consumers.

In sum, reformers in both countries tended to idealize the "classic" single-family household, with division of labor by gender and with fewer children but more intensive individual care of them. All the "classic" features were "regendered," that is, revived within the new context of modernized households and homes. Social rationalization, including self-improvement, was supposed to help create a "better family," which was seen as a "haven" in the hasty, restless, machine society that was emerging.[107]

The Impact of Social Rationalization

The movement toward social rationalization was not serene. The creation of a modern, "civilized," "socially rationalized" human being was not a natural process,[108] nor was it solely a result of market forces. Social reformers were certainly influential, and most people responded to their educational efforts with a mixture of acceptance and rejection. Open-mindedness and appropriation do not mean simple adoption but a complicated process of transformation. The history of the complex appropriation of social rationalization by various groups of people has not yet been written.

Some closing remarks might be added on the effects of the discourses about social rationalization. One can assume that efforts to educate people "from above" about modern ways were more successful in Germany than in the United States. "In a culture like Germany's, public control tended to beget obedience."[109] On the other hand, even

---

106. See Hayden, *Redesigning,* 207ff.

107. An informative introduction to the history of the family and modern historiography is provided by Tamara K. Hareven, "The History of the Family and the Complexity of Social Change," *American Historical Review* 96, no. 1 (1991): 95ff.

108. This is the impression left by the history of the process of disciplining human behavior. See Norbert Elias, *Über den Prozeß der Zivilisation,* 2 vols. (Frankfurt, 1976).

109. Seymour Toll, *Zoned America* (New York, 1969), 131.

Germans cannot be seen as objects easily molded by education and propaganda. They too were historical subjects who appropriated the rationalization of society in their own ways by assessing whether it suited them and critically rethinking the "advantages" of change.[110]

When working-class families in Germany moved to the new housing estates, they changed the matrix of their daily lives. According to Gerd Selle: "Working-class areas, with their historical memories and identity as neighborhoods in which workers had some roots, were replaced by sterile, anonymous housing estates, which seemed most intent on making social climbers feel at home who were eager to adopt the mentality of white-collar workers. . . . Nothing in the surroundings that could kindle any memories. . . . Functions and movements in the new housing were governed by ground plans that reflected the principles of Taylorism in factories but did not necessarily accommodate traditional lifestyles or provide relief from work and space for social interaction in the workers' families."[111] Although Selle's critical analysis highlights some important differences between the old and new experiences, it needs to be reworked and supplemented in light of the fact that most working-class people were affected only by the *idea* of a new life and not by any actual improvement in their living conditions. The exceptions were a relatively small segment of well-paid skilled workers. In addition, interviews with the inhabitants of the housing estates show that many felt quite at ease in their new surroundings. They recalled their arrival in the new estates as a positive experience, and this fact cannot be disregarded in any analysis.[112] The families that moved to new, well-equipped apartments were often quite pleased with the comfort of their new surroundings, despite the small size of many apartments (less than fifty square meters). The residents developed their own ways of making their new abodes feel like home. In doing so, they often ignored the rigid standards of behavior, especially insofar as questions of taste were concerned. Most families did not give away their old furniture and "dust catchers," if only because they often lacked money to buy new furnishings. We should keep in mind the considerable gap that existed in both countries between the image of domestic life projected in advertising and the actual ways in which most people lived.[113]

---

110. Edward Shorter asks a comparable question: "Were the lower classes merely aping the bourgeoisie, or did the evolution of their family patterns obey a dynamic of its own?" Edward Shorter, *The Making of the Modern Family* (New York, 1975), 231.

111. Gerd Selle (with Jutta Boehe), *Kultur der Sinne und ästhetische Erziehung* (Cologne, 1981), 150ff.

112. Peter Gorsen, "Zur Dialektik des Funktionalismus heute: Das Beispiel des kommunalen Wohnungsbaus im Wien der zwanziger Jahre," in Jürgen Habermas (ed.), *Stichworte zur "geistigen Situation der Zeit"* (Frankfurt, 1979), 2:688–707.

113. Cf. Fass, *Damned;* Wright, *Building the Dream,* 210.

While families were often quite resistant to the attempts to modernize taste, they were usually more receptive to the new standards in cleanliness and neatness, the modernization and rationalization of housework, and the intensification of family life.[114] There was a qualitative change in domestic life and its importance in women's lives, especially for those tenants in the new housing estates in Germany who had never previously experienced "good living conditions." Although the introduction of modern norms and values under the banner of social rationalization has been described as the "colonization" of everyday life,[115] one should remember that the "culture of appropriation" and all the continuing contradictions in women's lives and in consumer society prevented people from becoming pure objects of the reformers. Matthews expressed this point in respect to American housewives: "If one could accurately pinpoint the exact time when the phrase 'Just a housewife' made its first appearance, it seems likely that the period under discussion might have been at that time [i.e., the 1920s]. Certainly the likelihood that domesticity could be a fully adequate prop for female self-esteem had greatly diminished by 1930. The consumer culture along with the hedonism it spawned sounded the death knell both for housewifery as a skilled craft and for mothers as a moral arbiter."[116] Reformers had their best chances of succeeding if their efforts contained a promise of clear advantages, such as improved living conditions, and if the new norms they advocated (e.g., in regard to cleanliness) were accepted by the social and cultural milieus in which people, and especially women, already lived.

Conclusion

The U.S. efforts at social rationalization were limited in the 1920s by the lack of a large program to construct public housing, whereas the program in Germany was an effective means of social rationalization. In the United

---

114. Many of the tenants of the housing estates were white-collar workers or low-ranking officials. Their appropriation of modernity has been researched by, among others, Reinhard Spree. Reinhard Spree, "Angestellte als Modernisierungsagenten: Indikatoren und Thesen zum reproduktiven Verhalten von Angestellten im späten 19. und frühen 20. Jahrhundert," in Jürgen Kocka (ed.), *Angestellte im europäischen Vergleich* (Göttingen, 1981), 279–308.

115. See Jürgen Habermas, *Theorie des kommunikativen Handelns,* 3d ed., 2 vols. (Frankfurt, 1985); cf. T. J. Jackson Lears, *No Place of Grace: Antimodernism and the Transformation of American Culture 1880–1920* (New York, 1981), 10.

116. Matthews, *Housewife,* 193ff. Cf. also Robert S. Lynd and Helen Merrell Lynd, *Middletown* (New York, 1956). See also Mintz and Kellogg, *Domestic Revolution,* 117. The dilemma posed by women's emancipation and family work is discussed by, for example, Carl N. Degler, *At Odds: Women and the Family in America* (New York, 1978).

States, actual improvements and educational successes were concentrated in the new, white, middle-class suburbs and the few reform model-housing projects that were built. The government did not play a very big part in the construction of the suburbs, and the new way of life and modern domestic culture were not seen in the United States as a cultural obligation imposed "from above." The U.S. suburbs accordingly played a much less prominent role in the discourse on social rationalization than did the German housing estates. Social rationalization in the suburbs was carried out in a "softer," more market-driven way through such publications as the *Ladies' Home Journal* (including its numerous advertisements) and similar middle-class magazines. Although magazines and newspapers (especially the supplements with numerous pictures) also played an important role in Germany as "cultural transmitters," as could be seen in Hanover for instance,[117] the market mechanism had a far greater impact in the relatively rich United States than in Weimar Germany, with many consequences for the "culture of domesticity" and the culture of the public sphere. In contrast to the United States, social rationalization in Germany was linked to the new norms and values of the trade unions, the Social Democratic Party, the building cooperatives, the Bauhaus group, and the many reform-minded officials in state and local government. The discourse on social rationalization was therefore much more entwined with political parties, public authorities, and politics than in the United States.

In the United States as a whole, the attempts to rationalize everyday life were limited not only by the living conditions of the poorer workers (as in Germany) but also by the many ethnic communities in cities (in contrast to Germany)[118] that adhered to the standards and values of communal life.[119] The tension between family behavior in the dominant "WASP" (White Anglo-Saxon Protestant) culture and the traditional behaviors of African American families and immigrant families was a continuing fact of American life. Presumably, only those immigrants who wanted to improve their job prospects and were advised to look and live like "Americans" followed the advice of the reformers "voluntarily." "The need of conformity for success would overpower the remembrance of the old ways."[120] The limits on social rationalization

---

117. Von Saldern, "Reformwohnungsbau."

118. Except the neighborhoods of Polish and east European Jewish immigrants.

119. See for instance Ewen, *Immigrant Women*. As Kathleen Neils Conzen has pointed out, ethnic communities could maintain close interaction without residential concentration. Kathleen Neils Conzen, "Immigrants, Immigrant Neighborhoods, and Ethnic Identity: Historical Issues," *Journal of American History* 66 (1979): 613.

120. Doris Weatherford, *Foreign and Female: Immigrant Women in America, 1840–1930* (New York, 1986), 101.

can be seen in the various immigrant groups that needed their ethnic culture and milieus in order to survive in the United States. Despite some cultural resistance from them, the traditional idea of the United States as a melting pot (determined and dominated by "WASPs") was renewed and strengthened by the overarching, supposedly neutral concept of social rationalization and modernization. Seeing social rationalization as culturally neutral, the mostly white U.S. middle-class reformers were quite intolerant of the domestic cultures of immigrants and poor people and attempted to impose "white" middle-class norms and values.

Alongside these attitudes and the concept of Americanization of the immigrants, there was also a "pluralistic vision" in the 1920s that tolerated African American and other cultures to a certain degree. This tolerance did not extend though — and this is an important restriction — to white neighborhoods or to areas that seemed "disorderly" and "unclean."[121] Although this multicultural vision was very limited and in some ways just an image-polishing invention, it did not exist at all in Germany. Here the aim was for a nationally oriented "German modernity" achieved through social rationalization and new housing. The concept of harmonious, clean neighborhoods was inflated into a vision of a harmonized, "clean" *Volk* community. The social rationalization of everyday life and domestic culture led easily to a society planned in every way.

---

121. Fairbanks, *Better Citizens*, 35.

CHAPTER 6

The Poor and Homeless of Hanover in the Weimar Republic: The World of Gertrude Polley

Preliminary Remarks

Chapters 6 and 7 are closely related. The first is a study of poverty and homelessness in Hanover during the Weimar Republic. One of the poor and homeless people was Gertrude Polley, whose life story, and in particular the scandal she caused, is described in chapter 7.

The capitalist industrial society that had emerged since the mid–nineteenth century provided jobs and incomes for many people but required by its very nature that they be hired and fired in light of economic considerations and regardless of the need for employment. Loss of a job often led to poverty and sometimes homelessness, as it does today. Even relatively well-paid workers, such as mechanics and printers, often did not earn adequate incomes for their entire lives but just in their prime working years between the ages of about twenty and forty. Thereafter, they often found themselves sliding toward poverty, which could only be averted to some extent if their adult offspring could help.

For many people, in particular women, poverty was a regular part of the life cycle.[1] Older, single women were especially vulnerable.[2] People

---

1. Cf. in this regard David F. Crew, "'Wohlfahrtsbrot ist bitteres Brot': The Elderly, the Disabled, and the Local Welfare Authorities in the Weimar Republic 1924–1933," *Archiv für Sozialgeschichte* 30 (1990): 217ff.

2. Until 1929, more than half of the welfare recipients in Hamburg under the Weimar Republic were women. I am grateful to David Crew for pointing this out. See also Karen Hagemann, "'. . . wir werden alt vom Arbeiten': Die soziale Situation alternder Arbeiterfrauen in der Weimarer Republik am Beispiel Hamburgs," *Archiv für Sozialgeschichte* 30 (1990): 247ff.

gained access to the social insurance system through their jobs, and consequently all the women who did not have regular work outside the home were structurally disadvantaged. Women who were employed often received less pay than men and therefore benefited less from social insurance. The twentieth century did not bring any major changes to these basic patterns and even added another reason for impoverishment. As industry grew more sophisticated, it made more complex demands on its workers, which some were unable to meet for a variety of reasons—a phenomenon that is still with us today.

Introduction: Poverty and Homelessness in the Weimar Republic

Although the Weimar Republic claimed to be a welfare state from its inception,[3] poverty[4] and homelessness tended to increase rather than decrease throughout its history. Many people (and not just workers) who had previously managed to get along reasonably well found themselves unable to cope with the conditions in postwar Germany. There was a large political and sociocultural leap from the German Empire to the Weimar Republic, and many people failed to make it. Demobilization also had its effects. Many women who had worked at traditionally male jobs during the war were dismissed. By February 1919, there were more than seven thousand unemployed in Hanover and Linden, including about twenty-five hundred women.[5] During the inflationary boom in 1921–22, the number of unemployed sank temporarily in Hanover and elsewhere but only increased again during the hyperinflation of 1922–23. During this period, a process of impoverishment set in,[6] which

3. For the historical development of poor relief and welfare see Stephan Leibfried and Florian Tennstedt (eds.), *Politik der Armut und die Spaltung des Sozialstaats* (Frankfurt, 1985); Christoph Sachße and Florian Tennstedt, *Geschichte der Armenfürsorge in Deutschland,* especially vol. 2, *Fürsorge und Wohlfahrtspflege 1871–1929* (Stuttgart, 1988).

4. Poverty must be understood in historical terms, that is, the poverty line has to be measured by the standards of a given time.

5. Cf. Jochen Mignat, "Arbeitslosigkeit in Hannover 1877 bis 1989," *Hannoversche Geschichtsblätter* 44 (1990): 94ff., 100.

6. Ibid., 95. See also in this regard the article by Göran Hachmeister and Werner Kolbe, "Notsituationen im Hochinflationsjahr 1923," in Adelheid von Saldern (ed.), *Stadt und Moderne: Hannover in der Weimarer Republik* (Hamburg, 1989); Volker Seitz, "Notkriminalität in Hannover der Nachkriegs- und Inflationszeit," in the same volume.

ravaged not only workers but also the petite bourgeoisie and many families in other classes living on pensions and savings. Life improved somewhat for many Germans after 1923, when credits from the United States and the stabilization of the mark helped to fuel an economic upswing. However, numerous jobs were still lost in the rationalization of production and distribution that accompanied the upswing. There was a short worldwide economic downturn in 1926, which caused unemployment to spurt to previously unimaginable levels. These levels were dwarfed, though, by the Great Depression, beginning in 1929. Soon about every third person in the labor market in Hanover was jobless — a catastrophe as unfamiliar to people then as the hyperinflation had been a few years earlier.[7]

Number of Unemployed in Hanover (including Linden)

1919 (Sept.)	7,164
1923 (Nov.)	19,488
1926 (July)	27,103
1930 (Jan.)	25,300
1933 (Jan.)	58,340

The poverty of the 1920s was due primarily to the string of economic catastrophes that hit Germany. They were caused both by the business cycle and by more fundamental, structural problems. Particularly noticeable in the preceding figures for Hanover is the large number of people affected by the depression of 1926 and the consequences of rationalization.

Thanks to the social insurance system instituted by Bismarck and extended in 1927 to include unemployment insurance,[8] loss of a job did not automatically condemn a person to poverty. However, the gaping holes in the social safety net became apparent when people ran out of unemployment insurance and resorted to emergency welfare (*Krisenfürsorge*) or then fell back onto the lowest level of welfare, which was municipal welfare. It made a great deal of difference whether a person was supported by the Unemployment Insurance Corporation (unemployment insurance and emergency welfare) or the municipality (welfare for

---

7. Mignat, "Arbeitslosigkeit," 101. Hanover and Linden had about 400,000 inhabitants in 1925 and about 440,000 in 1933. In 1910 it had been 376,000.

8. Although regulations had been in effect since 1918–19 about support for the unemployed, the Act on the Procurement of Employment and Unemployment Insurance passed in 1927 marked a major new departure, although its positive effects were soon nullified by the severity of the Great Depression.

the unemployed and general welfare). As one fell further down the ladder, not only did the payments decrease — especially in Hanover[9] — but one was subject to more stringent controls on "shirkers" and the "dregs of society." In any case, unemployment meant that one's family was immediately thrown onto the slippery slope toward poverty, especially since many people did not have any savings or friends and relatives to whom they could turn for support. Those who did not qualify for unemployment insurance soon found themselves struggling just to survive, whether in Hanover or elsewhere.

The available support covered at most the cost of a poor diet. Housewives also felt pressured because they considered themselves primarily responsible for providing meals. The unemployed often fell into despair and apathy when no friends, neighbors, or extended family members could help and no opportunities could be found for odd jobs or earning a little on the side somehow. Suicide rates rose considerably in the Weimar Republic.[10] Social envy of people who did have jobs increased, as can be seen in the hysterical tones reached at times in the campaign against two-income families. The main goal of this campaign was to exclude married women from the labor force.

The new poverty was due primarily to the high rates of unemployment in the 1920s and early 1930s. However, there were other reasons as well why people could find themselves sliding into difficulty. The most important was the shortage of housing. Many families lacked homes of their own, and some even had no shelter at all.[11] There had long been a severe housing shortage, especially among the lower classes, but the

---

9. After the Emergency Decree of June 1931, the actual amount of support received on average by all recipients in Germany was 60.66 RM a month for unemployment insurance, 50.50 RM a month for emergency welfare, and 50 RM a month for municipal welfare for the unemployed. Heidrun Homburg, "Massenarbeitslosigkeit in Deutschland 1930–1933," *SOWI* 14, no. 3 (1985): 211. According to the Statistical Office in Berlin, at least 148 RM a month were needed in order to subsist; Hamburg, "Massenarbeitslosigkeit," 212. See as well Adelheid von Saldern, "Kommunale Verarmung und Armut in den Kommunen während der großen Krise 1928 bis 1933: Am Beispiel der Finanz- und Wohnungs(bau)politik," in *Soziale Bewegungen: Jahrbuch 3,* especially the part on Hanover, 76ff. (Frankfurt, 1987). The average amount of support received by people on general welfare in Hanover in 1931 was 39.20 RM a month, which was lower than in Hamburg or Kiel. In comparison, a warehouse worker earned a gross amount of 2,288 RM a year and a painter 3,106 RM. For more see Adelheid von Saldern, *Neues Wohnen: Wohnungspolitik und Wohnkultur im Hannover der zwanziger Jahre* (Hanover, 1993), 57.

10. The suicide rates for 1932 varied considerably from one country to another. Per million inhabitants there were 85 suicides in Great Britain, 133 in the United States, 155 in France, and 260 in Germany. Detlev J. K. Peukert, *Die Weimarer Republik: Krisenjahre der Klassischen Moderne* (Göttingen, 1987), 271.

11. In regard to this and what follows, see von Saldern, *Neues Wohnen.*

situation became worse in the early 1920s. Very few homes had been built during the war years, and although subsidies were provided in the first years thereafter, construction was severely limited by the period of inflation. While housing construction sagged, the need soared. The age structure of the population was changing, and there were fewer children now and more older people who needed homes of their own. The end of the war also brought a surge in the number of marriages and new couples who needed homes. In addition, Hanover was an attractive city for pensioners and other groups who moved from elsewhere and required housing.

A new program to build subsidized housing was launched in 1924, but in Hanover in particular, the homes that were built were targeted largely at the middle classes and the best-paid workers. This program did little, therefore, to relieve homelessness and the lack of housing. The state-subsidized apartments built in Hanover were relatively large, and the rent for them was beyond the means of poorer people. Hanover led the entire republic in the average number of rooms in the new housing and was last in the type of housing with just two or three rooms that working-class people might be able to afford.

The director of the welfare office in Schickenberg stated in 1930 that he could not see "any reduction in the severe problems facing needy families as a result of the new building program over the last few years."[12] How could things have been any different, one might ask, when Director of Municipal Construction Elkart insisted that the Housing Office only propose as tenants those people who were able to pay the rent, even in the case of apartments provided by the municipal building society. Otherwise, he said, the new housing would just become a welfare project, which was not the intention of the municipal authorities. Even the municipal housing in the suburb of Laatzen apparently did not accept poor tenants. Those who suffered the consequences were the neediest families, especially those living in emergency shelters. Unlike almost all other big cities in Germany, Hanover did not provide them with any rent subsidies, at least until the Great Depression hit. Needy families therefore had tremendous difficulty in finding housing, and many continued to live in shacks and emergency shelters.

There were high hopes for the "trickle-down effect,"[13] but it too did very little to relieve homelessness. In fact, in the years when a great deal of housing was built, homelessness only increased. Why did this happen? The passage of the Tenant Protection Act had been a great step

---

12. In ibid.

13. The "trickle-down" effect means that when richer people buy new housing, poorer people all down the income scale are able to move up to better housing. This theory is controversial because of the existence of relatively closed sections of the housing market.

forward after the war, but it was watered down in the aftermath of the shift in the balance of political power following the currency reform of 1924. Landlords who could show that they needed more space for themselves or that the rent had not been paid for a while were allowed henceforth to evict their tenants. If these so-called Exmittierte could not find another apartment (as was often the case), the responsibility for sheltering them fell to the municipality. It therefore set up a number of emergency shelters for families. By 1930, families with a total of 1,836 children were living in these shelters, some of which were former schools, poorhouses, shacks, railroad cars, and army barracks.[14] The city of Hanover had a total of 42,007 cases of homelessness on its hands by 1930, including repeat cases.[15] In general one can say that in the history of poverty and homelessness in twentieth-century Germany, a nadir was reached in the 1920s that is a black mark on the entire Weimar Republic and the history of the city of Hanover.

From Relief to Welfare

Before the First World War, the poor in Germany, and therefore in Hanover, were generally cared for by Armenkollegien. These councils consisted of municipal officials and employees assisted by *Armenpfleger,* or relief workers, operating in an honorary capacity according to what was called the "Elberfeld system."[16] The position of Armenpfleger was by no means voluntary; if someone did not want to take on this duty, he lost the right to vote or had to pay additional taxes.[17]

As much as possible, the Armenpfleger of the second half of the nineteenth century lived in the same part of the city as the families assigned to them and were supposed to assess the economic conditions and lifestyles of these families and either recommend them for relief or

---

14. A list of the municipal emergency shelters can be found in *Hannoversche Grundbesitzer-Zeitung,* June 28, 1930, in Hanover City Archives, BVC 62.

15. Angela Dinghaus and Bettina Korff, "Wohlfahrtspflege im Hannover der 20er Jahre: Kontinuitätslinien repressiver Armenpflege und sozialer Disziplinierung," in Adelheid von Saldern (ed.), *Stadt und Moderne: Hannover in der Weimarer Republik* (Hamburg, 1989), 223.

16. The so-called Elberfeld system had spread from Elberfeld to more or less all of Prussia since the 1850s. The core of this new approach to the poor lay in the use of people operating in an honorary capacity who were expected to get to know particular poor people and provide a better assessment of their actual needs, instead of the old system under which bureaucrats met at conference tables and divided up the meager municipal support for the poor. The municipal authorities also hoped that the new system would make it possible to reduce relief payments.

17. See Nancy Reagin, *A German Woman's Movement: Class and Gender in Hanover, 1880–1933* (Chapel Hill, 1995).

not. Each Armenpfleger was expected to oversee a maximum of four families. The city was divided into relief districts, which all met every month to discuss the individual cases. The Armenpfleger were instructed to provide the poor with nothing more than the bare necessities. The support that was provided should never leave the impression that relief was a substitute for "honest work." Layabouts, alcoholics, and the "immoral" were not eligible for assistance. This system of looking after the poor was certainly a two-edged sword, although it looks quite modern for the nineteenth century. The poor received the most intensive care possible, but on the other hand their daily lives were closely watched and supervised.

Besides municipal relief, there were also some charitable organizations at work in Hanover and elsewhere, for instance the Evangelische Verein. This Protestant association provided the poor with food, clothing, and money. In addition, the Verein für freiwillige Armenpflege (Association for Volunteer Care of the Poor) had been trying since 1885 to rationalize private-sector charity and entrench a private assistance and support system alongside municipal welfare. This association was staffed by volunteers who maintained close contacts with their municipal counterparts. While the people who worked in the front lines of municipal relief were all men, the Verein für freiwillige Armenpflege accepted women as well.

The relief system was reformed after the First World War. A new Welfare Office was built at 17 Friedrichstraße, and a Welfare Commission was established for each of the thirty districts in the city. These commissions had seven members, of whom one was the district welfare officer. At least one member was supposed to be a physician and one a teacher. The Welfare Commissions distributed the so-called visiting cards not by streets but by type of case, attempting to find the best possible match between the welfare workers and the poor people. Decisions about whether to provide support were made by the Welfare Office, and the members of the district commissions had only a right to be heard. However, the members of the commissions could raise or lower the regular welfare payments within certain limits or even cut them off entirely. If the Welfare Office disagreed with the decisions of a district commission, the Welfare Committee was summoned. This committee consisted of representatives of the municipal and city councils, as well as of various charities via the special committees.[18]

18. Wilhelm Schickenberg, "Die Vereinheitlichung der öffentlichen Wohlfahrtspflege und die Stadt Hannover," in *Festschrift zur Tagung des Deutschen Städtetages in Hannover (Sonderheft der Zeitschrift für Kommunalwirtschaft)* (Berlin-Friedenau, 1924), 14.

By 1928, more than seventy people wore the black and white garb of the welfare workers. Most of them were now women, although as usual the office was headed by a man. In Hanover, this man was a socially conscious public official named Wihelm Schickenberg. The major organizational changes in poor relief were, in Hanover as elsewhere, more female personnel and increasing professionalization and bureaucratization, in addition to the name change to "welfare."[19] Disputes frequently erupted over jurisdiction and coordination problems between the Employment Office, the Welfare Office, and the various private and church-operated charities in the city. With the advent of the new "welfare state," the role played by nongovernmental charities was clearly declining. These organizations were also weakened, in comparison with the prewar period, by a reduction in donations because of the impoverishment of parts of the middle class.[20]

Toward the end of the Weimar Republic, the welfare state began to crumble, and the advocates of private care for the poor again came to the fore with their calls for "help from one person to the next."[21] The National Socialists also played successfully on this theme before 1933, portraying the *Volksgemeinschaft,* or *"Volk* community," they advocated as the embodiment of similar ideals.[22] The Nazis were given a new opportunity when the welfare state began to disintegrate and the public debate over social problems turned increasingly to eugenics.

The Differentiation and Categorization of Welfare Recipients

One hallmark of modern welfare policy in the 1920s was the mounting tendency to differentiate among recipients and categorize them. This trend was prompted by the new kinds of people on welfare as a result of the war and the inflation as well as by the scientific or pseudoscientific

---

19. In general for this, see especially Christoph Sachse, *Mütterlichkeit als Beruf* (Frankfurt, 1986).

20. Mignat, "Arbeitslosigkeit," 99.

21. The discussions were mostly about the "proper" emphasis because private charities certainly played a role in the welfare system of the Weimar Republic.

22. I am grateful to David Crew for pointing this out. The Winter Relief Organization (*Winterhilfswerk*) played a major role in this connection. Cf. Wieland Elfferding, "Opferritual und Volksgemeinschaftsdiskurs am Beispiel des Winterhilfswerks," in Manfred Behrens et al. (eds.), *Faschismus und Ideologie (Argument-Sonderband AS 62),* (Berlin, 1980), 2:199–227. Many of these welfare workers were also very partial to the idea of some kind of *Volk* community. In addition, they stemmed for the most part from the middle classes and wanted to reserve the task of social work for themselves and thereby limit the influence of the Social Democrats. I am grateful to Nancy Reagin and Doris Schlüter for pointing this out.

urge to study and classify that had emerged in the nineteenth century. During the First World War, "war welfare" had been introduced as an offshoot of the newly developing *gehobene Fürsorge* (elevated welfare). The people who qualified could lay legal claim to war welfare and later to the payments made available to victims of the inflation. The recipients of this type of assistance did not suffer from the discriminatory practices that had typified relief in the nineteenth century. The purpose of gehobene Fürsorge was to prevent the recipients from sliding into the kind of poverty that would isolate them from their social peers, and it therefore entailed higher payments than normal. Most of the discriminatory practices and measures intended to discipline welfare recipients were also avoided.

While privileged groups received enough benefits to remain in touch, perhaps, with their traditional social peers, most people found themselves on *allgemeine Fürsorge,* or general welfare. The number of people drawing the two classes of welfare in Hanover can be seen in the relatively good economic year of 1928, when there were 533 people with war wounds and 6,794 people drawing small pensions and social security benefits versus 9,304 people who fell into the "others" category, meaning people who were on welfare because they had lost their jobs or were considered "antisocial" for other reasons.[23]

Not only was a distinction drawn between "elevated" and "general" welfare, but the latter was itself further subdivided into more and more categories. Under Section 13 in particular of the Reich Regulations on the Duty to Provide Welfare, people categorized as dissolute or reluctant to work were singled out for special treatment.[24] The subcategories into which people were thrust reflected the values and norms of bourgeois, capitalistic society. Particular emphasis was placed on cleanliness, orderliness, and willingness to work — as well as proper sexual behavior in the case of women. So-called layabouts and dissolute people were placed in the lowest subcategory of "general welfare," and their benefits were drastically reduced. The poor in this category were treated in the traditional way with an emphasis on discipline.[25] How, one might ask, could willingness to work be assessed? According to a Berlin newspaper, the Welfare Office in Hanover had "developed a special method of its own for determining whether the unemployed on municipal assistance really were willing workers. All men whose willingness to work came

---

23. See in this regard Dinghaus and Korff, "Wohlfahrtspflege," 196ff., 222.

24. Cf. Sachse and Tennstedt, *Armenfürsorge,* 2:151.

25. For social disciplining and its limits in the Weimar Republic using youth welfare as an example see Detlev J. K. Peukert, *Grenzen der Sozialdisziplinierung: Aufstieg und Krise der deutschen Jügendfursorge 1878 bis 1932* (Cologne, 1986).

into question were required every so often to chop wood in the asylum in Büttnerstraße for 1.65 marks per day. If they passed the test, they continued to receive welfare, but if they refused, their benefits were terminated."[26]

Needy people were divided therefore into various categories and treated quite differently by the welfare system in Hanover in the 1920s, as well as in other cities. For those in the lowest category, "the exclusionary methods of classical relief remained in force."[27] The categorization of welfare recipients was an outgrowth of the professionalization of the welfare system.[28] Welfare workers became better educated in the 1920s and developed the confidence to think that they could diagnose the problems of people on social assistance. To this end, welfare workers inspected the homes of beneficiaries and made inquires, not least of all among the neighbors. More than seventy of the reports that they drafted have survived—valuable and rather rare source materials that afford many insights into the living conditions of the poor. The following are a few examples.[29]

The living conditions of Family B. seem very miserable. They have just one small, narrow room and a similar kitchen. The eldest and youngest of the children are usually left all day in two baby carriages, while the middle child plays near the mother in the kitchen. The home appears very untidy, although this is probably due mainly to the lack of space. The air is almost unbearable, partly because of a breeding-cage for birds in the kitchen and partly because of poor ventilation and the three small children. Mrs. B., who is usually busy with the children's washing when we arrive for visits, has her hands full taking care of the small and in one case sickly children. She gets very little help, if any, from her husband. He is away all day. Mrs. B. apparently finds this perfectly acceptable and backs her husband in every way. In fact, though, his reputation in the building is not very good. Apparently, B. earns occasional, indeterminable amounts of money slaughtering animals. He never spends the money on his wife and children but drinks it away in the pub, according to credible people living in the building. Mrs. B. often

---

26. *Tempo,* April 29, 1929, first edition. In addition, there was compulsory labor. The number of people doing compulsory labor in Hanover rose from 118 in December 1929 to 378 in December 1931. Dinghaus and Korff, "Wohlfahrtspflege," 222.

27. Ibid., 195.

28. The training was provided in government-accredited schools.

29. Reports of welfare workers in the city of Hanover: *"Wie leben unsere Wohlfahrtserwerbslosen?" 73 Fürsorgerinnen berichten aus der Stadt Hannover* (Hanover, 1932).

used to accompany him, but has not been seen recently doing so because she is tied down by the smallest child. Very little can be said against the wife at this time because she literally works the whole day, but the husband is not adequately fulfilling his responsibilities toward his wife and children. This, more than unemployment, is the reason for their current sad circumstances. The sickly eldest child is being admitted to Mecklenheide,[30] which should provide some relief for Mrs. B. It is to be hoped that she will be able then to get her work done a little faster so that the two other children can be taken out regularly for some fresh air.

Mrs. B. has recovered fairly well from her last delivery, but the three children followed too closely upon each other. In addition, Mrs. B. is currently being treated as an outpatient at Hospital II,[31] something which I recently urged her to do. She says that her husband is healthy. I have often not been able to meet with him. I was not able to discover how many sick cards and insurance stamps there have been so far because Mrs. B. said that she did not know. Mrs. B. has been advised and urged to send her husband ahead to the appointments with the receipt book, but this has not happened yet. There seem to be some debts to a merchant. Mrs. B. did not have anything more to say about them. It is highly desirable that B. be assigned obligatory work as soon as possible to encourage him to get a regular job. The family will continue to be monitored. Occasional small donations of food and fuel coupons seem appropriate and will be made. There was a visiting card, which will remain in effect.

Another report stated that

K. has been known to us for years as a neat, modest, upstanding man. A visiting card is attached because K. approaches us on his own initiative with wishes and desires. He does not need any further support beyond occasional appropriations of various things. K. has lived in this area for a long time. He shares his room with another lodger. The room can be heated, but K. does not spend very much time there because he has not been given any coal yet at reduced rates. In my view, he should be granted the coal. K. goes to Leinstraße to eat, but would cook more often for himself if he had fuel. This would not be any cheaper, but it would be better for him. K. often has stomach problems and can't eat anything at all.

---

30. The Welfare Office's home for infants and small children.
31. The dermatology hospital in the city.

K. shows great interest in work groups, goes to presentations at the adult education center, and spends his evenings at the YMCA.

So far, K. washes, sews and darns his own things. He has done a pretty good job on his jacket and pants, but his underwear are ghastly. We give him some underwear from this office. . . . We also give him the shoes he needs. I consider him willing to work, but not very good at going out and finding it.

On the basis of this kind of ostensibly scientific analysis and categorization of welfare recipients, families deemed clean and willing to work stood a good chance of continuing to receive state welfare without undue infringement on their human dignity. However, those categorized as dirty, slovenly, and reluctant to work ran the risk of repression and even of being abandoned by society.[32] As the welfare system became more bureaucratic, there was a tendency to regard people who had fallen on difficult times primarily from an economic standpoint. Mignat pointed out in his study that even the many exchanges of letters among Social Democrats in Hanover did not show "any sign of human warmth." Welfare officials acted more like auditors toward the letters they received from the unemployed and treated them more like costs than people.[33]

In Hanover as in other cities, definite attempts were made to reintegrate certain categories of homeless people into society. Immediately after the First World War, *Kriegerheimstätten* were established (i.e., gardening areas were granted) to disabled ex-servicemen, although these gardening areas were created by federal legislation and did not include the really poor. The emergency shelter provided at the same time, for instance in the suburbs of Herrenhausen and Laatzen, met just the most basic of human needs, although it certainly helped to alleviate the suffering immediately after the war.[34] A more far-reaching attempt at reintegration into society can be seen in the establishment of a kindergarten in the railroad car project at Tönniesberg. At least the children were considered worth educating. Finally, plans were laid in 1930–31 to build housing for the "antisocial" in the suburbs of Ober-Ricklingen. This housing was intended for certain families from Tönniesberg that were considered

---

32. Dinghaus and Korff, "Wohlfahrtspflege," 204.

33. Mignat, "Arbeitslosigkeit," 108.

34. See in this regard and in respect to the following Sid Auffarth and Anna Masuch, "Stadtentwicklung in Demokratie und Diktatur," in Historisches Museum Hannover am Hohen Ufer (ed.), *Hannover im 20. Jahrhundert* (Hanover, 1978), 85ff. However, the families who lived here also had to be able to pay something toward the rent and therefore did not number among the poor in the strict sense.

neat, clean, and capable of reintegration into society. Three hundred tiny apartments were supposed to be built, complete with a day nursery and bathing facilities. In the end, though, only some of the housing was built, and the plans for shared-use facilities were canceled. However, the stigmatizing name "Antisocial Housing" stuck. Finally, we should mention the "Bemerode suburban housing estate" built during the Great Depression. Here the unemployed built 250 primitive houses largely with their own hands, using money from the federal government.[35] However, these undertakings were far from sufficient to deal with the problem of homelessness and the housing shortage.

Islands of Poverty

Emergency shelters were distributed more or less all around the city of Hanover, although with some noticeable concentrations in the Calenberger Neustadt area as far as Hanover-Linden. This sort of arrangement was common in Germany at the time and remains so to this day.[36] There was (and is) a big difference, therefore, between the so-called islands of poverty in Germany and the huge slums that arose in cities in the United States and the Third World. There were relatively few buildings in each island of poverty, and the islands were not very noticeable in the city as a whole.

One of these islands of poverty was the "Home for Willing Workers" at 30 Büttnerstraße, where poor drifters could spend the night.[37] The number of poor people wandering around Germany had increased throughout the nineteenth century,[38] and as a more bureaucratic approach was adopted toward caring for the poor, an organization was established especially for these drifters. Anyone who wanted to spend the night in one of the shelters for drifters had to chop wood for a few hours or clean the streets and then continue along a prescribed route to the next working shelter. The Act on Working Shelters for Drifters (*Wanderarbeitsstättengesetz*), passed in Prussia in 1907, established a rigid bureaucracy with

35. Mignat, "Arbeitslosigkeit," 110. The purpose was also to counteract the rapidly rising number of people who began squatting in small garden plots during the Great Depression.

36. This is the result of my own investigation of the 1920s. For an introduction to the Federal Republic see Laszlo A. Vaskovics, *Segregierte Armut: Randgruppenbildung in Notunterkünften* (Frankfurt and New York, 1976).

37. Another example already investigated is Marburg. Hubert Kolling, *Vom "Armenhaus" zur "Wanderarbeitsstätte": Ein Beitrag zur Sozialgeschichte der Stadt Marburg im 19. und 20 Jahrhundert* (Marburg, 1989).

38. The distinction between these people and journeymen learning their trade was vague at times.

a central association, the Gesamtverband Deutscher Verpflegungssta-
tionen bzw. Wanderarbeitsstätten. The people cared for by this association were generally not integrated into the capitalist industrial system,
whether for physical or mental reasons.

The Home for Willing Workers on Büttnerstraße was on the edge of
the city, not far from the Vahrenwald streetcar depot. About 200 people
could spend the night there under a strict set of rules. Infringements led
very quickly to the police being summoned. The home was supported by
the Association against Door-to-Door Begging and Homelessness. There
was another work home for drifters at 3 Goetheplatz. Some seven thousand overnight stays were counted there in 1907–8. A poorhouse could
also be found in Neue Straße. Poor or homeless people who did not have
families and were constantly on the move could also find shelter in a hut
built in 1922 on the grounds of the police station in Hardenbergstraße,
where 60 to 80 people could sleep. In this respect, Hanover was indeed
unique and could consider itself the only big city in Germany "where the
police provided their own social assistance for the homeless."[39] In addition, homeless people were often jailed for the night. In 1930, for example, 349 suffered this fate, and people "volunteered" another ten thousand times to spend the night in police cells.[40]

One institution that was unique to Hanover and controversial even
at the time was the Tönniesberg "housing estate." It stood out from all
the other emergency shelters scattered around the city because it consisted of old railroad cars. Each family was supposed to have an entire
car to itself, although more people were often squeezed in. There were
fifty cars in all, in which 144 families with 263 children were living
by 1930.[41] These "homes" were very narrow, of course; damp, and
crowded, and they stood on a slightly sloping meadow directly behind
the factories in Linden. The Tönniesberg estate looked more like a
camp, therefore, and stood out quite prominently. The visibility of this
social housing was unusual for German cities at the time, which had
undertaken in the nineteenth century to make poverty as imperceptible
as possible. Poorhouses and other kinds of asylums therefore often had
rather handsome facades. The written sources do not say whether there
was a fence around the Tönniesberg estate, but the photographs seem
to show one. In any case, the idea of fencing in the poor was certainly
not foreign to the Hanover police. As early as 1900, the chief of police

---

39. Hanover City Archives, Sozialamt, HR 136. The shelter for the homeless was
closed in 1932–33 and later torn down.

40. *Statistischer Vierteljahresbericht der Stadt Hannover 1932,* 3.

41. Hanover City Archives, Verwaltungsausschuß des Wohnungsamts, April 1930;
see also Dinghaus and Korff, "Wohlfahrtspflege," 213.

had developed a plan to intern "gypsies" (*Roms*) for the duration of their stay in the city on some land on Engelbosteler Allee and enclose it with a fence two meters high. A study was done of how thick and solid the materials would have to be.[42]

The Tönniesberg estate was infamous far beyond Hanover in circles interested in municipal politics. Voices from other cities joined the chorus of demands emanating largely from Social Democrats and Communists in Hanover that the railroad car estate should be dissolved as soon as possible. Emergency housing like this, they said, was no longer acceptable in Germany. Another scandal erupted when a typhus epidemic broke out in Hanover in 1926, raising eyebrows all across the republic. It was ultimately blamed on the municipal authorities, who had not ensured adequate supplies of quality drinking water in all parts of the city.[43]

Families that had long posed social problems lived cheek by jowl at Tönniesberg with others that had been evicted from their homes because of a lost job and thus joined the "new poor" of the times. Although the Housing Office tried sometimes to find adequate apartments for the latter, it had only limited success because rents remained high, despite the subsidies that were available. The inhabitants of the emergency shelters therefore came to regard them increasingly as permanent homes. At least the "rent" was less than even for old apartments.

If the Tönniesberg estate resembled a camp of some kind, other impoverished people lived in real barracks. This was the so-called Welfen Asylum in the former Barracks VI on Welfenplatz in Hanover. The families sent to this shelter were considered unworthy of any of the other municipal shelters, even Tönniesberg. For the most part, they either could not or would not pay the "rent" of 10 RM for one of the railroad cars. As a further deterrent to resorting to the Welfen Asylum, families were torn apart. Only women and children were admitted; husbands and fathers had to go elsewhere. Even in these most miserable categories of the poor and homeless, distinctions were therefore drawn between those families that paid the rent and those that did not. "Insofar as the social image of the inmates and the actual effects on them are

---

42. The plan was carried through. Ines Katenhusen, "'Die Herzader der Stadt.' Die Geschichte der Georgstraße," in Adelheid von Saldern and Sid Auffarth (eds.), *Wochenend und schöner Schein: Freizeit und modernes Leben in den Zwanziger Jahren: Das Beispiel Hannover* (Berlin, 1991), 131–41.

43. Cf. Regina Schramm, "Kommunale Gesundheitspolitik und Sozialhygiene im Hannover der 20er Jahre," in Adelheid von Saldern (ed.), *Stadt und Moderne: Hannover in der Weimarer Republik* (Hamburg, 1989), 117–54.

concerned, the 'Welfen barracks' ranked even below the shack settlements."[44] The barracking of people and tearing apart of "incorrigible" and "dissolute" families were not restricted to Hanover and could be found elsewhere in Germany as well.

In summary, one can say that although the poor and the homeless were relegated to the fringes of society, they were usually not pushed to the outskirts of the city, with the exception of Tönniesberg. Islands of poverty were scattered across the entire city, although they tended to be concentrated more in certain areas than in others, depending on the wealth of the neighborhood. Hanover stood out from other German cities in some regards in its approach to the poor, particularly in the close relations with the police, the tendency to use camps and barracks, and the rigid methods used to test willingness to work. In addition, the municipal bureaucracy was generally disinterested in social policy, with the exception of Schickenberg, who often found his hands tied. Although Hanover had some relatively dark sides, it did make some notable efforts as well, for instance the kindergarten in Tönniesberg, the emergency shacks and shelters, the "Antisocial Housing," and the suburban settlement in Bemerode. The modern welfare state, as implemented in and through the municipalities for the most part, proved to be a two-edged sword. Much more than before the war, strong distinctions were drawn among the beneficiaries: many were helped, but much greater efforts were made to exclude those considered dissolute and antisocial.

It became apparent that neither the federal government nor the municipalities were able to do enough to mitigate the poverty of a substantial proportion of the urban population. The 1920s were a time of poverty and despair for many people, despite the moniker of "the golden twenties." In many cases, these people became either politically radicalized or apathetic, especially the youth, who could not see much hope for the future either for society or themselves.

The effects of the provision of social assistance in a modern, industrial welfare state proved to be (and still are) ambivalent: on the one hand, help was provided, but on the other, this help was accompanied by repression, exclusion, and stigmatization. The social costs and benefits cannot be said to have offset one another because they affected (and affect) different groups of people. The repressive aspects of social assistance were not just vestiges of outdated attitudes, which would eventually disappear, but an integral part of modern social policy. There was

---

44. Dinghaus and Korff, "Wohlfahrtspflege," 217. Its capacity was about 100 to 120 families.

(and is) therefore always a danger of intruding too far and infringing on the inalienable dignity of the individual.

Looking ahead to the Third Reich

Under the Third Reich, the shack settlements in Hanover were largely dissolved. With no remaining constitutional restraints on the use of violence, homelessness could be rendered invisible. The small number of homeless families considered "worthwhile" were provided with housing; little is known about the fate of all the rest.

Policies toward the poor and homeless were soon bound up with plans to cleanse and purify the race. Many so-called racial and social hygienists and politicians with an interest in demographics felt that "cleansing the race" was a rational, modern way to solve social problems once and for all.[45] The fundamental differences between the Weimar Republic and the Third Reich in attitudes toward the poor and homeless were not always adequately understood at the time because various concepts of eugenics had already been circulating in the Weimar Repubic and needed "only" to be further developed. Under the Third Reich, "cleansing" was associated even more strongly "with the idea of health ascribed to it in the medical field."[46] Eugenics assumed a more prominent place in the public discourse in other countries as well, especially in regard to slum clearance. However, the negative influences of eugenics remained very limited in countries with democratic governments. The situation in Germany can only be understood, therefore, if the impact of the "Prerogative State"[47] imposed by the German fascists is adequately appreciated. The "Prerogative State" used its upper hand over the "Normative State" to sterilize so-called incorrigibly antisocial people (especially women) and ship those who did not qualify for the Reich Labor Service (or later the Wehrmacht) to concentration camps or camp settlements.[48] "Antisocial"

---

45. Cf. Detlev J. K. Peukert, *Max Webers Diagnose der Moderne* (Göttingen, 1989).

46. Dirk Schubert, "Gesundung der Städte: Stadtsanierung in Hamburg 1933–1945," in Michael Bose et al. (eds.), ". . . *ein neues Hamburg entsteht . . .*" *Planen und Bauen von 1933 bis 1945* (Hamburg, 1986), 80. Developing a "healthy" (Aryan) race seemed not only conceivable but actually achievable for the first time under a dictatorship. Cleaning up cities and cleaning up the race seemed to be similar aspects of modern planning. It is therefore not surprising that planning of this kind was put on an increasingly "scientific" footing with professionals carrying it out.

47. Ernst Fraenkel, *The Dual State: A Contribution to the Theory of Dictatorship* (New York, 1941).

48. Wolfgang Voigt describes a modern National Socialist camp in Bremen to which "antisocial families" were sent. Wolfgang Voigt, "Wohnhaft: Die Siedlung als panoptisches Gefängnis," *Arch+*, 16, no. 75–76 (1984): 82–89.

people were regarded as *volksschädigend,* or a blight on the German people that needed to be removed. This was not an outburst of premodernity or antimodernity but another face of modernity itself, a face that could lead to dehumanization and barbarism. The slide into barbarism was by no means inevitable or direct and was just one possibility among many. However, it was modernity itself, and especially the intrinsic hubris that everything could be done and controlled, that posed a tremendous temptation not only for National Socialists but also for many people who considered themselves apolitical experts in one field or another. They succumbed to the temptation and left millions of dead in their wake. While modernity was revealing its utmost potential for destruction, all countervailing forces were condemned to impotence through political and ideological dictatorship. Nazi social policy can be seen "as an anti-liberal variant of the modernization process and the outgrowth of a dehumanized variant of the rationalization movement."[49] The care afforded the poor in the Weimar Republic and developments in welfare policies and practices before 1933, especially the differentiated treatment given to various categories of the poor, did not lead directly to the "welfare policy" of the Nazis but did prepare the way to some extent. In the Weimar Republic, certain kinds of poverty were increasingly understood as an illness. Nineteenth-century liberals had tended to view poverty more as a moral question and as one's own fault. By the time of the Weimar Republic, though, criteria such as "curable" or "incurable" were coming to the fore. The modernization of social welfare, that is, the increasingly educational and medical approach taken toward individual cases, led to a greater emphasis on determining who could be cured and who could not. Those deemed "incurable" certainly faced a most difficult future.[50]

---

49. Peukert, *Diagnose de Moderne,* 82.
50. Cf. David F. Crew, *Germans on Welfare: From Weimar to Hitler* (New York and Oxford, 1998); cf. also idem, "Bedürfnisse und Bedürftigkeit: Wohlfahrtsbürokratie und Wohlfahrtsempfänger in der Weimarer Republik 1919–1933," *SOWI* 18, no. 1 (1989): 12–19.

CHAPTER 7

"A Sensation Comes to Naught": Gertrude Polley at the Center of a Discourse

with Karen Heinze and Sybille Küster

Introduction

On April 18, 1929, virtually a full-page article appeared in the *Hannoversche Kurier* under the headline "The Background to a Poster: The Polley Case — a Sensation Comes to Naught." The same day, the *Hannoversche Tageblatt* described an "incident in the Landtag," and one day later an article was published in the *Niederdeutsche Zeitung* under the headline "Accusations against the Housing Office: Incident in the Landtag: Gertrude Polley on Warpath." The day before the story first hit the headlines, an extraordinary disturbance occurred during a session of the Prussian Landtag in Berlin. In the middle of the debate over the budget for education and the arts, a woman from Hanover named Gertrude Polley threw a petition into the chamber from the spectator gallery. Social Democratic deputies picked it up and read it. In her petition, Polley begged the deputies for protection, shelter, and the return of her child, who had been removed from her custody. She tried as well to lower a large red poster into the chamber on a long string but was prevented from doing so at the last minute by guards who hurriedly appeared.

The press reports turned this "incident" into a cause célèbre, in which various organizations cast aspersions on each other, called upon witnesses, defended themselves, and played judge and jury. The municipal agencies, the press, and Gertrude Polley herself soon focused on the issue of who was "right" not just in a legal sense but in a moral sense as well.

Fig. 7.   Gertrude Polley and her son. (From Adelheid von Saldern, *Neues Wohnen in Hannover: Wohnungspolitik und Wohnkultur im Hannover der Weimarer Republik,* 73 [Hanover, 1993].)

In the following, we analyze the various interpretive models that the parties used in their approaches to this incident. The methodology that we employ is based on discourse analysis, which was first developed by literary scholars but has been used increasingly by historians as well. It is used here to investigate the ways in which historical power relationships were formed and represented in the language of institutions and individuals.[1] This methodology is based on the recognition that all source materials — whether Gertrude Polley's poster, newspaper articles, or statements by municipal government officials — say something about the social position and power of the person or institution that produced them. Power relationships are not only reflected but also reinforced or even originally constituted through the discourse. In order to decode the complex significations and their social functions, of which there are many kinds of traces in the discourse, the various levels of meaning in the text have to be tied to the discourses in it that structure and shape reality. This highlights the connections between the text, the discourse, and the social power structures. The "Polley case" serves accordingly to illustrate how existing hierarchies can be legitimized and reinforced through the power of definition and the categorization of people who challenge the social order and its institutions.

The discourse about the Polley case was heavily influenced by contemporary discussions of female virtues, especially motherliness. Close attention should therefore be paid to gendered interpretations that serve to validate hierarchical structures in the relationship between the sexes. Gender is understood here as a social category that is not biologically determined but rather given various contents over the course of time and therefore socially determined.[2] As we shall see, the media played and still play an instrumental role as producers and conveyors of gendered interpretations.

It is impossible to reconstruct Polley's previous life in detail because

---

1. For a basic discussion of the term *discourse* see Michel Foucault, *Ordre du discours, Inaugural Lecture at the Collège de France, December 2, 1970* (Paris, 1972). Here, discourse seems virtually overpowering in its determining materiality, although in later works Foucault discusses more the brokenness, dynamics, and changeability of (dominant) discourses. Idem, *Sexualität und Wahrheit*, vol. 1 (Frankfurt, 1977); vols. 2 and 3 (Frankfurt, 1986); and idem, *Madness and Civilization* (London, 1967). Two works that make excellent use of these insights are Carlo Ginzburg, *The Cheese and the Worms* (Baltimore, 1980); and Natalie Zemon Davis, *The Return of Martin Guerre* (Cambridge, 1983). We would like to thank Carola Lipp and Inge Marßolek for their criticism and encouragement.

2. Joan Scott was one of the first to develop gender as a socially constitutive category. See Joan W. Scott, "Gender: A Useful Category of Historical Analysis," *American Historical Review* 91, no. 5 (1986): 1053–76.

the records of the Housing and Welfare Offices were destroyed, as well as those of the Superior Court of Justice in Berlin and the state hospital in Hildesheim. Furthermore, no sources could be found in Lüneburg, where Polley lived for a while. Personal information and information about her various places of residence could be located only in the Hanover municipal office and in a report in the *Wohlfahrts-Woche,* a weekly published in Hanover by municipal authorites.[3] Some additional information is also available thanks to the interest that Berliners took in this case. The left-liberal daily newspaper *Tempo,* published in the capital by Ullstein Verlag, carried a series of articles about Gertrude Polley that began on April 17, 1929 (the day of the incident in the Landtag). The *Wohlfahrts-Woche* reacted harshly to one of these articles.

As a result of the interest taken by *Tempo,* Gertrude Polley attracted attention outside Hanover and became a cause célèbre in the press. Besides the previously mentioned reports in the middle-class dailies in Hanover — namely, the *Hannoversche Kurier* (sympathetic to the National Liberals and with a circulation of 50,000 to 60,000), the *Niederdeutsche Zeitung* (sympathetic to the German Nationals and with a circulation of around 15,000), and the *Hannoversche Tageblatt* (circulation of about 75,000) — reactions to the mounting conflict were also published in the Guelphic *Hannoversche Landeszeitung,* the *Hannoversche Volkszeitung* (sympathetic to the Center Party), and the independent *Hannoversche Anzeiger* (circulation 126,000).[4] It is striking that the Social Democratic *Volkswille* did not mention the Gertrude Polley case at all. The editors apparently did not find it a suitable platform from which to launch their criticisms of housing and social policies in Hanover. The Communist *Neue Arbeiter-Zeitung* reported only very briefly on Gertrude Polley, mentioning just the incident in the Landtag. The report did not say anything about her alleged hereditary problems or way of life and therefore aroused sympathy for her. It concluded with the following remark: "This is only one example of the scandalous housing policies of the Hanover City Council."[5] The *Neue Arbeiter-Zeitung* failed to keep its promise to explore the matter at a later time, apparently because the KPD felt that Polley did not provide good enough ammunition with which to attack the city authorities. The discourse over Polley was therefore confined primarily to the middle-class

3. We would like to thank the Hanover Registration Office and especially Mr. Rohde and his co-workers for their help.

4. The circulation of some newspapers is not known. For the others see Historisches Museum Hannover am Hohen Ufer (ed.), *Hannover 1933: Eine Großstadt wird nationalsozialistisch* (Hanover, 1981).

5. *Neue Arbeiter-Zeitung,* April 19, 1929.

newspapers and the *Wohlfahrts-Woche,* which was published by a municipal agency. Since two of the Hanover newspapers published word-for-
word transcripts, we have the complete text of her petition, which appears to be identical to the poster, as well as some additional comments
that she made. However, we do not have her other petitions and applica-
tions, apart from a few excerpts.

The Background to a Poster: Biographical Notes

Gertrude Polley's action in the Prussian Landtag was only the climax of
a nine-year battle with municipal government agencies in both Hanover
and Berlin.[6] She was born in 1887, married Adolf Polley, a factory
foreman, and came from Ortelsburg in East Prussia. She fled to Hanover in 1914 at the beginning of the First World War and moved very
often over the next few years. She moved seven times during just the
four years of the war. At first she received war relief, but then she
earned her own living from 1916 to 1918 as the "agent" of a bar li-
censee in the building that housed the Striel Orphanage at 4 Goseriede
Straße, often allegedly appearing drunk. When her husband returned
from the war in late 1918, he insisted that she give up this kind of job.
She did so, but he returned to Ortelsburg soon thereafter, while she
remained in Hanover.

At first Gertrude Polley received poor relief, but then she opened
an inn in Kohlrauschstraße, acting once again as an "agent." However,
the inn did not survive very long, and Polley then lived for a while with
her parents and brothers in emergency municipal accommodations in a
former army barracks. Through ways and means that cannot be clarified, she ended up a little later with a dilapidated, eleven-room house at
24 Sandstraße. Her father was entered in the land registry as the owner
of the house (allegedly only because of her impending divorce proceedings), and a down payment of four thousand marks was made on a

---

6. Unfortunately, some rather interesting questions cannot be answered because of
information that the media chose not to report. Our account of the Polley case is based
largely on the report in the *Wohlfahrts-Woche* of May 19, 1929, and on some information in
the files of the Hanover municipal office. Not all the references to these sources are
footnoted. The information in most of the Hanover press sounds very similar, although
sometimes it appeared in much shortened form. The newspapers differed in the amount
of information they provided. For the most part, we disregarded the articles in the
Hannoversches Tageblatt, Hannoversche Volkszeitung, and *Hannoversche Landeszeitung*
because they tended just to paraphrase or repeat in shortened form the longer articles in
the *Hannoverscher Kurier* and the *Niederdeutsche Zeitung.* It seems likely that all the
articles were based on a single informant, probably someone in the City of Hanover Press
Office, because much of the wording is identical.

purchase price of fourteen thousand marks. Gertrude Polley moved into this house on January 1, 1920, and opened a detective agency, but it too failed to do very well.[7]

Soon there was trouble at 24 Sandstraße with a tenant named Mrs. H., who allegedly reneged on the rent while her husband was in prison. Polley sought a notice of eviction and eventually succeeded in having it enforced by the courts. She was then assigned a compulsory tenant by the Housing Office, but she fought the assignment in court because the new tenant was said to be aggressive and violent. According to the *Wohlfahrts-Woche,* this tenant never moved into 24 Sandstraße because the eviction of Mrs. H. and her two-year-old child was postponed until January 1921. However, in December 1920, Polley's father and brother tore the windows and doors out of Mrs. H.'s apartment in an attempt to force her to leave. She still refused to go, and at this point Polley herself left. On April 1, 1921, the gardener "W." moved into Polley's apartment, after having purchased the building for twenty-five thousand marks and providing a down payment of five thousand marks. However, he then canceled the agreement because of the dilapidated condition of the building. A few months later, Polley's father sold it for thirty-three thousand marks to a prostitute, who would land in a workhouse in a few years. Polley lost all her assets at this time in ways that cannot be clarified[8] and was henceforth penniless and homeless.

At the same time, Gertrude Polley's family situation changed dramatically, according to the *Wohlfahrts-Woche* of May 19, 1929. The Allenstein District Court granted her husband a divorce in June 1921, and she was held the guilty party on the grounds of adultery. She then bore a son named Erwin on April 4, 1922. Her ex-husband did not officially deny being the father but was not bound in any case to provide child support. The natural father was alleged to be a wealthy merchant, who paid Polley a settlement that enabled her to give birth in a private, first-class maternity center. However, Polley was now a single mother, and her economic and social situation deteriorated. She lived with Erwin in her father's house and went on welfare in October 1922. In early 1923, Polley took to the road again, while Erwin stayed with his grandparents. She then returned to Hanover, quarreled with her parents in March 1923, and moved with Erwin to her sister's home, where she slept in a dark storeroom. She moved twice with her son to Kassel for short periods, where she lived with a new fiancé at his sister's place. When he apparently suffered an attack of delirium and acted terribly in front of

---

7. For another version see *Tempo.*
8. Gertrude Polley blamed her father in part and the authorities in part.

Polley and her child, she moved in with his mother. Her fiancé allegedly staged some horrible scenes here as well, and in any event, her bed was bug ridden.

According to the *Wohlfahrts-Woche* of May 19, 1929, Polley returned to Hanover, where she lived in cheap hotels and left her son with foster parents. At times she earned a living as a domestic in a "house of ill repute" in Lüneburg. She was suspected of prostitution and in 1923 was sentenced to prison for two weeks by the jury court in Lüneburg. In May 1924, official notification was received that she was leaving Hanover. She traveled back to East Prussia by way of Berlin. Her son, Erwin, was taken to a children's sanitarium in early June 1924, and then his grandparents took him in again. At this point, Polley's former husband was apparently supposed to be compelled to contribute to the costs of child care. Soon thereafter, Polley returned to Hanover and sought accommodations, which the Housing Office provided in late November 1924 in a former epidemic shelter at 92 Bischofsholer Damm, which had been converted into emergency housing. In December 1925, Erwin entered the city's Mecklenheide children's home because of anemia and was then hospitalized for three months. He was subsequently taken to his aunt's home.

When Gertrude Polley refused to pay the fee for her emergency accommodations, she was forced to move again and beginning on June 8, 1926, had to make do in an even worse public shelter. She was assigned to what the *Hannoversche Kurier* called the "well-maintained railway car settlement" at Tönniesberg but which she considered a "horrible cattle-car settlement." She had further run-ins with Housing Office officials. She was accused of insulting civil servants and sentenced to four weeks in jail. She proved rebellious on other occasions as well. Housing Office officials once had to call the police, apparently, to have her "removed from the building because she was calling people names like 'beast' and 'monstrosity.'"[9] All the while she and her child were reliant on the assistance of the Welfare Office.

Erwin shuttled back and forth between Tönniesberg and his grandparents' apartment. When the grandparents made more and more problems for the welfare inspectors, the Hanover Youth Welfare Department applied to the district court in Neukölln (Berlin) to have Polley deprived of the custody of her child on the basis of Section 1666 of the Bürgerliches Gesetzbuch. The district court ruled on August 18, 1927, that both Gertrude Polley and her former husband should be stripped of custody, at least temporarily. Gertrude Polley protested but was

---

9. *Hannoverscher Kurier,* April 18, 1929.

turned down by the Berlin 2 District Court on November 29, 1927. The Hanover Youth Welfare Department took custody of six-year-old Erwin and on March 5, 1928, placed him in the city's Kleefeld Youth Home at 13 Kirchröderstraße. The newspapers cited a variety of reasons for this fateful decision. The *Hannoversche Anzeiger* pointed to the domestic lives of Gertrude Polley and her parents and said that the constant quarreling had become intolerable and the child was in physical and spiritual danger.[10] The *Niederdeutsche Zeitung* claimed that Erwin was suffering from physical and moral neglect.[11] However, *Tempo* in Berlin maintained that he was sent to the youth home because his mother was hospitalized.

Erwin Polley eventually fell extremely ill, and the Youth Welfare Department released him for Easter Sunday, April 7, 1928, at the wish of his mother, who "had now found accommodations with her father and sister."[12] However, Gertrude Polley did not return her son to the home for youth and took him with her to Berlin. Here, for the first time in almost ten years, she got a job. She was employed in the housekeeping department of the Lichtenrade sanitarium.[13] Erwin was placed in private care. However, Gertrude lost her job after only four weeks when she fell ill and was admitted to the Pankow hospital. Her son, who also became sick, entered the Buch Children's Hospital. Gertrude left the hospital in October 1928, but her son, who had already been taken into custody by the welfare authorities in Berlin in July 1928, was sent to the orphanage on Alte Jacobistraße, at the urging of the authorities in Hanover. He was then sent to the Heinersdorf home for juvenile delinquents and children on welfare. Gertrude Polley resisted this decision as well. "The child was subsequently sent back to the orphanage, but since 'no foster home could be found,' was returned to Heinersdorf,"[14] where he could still be found at the time of the incident in the Landtag. On February 2, 1929, the Neukölln district court deprived Polley of custody for good.

Polley's life to that point had been a regular odyssey from one city to the next, with serial accommodations in cheap hotels, private homes, emergency shelters, and hospitals. She had other people in her life, and her individual story was also the history of a dysfunctional family. Her personal crises and frail physical and mental state — she herself said that she suffered from a serious nervous disorder — led constantly to situations

10. *Hannoverscher Anzeiger,* April 19, 1929.
11. *Niederdeutsche Zeitung,* April 19, 1929.
12. *Tempo,* April 17, 1929, first edition; *Hannoverscher Anzeiger,* April 19, 1929.
13. Gertrude Polley's motivations for moving to Berlin are not clear. According to *Tempo,* she "fled" to Berlin because she was persecuted by officials in Hanover.
14. *Tempo,* April 17, 1929.

in which municipal agencies in Hanover and Berlin felt obliged to intervene. Her child suffered especially severely. He changed homes constantly as he was shunted back and forth between his mother, aunt, and grandparents, as well as foster parents, hospitals, and youth homes. It is hardly surprising that Erwin was sickly.

Polley was in a daunting social and financial situation by 1928. She faced incalculable perils and hazards as a single parent with a criminal record who had been found the guilty party in divorce proceedings. She did not benefit from the relative stability of the Weimar Republic between 1924 and 1928–29, and her living conditions actually deteriorated. The assistance from her family was evidently insufficient to stabilize her circumstances. Despite this assistance, there was also much quarreling and even violence in the family. The mutual reproaches were endless. According to the May 19, 1929, edition of *Wohlfahrts-Woche,* Polley's sister maintained that their father had defrauded the state over war injuries and their brother had looted during the war and later stolen from his employer. The latter allegation was confirmed by Gertrude Polley as well. The brother thereupon took successful legal action against his sisters. He alleged in turn that Gertrude was unwilling to work, sustained herself in dubious ways, and was best sent to a workhouse. Their father, in his view, belonged in an insane asylum because he had smashed a large hole in his son's head with a hammer. The mother too was not spared. According to Gertrude Polley, she had committed adultery with her brother-in-law and then attempted to induce him to carry out a murder. She had also encouraged Gertrude's brother to murder her sister. According to the *Wohlfahrts-Woche,* the mother had also reported Gertrude to the police for incest with her father, while her father had reported Gertrude for having an abortion. The family seemed to live together only because forced by circumstances to do so. A welfare worker described the situation as follows in a report written in January 1928: "Father S. and Gertrude Polley live together in two rooms in the apartment and have the child with them. Mother S. lives with the son in the room they use as a store and in the cellar, where they took their beds because Gertrude Polley removed them at one point. They hit each other with coal shovels, throw water at each other, and so forth." Even if only half these stories are true, it is remarkable that the "family" continued to get back together so often, as the *Wohlfahrts-Woche* itself noted.

Similar problems existed in Gertrude Polley's friendships, especially with her "fiancé" in Kassel. This liaison apparently failed to improve Polley's life and if anything made it worse. There is also no sign of a mutually supportive neighborhood, which could have helped with child care while Gertrude worked outside the home. Her social isolation can be seen in her repeated efforts to find a place that could take care of her son. Polley apparently attempted to break out of her isolation and position as an outsider by cultivating contacts with Communist deputies. She was even described as an "enthusiastic co-worker" of the Communist Arbeiterzeitung in Hanover.[15]

Polley could not expect ever to regain custody of her son because the Youth Welfare Department regarded her with particular suspicion as a welfare recipient with a criminal record. She looked, for her part, with very mixed feelings on the agencies with which she dealt. She was dependent on welfare as a single mother but also felt victimized by the authorities. It was they, after all, who had deprived her of her son, and the Housing Office had attempted to force her to accept particular tenants when she did have a home. Later, however, the circumstances were reversed, and the same office found emergency shelter for her when she became poor and homeless. When she had run-ins with the Housing Office, it was supported by various other municipal institutions, including the Welfare Office, with its obtrusive social workers; the Youth Welfare Department; the municipal youth home, the courts; and finally the jail. In Polley's eyes, the various municipal agencies and institutions all merged into a single entity, "the authorities." They would wreak revenge, she feared, and bring down untold suffering and misfortune upon her. The "authorities" appeared endowed with great power, and she sought desperately to defend herself.

Polley resorted to various means in her struggle with the authorities. According to the *Wohlfahrts-Woche* of May 19, 1929, she showered various department heads and public figures with letters and complaints, including the Prussian minister of welfare, the county manager for Hanover, and the mayor of the city of Hanover. She allegedly wrote nearly three hundred pages over the years. In her letters, Polley sprayed invective at the officials, decrying them as "criminals" and "idiots," and tried to take advantage of the traditional hard feelings between Prussia and the former Kingdom of Hanover. When in Berlin in 1926, she said that she wanted to use "printed posters to publicly disgrace those Prussian haters, the Hanover municipal executive."[16] She also tried to have criminal charges laid. In January 1927, she charged a department head in the Housing Office with assault and the director with physical coercion and

---

15. *Niederdeutsche Zeitung,* April 19, 1929. It is impossible to determine whether Gertrude Polley actually worked for the Communist newspaper at the time. It did not do very much to support her in her struggle with the authorities, despite a brief initial mention, and therefore does not seem to have had close contacts with her.

16. In *Wohlfahrts-Woche,* May 19, 1929.

trespass. However, this backfired when she, not the officials, was sentenced to six weeks in prison. The sentence was reduced on appeal to four weeks and then appealed again on a point of law. In a letter of November 1, 1926, to the Hanover municipal executive, she demanded compensation of thirty-six thousand marks for the injustice done to her and her child.[17]

In her struggle with the authorities, Polley also attempted to exploit to the hilt all the opportunities afforded by the Weimar welfare state. She went to see officials repeatedly. From the Welfare Office, she demanded higher support payments, various medical specialists, baths, and massages. In order to circumvent the requirements, she resorted to what the authorities called "boundless exaggerations of her illnesses," for instance, when she was told that she had to work.[18] Finally she turned to the public. On March 5, 1929, the day when her son was forcibly removed to the Kleefeld Youth Home, Polley tried to deliver a speech from the public gallery of the Hanover municipal councils during the budget debate. When this demonstration failed, she began planning the petition that she dropped on the Prussian Landtag. "After a terrible inner struggle, I have decided to go public."[19]

"Obvious Crimes of the Authorities"

Polley's petition drew the attention of the Prussian Landtag to the alleged failings of municipal agencies and to the painful gap between her entitlements under the welfare state and what the bureaucracy actually provided. She hoped that if the democratically elected legislature, or at least some deputies, intervened on her behalf, her claims would be greatly strengthened. She stated:

> I appeal hereby to the hearts of all the deputies and request protection for me and my child against the obvious crimes of the authorities. Through my nine-year struggle for a home and vain complaints to parliament and ministers, I have brought down upon myself the vengeance of the authorities in Hanover, thanks to whom in 1920 I lost my house, abode and property in Sandstraße in a perversion of justice in an eviction case. As a result of my temporary stay in 1924 in the epidemic ward (previously called Bult barracks) of a former isolation hospital at 92 Bischofsholer Damm, and after the Housing Office forcibly removed me to a

17. Ibid.
18. Ibid.
19. Ibid.

quasi cattle car in that horrible cattle-car settlement of Tönnies-berg, the Hanover Housing Office seized the opportunity to make accusations over my nine-year struggle for a place to stay and had me sentenced to four weeks in prison. Similarly, the Youth Welfare Department tore my beloved only child from me at the age of six. I did nothing wrong in his upbringing, but it committed crimes against the child. The Youth Welfare Department on Danziger Straße is dragging him now as a hostage and prisoner from one institution to the next in Berlin. He is already wasting away and is seriously ill. After my nine-year struggle, I beg you for protection and for a home for me and my child so that we are finally free from the crimes of the authorites. I beg on behalf of my unhappy child. I beg for some compensation for the damage to my health and finances in nine years of homelessness. I beg for protection for me and my child against further crimes.

Respectfully yours, Mrs. Gertrude Polley of Hanover.

In her petition, Polley made an emotional appeal first "to the hearts" of the deputies and to their sense of honor as men that they should help a persecuted mother begging for protection for herself and her "unhappy child." She said that she was a victim of the "vengeance of the authorities," in particular the Housing Office. As a result of its unjust interference ("a perversion of justice"), she was no longer a homeowner and found herself in need of housing. Polley behaved as if she had a right to housing. Perhaps she understood the Weimar constitution in this way. The constitution stated in Article 155: "The distribution and use of land are supervised by the state in such a way as to prevent abuses and pursue the goal of providing every German with healthy housing and every German family, especially those with many children, with a place to live and work that meets their needs." But did this article apply to her? She was "German" no doubt, but the German text used the masculine form of the word, and she was a woman. Did this make a difference? Did male linguistic forms really include women, as generally maintained? Furthermore, Polley was a single mother. Did she and her son constitute a family? She certainly did not have "many children." In any event, Polley could not claim that she was legally entitled to housing on the basis of the Weimar constitution, as the *Wohlfahrts-Woche* of May 19, 1929, made perfectly clear in its comments on the "Polley case." "Nobody in Germany," said the journal, "has a right to housing." According to it, Polley was not even entitled to be on the priority list because her father had said that she could always live with him and had put two rooms at her disposal. "Only when she submitted a statement from the district attorney to the effect that her parents and brother had reported her to the police more than ten times — a sign of the enormous hostility in which they lived — did the Housing Office grant Mrs. Polley priority for a kitchen-living room and a bedroom. Finding such a place was naturally *her* responsibility." As shown by the reports on the actual practices followed in the distribution of housing, Polley had virtually no chance of finding an apartment on her own.

Like many other people, she landed in a municipal emergency shelter. She thought that it was "completely overrun and infested with vermin" and that, as a "former epidemic shelter," it was far from "healthy housing." Polley transferred her anger over the conditions to the authorities. In her view, they were engaged in a kind of criminal conspiracy, committing crimes, bending the law, seeking revenge, and violently punishing any resistance. In this context, a child could be seen as a hostage, dragged away and held captive. Polley did not confine herself to an appeal for shelter and included a demand for financial compensation as well. A monetary award would have not only rescued her from her economic plight but also would have been of great symbolic value for her. She wanted symbolic punishment for the injustice that she had suffered and official acknowledgment of the legitimacy of her accusations.

Gertrude Polley portrayed herself as the innocent victim of despotic officials. Her actions and the text of her petition attested to her unbroken determination to defend herself. She mentioned three times in the relatively short text on the poster that the struggle had continued for nine years. She thought that her tenacity was the reason why the authorities were determined to seek revenge, and she regarded her dramatic action in the spectators' gallery as only the logical consequence of the failure of more orthodox methods.

The *Hannoversche Kurier* gave Gertrude Polley a broad hearing and, in addition to her poster text, printed other statements detailing her accusations against various youth welfare departments. She angrily described the conditions in the orphanage in which her son lived as no better than in the "Wild West." Her son had lost "a terrible amount of weight," and his bones were "underdeveloped." He had been "badly beaten about the head" and had "an abscess of the middle ear." The orphanage had not only disregarded its duty to care for his physical needs but had also committed moral offenses. "Young boys must bathe together with adults in one room without any supervision; this is an overt offense against morality and modesty. What does the article of the law on trashy literature say about this? The children are defenseless and exposed in their nudity to severe abuse from the adults. Despite his run-down condition, my little son, who is seven years old now, was beaten with brushes by adults in the bathroom."[20] As evidence that her accusations were not pure invention, she described another case in which a child was so badly beaten that it had to be taken to a hospital in serious condition. According to Polley, there was systematic neglect of the children, and the abuse of her son was no exception.

Polley couched her complaints in legal language and referred explicitly to particular articles in the legislation. Her accusations could easily be translated into criminal charges, for instance the alleged failure to fulfill the duty of care toward the children in regard to their clothing and food, the moral offenses, the child abuse, and the failure to intervene and prevent these crimes. In her view, these infractions should have compelled the legal system to take action. Did the Juvenile Welfare Act of 1922 not promise that "all German children have a right to be raised in such a way that they are physically, spiritually, and socially sound"?[21] And did the "care" provided to her son, who had been removed from her custody, not infringe on the constitutionally guaranteed protection of youth in Article 122 against "moral, mental or physical neglect"? The "Polley case" highlighted the inconsistencies between the claim of the Weimar Republic to be a welfare state and actual practices in many cases.[22]

Article 119 of the Weimar constitution described the "preservation of cleanliness and health and the social advancement of the family" as duties of the state. However, the implementation of this article was left largely to the municipalities, as was social policy in general. Under the Reich Regulations on the Duty of Care (RFV) from 1924 and the Reich Principles on the Conditions, Type, and Amount of Public Welfare from 1923, responsibility for public welfare fell to district agencies in the cities and rural areas.[23] Local authorities therefore had broad legal scope to implement social programs, but they lacked financial resources.[24] The

---

20. *Hannoverscher Kurier,* April 18, 1929.

21. A critical view can also be taken of the first article of the Juvenile Welfare Act. Although appearing to concentrate on the personal development of children, it required an upbringing that would produce "sound" youth as socially defined. Detlev J. K. Peukert, *Die Weimarer Republik: Krisenjahre der klassischen Moderne* (Göttingen, 1987).

22. Ibid., 221.

23. Regina Schramm, "Kommunale Gesundheitspolitik und Sozialhygiene im Hannover der 20er Jahre," in Adelheid von Saldern (ed.), *Stadt und Moderne: Hannover in der Weimarer Republik* (Hamburg, 1989), 122ff.

24. Adelheid von Saldern, "Kommunaler Handlungsspielraum in der Wohnungspolitik während der Zeit der Weimarer Republik," in Christian Kopetzki et al. (eds.), *Stadterneuerung in der Weimarer Republik und im Nationalsozialismus* (Kassel, 1987), 239–56.

already excessive demands on municipalities were further aggravated by the various crises through which the republic passed before 1924 and, even more devastatingly, after 1929. During these periods of crisis in particular, entire population groups were socially marginalized. Unemployment and homelessness often went hand in hand.[25]

Social programs failed to live up to the progressive ideals of the constitution not only because of insufficient financial resources but also because of the conservative attitudes and behavior that often characterized the civil service machinery. What purposes were social programs supposed to serve? Should people receive benefits who were at fault for straying from the path of middle-class rectitude? If so, in the minds of most officials, then only in conjunction with some supervision of their lives. Some control had to be exercised over the affairs of marginal groups and people who had come down in the world.

Gertrude Polley: "The Taming of the Shrew" in Public Discourse

By infringing on the decorum of the Landtag, Gertrude Polley ended the anonymity in which most welfare recipients lived and attracted not only the passing attention of the deputies but also the interest of the public. The following is a list of the press articles devoted to her in 1929.

> April 17: *Tempo:* "A Mother's Cry for Help: Robbed of Her Child by the Housing Office: A Shocking Tragedy" (on the same day when Polley went to the visitors' gallery)
> April 18: *Hannoverscher Kurier:* "Background to a Poster: The Polley Case — a Sensation Comes to Naught"
> *Hannoversches Tageblatt:* "An Incident in the Landtag: A Visitor in the Gallery from Hanover Throws a Petition into the Chamber and Accuses Hanover Officials"
> *Tempo:* "A Mother's Cry for Help" (with photo).
> *Hannoversche Volkszeitung:* "Incident in the Landtag: A Visitor in the Gallery from Hanover"

---

25. The contradiction between the far-reaching aims of social policy and the need to back away from them in times of economic crisis was symptomatic not only of the Weimar welfare state but of the modern welfare state in general. Cf. Detlev J. K. Peukert, *Die Weimarer Republik: Krisenjahre der klassischen Moderne* (Göttingen, 1987). A more detailed description of welfare practices in Hanover can be found in Angela Dinghaus and Bettina Korff, "Wohlfahrtspflege im Hannover der 20er Jahre: Kontinuitätslinien repressiver Armenpflege und sozialer Disziplinierung," in Adelheid von Saldern (ed.), *Stadt und Moderne: Hannover in der Weimarer Republik* (Hamburg, 1989), 189–223.

April 19: *Niederdeutsche Zetung:* "Accusations against the Housing
  Office in Landtag Incident: Unfounded Attacks on the Local
  Housing Office by Mentally Deficient Woman"
Neue Arbeiter-Zeitung: "Hanover's Housing Policy Attacked in
  Prussian Landtag"
Hannoversche Landeszeitung: "A Mother Looks for Her Child:
  Incident in Prussian Parliament: A Petition for the Deputies"
April 24: *Tempo:* "Erwin Polley" (with photo)
April 27: *Tempo:* "How Officials Fight Back against Mrs. Polley:
  The Ugly Casting of Moral Suspicion"
April 29: *Tempo:* "The Cry for Help from the Cities"
May 1: *Wohlfahrts-Woche:* "Smut and Trash"
June 9: *Wohlfahrts-Woche:* "Temperate 'Tempo'"

The press coverage casts further light on the Polley case. The Berlin
daily *Tempo* published its first article on April 17, 1929, the day of the
incident in the Landtag. According to the editor in chief, his attention
was drawn to Polley's previously futile struggle by an open letter. "At
that time, letters were sent out to all newspapers and deputies, the final
cry for help from a mother fighting for her child."[26] This can only mean
that Polley had prepared her action well and was attempting not only to
gain the help of some deputies but, most important, to arouse public
opinion.

Despite their contrasting political sympathies and publishing methods, all the press organs that took an interest in Polley's action in the
Landtag placed it in the context of her ongoing struggles with the bureaucracy. However, they differed in their judgments of who was the victim
and who was truly responsible for the situation. The Hanover publications based their articles on the files, records, and comments of the
municipal agencies and the courts that had dealt with Polley. They did not
conduct any independent investigations and tended to compare Polley's
version of events to the supposedly "objective" official record. The
Hannoversche Tageblatt and *Niederdeutsche Zeitung* set out explicitly to
reveal "what sort of a person this woman is" by reporting various inci-
dents culled from the records of Polley's conflicts with the authorities
over nine years.[27] Polley's accusations against the Housing Office were
mentioned only in passing and in reference to the lack of any further
information. Polley had not lost her house because of any perversion of
justice but "for some reason or other." The doubt cast on Polley's version

---

26. *Tempo,* April 17, 1929.
27. Here and for the following see *Niederdeutsche Zeitung,* April 19, 1929.

of events can be seen as well in the comment "whether she bought a house here [in Hanover] . . . is not known." The editors could not find any information about the house on Sandstraße and implied therefore that Polley could not possibly have been evicted from it. Instead, she had been evicted from the former isolation hospital because she had "constantly failed to pay the low shelter fee." The *Niederdeutsche Zeitung* claimed that these accommodations were not "vermin infested," as Polley had alleged, but "properly maintained."

The *Hannoversche Kurier* took a similar tack.[28] First, it pointed out a contradiction between Polley's statement on the poster and an earlier statement that she had made. Then it described her character on the basis of information obtained from the various municipal agencies involved. The heading "Background to a Poster" did not herald any independent investigation into conditions in the orphanage but rather information about Polley's former "immoral" lifestyle and unreasonable behavior toward the authorities. The reports in the three Hanover dailies aimed generally to discredit Polley's accusations by portraying her as untrustworthy. The *Hannoversche Kurier* delved even less than the *Niederdeutsche Zeitung* into Polley's accusations, but it did absolve her to some extent of responsibility for her actions. Although she was certainly "somewhat hysterical by nature," most of the blame lay with the miserable times. The confusion sown by the war and postwar society had made Polley unable to "reconcile herself mentally to what is possible and just and voluntarily submit to it." The association in the daily between Polley's individual plight and the overall political and economic circumstances culminated in the far-fetched claim that only a peace treaty (with the Entente powers) could improve the situation. Complex issues were thereby simplified and reduced to the question of reparations. A direct relationship was established between reparations and social problems under the assumption "no payments—no misery."

Only the Berlin daily *Tempo,* the "Newspaper of the Times," sided with Gertrude Polley and attempted to view the situation from another angle, as shown by headings such as "A Mother's Cry for Help," "How Officials Fight Back against Mrs. Polley," and "Robbed of Her Child by the Housing Office." *Tempo* seemed interested most of all in "portraying a life whose course has been set by conflicts with the Housing Office."[29] The Housing Office was seen as the source of all the events, including the loss of child custody. The editor in chief in Berlin criticized the way in which the Hanover newspapers were handling the case, alleging that

28. Here and for the following see *Hannoverscher Kurier,* April 18, 1929.

29. *Tempo,* April 17, 1929, first edition; *Tempo,* April 27, 1929, first edition; *Wohlfahrts-Woche,* June 9, 1929.

they were prejudicing their readers against Polley. He claimed that, in contrast to his colleagues in Hanover, he was acting in accordance with the principles of objective journalism, and he even wrote letters to the Press Office of the city of Hanover defending his portrayal of the case. In contrast to the newspapers in Hanover, *Tempo* was a tabloid aimed at attracting a broad spectrum of big city readers. It was accordingly far from unbiased, and its articles appealed heavily to the emotions in order to generate sympathy for Polley. One headline screamed: "Shattering Life Tragedy."[30] In accordance with Polley's own accounts of her life, the paper portrayed her as an innocent victim persecuted by the bureaucracy. The difference in the use of photographs is also noteworthy. On two occasions, *Tempo* published photographs of Polley and her son and took advantage of the opportunity to remind its readers of the scandal surrounding her. In an age of magazines and "moving pictures," no tabloid could do without photographs any more, and in this case, they were used quite consciously to maintain the readers' interest in the story of Gertrude Polley.

The attacks in the Berlin press did not go unheard or unanswered in Hanover. Officials defended themselves in the *Wohlfahrts-Woche,* questioning the objectivity of *Tempo* itself and denouncing its "fraudulent distortions." The editor in chief had allegedly asked questions out of context, thus making it clear "that he was interested only in spreading explosive materials around."[31] *Tempo* was using the story to increase its own profits. The Berlin tabloid was also indirectly taken to task by the *Hannoversche Kurier,* which claimed that it wanted to avoid "sensationalizing" the story and regretted that a child was the subject of "garish posters and sensational articles." The Hanover dailies therefore upheld the values of their middle-class readers, although with slightly different emphases, while *Tempo* was far enough removed from the bureaucracy in Hanover to seize upon Polley's accusations and portray what had happened to her as an exemplary case of injustice.

"Mrs. Polley on the Warpath"

We shall turn now to the kinds of explanations that the newspapers provided of the incident in the Landtag and the methods that they used to support or undermine the legitimacy of Gertrude Polley's demands. The *Hannoversche Kurier* explained in the very first lines of its commentary why it was quoting Polley in detail: "We would certainly not repeat this

30. *Tempo,* April 17, 1929, first edition.
31. *Wohlfahrts-Woche,* June 9, 1929.

rather unpleasant description [of conditions in the Berlin orphanage], out of sheer sensationalism for instance, if it did not clearly contradict what Gertrude Polley once said about Berlin when she was trying to turn the treatment that she received there against Hanover. After indulging in a vile 'barrage of abuse' against the 'murderers' in Hanover, as the report stated, she said that her treatment in Berlin was lovely in contrast and officials had virtually fought for the honor of serving her."[32] The implication to the readers was that there was no further need to investigate her accusations. Quotations were used primarily to prove Polley's dishonesty. The contradictions in her statements — at times praising the conditions in Berlin and at times condemning them — were taken as evidence that she tailored whatever she said to particular audiences in order to derive the greatest advantage. By highlighting her self-contradictions, the *Kurier* attacked Polley for her ability to act in situation-specific ways. The newspaper went on to remark laconically: "It is strange that everybody seems to be repaid with a lack of gratitude."[33] What seemed so unusual to the editors was Polley's presumptuousness and lack of obsequiousness and gratitude. "Appropriate behavior" would have been subordination, supplication, thankfulness, and respect for authority. It was completely "inappropriate," on the other hand, for Polley to question authority, instruct officials in their duties, portray herself as competent in questions of constitutional rights, act as a claimant, and insult people when her pride was hurt or she felt that an injustice had been done.

The *Niederdeutsche Zeitung,* for its part, looked even more deeply into Polley's "career with agencies" prior to the incident in the Landtag. It pointed out that she had been fighting for years with not only one agency but a number that had been involved in her case. "Mrs. Gertrude Polley has already proved a handful for the authorities. There are a multitude of files about her in all sorts of agencies and courts."[34] Although no precise information was added, the reference to the courts left the impression that Polley was criminally inclined. The *Niederdeutsche Zeitung* also attempted to explode the notion that Polley's action in the Landtag was an extraordinary deed on the part of a desperate woman by carrying a report that she had "already attempted a similar maneuver in Hanover."[35]

The impression was thus given that Gertrude Polley was a perpetual complainer and crank, an idea reinforced by the statement that she had quarreled "with all the authorities in the world." The polemics of the

---

32. *Hannoverscher Kurier,* April 18, 1929.
33. Ibid.
34. Here and for the following see *Niederdeutsche Zeitung,* April 19, 1929.
35. *Niederdeutsche Zeitung,* April 19, 1929.

Hanover newspapers made Polley look like some kind of savage on the "warpath" in her struggle for her child and housing. Finally, she was made to look silly as well. Gertrude Polley, "who wants to set herself up as judge over all of us in Germany," should not "appeal immediately to the League of Nations because of a difference of opinion about whether some furniture was damaged or not."[36]

Not only did Gertrude Polley disregard all that is "possible and just"[37] in her choice of methods, but her demands on the Welfare Office were wildly exaggerated, in the eyes of the Hanover newspapers. They reported that she had once told it that she was starving and desperate for help but the social worker who was sent out to check the situation found "the whole family gathered happily around the table, enjoying coffee and cake."[38] They reported further that Polley "wore very elegant clothes and often frequented cafés" and thus clearly indicated that her lifestyle was not in keeping with her alleged circumstances. She wore "elegant, chic clothing" when she went out and had "coquettish hairdos."[39] She had even written to the municipal authorities: "I shall leave my accommodations at Tönniesberg as soon as possible after my return because it does not seem appropriate for me to be in such a place in my elegant clothing."[40] One of her letters had been penned from the exclusive Hotel Adlon in Berlin. Gertrude Polley seemed to live in two different worlds, as though she wanted to flaunt the last of her cultural capital (Bourdieu's term) or hoped that expensive clothing would provide some kind of symbolic relief from her misery since there was no prospect of any real change. Journalists and government officials found such behavior inexplicable and irrational, including her incessant letter writing. According to one commentator, she seemed to spend her mornings either sleeping or writing letters.[41]

Nobody gave much thought to why Polley acted as she did. It appears, though, that writing letters released her from her role as a victim and an object and gave her an opportunity to express her thoughts without contradiction. She liked in her letters to associate her life with well-known events, including for instance the Haarmann murders (spectacular mass murders that took place in Hanover) and the typhus epidemic in Hanover. At times her writings took on religious and even apocalyptic overtones: "Punishment will descend upon Hanover." Society and the

---

36. *Hannoverscher Kurier,* April 18, 1929.
37. Ibid.
38. Here and for the following see *Niederdeutsche Zeitung,* April 19, 1929.
39. *Wohlfahrts-Woche,* May 19, 1929.
40. Ibid.
41. Ibid.

individual, fact and fantasy were intertwined. "I do not want to become famous and am not a professional fortune-teller, but revelations are made to me in a dreamlike state."[42] Reality mingled with reverie: "The day before yesterday the newsstands [in Berlin] were overflowing, cursing fists reached for the sky, mothers cried for me and my child. . . . My and my child's cruel fate are going to be performed in the theater, plainly and truthfully."[43] Was it truth or fiction when Polley spoke here of an imminent contract for a play depicting her suffering and that of her son? The answer is of little import, given that her main concern was to publicize in a spectacular way the fate visited upon her and her son and etch it indelibly in the collective memory.

Municipal officials in Hanover reacted in a telling way, as preserved in the *Wohlfahrts-Woche* of May 19, 1929: "Why wouldn't there be some trashy playwright in Berlin who wants to earn money from this smut? This is hardly surprising in view of all that we have seen over the last few years." The very title of the article evoked associations with the Trash and Smut Act of 1926, which was supposed to place morally offensive literature on prohibited lists, although no clear definitions were provided.[44] The view of art expressed here in the *Wohlfahrts-Woche* was that it is little more than a banal replication of real life: only a "trashy" playwright could write a play about a "smutty" subject, and the resulting work of art could only be filth. Overtly the municipal officials adhered to the cultural canon of the well-educated bourgeoisie and looked to the theater for edification and representations of the sublime, not the "smut" of everyday life.

Municipal bureaucrats also noted that Gertrude Polley was very conceited. In a letter describing herself in 1914, she had allegedly said that she was well off, young, beautiful, and full of life. The *Wohlfahrts-Woche* of May 19, 1929, also brought up the change in her first name from the regular German "Gertrud" to "Gertrude." Everything that she did allegedly smacked of attempts to make herself appear intriguing.

The inclusion of Gertrude Polley's character and way of life in the discussion of her case was not just a journalistic whim. Municipal authorities were making real evaluations of her with definite material consequences. The Reich Regulations on the Duty to Provide Welfare of 1924 defined various categories of recipients. "Victims of the war and the

---

42. Gertrude Polley's letter, November 1926, in *Wohlfahrts-Woche,* May 19, 1929.

43. *Wohlfahrts-Woche,* May 19, 1929.

44. For the Trash and Smut Act of 1926 see Detlev J. K. Peukert, "Der Schund- und Schmutzkampf als 'Sozialpolitik der Seele,'" in *"Das war ein Vorspiel nur." Bücherverbrennungen Deutschland 1933. Voraussetzungen und Folgen. Ausstellung der Akademie der Künste, 8. Mai bis 3. Juli 1983* (Berlin and Vienna, 1983), 51–64.

inflation" were entitled to *gehobene Fürsorge* (elevated welfare), while all others received only *allgemeine Fürsorge* (general welfare). Individuals who "dodged work" or were "reluctant to work" received lower payments. The welfare authorities in each municipal district in Hanover employed a social worker who helped to determine the categories into which various individuals fell. The social worker made unannounced visits and checked on the applicants' accommodations and circumstances, their willingness to work, their morals, and their attitudes (largely political). The social worker then drafted reports, which were forwarded to the Welfare Office and which categorized people in an apparently rational way on the basis of such criteria as "tidy" or "untidy" and "willing to work" or "unwilling to work." The newspaper descriptions of Gertrude Polley were therefore not just personal defamations by particularly presumptuous journalists or municipal officials but a product of this system of "rational" categorization. It had a particularly devastating effect on Polley because she was placed in the lowest category.

Among the worst things that could happen to a welfare recipient was to be categorized as lazy and reluctant to work. This was the reproach leveled at Gertrude Polley in the *Wohlfahrts-Woche* of May 19, 1929: "She occasionally sold bottled beer and cigarettes and probably sewed as well for a ready-made clothing store. However, everyone who observed her agreed that this was only a scam." While the other publications usually depicted her as ill and suffering from a nervous disorder, the *Wohlfahrts-Woche* of May 19, 1929, dug up a medical report from a staff physician that certified quite the opposite. According to it, she was 80 percent capable of gainful employment in January 1925 and even 100 percent capable in the area of the catering trade. In May 1926, she was deemed completely healthy. During treatment with Salvarsan[45] for syphilis, she was declared 70 percent fit for work in June 1926 and then reclassified as completely fit. In January 1929, she was examined by two staff physicians. One of them declared her exactly 66 2/3 percent fit for work if she was given arch supports, which she then received according to the *Wohlfahrts-Woche*. The other went straight to the point: "Very much a perpetual complainer about everything. Moderately fallen arches, obese, and depressed state of mind. Eighty percent fit for work."

Tempo saw the situation quite differently from the authorities. It depicted Polley as doubly victimized, first by social conditions (as she was by the *Hannoversche Kurier* as well) and second by officialdom. "No agency or municipal body can be held responsible for the catastrophic housing conditions, which have caused infinite suffering and misery and

---

45. Salvarsan was a medication for recurrent fever and syphilis.

destroyed so many lives. But the men entrusted by the city with overseeing the public good must be able to demonstrate one thing: an understanding for desperate people and wasted lives and an ability to put their own oversensitivities last."[46] What other newspapers saw as gross impertinence on the part of Gertrude Polley, *Tempo* portrayed as an oversensitive reaction to a "rash comment from a woman who had earned her own living from earliest childhood and never learned to choose her words carefully."[47] In *Tempo*, it was always the officials who were unjust to Gertrude Polley, rather than the reverse. She was portrayed as having been "robbed" of her home and her right to raise her own child.[48] Officials were accused of making themselves "judges over their fellow man," without endeavoring to discover "the deeper emotional reasons for particular actions." The authorities were perfectly capable of destroying the lives of other people "out of their own class snobbery or because something seems, when viewed superficially, to be against the rules."[49]

Tempo took an extremely critical view of the authorities and was therefore receptive to the idea that it was they who had made Polley a social outcast. She was labeled a crank and perpetual complainer because of her constant attempts to find justice. Her medical history raised "some doubts in superficial observers about her soundness of mind," and because of her conviction for insulting an official, she had a criminal record and "was still viewed by every authority with distrust."[50] The article concluded that such people had no chance "of finding more peaceful conditions" and "settling down in quiet respectablity." They would always be haunted by their pasts, and this was a "devastating tragedy in life."[51]

The municipal authorities in Hanover refused to be swayed from their positive view of conditions at the Tönniesberg estate. In their dispute with *Tempo* over the Polley case, they praised the "exemplary achievements of the city of Hanover" and noted sarcastically: "We are convinced that most of the 22,000 families living in cellar apartments in Berlin, according to the housing census of 1925 (in Hanover there were 200), would fight for places in the freight cars at Tönniesberg if we made them available."[52] There were overtones of the competition between the cities in the dispute, and Hanover was determined not to be criticized for its housing policies. The importance of this aspect of the dispute can

46. *Tempo,* April 27, 1929, first edition.
47. Ibid.
48. *Tempo,* April 18, 1929, third edition.
49. *Tempo,* April 27, 1929, first edition.
50. Ibid.
51. *Tempo,* April 17, 1929, first edition.
52. *Wohlfahrts-Woche,* June 9, 1929.

be seen in the fact that the Berlin newspaper had tried to do just this in writing that "a mother's cry for help" had become the "cities' cry for help." [53] This article described the housing situation in Hanover and took a few jabs at the welfare policies of municipal officials.

"The Ugly Casting of Moral Suspicion"

The Hanover newspapers frequently besmirched Polley for her "immoral way of life." The *Hannoversche Kurier,* for example, reduced thirteen years of her life to the following: "While her husband was away at war, Mrs. Polley led an irregular life. She acted as an agent for a bar, entertained gentlemen in her apartment, and later opened a detective agency. She was divorced in 1921 for infidelity and was found the sole guilty party. The consequence of her infidelity is the child, over whom she is now fighting with all the authorities in the world. It is impossible to determine the father. Her divorced husband—an honest foreman—refuses to pay child support. Mrs. P. was sentenced for prostitution in 1923 and was severely ill in 1926 and 1927."[54]

Even more than what was said, it was what was left unsaid that gave free rein to the imagination and allowed readers to fill the gaps in this short biography. The newspaper implied that the Polleys were hardly a model bourgeois family in which the husband was the sole provider. While still married, Gertrude Polley made herself independent. She earned a living in dubious ways, acting as a bar agent, which sounds rather illicit; working as a detective in a male-dominated occupation on the fringes of the underworld; and finally entertaining "gentlemen" in return for pay, it seems, when this is included in her list of occupations. The latter suspicion was fueled by information about her family circumstances. She was divorced by her husband because she broke the commandment of fidelity. The newspaper connected her "adultery" with "gentlemen visitors" and implied that it was not a question of a single indiscretion but of "fornication" on a regular basis: that is, prostitution. Her immorality was evidenced by her regularly changing sexual partners, her venereal disease, and the alleged doubt about who fathered her son. The mention of veneral disease and other diseases in this context is clearly defamatory.

The *Niederdeutsche Zeitung* also alluded to the suspicion of prostitution when it reported that Gertrude Polley had worked as a domestic "in a house of ill repute," her "way of life left much to be desired, according

---

53. *Tempo,* April 17, 1929, first edition; *Tempo,* April 19, 1929, first edition.
54. *Hannoverscher Kurier,* April 18, 1929.

to official reports," she "never held a proper job," and she "earned her living for the most part in dubious ways."[55] She was not only morally unreliable but politically unreliable as well because she maintained close contacts with Communist deputies. The impression was thereby created in the minds of readers that the Communist Party was morally depraved.

The newspaper reports never described Polley directly as an adulteress or a whore. These impressions were raised instead through insinuations intended to fire the imaginations of the readers ("gentlemen visitors" and "male acquaintances"), as well as through the well-mannered euphemisms used to describe her activities (her "roaming" and "dubious occupations"), and finally allusions to her shady places of work ("apartment" and "bar").[56] The language used to describe her suspected activities was also very bureaucratic ("commercial fornication"). In using this temperate, middle-class language, the newspaper reporters distanced themselves linguistically from Gertrude Polley and contented themselves with mere allusions to her "unspeakable" activities.

No aspersions at all were cast on Polley's husband, who was portrayed as an "honest foreman" with a respectable occupation who had originally provided for his wife. He was not responsible for his wife's "irregular" way of life because it started while he was in the war. This gendered version of the "stab-in-the-back" myth was widespread in conservative circles and was indicative mostly of male anxieties about the increasing independence of women.[57] Gertrude Polley was portrayed accordingly as one of those women who allowed the homeland to sink into vice and immorality while their husbands were serving at the front. Her husband's blamelessness had been confirmed, after all, by the courts in the divorce proceedings. His refusal to support a stranger's child was considered a legitimate and understandable reaction on the part of a cuckolded husband.

In the eyes of the Hanover press, Gertrude Polley's immorality inevitably cast a pall over the upbringing of her son. According to the *Hannoversche Kurier,* Polley's way of life was the immediate reason why she was deprived of custody.[58] "All of this was reason enough in both Hanover and Berlin (Neukölln District Court) for the child to be placed in other hands on account of moral endangerment." The newspaper added: "The boy shows some nice aptitudes and the Hanover Youth

55. *Niederdeutsche Zeitung,* April 19, 1929; see also *Hannoversche Landeszeitung,* April 19, 1929.

56. The *Niederdeutsche Zeitung* clearly labeled her workplace a "house of ill repute."

57. In general, see Ute Daniel, *Arbeiterfrauen in der Kriegsgesellschaft: Beruf, Familie, Politik im Ersten Weltkrieg* (Göttingen, 1989).

58. *Hannoverscher Kurier,* April 18, 1929; *Hannoverscher Anzeiger,* April 19, 1929.

Welfare Department would have liked to continue caring for him in the Kleefeld Youth Home, but Mrs. P. did not want to leave her son and took him to Berlin. The *Niederdeutsche Zeitung* referred to the Welfare Office and its fear for both the moral and physical health of the boy as the reason why he was placed in a home. Only after he had become "very run down" in the care of his mother was he placed for a second time in the custody of municipal welfare officials in Berlin.[59]

The Hanover newspapers stressed the credibility of Gertrude Polley's opponents by referring to their academic titles and lofty positions, for example, "Director of the Housing Office Dr. Jordan."[60] On the other hand, they permanently damaged Polley's credibility by reporting professional medical assessments. "A medical expert described her as abnormal and suffering from severe hereditary problems."[61] Her mental state had evidently been assessed during her imprisonment. Physicians and psychologists in particular wielded enormous power of definition within the bureaucracy and helped to stabilize the existing social order by justifying the measures taken by the state against people who were troublesome and nonconformist. In addition, medical experts were almost always men who looked at the lives and health of women from a male perspective. By delegitimizing on medical grounds behaviors that conflicted strongly with the existing norms, public authorities could easily reassert the social order and concept of normality that had been challenged.[62] In the public discourse over Gertrude Polley, expert medical reports were used to explain her behavior. An authoritative picture was drawn of a mentally ill person whose actions were due to abnormality and heredity and no longer solely to the dire social straits in which she found herself. As the *Hanoversche Kurier* concluded: a "picture thus emerges of a woman who is by nature somewhat inclined to hysteria."[63] Elements from modern medicine had entered the popular understanding of hysteria, which was traditionally attributed more to women, and the authority of science could henceforth be invoked to stigmatize nonconformist female behavior as unhealthy and sick.[64]

---

59. *Niederdeutsche Zeitung,* April 19, 1929.

60. Ibid.

61. Ibid.

62. For the connection between the rise of the medical profession and the use of its power of definition to serve the state see Gerd Göckenjan, *Kurieren und Staat machen Gesundheit und Medizin der bürgerlichen Welt* (Frankfurt, 1985).

63. *Hannoverscher Kurier,* April 18, 1929. Although the paper blamed Polley's hysterical behavior mostly on her own predisposition, it qualified this opinion somewhat by pointing as well to the confusion of the times.

64. For the use of medical discourse and the exclusion of the insane in order to stabilize society, see Michel Foucault, *Madness and Civilization* (New York, 1965); for

It is no longer possible to determine when exactly Polley's son fell ill and who neglected his or her duty toward him. What we can say is that a particular view of middle-class, respectable femininity was at work here, according to which "motherhood" could not be reconciled under any circumstances with a variety of sexual partners. Devoted mothers and immoral prostitutes, Madonna figures and whores were considered mutually exclusive patterns of female behavior, although in reality, women's historical experiences have been much more complex than this paradigm would lead one to believe. As a single mother, Gertrude Polley might well have become a prostitute in order to support herself and her child in desperate times, like so many other women in the first few years after the war. However, the authorities did not base their decision to send Erwin Polley to a youth home on Gertrude's subjective reasoning but rather on their own monopolistic definition of what constituted moral endangerment of a child. Polley's case demonstrates once again that officials predicated their decisions on a moralistic view of women, in which sexual practices were the most important criterion. Polley's sentence for prostitution was reason enough for the Welfare Office to doubt her ability to raise a child.

In the eyes of the authorities in Hanover, it was "silly" for *Tempo* to make Gertrude Polley, of all people, the heroine of a series of articles. The female norm that should prevail in their view soon became apparent: "If the dissolute life of this woman is supposed to be typical of our German mothers, then we are finished."[65] As the authorities announced in the *Wohlfahrts-Woche,* they still considered Polley "mentally inferior and hardly responsible for her endless scribblings."[66]

The newspaper reporters in Hanover worked hand in glove with the officials whose decisions were being questioned. In explaining for their readers why someone like Polley would appeal to the Landtag in such an unusual and dramatic way, they painted a picture of someone who lived totally outside the norms of regular life, as they themselves conceived of these norms. Not only was she an adulteress, a prostitute, a Communist, a savage, and a bad mother, she was also insane. By discrediting Polley in this way, they made it easy to dismiss her accusations against the Housing Office without ever investigating them.

The issues of "femininity" and "motherhood" were raised by Gertrude Polley as well but in her defense. In attempting to justify what she

---

hysteria in particular see 285ff. See also Martin Hewitt, "Bio-Politics and Social Policy: Foucault's Account of Welfare," in Mike Featherstone et al. (eds.), *The Body: Social Process and Cultural Theory* (London, 1991), 225–55.

65. *Wohlfahrts-Woche,* June 9, 1929.
66. Ibid.

had done, she repeatedly stressed that she was concerned as a mother and thus tried to appropriate an aspect of femininity that was seen in a very positive light. Her pleas were not just for herself but most of all for her mistreated child, in whose upbringing she never "did anything wrong." In saying this, she was appealing — just like the municipal officials and newspaper reporters — to the high social regard for mothers devoted to their children. The cultural hegemony (Gramsci's term) of certain ideals and norms is very apparent here, and neither individuals nor groups could escape them. Polley played upon her motherhood as much as possible, claiming that she had sent her son regular parcels of clothing and shoes even when he was in the orphanage and no longer her responsibility. She attempted to ward off any accusations that her spectacular action in the Landtag served only her own material, egoistic interests by keeping her son in the forefront of her dispute with the authorities. In this way, Polley reversed the roles and became the accuser instead of the accused. The authorities claimed that she was failing as a mother, but she insisted that it was the Youth Welfare Departments that were neglecting their duty. Municipal agencies were there to provide help in emergency situations, but they just created those situations in the first place through their criminal methods.

Tempo also seized upon Polley's way of life and attempted to market it. Under the heading "The Ugly Casting of Moral Suspicion," it described the doubts about Polley's morals as slanderous and libelous.[67] The *Tempo* journalist could not resist discussing Polley's life as well, although he defended it, claiming that her child custody files contained a police report saying that no fault could be found with her. Having overcome "a frightful home life and a terrible marriage," she had only attempted as a divorced woman to satisfy her longing for a child.[68] *Tempo* also denied the accusation in the Hanover press that Polley suffered from venereal disease, referring to various authorities and expert medical opinions and thus attempting to carry the day by using the same method as the Hanoverians.[69]

Tempo took part as well in the discourse on Polley's virtues as a woman and a mother. It described how she had fought for her child, who was "all that she really had in life."[70] Her story was "a mother's cry for help" and a "mother's tragedy."[71] Many details were added to show that Polley was a devoted mother who thought only of her child.

---

67. *Tempo,* April 27, 1929, first edition.
68. Ibid.
69. Ibid.
70. *Tempo,* April 27, 1929, first edition.
71. *Tempo,* April 17, 1929, first edition.

Tempo apparently adopted unquestioningly Polley's own interpretation of events. However, what seemed in her mouth like an exercise in calculated self-justification appeared more akin in the newspaper to trite sensation mongering, despite the criticism of municipal government officials. The paragraph headings read as follows: "An Undaunted Refugee from East Prussia," "In the Cattle Car," "The Hunt for Her Child," and "Flight to Berlin."[72]

Although the Hanover press clearly disagreed with *Tempo* and Gertrude Polley about the proper interpretation of the incident in the Landtag, they all judged it in terms of the same social values. It was a question for all of them of justice, order, health, morality, moderation, and normality versus injustice, crime, sickness, immorality, vice, abnormality, smut, trash, and inappropriate methods.

Epilogue

Who was Gertrude Polley in actual fact: a paranoid hysteric who made inordinate demands and insisted that she was persecuted even though officials' criticisms were well deserved; or a victim of willful and arbitrary officialdom and a desperate mother who fought for her rights and showed great courage in turning to the public to protect herself and her child?

This is the wrong question to ask because it is based on a false dichotomy. Polley presumably had a very complex and contradictory personality, which cannot be clearly determined in any case. Her personality also changed apparently under the impact of her experiences in these difficult times. So far as can be reconstructed, her life deteriorated only slowly to a point that she herself experienced as catastrophic. The interaction of social conditions, individual dispositions, Polley's experiences with government officials, and their subjective interpretations propelled her into a downward spiral that eventually turned her indeed into a perpetual complainer or crank.

What is a "crank" (*Querulant*)? There was no official or legal definition at the time, nor does one exist today. All we have are descriptions of some supposedly typical behaviors of cranks and experiences with them. "In the life of every crank, a key initial experience of an injustice that is never set right plays a triggering role."[73] As we now know, most cranks are not mentally ill but "live constricted lives and make their personal problem the center of the universe."[74] Polley's key initial experience was

---

72. *Tempo,* April 17, 1929, first edition.
73. *Die Zeit,* January 11, 1991.
74. Ibid.

probably the loss of her house and home. According to the same source, cranks are prolific writers who are well aware of their rights. This was certainly true of Gertrude Polley. "Cranks usually do not hesitate to put pen to paper and sublimate their self-tormenting despair in a nonviolent way by writing legalistic letters."[75] Their incessant exaggeration soon leaves them "extremely isolated." The main opponents of cranks are nearly always public officials and institutions that figure ever more prominently in the everyday lives of the general population as the modern welfare state develops. Both Max Weber and Michel Foucault analyzed this development in modern society and its consequences, although in very different ways. Jürgen Habermas spoke of the "colonization of everyday lives," although this should not lead to the conclusion that people lost their status as subjects. Anyone who keeps an eye on the power of the municipal authorities can view cranks as very delicate sensors who react in exaggerated but usually nonviolent ways to aspects of society that deserve criticism and therefore affect more than just them. This was true of Gertrude Polley. She and most cranks are Davids fighting the Goliath of the authorities, even if all the legalities are upheld. The more effective that cranks are in accusing the authorities of abuses, the more dangerous they seem and the more officials want to get rid of them.[76] In Polley's time, like today, cranks were therefore easily declared insane. The legal sociologist Wolfgang Kaupen views cranks primarily as a "result of a labeling process." In his view, the authorities that are responsible for upholding the social order, especially courts working together with psychiatrists, often react to uncomfortable criticism or uncomfortable people "by declaring them mentally disturbed . . . and therefore not to be taken seriously."[77]

Without realizing all the consequences, Gertrude Polley achieved her aim of putting herself in the middle of a public discourse. She expected to participate in this discourse and hoped that it would provide the ultimate solution to her problems. However, it just sealed her fate and changed her personality as she began to resemble the image painted by the authorities and the press of certain kinds of women. Polley increasingly became a mere exhibit in a discourse focusing more on social values and norms than on her particular person. Some people used the "Polley case" to reinforce the existing social order, while others used it to criticize public officials, whose influence was becoming very strong in modern society and everyday life.

Little is known about the rest of Gertrude Polley's life. After 1929,

75. Ibid.
76. Ibid.
77. Ibid.

she dropped totally out of sight for three years. The Housing Office noted that she had "moved to unknown." Was she imprisoned because of the incident in the Landtag? Polley was mentioned again in 1932 as living in Mechtspringe. We also know that at the age of forty-five in November 1932 she married Christoph Barkefeld, who was eighteen years her senior. While she lived in Hanover, probably with her second husband, her son was in Ihme-Roloven. It is impossible to determine, though, whether he was institutionalized or living with friends or relatives. Housing Office information also makes it clear that she did not regain custody of her son after 1929, despite her success as reported by *Tempo*. Her struggle in this regard was therefore all in vain.

After the National Socialists came to power, Polley entered the mental institution in Hildesheim in July 1933. We cannot determine whether she did so of her own accord (which seems improbable), whether a state order was obtained, or whether her relatives had her committed. Polley's disputes with the authorities make it likely, though, that she was classified as "antisocial" and became one of the many victims of Nazi "cleansing."[78] She had finally become an official social outcast and was largely deprived of her status as a subject. Her struggle with the authorities was decided once and for all. Well before the terrorist Nazi regime took power, though, she was heading toward committal to a closed facility. The *Wohlfahrts-Woche* noted as early as its May 1929 issue and at the end of a long article: "It seems to us that it is time, even before passage of the Protection Act, to consider sending this incurable crank Gertrude Polley to a closed facility for her own sake and in order to save administrative and court costs." Precise calculations showed that Polley cost "year in, year out, 3,000 marks in administrative and court expenses." Besides all the other measures usually taken against cranks, it seemed reasonable from a utilitarian, administrative point of view to have Polley committed against her will in order to save money.[79]

The final surviving document states that Polley was divorced in December 1936. It is not clear whether this was in response to state pressure. Polley's divorce probably reduced her contact with the outside world and made her increasingly lonely. The Hildesheim State Hospital, the successor institution, and the Hildesheim Registration Office have no records of Polley's ultimate fate. Like so many cranks before and after her, Polley returned to anonymity: a sensation come to naught.

---

78. In general, see Klaus Scherer, *"Asozial" im Dritten Reich: Die vergessenen Verfolgten* (Münster, 1990); Gisela Bock, *Zwangssterilisation im Nationalsozialismus* (Opladen, 1986).

79. Cf. Detlev J. K. Peukert, *Max Webers Diagnose der Moderne* (Göttingen, 1989).

POPULAR CULTURE AND POLITICS

CHAPTER 8

Sports and Public Culture:
The Opening Ceremonies of the
Hanover Stadium in 1922

Introduction

The stadium of interest to us here was renamed on a number of occasions. In 1916 it was originally supposed to be called "Hindenburg Stadium," but at the opening ceremonies in 1922, it was named "City of Hanover Stadium." In 1933–34, the stadium was rebaptized the "Hindenburg *Kampfbahn*,"[1] and the old name chiseled into the entranceway was altered. After 1945, the name was officially changed again to "Stadium of the Capital City of Hanover," but in the end, people just called it "Eilenriede Stadium" after the nearby urban forest. In this chapter, we focus primarily on the original name for the stadium before it was completed, the name that it was given at the opening ceremonies, and the great dispute surrounding this change.[2]

---

1. Mayor Menge ordered the name change in 1934, thereby following the example set by other cities. Cf. *Muttersprache: Zeitschrift des deutschen Sprachvereines* 49, no. 11 (1934): 390.

2. The following is not only a study of a particular event but also an attempt to analyze the discourses surrounding it in a Foucaultian or post-Foucaultian way. Although there is considerable disagreement among German historians about the epistemological value of this methodology, it is already heavily influencing the research in the guise of "new cultural history," especially abroad and not least of all in the United States. Good overviews can be found in Nicholas B. Dirks, Geoff Eley, and Sherry B. Ortner (eds.), *Culture/Power/History: A Reader in Contemporary-Social Theory* (Princeton, 1994). In the introduction to their volume, Richard Wightman Fox and T. J. Jackson Lear state that "historians must become more 'cultural' in attending to private as well as public life, and in paying close attention to the ways in which meaning is layered into the documents (of all kinds) that we use and that we write. We also share the conviction that becoming 'cultural' must not lead to the neglect of power. Cultural meanings have social and political origins and consequences,

Names are symbols and have meaning. By the time of the official opening, the name "Hindenburg" had come to stand for the martial culture of Wilhelminian Germany and its desire to become a world power. People on the political right could identify with such a name, but there was a new wind blowing in Germany in the aftermath of its defeat in the war. The republic born of the revolution of 1918–19 was anything but solid. Workers and politicians to the left of the Majority Social Democrats sought even greater political and social changes, often resorting to nonparliamentary means in their efforts to achieve their ends. Meanwhile, the republic was badly damaged by politically motivated murders carried out by right-wing extremists. The best-known victims were the Center Party politician Matthias Erzberger (1921) and the foreign minister, Walter Rathenau (1922). The unsuccessful Kapp Putsch against the Reich government and the ensuing disturbances in the spring of 1920 showed that violent opposition could be expected from far more than just a few scattered individuals on the extreme right. The situation degenerated into a virtual civil war.[3] It soon became clear, though, that the extreme right could not stir up enough antirepublican sentiment in the general population to seize power — not even in 1923 when the French occupation of the Ruhr and hyperinflation threatened to destroy the entire social and political order.[4] Many right-wing politicians may have eyed Mussolini with considerable envy therefore when, in the year of the inauguration of City of Hanover Stadium, he successfully completed his "March on Rome." Nothing of this kind seemed possible at the time in Germany. To all appearances, the Weimar Repubic survived its troubled infancy in relatively good condition. There was considerable doubt, though, about how deep the support for the new republic was among its own civil servants and the general population. Could the regime survive with the support of *Vernunftsrepublikaner* (republicans by rational conviction), or did it need to win over their hearts as well as their minds?

A study of public culture can show us how people generally felt about the republic and whether it was succeeding in appealing to them

in private and public realms alike" (Richard Wightman Fox and T. J. Jackson [eds.], *The Power of Culture: Critical Essays in American History* [Chicago and London, 1993], 4). I would like to thank Inge Marßolek, Uta C. Schmidt, Monika Pater, Daniela Münkel, Ines Katenhusen, and Cosima Winkler for their criticisms and encouragement.

3. For the civilian militias see the monograph by Andreas Brundiers, *Gegenrevolution in der Provinz: Die Haltung der SPD zu den Einwohnerwehren 1919/20 am Beispiel Celle* (Bielefeld, 1994); for the "War in the Ruhr" see Erhard Lucas, *Märzrevolution 1920*, 2d ed., 2 vols. (Frankfurt, 1970–73).

4. For a good introduction to the history of the Weimar Republic, see Detlev J. K. Peukert, *Die Weimarer Republik: Krisenjahre der Klassischen Moderne* (Frankfurt, 1987).

on an emotional level.[5] The politicians who championed the German republic clearly recognized the problem. In the same year in which the Hanover stadium opened, President Friedrich Ebert announced that the "Deutschlandlied" would be Germany's official national anthem, replacing "Heil Dir im Siegerkranz," which had often been played under the empire. In addition, the government organized constitutional celebrations to encourage people to identify with the new republic. What happened, though, at "apolitical" public gatherings? What political and cultural values did they convey? How did Germans describe their nation, how did they handle the symbols of the past, and how did they conceive of the future?

Berlin was the heart of the new political system and a major European metropolis. The world press closely followed what happened there. Less attention was paid to events elsewhere, although these events are no less important to researchers, especially if they want to learn something about public culture in various regions of the young republic. What follows is a contribution to this area of study. We hope to reconstruct the thought patterns and actions of Germans as revealed in public culture. The research is based largely on newspaper reports. Further materials were also found in the Hanover City Archives, which became especially important because they alone reveal how the opening ceremonies teetered between high political scandal and provincial farce (see section 1).

The new stadium in Hanover was a sign of the importance that sports were gaining as a major part of popular culture, whose great breakthrough came in the 1920s (see section 2). Cities attempted to respond to the new demand. In the late nineteenth century, urban centers that aspired to be "modern" had to be able to boast gas works and electrical power stations, opera houses, train stations, museums, and theaters. Under the new political winds blowing in the Weimar Republic, cities felt a greater need not only for adult education centers and

---

5. The term *public culture* includes more of society than the term *political culture*. For the concept of public culture see Jürgen Habermas, *Strukturwandel der Öffentlichkeit: Untersuchungen zu einer Kategorie der bürgerlichen Gesellschaft* (Darmstadt and Neuwied, 1962); Oskar Negt and Alexander Kluge, *Öffentlichkeit und Erfahrung: Zur Organisationsanalyse von bürgerlicher und proletarischer Öffentlichkeit* (Frankfurt, 1972); cf. in this regard Donald Horne, *The Public Culture* (London, 1986); Theodore Mills Norton, "The Public Sphere: A Workshop," *New Political Science* 11 (spring 1983): 75–84; Craig Calhoun (ed.), *Habermas and the Public Sphere* (Cambridge, 1992); Geoff Eley, "Nations, Publics, and Political Cultures: Placing Habermas in the Nineteenth Century," in Nicholas B. Dirks, Geoff Eley, and Sherry B. Ortner (eds.), *Culture/Power/History: A Reader in Contemporary Social Theory* (Princeton, 1994), 297–336. For the social problems in Germany and questions of public morality after the First World War see Richard Bessel, *Germany after the First World War* (Oxford, 1993), especially chaps. 8 and 9.

public libraries but also for swimming pools and athletic facilities. The range of infrastructure needed to polish a city's image expanded enormously (see section 3).

Although the balance of power in municipal politics had swung toward the labor movement and the Majority Social Democrats (this was the new name of the SPD following the split of 1917) in the aftermath of the revolution of 1918–19, the deep-rooted traditions of Wilhelminian class society times continued to weigh heavily, here as in other areas of life (see section 4). Nevertheless, both the Majority Social Democrats and the middle-class parties attempted to practice pluralism on the municipal level, at least insofar as formal public culture was concerned (see section 5). A look at the press coverage of the opening ceremonies also enables us to comment on the prevailing views of the sexes (see section 6). Finally, the questions raised about Hindenburg in part 1 of this chapter are addressed again, although this time in a way that is less related to him in particular. We are more interested in conservative, militaristic public culture during the early years of the new republic and the related political values and hopes for the future (see section 7).

Ritual processes, such as the opening ceremonies of a stadium, work primarily on the symbolic level. The messages conveyed to spectators, radio listeners, and active participants in particular are often vague and diffuse, appealing directly to the emotions. For this reason, ritual processes create new communication nodes. According to the concepts of Victor Turner and others, ritual processes create a "communitas," which is different from the structured communities in which people otherwise live. The "communitas" created by rituals binds together symbols, rites, and interpretations that otherwise appear in very different cultural contexts. In this way, semantic systems of central, polyvalent myths and symbols are created that generate an enormous inner sense of belonging. According to Turner, "communitas" provides a model of social relations that is not based on status, role, and office, that is, on social structures. A society needs both models of social relations and cannot do without the interplay between the "communitas" evoked by rituals and the social units based on structures. It is precisely because these social models are very different and mutually exclusive that people develop a "need" for both kinds of relationships.[6]

As a result of the kind of analysis advanced by Turner, historians have developed a new sensitivity to ritual processes in the public culture

6. Victor Turner, *The Ritual Process: Structure and Anti-Structure* (Chicago, 1969), 96, 193.

of secularized, modern societies. This sensitivity heightens our awareness of how nations and national identities[7] are forged through particular symbols, forms, and contents and carries us far beyond the older theories about propaganda and manipulation. However, insights into the social importance of rituals and celebrations do not say anything about how the thoughts and ideas that they conveyed should be assessed. This is also a task for historians, who understand symbols and the contents they convey not as anthropological constants but as expressions of a given time and place. Cultural practices need to be confronted with the alternatives available at the time, even though the latter were not adopted. The theories outlined here are clarified and made more concrete in the following discussion of the grand opening of the stadium in Hanover.

1. Hindenburg as Symbol and Myth: The Dispute over the Inscription and Name of the Stadium

The grand opening of the stadium would not be half so interesting from a historical point of view if not for the scandal over the name. Scandals are events that come quickly to public attention and reveal that influential people have blatantly violated social values and standards of one kind or another. In general, scandals are socially significant because they expose matters that are normally kept hidden or are hard to prove and because they are often considered just "the tip of the iceberg" and indicative of far more extensive problems. Scandals exert a broad fascination and bring the various publics in society together for a short time through the media and communications, in a way that can only be compared to major events, disasters, and sensations.[8]

There is a saying that "whoever pays the piper calls the tune," but thorny problems may sometimes arise, as in the case of the Hanover stadium. At first, the situation seemed crystal clear. In 1916, in the middle of the war, a wealthy Hanoverian named Gustav Brandt donated three hundred thousand marks for the construction of a stadium,[9] on condition that the work be completed within five years. He died in 1918, the year of Germany's defeat. Three years remained to build the

---

7. In general see John Tomlinson, *Cultural Imperialism: A Critical Introduction* (Baltimore, 1991), especially 84.

8. For the Wilhelminian SPD, see in this regard Alex Hall, *Scandal, Sensation, and Social Democracy: The SPD-Press and Wilhelmine Germany 1890–1900* (Cambridge, 1977).

9. Brandt was unmarried and estranged from his relatives. His fortune amounted to 6 million marks.

stadium, but spiraling prices drove the cost up considerably. The city authorities appropriated an additional eight hundred thousand marks in 1920 but in so doing complicated the situation: who would call the tune now? The problem was not so much one of time—after all a world war had been lost and Brandt's heirs had graciously agreed to an extension until 1923. The real difficulty lay in the reason for the donation, which was to mark the jubilee on April 7, 1916, of Field Marshal von Hindenburg's first enlistment in the army. The Majority Social Democrats had managed to work together relatively well with the old civil service elites and even parts of the old military leadership during the revolution,[10] but this did not mean that they could easily accept Hindenburg as a suitable person after whom to name the stadium.

It was true that the field marshal certainly occupied a special place in the hearts of Hanoverians. He lived in the city from 1919 to 1925, and nowhere else in the republic was he held in such high esteem. He moved to Hanover shortly after the end of the revolution, and his arrival on July 3, 1919, was greatly celebrated.[11] When his wife was laid to rest in Hanover in May 1921, the ceremonies were attended by the Stahlhelm (a right-wing paramilitary unit), student fraternities, soldiers' associations, and delegations from the schools. The *Hannoversche Tageblatt* got to the heart of the great display of mourning when it wrote: "The faithful wife of our Hindenburg is dead" (May 19, 1921). She was seen less as a personage in her own right than as an appendage to the great field marshal, who remained the actual object of adoration.

One year before the opening ceremonies of the stadium, all seemed to be unfolding as Brandt had wished, at least insofar as the name was concerned. On July 6, 1921, the municipal executive wrote to Hindenburg as follows: "We are pleased to fulfill the donor's condition in regard to the name because none could be more suited than that of Your Excellency to an edifice devoted, after the huge losses of the world war, to strengthening a new generation."[12] The message conveyed here could be summarized as follows in only slightly overstated form: the old warlike, militaristic culture of the empire should shape the future of the new Germany as well through the personage of Hindenburg; we want to make up the losses suffered in the war, and this is the main purpose of sports and the new stadium. Hindenburg thanked the city for the great

---

10. We should recall in this regard the agreement reached on the telephone between the Chancellery (Ebert) and army headquarters (Groener) on November 10, 1918.

11. See in this regard Sabine Guckel, "'Vergnügliche Vaterlandspflicht': Hindenburg-Kult am Zoo," in Hannoversche Geschichtswerkstatt (ed.), *Alltag zwischen Hindenburg und Haarmann* (Hamburg, 1987), 13–19.

12. Hanover City Archives HR 20, no. 818.

honor it wished to bestow upon him and expressed his willingness to lend his name to the project.[13]

However, a great row soon erupted. A Social Democratic alderman named Bromme said that he was astonished at this choice, about which nothing had been said. If city council had known, in his view, it would never have given its approval to build. "Hindenburg was a pillar of the nationalistic movements, and the stadium was therefore being given a political coloration that Bromme could not approve."[14] The sitting director of municipal construction, Paul Wolf, finally admitted that the full wording of the original donation had not been read out when council had approved the emergency construction work.[15] This admission soon brought the row to full boil.

Among the leading opponents of the name was the Kartell für Sport und Körperpflege (Syndicate for Sport and Care of the Body), the federation of all workers' athletic clubs.[16] Even though the name "Hindenburg" had already been chiseled into the pillar in the entranceway to the stadium, the syndicate demanded that it be erased. At this, the representatives of sports in the armed forces stood up and stalked out of the meeting held to discuss the name. The chairman of the Hauptausschuß für Leibesübung (Central Committee for Physical Exercise), Professor Kohlrausch, was only echoing the sentiments of his members when he expressed his outrage that the naming of the stadium had led to "attacks on the personage of Hindenburg."[17]

---

13. Only Theodor Lessing expressed his objections in 1925, whereupon an anti-Semitic campaign was launched against him. See Rainer Marwedel, *Theodor Lessing 1872–1933: Eine Biographie* (Frankfurt, 1987), 244.

14. Hanover City Archives, HR 20, no. 818.

15. Hanover City Archives, HR 20, no. 818. This is confirmed as well by the minutes of the joint session of the municipal councils on September 9, 1920. Hanover City Archives, Städtische Kollegien 1920, vol. 4. For Wolf, see Eva Benz-Rabahah, "Paul Wolf, ein Städtebauer zwischen Tradition und Revolution," in Sid Auffarth and Adelheid von Saldern (eds.), *Altes und neues Wohnen: Linden und Hannover im frühen 20. Jahrhundert* (Seelze-Velber, 1992), 144–56.

16. Among the duties of the Kartell were representing the clubs before the authorities, leasing and renting sports fields and gymnastics halls, corresponding with the Bundeszentrale der Arbeiter, and organizing advertising campaigns. Hartmut Lohmann, "Organisierter Arbeitersport in Hannover in den 20er Jahren," in Adelheid von Saldern (ed.), *Stadt und Moderne: Hannover in der Weimarer Republik* (Hamburg, 1989), 253–85; for further general literature about workers' athletics see among others Christiane Eisenberg, "Massensport in der Weimarer Republik: Ein statistischer Überblick," *Archiv für Sozialgeschichte* 33 (1993): 137–79; Herbert Dierker, *Arbeitersport im Spannungsfeld der Zwanziger Jahre: Sportpolitik und Alltagserfahrungen auf internationaler, deutscher und Berliner Ebene* (Essen, 1990).

17. Note taken by Wolf at the meeting of the building commission on December 1, 1921. Hanover City Archives, HR 20, no. 818.

However, the Kartell für Sport und Körperpflege would not be intimidated. Its spokesman, Hermann Schönleiter, argued that city council had a right to name the stadium and that the name "Hindenburg" was tarnished and totally unacceptable. It was a reminder of a man "who, vastly overestimating the strength of the German people and blinded by initial military successes, contributed irresponsibly to ruining the health of the people. We would fail to do justice to our German comrades who fell for the fatherland if, through quiet acquiescence in this name for the stadium, we honored a man who heartlessly tore them from their loved ones and drove them to a cruel death."[18]

The emotionally charged tone of this speech is noteworthy. Impassioned rhetoric was quite common at the time — a sign that feelings were still raw. No great martial virtues were evoked in this speech. Soldiers became "German comrades who fell for the fatherland." Much is covered over by the use of the latter term. No mention is made of Germany's primary responsibility for the war or of the senselessness of the sacrifices that were made. Hindenburg's faults are restricted to his lack of realism in the conduct of the war and the fateful consequences for Germany. Those people who revered Hindenburg for his (and Ludendorff's) military successes at Tannenberg thought in similar terms and used much the same language, although with contrasting contents. The emphasis in Schönleiter's argument is on personal misbehavior and character weaknesses, and it is therefore virtually just the reverse of the argument advanced by those who admired Hindenburg. One could therefore almost speak of a kind of "negative adulation" for the field marshal.

The city executive pointed out cautiously in its letter of response that the name of the stadium had been agreed upon with representatives of the Social Democratic Party.[19] However, this failed to satisfy the Kartell für Sport und Körperpflege, which remained at loggerheads with the Hauptausschuß für Leibesübung. The two organizations were quite different in size, with the Hauptausschuß able to muster some thirty-five thousand members in comparison with the Kartell's six or seven thousand. Size, though, was not everything, and the Kartell was able to point out that the Majority Social Democrats were largely responsible for building the stadium.

One day, it happened: the inscription in the entranceway was actually chiseled out. The balance of power in the city of Hanover was evidently such that the Kartell was able to carry the day with the help of the Majority Social Democrats. In place of the old name was now "City

18. The crucial letter was written on December 9, 1921. Hanover City Archives, HR 20, no. 818.
19. Hanover City Archives, HR 20, no. 818.

of Hanover Stadium." What looked like a stunning victory was actually more limited in scope because the inscription was expanded to include the original reason why the stadium was built, thereby giving public expression to the adulation of Hindenburg. However, this compromise was still too much for conservative, middle-class circles. They remained furious over the chiseling away of the old name,[20] and the bourgeois newspapers continued to refer to the "Hindenburg Stadium." One commented that "all German athletes who still have a glimmer of patriotic honor consider the removal of the name 'Hindenburg Stadium' a stinging disgrace, a slap in the face of the entire nation. In their circles, the name will forever be 'Hindenburg Stadium,' although the stone has been chiseled away. For the name 'Hindenburg' is carved on the heart of the German people. Deep into even Social Democratic circles, people simply cannot understand how a group of fanatical hatemongers could do such a thing before the city authorities had even spoken on the issue."[21]

The dispute was at least located here on the level where it belonged, namely, political culture, but how was this done? There is no shortage of emotionally charged words, such as *honor, patriotic, heart, disgrace,* and *fanatical hatemongers*. Political opponents are ostracized and defamed. They are ostracized through the suggestion that since even many Social Democrats supported Hindenburg, those people who did not must be fanatical hatemongers and of questionable sanity. The figurative language is also noteworthy: the stone inscription may have been chiseled away but not the carving on the heart of the German people. The "fatherland," the "nation," and the "people" are equated with one another in a homogeneous way and held aloft in the same old spirit; any other interpretations of the "nation" are not considered.

The dispute over the name of the stadium expressed and symbolized the deep split in the political culture of the young republic. It cast a revealing light on the balance of power: the Majority Social Democrats may have emerged victorious on a formal level, but they still could not dominate public culture. In addition, the artistic avant-garde (Kurt Schwitters and others) in Hanover who had caught the public eye during the early days of the republic apparently had nothing to say. During the revolution of 1918–19, the artistic avant-garde in the Arbeitsrat für Kunst (Workers' Council for the Arts) in Berlin had attempted to bring art, politics, and society closer together through their utopian designs. After the Weimar Republic was founded, though, such impulses seemed to fade, or they

---

20. *Nordwestdeutsche Nachrichten,* February 12, 1922.

21. *Hannoverscher Kurier,* February 12, 1922. The *Hannoversche Kurier* played an especially prominent role in this regard, even commenting on an onslaught by "fanatic antimilitarists."

Fig. 8. Hindenburg's reception at the Hanover station, July 4, 1919. (From Hans-Dieter Schmid [ed.], *Feste und Feiern in Hannover*, 179 [Bielefeld, 1995].)

never really emerged in the first place in cities like Hanover. The Hanover avant-garde was particularly interested in working creatively with the everyday materials of the new mass society and had every reason therefore to develop links with representatives of popular sports. It was no coincidence that Bertold Brecht, for example, developed a particular interest in boxing, the spectator sport par excellence of the 1920s. In Hanover, however, the artistic avant-garde chose to remain quite aloof from political culture, and even a great scandal could not change this.

2. Sport Reigns Triumphant: The Opening Ceremonies

The highlight of the opening ceremonies was the parade of countless athletes into the new stadium. The first of the sports clubs to enter was the North German Soccer Association, followed by the North German Rugby Association.[22] The organizers considered it a matter of honor to have all sports clubs represented.[23] Many schoolchildren were also present, as well as the massed chorus of the Hanover Singers.[24]

Then came the demonstrations, which transported the crowd into the beckoning world of spectator sports. Three thousand schoolchildren performed free gymnastics, followed by "happy games." The massed chorus of the Hanover Singers also gave of its best. The sports program followed, with an array of events demonstrating the diversity of sporting life. There were a race of three hundred track-and-field athletes, a 100-meter sprint, long jump, javelin, apparatus gymnastics, so-called people's gymnastics, various ball games such as Schlagball and Faustball, women's Faustball, relay races, pole-vaulting, and finally a "rugby football match" between the Schwalbe-Döhren and Victoria-Linden clubs.

The stadium was sold out, and fifteen thousand spectators of all ages and social classes attended.[25] The huge interest in the stadium is not surprising. In a total German population of about 60 million, some 20 million were considered sports fans,[26] and Hanover was no exception. As mentioned earlier, spectator sports achieved their great breakthrough in the 1920s and became an important part of popular culture. Not only sports (especially spectator sports) but also movies, radio

---

22. *Hannoversche Landeszeitung,* May 23, 1922. The fact that the first association to enter was the soccer club could be seen as symptomatic of the sharply increased interest in soccer in the 1920s.

23. *Hannoversche Landeszeitung,* May 25, 1922.

24. *Hannoversche Landeszeitung,* May 28, 1922.

25. *Hannoverscher Anzeiger,* May 27, 1922.

26. In 1933, some 7.1 million people are said to have belonged to athletic clubs. Ernst Bayer, "Sport, Politik, und Presse" (Ph.D. diss., Heidelberg, 1936), 25; more accurate research with similar results in Eisenberg, "Massensport," 146ff.

(after 1924), magazines, and pulp novels were changing the way in which people lived and perceived the world, commercializing everyday human needs and creating leisure activities that transcended the traditional class boundaries and social circles. The opening ceremonies therefore epitomized modern spectator sports and commercialized leisure culture, which was expanding rapidly despite the straitened economic circumstances at the time.

Spectator sports themselves resulted from the increasing professionalization and commercialization of cultural practices.[27] Professionals could produce top-flight performances, and top-flight performances were good for business. The greater the supply, the more spectators came to demand performances that were always getting better. The interaction of order and discipline, play, and the struggle to the finish was very appealing. "While experiencing the tumult of competition, spectators look forward to the emergence of a new order. The feelings of fear, uncertainty and aggression aroused by the events of the competition are resolved in a feeling of security. When sporting events unfold within a fixed framework, they transform the fear generated by the struggle into hopes for an order that will triumph over the tumult."[28] This jumble of mechanisms and effects found expression as well in the speeches delivered at the ceremonies, for instance in the talk of "games of competition and celebration" or of the "noble struggle." Nothing could be grander than these "German Olympic Games," which — as was immediately added — should have been held already under the empire.[29]

Although spectator sports had begun to emerge before the war, the public was still unaccustomed to many aspects of them. This lack of familiarity became apparent at the opening ceremonies during the game of rugby, a sport that was not played very much in Germany but had some following in Hanover. According to press reports, the spectators gave the impression that they had never seen such a thing. At first, they seemed to think that the game was a kind of slapstick humor because of all the tumbles, and only gradually did they begin to watch excitedly and applaud the play.[30]

A truce was even struck for the opening ceremonies between the

---

27. The term *culture* is understood in the broad sense here and in what follows. For an introduction to this see Ute Daniel, "'Kultur' und 'Gesellschaft': Überlegungen zum Gegenstandsbereich der Sozialgeschichte," *Geschichte und Gesellschaft* 19, no. 1 (1993): 69–99. For spectator sports in general see Gunter Gebauer and Gerd Hortleder, "Die Epoche des Showsports," in Gunter Gebauer and Gerd Hortleder (eds.), *Sport—Eros—Tod* (Frankfurt, 1986), 82.

28. Ibid., 85.

29. Fink, quoted in *Hannoversches Tageblatt,* May 26, 1922.

30. *Hannoverscher Kurier,* May 26, 1922.

gymnasts and the athletes. Gymnasts tended still to be somewhat hostile toward sports, which were threatening the traditional preeminence of their pastime in Germany. Expressions of goodwill were therefore not necessarily assured. While many educators and functionaries of the old school were still caught up in the rivalry between sports and gymnastics, "modernists" hoped that sports, and even spectator sports, would boost the "culture of physical exercise" in general. Many people who were concerned about Germany's future viewed spectator sports less as an aspect of commercial, professionalized popular culture than as an opportunity to activate their fellow citizens and get them involved in gymnastics. This desire can be seen in the previously mentioned letter to Hindenburg from the city executive and again in the address delivered at the opening ceremonies by Senator Fink, a right-wing Liberal. He lamented "the lethargy and indifference toward physical exercise still found in all social classes." According to the senator, "gymnastics, sports and games" were a good antidote to the "nervousness, haste and restlessness brought by modern developments into the life of the *Volk.*"[31] Professor Kohlrausch spoke in turn about gymnastics and sports as the "fountain of health of the German people,"[32] mixing old ideas about the need for physical training prior to induction into the army with social reform concepts that were revived after the war to improve the health of the general population. Fink found similarly equivocal words, this time addressed specifically to the youth, Germany's supposed future wealth, whom he encouraged to adopt a "moderate, natural way of life," including "exercise and activity amidst nature, in the sun and air."[33] The opening ceremonies and some passages from the speeches illustrated, once again, the multiplicity of meanings and functions attributed to sports and gymnastics in postwar German society.

3. Big City Image Polishing and the Bold Decision to Build the Stadium

Even though Germany had lost the war and was strained to the limit by the housing shortage and high unemployment, Brandt's donation from

---

31. *Hannoversches Tageblatt,* May 26, 1922. Fink was a member of the National Liberals under the empire and of the German People's Party during the Weimar Republic.

32. Kohlrausch, quoted in *Hannoversches Tageblatt,* May 26, 1922. For an introduction to the Lebensreform movement, see Wolfgang R. Krabbe, *Gesellschaftsveränderung durch Lebensreform* (Göttingen, 1974); Ulrich Linse, "Lebensreformbewegung," *Archiv für Sozialgeschichte* 17 (1977): 538–43; for public health policies — using Hanover as an example — see for instance Regina Schramm, "Kommunale Gesundheitspolitik und Sozialhygiene im Hannover der 20er Jahre," in Adelheid von Saldern (ed.), *Stadt und Moderne: Hannover in der Weimarer Republik* (Hamburg, 1989), 117–55.

33. Fink, quoted in *Hannoversches Tageblatt,* May 26, 1922.

1916 was enough to prompt the Hanover municipal authorities to appropriate an additional eight hundred thousand marks in 1920 and begin construction.[34] Already under the empire, cities across Germany competed in image polishing and were eager to rank high among the leading centers in the nation. A positive image was good for tourism and helped to attract both industry and wealthy pensioners. A city's image depended for the most part on having a modern infrastructure, while the terrible conditions often found in working-class neighborhoods mattered much less, if at all. Cities had been compared and statistics produced already in Wilhelminian times,[35] but the revolution of 1918–19 added a whole new dimension. Social infrastructure, in the broadest sense, became a political rallying cry — not least of all in order to avoid a revolution like that in Russia. Public libraries, public schools, and social housing ranked high on the list of needs, but sports fields and swimming pools also figured prominently.[36] While Frankfurt, Cologne, Nuremberg, and other cities could already boast of "spacious, often overly well-equipped stadiums,"[37] Hanover looked like a poor cousin. At first it concentrated its efforts on numerous exercise areas, 121 in all, scattered across the city. If these areas are lumped together with playing fields, Hanover was providing 4.3 to 4.5 square meters of space per inhabitant for athletic endeavors, at a time when the generally accepted standard was only 3 square meters. It was probably the only large city in Germany that surpassed the standard and accordingly earned the moniker of the Großstadt im Grünen (the city amid the green) — even though the greenery was far from evenly distributed, with middle-class neighborhoods better endowed than their working-class counterparts.[38]

There was no reason, therefore, for the city of Hanover to fear

34. Alderman Demmig and former city manager Tramm spoke out against the timing of the project. Joint session of the municipal councils on September 9, 1920. Hanover City Archives, *Städtische Kollegien 1920,* vol. 4.

35. See in this regard Heinrich Silbergleit, *Preußens Städte* (Berlin, 1908); and *Statistisches Jahrbuch deutscher Städte,* published since 1890.

36. Some initial insights into this can be found in Sid Auffarth and Anna Masuch, "Stadtentwicklung in Demokratie und Diktatur," in *Hannover im 20. Jahrhundert: Aspekte der neueren Stadtgeschichte (Beiträge zur Ausstellung)* (Hanover, 1978), 85–108. In later years, there was some conflict over this kind of municipal image polishing with captains of industry and Reich president Schacht, who saw these sorts of facilities as wasteful spending that the German people could not afford. See in this regard Carl Böhret, *Aktionen gegen die "kalte Sozialisierung" 1926–1930: Ein Beitrag zum Wirken ökonomischer Einflußverbände in der Weimarer Republik* (Berlin, 1966).

37. *Bauamt und Gemeindebau* 13, no. 3 (February 6, 1931): 42.

38. Ibid.; for green spaces and open spaces see Ulfert Herlyn and Ursula Poblotzki (eds.), *Von großen Plätzen und kleinen Gärten: Beiträge zur Nutzungsgeschichte von Freiräumen in Hannover* (Munich, 1992).

comparison with other German cities in respect to opportunities for sports and exercise. Nevertheless, it did not have one of the large, impressive facilities for spectator sports that were considered the wave of the future. Only a stadium would do. Spurred on by the 1916 donation, Hanover became the first city after the war to undertake such a mammoth project, as was proudly reported in the local press.[39] No construction workers were available at first because of the crying need at the time for emergency housing and small apartments, and so the city had to rely on so-called irregular work.[40] Money was saved on the fittings and the roof, which was initially entirely omitted. When completed, the stadium accommodated twelve thousand standing but only three thousand sitting. This was both too many and too few: too many for everyday athletic events but already too few for the very large international matches being held.[41]

In conclusion, the building of the Hanover stadium should be seen in a general context of image polishing and urban infrastructure. At the time, municipal politics were devoted in considerable part to such questions as which facilities the city should finance, what elements of the population benefited most from these facilities, and how the city's reputation could be enhanced, with different groups having very different interests. It was relatively easy, however, to rally support for a stadium, not just because of the donation of 1916 but also because interest in sport transcended the social classes and the stadium was to be a multipurpose facility.

4. The Fissures in Class Society: The USPD Turns Its Back on the Opening Ceremonies

The class system of Wilhelminian times had left deep divides in society that were only exacerbated by the plan to name the stadium after Hindenburg. The labor movement considered the aging field marshal a symbol of the prewar society and the strong class system that had prevailed then. In those days, Social Democrats were often snubbed as nothing more than troublemakers who did not deserve even to be considered serious political opponents. They were politically and culturally ostracized and regularly humiliated, discriminated against, and harassed. This situation changed in the wake of the revolution of 1918–

---

39. *Hannoversches Tageblatt*, March 4, 1919.

40. Unemployment rose sharply in the late summer of 1920.

41. The city authorities would not accept more seats in the stadium. Joint session of the municipal councils, September 9, 1920. Hanover City Archives, *Städtische Kollegien 1920*, vol. 4.

19,[42] when the Social Democrats and labor unions became the acknowledged representatives of the working class. (After all, the middle classes and factory owners had a lot to lose if the revolution went too far.) However, the bitter experiences under the extremely rigid class system of the German Empire were not easily forgotten. The residual anger was most evident within the USPD (the Independent Social Democratic Party of Germany), to the left of the Majority Social Democrats. It refused to have anything to do with the opening ceremonies, ostentatiously spurning any invitations before they were even issued. This decision was not predicated solely on historical bitterness, however, and current political calculations also played a role.[43] Party headquarters had issued instructions that joint events with the bourgeoisie should be avoided. The mayor of Hanover, a Majority Social Democrat named Leinert, attempted to mediate but to no avail. The bourgeois press showed no understanding of the feelings of the USPD members, commenting spitefully on their "sullen refusal to attend."[44]

Unlike the USPD to their left, the Majority Social Democrats were divided in their attitude toward the opening ceremonies. As the leading party on city council, they were chiefly responsible for the building of the stadium,[45] but the "Hindenburg issue" proved very difficult. In the end, many Majority Social Democratic aldermen and members of the municipal executive apparently boycotted the opening ceremonies, as did Mayor Leinert himself, who claimed he was prevented from attending but probably thought it wise under the circumstances not to appear. Other party members apparently felt otherwise: Senator Sporleder and

---

42. For the revolution in Hanover see Werner Heine, *Verlauf und Auswirkungen der Novemberrevolution 1918 in Hannover* (Hanover, 1978). In the first municipal elections after the war in 1919, the Majority Social Democrats reaped 47.2 percent of the votes.

43. The Independent Social Democratic Party, which had split from the old SPD in 1917, advocated various kinds of workers' councils during the revolution of 1918–19. It benefited tremendously in the Reichstag elections of June 1920. However, its good fortune did not last for long. Squeezed between the Communist Party on one side and the Majority Social Democrats on the other, the Independent Social Democrats proved unable to develop credible political alternatives of their own. Some members defected to the Communists in 1920–21, and what remained of the party joined the Majority Social Democrats in September 1922. The Independent Social Democrats had little recognizable support in Hanover, winning only two of eighty-four seats in the municipal elections of 1919. *Hannover im 20. Jahrhundert,* 80. The Communist Party was not represented at all on city council.

44. *Hannoversche Landeszeitung,* May 28, 1922.

45. There was broad majority support, however, in the municipal councils. Joint session of the municipal councils on September 9, 1920. Hanover City Archives, *Städtische Kollegien 1920,* vol. 4.

Alderman Kleinert were spotted among the honored guests at the grand opening, thereby demonstrating their "manly courage" according to the middle-class press.[46] While the opening ceremonies received lavish coverage in the middle-class press, the Social Democratic *Volkswille* devoted only nine lines to them, published three days later.

While most of the Majority Social Democrats on the city council and municipal executive who refused to attend were reacting to the brouhaha surrounding the name of the stadium, the Kartell für Sport und Körperpflege, which was close to the Majority Social Democrats, had further, more principled objections. Its refusal was rooted as well in the conceptual disagreements and ill will between middle-class athletic clubs and workers' clubs, which had finally led to a formal decision by headquarters in Leipzig that workers' clubs should not participate in the events with "bourgeois" clubs.[47] The thought patterns engendered by class society evidently lived on in the realm of sport.[48] The reasons advanced for keeping one's distance from bourgeois clubs can be summarized as follows: bourgeois clubs embraced competition, encouraged high-performance athletes, and staged ceremonies honoring individual champions, while the workers' sports and gymnastics clubs emphasized mass participation and cultivated a working-class culture of solidarity and community.

The workers' sports and gymnastics clubs were quite successful in their attempts to make sport an integral part of everyday working-class culture in the Weimar Republic, eventually signing up about a million members. However, the bourgeois clubs were even more successful, counting about 7 million members. Superior working-class athletes often felt attracted to the bourgeois clubs, mostly because of the emphasis on individualism and high performance but also because of the quality of their equipment, and many eventually went over to the "class enemy." This step was facilitated by the fact that at least some bourgeois clubs welcomed working-class athletes and held themselves out as apolitical. Although their politically active members supported the middle-class parties, the bourgeois clubs generally subscribed to the belief that sports

---

46. *Hannoversche Landeszeitung,* May 28, 1922.

47. Horst Ueberhorst, *Frisch, frei, stark und treu* (Düsseldorf, 1973), 210. The cleavage between the working-class and middle-class athletic movements in Hanover was also apparent at the constitutional celebrations of 1929, which were held in the new stadium. However, the stadium was certainly used by working-class athletic clubs as well in the 1920s.

48. Under the empire, working-class and middle-class athletics were kept strictly separate.

should not be used directly for partisan political purposes, a conviction quite in keeping with the cultural norm. The image that arose therefore was that sports and politics had nothing to do with each other.[49] It would have been unthinkable for a Social Democratic or Communist athlete to become president of a middle-class club, but that was never a serious possibility anyway and therefore easy to disregard. Although workers' athletic clubs rooted in a strong class-consciousness were still very popular in the Weimar Republic, they were eventually driven onto the defensive, at least among the multitudes of workers without ties to the labor movement, by the (ideologically motivated) belief that sport was all that mattered.

The new popular culture, and especially sports, created areas of life in which the class system broke down to some extent. Here the differentiation into various classes and social strata was "solely" through the "invisible hand" of the market and prices, although even this mechanism did not always work. The new reality was described by Siegfried Kracauer, in reference to an automobile exhibition: "If I had not already known, I would now be finally convinced, after visiting the International Automobile Exhibition at Kaiserdamm, that automobiles are one of the few things that are universally revered nowadays. . . . Taxi drivers and gentlemen who drive their own automobiles, young fellows looking very proletarian and squads of police officers, elegant dandies and aspiring motorcyclists — people who would otherwise have nothing to do with each other — file religiously through the hallways, doing their devotions before radiators, ignitions and bodywork."[50]

The opening ceremonies were also boycotted by people on the other side of the political spectrum. One striking absence was that of Hanover's most powerful politician of Wilhelminian times, City Manager Tramm, who was finding it difficult to come to terms with the new political circumstances and his loss of influence.[51] Hindenburg too declined his invitation in the end, allegedly because it arrived too late.[52] His absence could certainly not be ascribed to any lack of interest in sports, although his tastes ran more to steeplechase.[53]

---

49. Organizations that are unquestionably part of the dominant public culture do not need to draw a direct connection between their activities and politics, as Gramsci pointed out. After 1933, it became particularly apparent that the separation of sports and politics was an illusion. The supposedly "apolitical" athletes competed for Nazi Germany as if nothing had changed.

50. *Frankfurter Zeitung,* February 24, 1931.

51. *Hannoverscher Kurier,* May 27, 1922.

52. Letter from May 30, 1922. Hanover City Archives, HR 20, no. 818.

53. "Hindenburg's interest in sport" was acclaimed when, for example, he went to Hanover for the steeplechase in 1928. *Weltschau,* May 19, 1928.

5. The Beginnings of Pluralism in Politics? Speeches Free from Political Attacks

While behavior marked by past experiences with class society was certainly one sign of the times, another was grudging acceptance of municipal democracy and pluralism as a result of more democratic electoral laws. Public opinion under the empire, strongly influenced by the middle classes, had always held that municipal politics was and should be apolitical. This view was due in part to the fact that workers were usually not represented at all on city councils or, if so, then only in very small numbers.[54] There were disagreements over municipal politics within the middle classes, of course, but they could always agree more or less on such fundamental issues as the distribution of resources between them and the working class or the preservation of the undemocratic electoral law. Middle-class officials were convinced in their own minds that they acted "apolitically" on behalf of the entire community. The cities, with their new cultural edifices, were bastions of middle-class power. The revolution of 1918–19 put an end to this state of affairs, at least in theory. The municipal franchise was extended in January 1919, in a step often lamented in middle-class circles as an unfortunate politicization of municipal life. However, closing middle-class ranks in opposition to the expanded franchise seemed dangerous and inopportune in view of the recent revolutionary events.[55] There was still a need to bolster the very moderate Majority Social Democrats or join in a consensus with them against the radical Left, which posed the severest threat to the middle classes. The attempts to form a consensus were somewhat successful, as could be seen in the efforts to compromise at the opening ceremonies of the stadium.

In accordance with this desire to preserve an atmosphere of goodwill, the city authorities agreed in advance that the orators asked to speak at the opening would refrain from all cutting remarks. They agreed further that the name "Hindenburg" should not be mentioned at all.[56] Under the circumstances, it seemed for the best that the most

---

54. See in general in this regard Adelheid von Saldern, "Geschichte der kommunalen Selbstverwaltung in Deutschland," in Roland Roth and Hellmut Wollmann (eds.), *Kommunalpolitik: Politisches Handeln in den Gemeinden* (Opladen, 1994), 2–19; for Hanover see Waldemar R. Röhrbein, "Verwaltung und politische Willensbildung," in *Hannover 1913: Ein Jahr im Leben einer Stadt: Beiträge zur Ausstellung, Historisches Museum* (Hanover, 1988), 61ff.

55. Not until the elections of 1924 did the middle-class parties form a so-called Ordnungsblock directed against the Social Democrats.

56. Minutes of the meeting of municipal authorities on May 16, 1922. Hanover City Archives, HR 20, no. 818.

prominent adversaries in the conflict over the stadium chose to absent themselves, as well as Hindenburg himself. Among the guests of honor who did appear was state governor Gustav Noske of the Majority Social Democrats, who apparently was not put off by the quarrels over the name of the stadium. He had been offered the position of governor when it became clear that his position as minister of the Reichswehr was no longer tenable.[57] Another guest of honor was Brigadier-General Voigt, as the representative of the local garrison. It was probably no coincidence that the *Hannoversche Landeszeitung* listed him first among all the guests. Also in attendance were the county manager, Fritz von Velsen; the chief of police, Rudolf von Beckerath; various city senators; members of the city school board Wespy and Grote; and a few aldermen. We will not delve into the issue of how many of the non-SPD guests of honor were strong supporters of the new republic, but it was probably very few.[58]

The first speaker at the opening ceremonies was Director of Municipal Construction Paul Wolf. He mentioned the origins and construction of the stadium and thanked all those who had lent a hand. Then came the keynote speaker, Senator Fink, representing the city. He discussed the history of the efforts to provide physical training, drawing a connection between the stadium and the "beloved fatherland." Privy Counselor Kohlrausch then offered his observations as chairman of the Hauptausschuß für Leibesübungen, concluding with a cheer for the city of Hanover, which was enthusiastically received.[59]

57. For Noske see in particular Wolfram Wette, *Gustav Noske: Eine politische Biographie* (Düsseldorf, 1987). His downfall came as a result of his decision to use the extreme right-wing Free Corps to put down supposedly radical workers in actions that led to much bloodshed, especially in the so-called Ruhr War (1920). The cruelty with which the Free Corps set about its task can be seen in a letter from a young student, in which he writes that he and his comrades even shot the wounded and ten Red Cross nurses during the Ruhr War against leftists. In regard to the latter, he writes: "We shot with pleasure on these disgraceful creatures. How they cried and begged. . . . We were much more noble toward the French on the battlefield." Josef Ernst, *Kapptage im Industriegebiet* (Hagen, 1921), 68. We still do not have a recent overview of the "white terror" of those years.

58. There is still a need for more detailed research into the public servants in Hanover who continued in their positions, a topic that we cannot explore any further here. It can be assumed that there was insufficient turnover at the time of the revolution in the old elites in society and the public service. This has often been described in the literature as a birth defect of the young republic, which later contributed to its downfall. See in this regard Reinhard Rürup, *Probleme der Revolution in Deutschland* (Frankfurt, 1986); Wolfgang Runge, *Politik und Beamtentum im Parteienstaat* (Stuttgart, 1965); and Wolfgang Elben, *Das Problem der Kontinuität in der deutschen Revolution: Die Politik der Staatssekretäre und der militärischen Führung vom November 1918 bis Februar 1919* (Düsseldorf, 1965).

59. *Hanoversche Landeszeitung*, May 28, 1922.

The various speakers refrained from political digs but also maintained a curious distance from the new republic. Much of what they said seemed more inspired by the past and what they claimed to be "eternally valid." Not worth mentioning, apparently, were any reflections on the role of sports in a democratic society.[60] The attempts to preserve a moderate tone and contribute to the political compromise were relatively superficial, inspired more by a desire not to spoil the show than by any real desire to explore what democratic pluralism might mean in sports and the public culture of the new republic.

6. Social Constructs of Femininity: The Reporting of the Opening Ceremonies

The newspaper reports of the opening ceremonies are excellent sources of information about the prevailing concepts of women and femininity. Particularly interesting is the way in which these concepts interacted with the relatively new phenomenon of sports. One notices immediately that sports were associated with men and any female athletes were seen as exceptions to the rule that needed special linguistic markers. For instance, men played "volleyball" while women played "women's volleyball";[61] men engaged in "gymnastics" and women in "women's gymnastics."[62]

The tone of the reporting was also different for men and women. The men's competitions were reported in an objective way, for instance: "Masses of gymnasts on the horizontal and parallel bars and on the horse demonstrated only a fraction of apparatus gymnastics, but it elicited pure joy and honest applause. What had been achieved in long, quiet hours of work behind closed doors in the clubs was put on display. In between, the 100-meter sprint was held, as well as the long jump and the javelin. Replacing the Leinhäuser teams, which backed out at the last minute, Turnclub Linden faced a combined rounders team but squeezed out a victory. The Turnclub and Turnerschaft 52 played a hard-fought volleyball match, which the Turnclub won by a whisker."[63]

The reporter's tone changed when women became the subject: "then the women and girls of the gymnastics associations filled the field

---

60. Wolf, quoted in *Hannoversches Tageblatt*, May 26, 1922. What was new in German society was mentioned only once and even then in connection with the old. Reference was made to the proximity of the new stadium to the municipal hall, which had been built in the old days of Wilhelmine society.

61. *Hannoversche Landeszeitung*, May 28, 1922.

62. *Hannoversches Tageblatt*, May 25, 1922.

63. *Hannoversches Tageblatt*, May 26, 1922.

with life. About 300 women from all district associations demonstrated Indian club swinging that was perfect in form. Gymnastics coach Loges kept the throngs firmly under control, but earned even greater applause next with his master class. One hundred and fifty female gymnasts from all clubs demonstrated a variety of rhythmic gymnastics to the sound of waltz melodies, in a display that will do much to promote female gymnastics. Among other things, there were also exercises on 15 parallel bars. Hopping and interpretive exercises to the sound of Schubert's "Marche militaire" closed the brilliantly successful performances of the master class under the outstanding leadership of gymnastics coach Loges."[64]

"Gymnastics coach Loges" felt that the emphasis in gymnastics should be on movement, and he had worked to reform women's gymnastics at the Hanover Master Gymnastics School he founded in 1921, especially by promoting rhythmic gymnastics. Like modern interpretive dance, which was also particularly popular in Hanover thanks to the influence of the famous expressionist dancer Mary Wigman, this type of gymnastics was the sort of modernism that many felt was especially suited to German culture. Loges also favored mass demonstrations of gymnastics.[65] Shows featuring various configurations of club-swinging women became very popular in the Weimar Republic, not to mention the Third Reich.

Strenuous physical exercise and competition were generally associated with male athletes, whose individual natures were allowed to shine through in the reporting.[66] In the reporting on women, physical exertion was downplayed as much as possible, and the individuality of the athletes was submerged in a sea of generalizations, clichés, and general descriptions of the beauty of the scene. In the report quoted earlier, the movement of the female bodies is examined, with the emphasis on all that is aesthetic and womanly, and the presentation is finally judged "perfect in form." Many reporters, including the one quoted here from the *Hannoversche Tageblatt,* waxed enthusiastic about the perfection of the technique, supposedly the result of much hard work, stamina, and

---

64. Ibid.

65. Later, in the Third Reich, Loges assumed the position of 'Women's Warden for Gymnastics and Dance" on the board of the German Gymnastics Association, where he aligned himself with the Nazi conception of sport. See Arnd Krüger, "'Die Gesetze der Schönheit in der Bewegung sind es wert, daß sie verbreitet werden': Carl Loges und die Musterturnschule," in Niedersächsischen Institut für Sportgeschichte, Hoya e.V. (ed.), *Sport in Hannover: Von der Stadtgründung bis heute* (Göttingen, 1991), 136–39; and Kurt Hoffmeister, "Carl Loges (1887–1958)," in the same volume, 140.

66. Heike Hanisch, "Geschlechterverhältnis und Sportöffentlichkeit in der Weimarer Republik am Beispiel von Leichtathletikwettkämpfen" (master's thesis, University of Hanover, 1993), 38ff.

an ability to subordinate oneself. The reporter maintained the same tone, although from the opposite point of view, in mentioning that "one lady" had suffered "a slight mishap" during the club swinging.[67] In short, reporting on female gymnastics and sports generally focused on aesthetic concepts of female grace and charm.[68]

Female participants in sports and gymnastics were not only described from aesthetic points of view and often in sexualized contexts but also were referred to as potential mothers. There was much talk at the time about the effects, for better or worse, of sports and gymnastics on the womb.[69] This kind of concern creeps into the newspaper report quoted previously when the reporter says that the women "filled the field with life," in what was probably an unconscious association with the life-giving womb. The introduction of Mother's Day in the same year bespeaks the same spirit, although it was not explicitly mentioned in the reporting of the opening ceremonies.[70] The exaltation of women as mothers or potential mothers reached its peak in Senator Fink's address to the assembled crowds, when he evoked the image of an all-encompassing mother of the *Volk* and tribe. He encouraged them to see themselves "as sons and daughters of a German mother, as members of a tribe."[71] The attempts to reconcile modern popular culture with these anachronistic images reminiscent of ancient myth are remarkable.

From the point of view of their effects on the womb, female gymnastics were now considered acceptable and even desirable if not overdone, partially as a result of the ideas about the body propagated by the "life reform movement." The newspaper report quoted earlier encouraged women to imitate their fellows and take part in gymnastics, including the comment that the opening ceremonies did much "to promote female

---

67. *Hannoverscher Kurier,* May 26, 1922. Connotations are evoked that have nothing to do with sport precisely because it is not plainly stated what her "slight mishap" was.

68. We will not delve any further into the extent to which the image of club-swinging women kept "under firm control" by a man was an appeal to sexual fantasies.

69. Cf. as well Krüger, "Gesetze," 136.

70. For Mother's Day, see Karin Hausen, "Mütter, Söhne, und der Markt der Symbole und Waren: Der deutsche Muttertag zwischen 1923–1933," in Hans Medick and David Sabean (eds.), *Emotionen und materielle Interessen* (Göttingen, 1984), 473–523; Karin Hausen, "Mütter zwischen Geschäftsinteressen und kultischer Verehrung: Der 'Deutsche Muttertag' in der Weimarer Republik," in Gerhard Huck (ed.), *Sozialgeschichte der Freizeit: Untersuchungen zum Wandel der Alltagskultur in Deutschland* (Wuppertal, 1980), 249–81. For more information see Karin Hausen, "Die Sorge der Nation für ihre 'Kriegsopfer': Ein Bereich der Geschlechterpolitik während der Weimarer Republik," in Jürgen Kocka et al. (eds.), *Von der Arbeiterbewegung zum modernen Sozialstaat: Festschrift für Gerhard A. Ritter zum 65. Geburtstag* (Munich, 1994), 719–40, especially 734ff.

71. Fink, quoted in *Hannoversches Tageblatt,* May 26, 1922.

gymnastics." Women's gymnastics did grow rapidly in the Weimar Republic, and by 1930 some eighty-five thousand women were officially involved.[72] At the same time, though, gymnastics became strongly associated with women, with the result that male participation dwindled to only six thousand. The new popular culture perpetuated, although in modernized form, the division of activities by gender, which had grown much more pronounced with the emergence of bourgeois society in the nineteenth century.[73]

Although gymnastics were considered an acceptable and even desirable activity for women, there was strong public resistance to female participation in track and field, even though some sixty-two thousand women did become club members.[74] Physicians were particularly opposed, claiming that track-and-field competitions would make women mannish, damage their reproductive organs, and injure their delicate nervous systems. Other critics were more concerned about the sexual order, claiming that athletic clothing was a threat to morality and that the existing hierarchies and spheres of interest of the genders were called into question.[75] Similar arguments could be heard about other kinds of sports.

However, the picture painted so far of athletics in the Weimar Republic is too one sided. Despite all the foot-dragging, athletics opened to women in the 1920s, at least to some extent and even though the leaders generally remained men.[76] The 27,000 female members of athletic clubs in 1914 climbed to 201,000 in 1930. The figures are somewhat misleading, though, because about 25 percent of these women were members of tennis, field hockey, or golf clubs.[77] In addition, despite the impressive

---

72. Krüger, "Gesetze," 136.

73. In other areas as well, modernization and traditional sexual roles were combined in new ways in the 1920s, for instance in domestic culture. In keeping with traditional standards and values, women remained solely responsible for housekeeping, although they were now supposed to be "modern" in their approach thanks to mechanization and professionalization. See in this regard as well Adelheid von Saldern, *Neues Wohnen: Wohnungspolitik und Wohnkultur im Hannover der Zwanziger Jahre* (Hanover, 1993), 148ff.

74. Eisenberg, "Massensport," 161. There were forty-five thousand women in the German Swimming Association.

75. Hanisch, "Geschlechterverhältnis," 64; for a basic discussion see Gertrud Pfister, "Zur Geschichte des Diskurses über den 'weiblichen' Körper (1880–1933)," in Birgit Palzkill et al. (eds.), *Bewegungs(t)räume: Frauen—Körper—Sport* (Munich, 1991); Gertrud Pfister and Hans Langenfeld, "Vom Frauenturnen zum modernen Sport: Die Geschichte der Leibesübungen der Frauen und Mädchen seit dem Ersten Weltkrieg," in Horst Ueberhorst (ed.), *Geschichte der Leibesübungen* (Berlin, 1982), 312:977.

76. See in this regard Sigrid Block, *Frauen und Mädchen in der Arbeitersportbewegung,* (Münster, 1987), 211ff. and the related tables in the appendix.

77. Eisenberg, "Massensport," 159ff. The basis on which the figures were determined differs so much from one case to the next that they cannot be directly compared.

growth in the number of female members of athletic clubs, the "disparity in comparison with men since 1913–14" did not decline and even increased. Although the proportion of female members of athletic clubs increased substantially until 1930, "the gender gap increased in terms of absolute numbers because the total number of female athletes was originally so small."[78]

Like the movies, sports did much to expand the range of activities in which women could participate, thereby helping to undercut the gendered division of life into a "domestic sphere" dominated by women and a "public sphere" dominated by men.[79] A young, self-confident "new woman" was said to be rising above the traditional female roles, taking advantage of the innovations and opportunities afforded by the times, whether in careers for women, the fashion industry, or athletics. Although the "new woman" was more a social construction composed of various images of women than a type who really existed, the coining of this term was a sign that relations between the sexes were beginning to change in the 1920s. Many working-class women, whose everyday lives were filled with drudgery and overwork, drew from the concept of the "new woman" some hopes (although fleeting and internally inconsistent) that life could be freer and better for themselves or their daughters, whatever their specific individual hopes may have been.[80]

On the other hand, cultural conservatives[81] of both sexes inter-

---

78. Ibid. There were about 3 million active male athletes in the Weimar Republic by the time of its collapse, a figure that was not reached and surpassed by women until between 1970 and 1975.

79. In regard to movies and the cinema and the unprecedented influence of the new media on the private and pubic spheres, see for early movies among others Miriam Hansen, "Early Silent Cinema: Whose Public Sphere?" *New German Critique* 29 (1983): 147–84; and Heide Schlüpmann, "Kinosucht," *Frauen und Film* 33 (October 1982): 45–52.

80. This is one of the conclusions of a study of Social Democratic working-class women in the Weimar Republic: "Ideals and standards, and therefore their expectations of everyday life, clearly changed faster in the first three decades than the reality of their lives. As a result, the inconsistencies and contradictions in their everyday experiences only increased." Karen Hagemann, *Frauenalltag und Männerpolitik: Alltagsleben und gesellschaftliches Handeln von Arbeiterfrauen in der Weimarer Republik* (Bonn, 1990), 651. Hagemann, to be sure, is referring here more to the welfare state than to changing cultural values. However, these two realms are interconnected through the realm of consumption. Although women expected to benefit from cultural change, they still criticized individual aspects of it. Social Democratic women had negative observations, for instance, about "shallow popular culture" and the Americanization of women. For more see Atina Grossmann, "Girlkultur or Thoroughly Rationalized Female: A New Woman in Weimar Germany?" in Judith Friedlander et al. (eds.), *Women in Culture and Politics: A Century of Change* (Bloomington, 1986), 62–80.

81. *Cultural conservative* was a contemporary term. It is not limited in scope to the members and supporters of the conservative parties but also includes numerous supporters from the liberal parties. See in this regard chapter 10 in this volume.

preted most aspects of the trend to the "new woman" as a threat to the family and therefore to the basic social order and the relationship between the genders. Their cultural ideal remained a polarized relationship of the sexes with special spheres of activity, although, to be sure, in expanded and "modernized" form.[82]

7. Conservative, Militaristic Public Culture: Values and Hopes

Although municipal politicians in Hanover certainly went out of their way to mitigate the political confrontation at the opening ceremonies, the conservative, militaristic mind-set that dominated public culture seemed to be taken for granted.[83] This mind-set included a negative attitude toward political parties and their competing policies, as could be seen when Senator Fink expressed the hope that the stadium could be kept free of "party quarrels." His thoughts were based on the supposed need for harmony, and he called for "peace and unanimity" and expressed his hope that the stadium would "serve the best interests of the whole of society." All social strata should come together in the stadium.

This concept could be interpreted as typical of modern sport, which cut across class lines. However, in the context of the other statements quoted earlier, another image emerges as well. What sounds conciliatory at first is actually a call, when read against the grain, for a unitary, apolitical *Volk* that, "in true love of the fatherland," sees itself as "members of a tribe."[84] Reading between the lines, we see here a total lack of understanding of the young democracy, which required political parties and disagreements, as well as a culture of dispute and compromise. Instead of this, dubious concepts such as "fatherland," "nation" "*Volk*," and "tribe" were held out as unifying principles, which, even after the experiences of the world war, were still considered beyond all question. This was the basis on which an attempt should be made to build a "communitas," in the words of Victor Turner discussed earlier. Apparently, this attempt proved quite successful. Many of the spectators seemed to share Senator Fink's approach, and according to newspaper

---

82. The Nazis too picked up on this, giving racial overtones to the "mother of the nation."

83. For conservative, militaristic local cultures after 1924–25 see Peter Fritzsche, "Between Fragmentation and Fraternity: Civic Patriotism and the Stahlhelm in Bourgeois Neighborhoods during the Weimar Republic," *Tel Aviver Jahrbuch für deutsche Gerchichte* 17 (1988): 136ff.

84. Fink, quoted in *Hannoversches Tageblatt,* May 26, 1922. This expression may just have been a meaningless cliché of the times, but its use to characterize political parties is no less instructive.

reports, his "cheer for the German fatherland was echoed by many thousands of voices and everybody rose to sing the "Deutschlandlied" with great gusto."[85]

It seemed only natural that the opening ceremonies were embedded in the old military culture. Although many people certainly pondered their own biographies in the light of the disastrous war, they continued to identify with the military.[86] This was probably due in large part to the "Bolshevik threat,"[87] which had enabled the high command, with the help of the "Free Corps," to reassert itself during the revolution of 1918–19 as the government's partner in the struggle to keep power and maintain order. The military therefore remained in the forefront of people's minds.[88] Rhetorical flourishes such as "the tragic outcome of the war"[89] or the statement that Germany had been "hurled by grievous fortune from the proud heights into the depths of the abyss" show that no attention was paid to the responsibility of Germany, and especially the high command, for the outbreak and conduct of the war. As was already mentioned in part 1 with examples from other sources, the primary emphasis was not on building a new, peaceful, democratic Germany but on regaining the old position of power. According to Fink, a "ray of hope" lay in the "gathering strength of our people," if "we keep our faith in our ascent and recovery from the severe illness that has shattered our people." The aim was "the delivery of the German people from misery and humiliation, the return of our fatherland to the object of our desires: the glories of old."[90] The phrase "glories of old" shows that Fink did not distance himself in the slightest from the semiautocratic system that had prevailed under the empire. His address was therefore actually an affront to the new Social Democratic government.

There were also strong military overtones to the way in which the

85. *Hannoversche Landeszeitung,* May 28, 1922; a similar description also appears in the *Hannoverscher Anzeiger,* May 27, 1922. In the early Weimar Republic, the anniversaries of the Battle of Sedan, the founding of the German Reich, and Bismark's birthday provided welcome opportunities for nationalistic and militaristic circles to gather and celebrate the occasions together. See Fritzsche, "Fragmentation," 136.

86. This was made easier by the "stab-in-the-back" legend, referring to the untenable thesis that Germany suffered military defeat largely because of revolutionary agitation at home, which sapped the strength of the armed forces. Hindenburg quoted a British general as saying: "The German army was stabbed in the back." [Bodo] Harenberg, *Schlüsseldaten 20. Jahrhundert* (Dortmund, 1993), 142.

87. Still informative in this regard is Peter Lösche, *Der Bolschewismus im Urteil der deutschen Sozialdemokratie 1903–1920* (Berlin, 1967).

88. This is not the place to look any further at the drastic cuts to the military as a result of the Treaty of Versailles.

89. Wolf, quoted in *Hannoversches Tageblatt,* May 26, 1922.

90. Fink and Wolf, quoted in *Hannoversches Tageblatt,* May 26, 1922.

ceremonies were staged. In the great parade of athletes and school-children, it was no coincidence that the military athletic association was the first group to enter the stadium, accompanied by "the merry sound of marches." The orators at the ceremonies and the newspaper reporters frequently resorted to military terminology, speaking of the "march past" and the "command" to sit down, "bloodless battle," "exercises to steel the body," and the "quality of the . . . human matériel."[91] In addition, so-called military competitors made an appearance.

Nevertheless, the military culture was toned down somewhat at the opening ceremonies, and there were definite signs of the new era. The stadium itself would have been very different if the times had not changed. Originally, during the war, Director of Municipal Construction Wolf had planned to build the stadium in the Döhren marshlands near the Döhren Tower along with a "war memorial" or "commemorative grove for the sons of the city who fell in the world war."[92] These so-called heroes' groves typically eschewed architectural elements or monuments in favor of oak trees meant to symbolize strength, might, endurance, and unity.[93] There were many proponents of this kind of "heroes' grove" during the war, including none other than Field Marshal von Hindenburg himself. Many were actually laid out,[94] and for the fiftieth jubilee of his induction into the army, the city of Hanover planned to build a great ring road on its southeastern edge lined with "heroes' groves" in "homage to Hindenburg." The work was to be financed through donations.[95] However, this and similar ideas never got beyond the planning stage. In March 1919 (i.e., *after* the revolution), circles close to Director of Municipal Construction Wolf were still thinking of constructing "a huge monument in honor of our fallen local heroes as the focal point of a spacious park, with gardens, a heroes' grove, swimming pools and playgrounds grouped around it."[96] In the end, this plan was also jettisoned, if for no other reason than that the ground was very soft and building such a monument would have been prohibitively expensive.[97]

---

91. *Hannoversche Landeszeitung,* May 28, 1922.

92. Wolf, quoted in *Hannoversches Tageblatt,* May 26, 1922.

93. For a relevant, comprehensive discussion: Gerhard Schneider, ". . . *nicht umsonst gefallen"? Kriegerdenkmäler und Kriegstotenkult in Hannover* (Hanover, 1991), 148–53.

94. George L. Mosse, *Fallen Soldiers: Reshaping the Memory of the World Wars* (New York and Oxford, 1990), 88.

95. For more see Walter E. W. Saal, "Bernhard Hoetger: Ein Architekt des norddeutschen Expressionismus" (Ph.D. diss., Bonn, 1989), 121ff.

96. *Hannoverscher Kurier,* March 2, 1919. This newspaper advocated many sports fields but not necessarily a stadium.

97. Wolf, quoted in *Hannoversches Tageblatt,* May 26, 1922.

Some remnants of military culture still clung, though, to the stadium that was built. Sports continued to be closely associated with war, struggle, and sacrifice. The stadium was occasionally referred to as a "battleground" (*Kampfstätte*),[98] and the pillar in the entranceway bore the inscription "Erected in the time of need of the German people, may this be a site of joyful struggle for the youth. Help us to raise a strong new generation following the wounds of the war, one that is grateful for the sacrifices of their fathers and proves itself worthy of them."[99] Even after the war, self-sacrifice was still extolled as a great virtue.[100] Some secondary virtues that were supposedly quintessentially German were also lauded at the opening ceremonies. One orator claimed, for instance, that things had been done "in the German way, with self-discipline and strict devotion to duty."

The speeches also made particular mention of the youth, which needed to be "strengthened and steeled."[101] The ultimate purpose was apparently to toughen up large numbers of the youth in order to magnify the power of the German people, which, as was claimed elsewhere, "could be equated with the power to defend ourselves."[102] The idea was to raise a "strong, young generation after the losses of the war."[103] Thought processes of this kind were very common in public speeches, although they could be interpreted in different ways ranging from civilian and social reformist to militaristic and revanchist. Common to all of them was often a biological element, for instance when it was said that a healthy mind required a healthy body. There was also a touch of social Darwinism, which found expression in statements about the "struggle for survival."[104]

Sports and war continued to be closely associated in the minds of many people. There was a certain tradition to this in Germany where, ever since the nineteenth century, physical education in secondary schools had been seen as preparation for induction into the army. Director of Municipal Construction Wolf was apparently one of those who took connections of this kind for granted.[105] Although no "heroes'

---

98. Cf. for instance the joint session of the municipal councils. Hanover City Archives, *Städtische Kollegien 1920,* vol. 4.

99. In *Hannoversches Tageblatt,* May 26, 1922, and repeated in Wolf's address.

100. See in this regard for the period before the war Wolfram Siemann, "Krieg und Frieden in historischen Gedenkfeiern des Jahres 1913," in Peter Düding and Paul Münch (eds.), *Öffentliche Festkultur: Politische Feste in Deutschland von der Aufklärung bis zum Ersten Weltkrieg* (Reinbek, 1988), 298–320.

101. Fink, quoted in *Hannoversches Tageblatt,* May 26, 1922.

102. *Hannoverscher Kurier,* March 2, 1919.

103. Wolf, quoted in *Hannoversches Tageblatt,* May 26, 1922.

104. Fink, quoted in *Hannoversches Tageblatt,* May 26, 1922.

105. See in this regard Schneider, *"Nicht umsonst,"* 122ff., 161.

grove" was built in the end, a war memorial was constructed very close to the stadium to ensure that the link between physical exercise and warfare was preserved for future generations.[106]

Conclusion

The official opening of the stadium in 1922 showed that the old Wilhelminian way of celebrating important events could not be totally preserved after the First World War, although many traditional practices survived. More of these practices would have continued, in all likelihood, if the labor movement had not gained considerable influence over public culture thanks to labor's position of relative strength after the lost war and the inability of its political enemies to continue ignoring it. The Social Democrats, who had long been decried as *vaterlandslose Gesellen* (unpatriotic), had very ambivalent feelings about patriotism and the military. However, they had been deeply moved in many cases by their experiences in the Great War, not least of all—despite the horror of war—by their experience of the "community of the front" spanning all social classes. These experiences, together with the harshness of the Treaty of Versailles and the constant hostility of opponents of the republic, induced the Majority Social Democrats largely to forgo thorough public analysis of Wilhelminian militarism and imperialism and a clear, public interpretation of what the democratic, republican nation was all about.[107]

There were still strong differences, though, between the Majority

---

106. There had previously been shooting ranges on the land where the stadium was built. Military culture was given a boost in Hanover when Hindenberg, an honorary citizen of the city to whom the city had presented a villa and a German shepherd dog, was elected Reichspräsident in 1925. He failed to receive a majority in the city that supposedly so revered him, but this only caused conservatives to howl all the more about the need for an "inner Tannenberg" (in reference to the great victory gained under the leadership of Hindenburg and Ludendorff at the Battle of Tannenberg in East Prussia on August 31, 1914). A three-hour march past before Hindenburg's house in Seelhorststraße (today: Bristolerstraße 6) reveals the extent of the affection for him. See also Waldemar Röhrbein, *Hannover, so wie es war,* 2d ed. (Düsseldorf, 1980), 87. It was said at the time that "All our good sides, our trust in God, love of the fatherland, courage, selflessness, devotion to duty, sense of order, and inner urge toward purity of the soul live in him and elevate him for us to the heights of the ideal human being." Marwedel, *Lessing,* 256.

107. It is noteworthy that during the revolutionary months of 1918–19, the Majority Social Democrats did not attempt in their writings and speeches to invoke the French Revolution and the founding of the nation on it. See in this regard Adelheid von Saldern, "'Nur ein Wetterleuchten': Zu den historischen Komponenten des 'Novembergeistes' von 1918/19," in Jürgen Kocka et al. (eds.), *Von der Arbeiterbewegung zum moderne Sozialstaat: Festschrift für Gerhard A. Ritter zum 65. Geburtstag* (Munich, 1994), 104.

Social Democrats' conceptions of what the political culture should be and the conceptions of the Conservatives or Conservative-Liberals — as can be seen in the scandals surrounding the opening ceremonies. The chiseling in and chiseling out of the name "Hindenburg" and the way in which the field marshal's persona hung over the opening ceremonies, despite his physical absence, are testimonials to these differences. The dispute over the name of the stadium developed into a struggle over the direction that public culture would take, which was beginning to include spectator sports and, along with them, popular culture.

There were attempts to use athletic ceremonies in order to ritualize nationalism and put it on a modern footing.[108] Values that had grown dubious, such as "fatherland," "the strength to defend oneself" (*Wehrkraft*), and "combative spirit" (*Kampfgeist*) could survive in this way as an apparently natural part of public culture. The tensions surrounding the opening ceremonies were due to the fact that these values continued to thrive, even though the Social Democrats supposedly held the upper hand in municipal politics in Hanover. The Social Democrats could prevent the worst from happening, that is, naming the stadium after Hindenburg, but they could not (and did not want to) determine by themselves what public culture should be and what the "nation" should mean in a democratic republic.[109] In the middle-class parties, no politicians stepped forward who were out-and-out democrats and not just *Vernunftrepublikaner.* No symbols grew up around the young republic, democracy, and the ideal of a civil society that could capture the public imagination. Concepts and ideas paving the way to the future remained poorly developed. No one felt proud of the fact that a semiautocratic, militaristic government had been overthrown in virtually bloodless revolution. What a contrast to the political culture in France, where the national identity revolved around the glorious *révolution,* despite all the lives it cost!

Thirty-two years later in 1954, at the opening ceremonies of Lower

---

108. Cf. in general Harry Pross, "Ritualisierung des Nationalen," in Jürgen Link and Wulf Wülfing (eds.), *Nationale Mythen und Symbole in der zweiten Hälfte des 19. Jahrhunderts* (Stuttgart, 1991), 94–106.

109. Whether and to what extent the local Social Democrats realized that this was a problem is an open question. On the national level, the SPD attempted to avoid any clarifications of war guilt, although clearly distinguishing itself in this regard from the parties on the right. By contributing to the national consensus that developed around rejecting responsibility for the outbreak of the war, the SPD missed an opportunity to help forge a "new, republican beginning." See Gottfried Niethart, "'So viel Anfang war nie' oder: 'Das Leben und nichts anderes': Deutsche Nachkriegszeiten im Vergleich," in Gottfried Niethart and Dieter Riesenberger, *Lernen aus dem Krieg? Deutsche Nachkriegszeiten 1918 und 1945* (Munich, 1992), 27.

Saxony Stadium in Hanover, no marches were played. Some symbolic connections were still visible between sports and war since the fanfares were played, alongside police bands, by musicians from the Federal Border Guard, in an allusion to the Cold War. For the most part, though, military culture had been dropped in favor of the politically inoffensive "eternal" values of Western, Christian civilization, as symbolized in the concluding song by Hermann Claudius, "Wenn wir schreiten Seit an Seit, . . . mit uns zieht die neue Zeit" (When we stride side by side, . . . the new times are with us).

Henceforth, sports and politics were supposed to be mutually exclusive. Athletic events were expected to bring the social classes together, a task made all the easier by the fact that working-class sport, once suppressed by the Nazis, failed to revive after 1945, with only a few exceptions. Folk dancing and local costumes were very much in evidence at the opening ceremonies and were the only traditional elements that seemed to have survived the intervening years with their reputations still intact.[110] Their inclusion in the opening ceremonies symbolized the notion that folk culture — or what was defined as such — was beyond politics, a view that was clearly not right with respect to the Third Reich.

There were no long-winded speeches, just a few introductory remarks and the conveyance of the stadium to the athletes. The demonstrations and competitions began immediately.[111] The speeches may have been cut short by the heavy rain, but lack of eloquence was also possibly a sign that the Third Reich had destroyed forever the traditional kind of political celebrations in Germany.[112] Director of Municipal Construction Hillebrecht did mention in passing that the rubble used to build the stadium was mixed with blood and tears.[113] A democrat by now, he too used language intended to keep alive the memory of those who had perished in the Second World War, according to the newspaper report, although he failed to mention who was actually responsible for the war or who were the true victims of the Nazi regime. Instead, Germans in general were remembered as victims, that is, primarily as victims of the bombs dropped by the Allies. Here we see a way of dealing with the Third Reich that was very typical of public culture in the Federal Repub-

---

110. For the folk dancing, see *Hannoversche Allgemeine Zeitung,* September 25–26, 1954.

111. *Hannoversche Presse,* September 25, 1954; *Hannoversche Allgemeine Zeitung,* September 27, 1954.

112. Cf. in this regard the overview by Michael Maurer, "Feste und Feiern als historischer Forschungsgegenstand," *Historische Zeitschrift* 253 (1991): 103–30.

113. *Hannoversche Presse,* September 27, 1954.

lic at that time and, to some extent, still is today.[114] At the original opening ceremonies in 1922, the war had been interpreted primarily as a matter of fate and misfortune, whereas now the emphasis was on blood and tears. In both cases, though, Germany was portrayed as a passive victim. There were therefore certain similarities on the formal level in the ways in which the wars were interpreted. The two postwar cultures were very different, though, in other respects, for instance the role of militarism and quest for great power status; the kinds of monuments raised to the fallen soldiers; and, most of all, the disassociation of sports from any idea of training and toughening up the youth for war and instead their confirmation as an important part of popular culture.[115]

---

114. One could point in this connection to the commemorations in Bitburg in 1985 and at the Neue Wache in Berlin, which was inaugurated in November 1993.

115. For the first two aspects see Wolfram Wette, "Die deutsche militärische Führungsschicht in den Nachkriegszeiten," in Gottfried Niethart and Dieter Riesenberger, *Lernen aus dem Krieg? Deutsche Nachkriegszeiten 1918 und 1945* (Munich, 1992), 39–67; and Sabine Behrenbeck, "Heldenkult oder Friedensmahnung? Kriegerdenkmale nach beiden Weltkriegen," in the same volume, 344–65.

CHAPTER 9

Popular Culture: An Immense Challenge in the Wiemar Republic

Introduction

Although the origins of the new popular culture reached back to prewar days, it did not begin to spread rapidly until the 1920s, when both public and private life were deeply influenced. Radio, records, movies, jazz, new dances, shows, high fashion, pulp magazines, spectator sports, advertising, and other developments revolutionized perceptions of the world or what could be called the culture of the senses.[1] Increasing amounts of leisure time were devoted to popular culture.[2] According to contemporary estimates, about 2 million people a day were going to the

Earlier versions of this article were discussed in 1989 in the history departments of various U.S. universities, including Johns Hopkins University in Baltimore, the University of Nebraska—Lincoln, the University of Texas—Austin, Yale University, Harvard University, the University of California—Berkeley, Stanford University, the University of Chicago, New York University, and others. An earlier version also served as one of the discussion points at two conferences of scholars from East and West Germany on continuity and change in working-class culture. These conferences in Hanover in 1989 and Berlin in 1991 were organized by Dietrich Mühlberg and myself with the financial support of the Volkswagen Stiftung. I would like to thank everyone involved for the critiques offered on these occasions. I would also like to thank Imke Jungjohann for her help with the research.

1. Gerd Selle (with assistance from Jutta Boehe), *Kultur der Sinne und der ästhetischen Erziehung: Alltag, Sozialisation, Kunstunterricht in Deutschland: Vom Kaiserreich zur Bundesrepublik* (Cologne, 1981); cf. Siegfried Kracauer, *The Mass Ornament: Weimar Essays* (Cambridge, MA, 1995).

2. For reasons of space, this aspect is not discussed any further here. The questions of how various social strata used their leisure time and the role that popular culture played are just as important, however, for a description of life in the Weimar Republic as the question discussed here, namely, the impression that the public had of popular culture and of its effects on the general population.

movies by the mid-1920s.[3] By early 1927, there were 1.4 million radio sets in Germany and about 3.7 million listeners, including large numbers of working people.[4]

The everyday lives of many Germans were deeply affected by the media, which "provided other social spaces, other ways to spend time and socialize, and new leisure activities. They created, one would expect, different personalities after which to model oneself, including the behaviors seen in the movies, and they trained their audiences to see the world in a faster, more disjointed, more reflexive way."[5] Popular culture was very controversial, though, and there were various attempts to influence it in one direction or another. Should it be encouraged, contained, channeled, reworked or refined?"[6]

The term *popular culture* and its meaning are vague, equivocal, and controversial and can only be adequately understood in historical context. The term is used here in reference to cultural artifacts that were produced in industrial and commercial ways or by new technological inventions and consumed by large numbers of people.[7]

Popular culture was distinguished not only from "high culture" but also from folk culture and labor movement culture, although the boundaries were fluid because of the mutual influences on form and contents.[8]

---

3. Dieter Langewiesche, "Freizeit und 'Massenbildung': Zur Ideologie und Praxis der Volksbildung in der Weimarer Republik," in Gerhard Huck (ed.), *Sozialgeschichte der Freizeit: Untersuchungen zum Wandel der Alltagskultur in Deutschland* (Wuppertal, 1980), 223–49.

4. In Dieter Langewiesche, "Politik — Gesellschaft — Kultur: Zur Problematik von Arbeiterkultur und kulturellen Arbeiterorganisationen in Deutschland nach dem Ersten Weltkrieg," *Archiv für Sozialgeschichte* 22 (1982): 397. Radio in Germany was not commercial. The Reich and the various governments held a majority interest in all radio companies under the radio regulation of 1926. The holding company Reichs-Rundfunk-Gesellschaft considerably increased the ability of the state to influence radio broadcasting. In 1932 radio became entirely government operated. Winfried B. Lerg, *Rundfunkpolitik in der Weimarer Republik* (Munich, 1980), 267ff.

5. Erhard Schütz, "Medien," in Dieter Langewiesche and Heinz-Elmar Tenorth (eds.), *Handbuch der deutschen Bildungsgeschichte* (Munich, 1989), 5:372.

6. The term *refinement* (Veredelung) was current at the time. What reformers meant by it was ridding popular culture of kitsch and making popular culture "moral."

7. The use of *popular culture* here is neutral and therefore different from the uses, especially by the Frankfurt school, in which the equivalent term *Massenkultur* almost always has largely negative connotations.

8. For theoretical positions see, on the one hand, Max Horkheimer and Theodor W. Adorno, "Kulturindustrie: Aufklärung als Massenbetrug," in Max Horkheimer and Theodor W. Adorno, *Dialektik der Aufklärung*, new ed. (Frankfurt, 1971), 108–51; and, on the other hand, Umberto Eco, *Apocalittici e integrati* (Milan, 1964). For an introduction to the current state of theoretical views of popular culture, not least of all from a historical perspective, see the contributions of Lawrence W. Levine, Robin D. G. Kelly, Natalie

Popular culture was and remains rather ambiguous from a political perspective because it can coexist with a variety of political systems. It did not develop on politically or culturally neutral ground because the cultural industries quickly became relatively expensive, and capitalists certainly had greater opportunities to shape it than did workers or the labor movement.[9]

In the following we wish to look at how culturally active representatives of the (well-educated) bourgeoisie, the artistic avant-garde, left-wing intellectuals, and the labor movement responded to the phenomenon of "popular culture." At the heart of the discussion are the so-called cultural conservatives[10] because they generally set the tone of the debate, especially in the Reichstag and Prussian Landtag. Attitudes toward popular culture are generally studied by means of three examples: pulp fiction (*Trivialliteratur*) (especially that sold door-to-door), movies, and radio. While movies and radio were totally new forms of popular culture, pulp fiction had developed from older models. Nevertheless, it was mass-produced pulp fiction that the well-educated bourgeoisie seemed to find most objectionable.

Cultural Interventionism

Ruling circles have always concerned themselves with the morals, customs, and cultural lives of the people they govern and have attempted to intervene in various ways in their culture.[11] However, the challenge posed by modern popular culture was unprecedented because it threat-

---

Zemon Davis, and T. J. Jackson Lears in *American Historical Review* 97, no. 5 (1992): 1369–431; and Michael Denning, Janice Radway, Luisa Passerini, William R. Taylor, and Adelheid von Saldern in *International Labor and Working-Class History* 37 (spring 1990): 2–41. Further reference to the literature can be found in the two journal articles just mentioned.

9. For this reason, Eco's conception of popular culture as an "open culture" must be limited and thereby modified as a result of this difference in opportunity; Eco, *Apocalittici*, 15. For contemporary understandings of the terms *popular culture* and *the masses* and the related hopes and fears of the left-liberal bourgeoisie, see Dieter Mayer, *Linksbürgerliches Denken: Untersuchungen zur Kunsttheorie, Gesellschaftsauffassung, und Kulturpolitik in der Weimarer Republik (1919–1924)* (Munich, 1961), for instance 219, 224.

10. The term *cultural conservatism* was in use at the time. For instance, it was used in the sense in which we use it by Gerhard Stiebler, "Kultur-Konservatismus," *Kulturwille: Monatsblatt für Kultur der Arbeiterschaft* 8, no. 7–8 (1931): 105.

11. For the late nineteenth century see for instance Jürgen Reulecke, "'Veredelung der Volkserholung' und 'edle Geselligkeit': Sozialreformerische Bestrebungen zur Gestaltung der arbeitsfreien Zeit im Kaiserreich," in Gerhard Huck (ed.), *Sozialgeschichte der Freizeit: Untersuchungen zum Wandel der Alltagskultur in Deutschland* (Wuppertal, 1980), 141–61.

ened to bring about a fundamental shift in the cultural values of society. The times were unusual, said Reich minister of the interior Dr. Külz of the German Democratic Party, in 1926: "Never has German literature, never have art and science been so impeded by smut, trash and kitsch as they make their way to the people."[12]

There were no historical precedents for a challenge of this kind. Ruling circles had to gain some experience first, remaining as flexible and capable of learning as possible, understanding popular culture as a process, and discovering how to see through the complex relationship between popular culture and the power structure. This task was not easy, especially since popular culture made its breakthrough in Germany at a time when the traditional political and cultural system of the empire had collapsed and the middle classes were nursing traumatic memories of the lost war and revolution. The discussion about popular culture in the 1920s could build in many ways on similar discussions under the empire, but these discussions had always been held on what seemed like a firm footing from the perspective of the ruling classes. Now there was a "discourse without any solid ground" on which to stand, at a time when popular culture was expanding rapidly. The resulting situation was often considered dangerous. It was under these unstable conditions for the bourgeoisie, and especially the well-educated bourgeoisie, that the debates raged about good taste, morality, and kitsch[13] and the new mass media of movies, radio, and pulp fiction. We will examine these debates in more detail subsequently.

The arrival of strong U.S. influences in popular culture, especially in regard to movies, the "girl cult," and lifestyles (the "American way of life"), aroused concern in many middle-class circles about cultural domination. Germany's relations with the United States remained quite good on the political and economic levels, at least while the Dawes Plan was still in effect (1924–30), and reactions to the "Americanization of German culture" tended to be more mixed[14] than reactions to influences from Soviet Russia, which were much easier to decry as "cultural Bolshevism" and push to the cultural and political fringes. "Cultural

---

12. Dr. Külz, minister of the interior, German Democratic Party, *Verhandlungen des Reichstag, Stenographische Berichte,* vol. 391, 239th session, November 26, 1926, 8213.

13. "Kitsch arises when a stylistic device is taken from one context and inserted into another, whose structure does not have the same homogeneity and necessity as the original, while the message is offered, on the basis of the insert, as an original work conveying new experience." Eco, *Apocalittici,* 88.

14. For more see Adelheid von Saldern, "Überfremdungsängste: Gegen die Amerikanisierung der deutschen Kultur in den Zwanziger Jahren," in Alf Lüdtke, Inge Marßolek, and Adelheid von Saldern (eds.), *Amerikanisierung: Traum und Alptraum im Deutschland des 20. Jahrhunderts* (Stuttgart, 1996), 213–45.

Bolshevism" gradually assumed greatly inflated meanings. For instance, according to the writer and Center Party deputy Josef Joos, it meant the "dissolution and disappearance of deep moral traditions in marriage and the family, the state and the church."[15] His fellow party member Georg Schreiber, a professor of theology from Münster, stated quite clearly what actually lay behind the struggle against "cultural Bolshevism" insofar as he and similarly minded people were concerned, when he proclaimed in the Reichstag in 1929 that "Christianity and German culture have gone together in all ways. Their fates are uniquely intertwined and this must remain so."[16] However, Wilhelm Sollmann, a Social Democrat and merchant by trade who later became the editor in chief of the *Rheinische Zeitung,* criticized the indiscriminate use of the term *cultural Bolshevism* because, as one might assume, cultural practices revolving around the SPD ran the risk of being swept up in overly expansive definitions. Sollmann saw the dispute over "proper" cultural practices as an attempt on the part of cultural conservatives, especially those in the Center Party, to impose "cultural dictatorship by the orthodox Christian worldview."[17] These were the parameters within which at least part of the public discussion raged. The resistance of the church and the faithful to the ever broader and deeper secularization of cultural life led to demands for far-reaching government intervention.

Greater state invention in culture was justified in other ways as well. For instance, parallels were drawn between the duties of a "modern *Kulturstaat,*" especially insofar as youth were concerned, and those of the modern welfare or constitutional state.[18] The state "very much has a duty nowadays . . . to pursue a conscious cultural policy."[19] Theodor Heuß, a German Democratic Party deputy in the Reichstag, was reflecting much of public opinion when he spoke of a "social policy of the soul"[20] in connection with government intervention in culture.

People who wanted to see Germany regain a leading role in the world also called for government intervention in culture. Center Party

---

15. Joos, Center Party, *Reichstag,* vol. 428, 178th session, June 18, 1930, 5584. Individual examples appear here.

16. Dr. Schreiber, Center Party, *Reichstag,* vol. 425, 79th session, June 7, 1929, 2181; for similar comments see Mumm, German National People's Party, *Reichstag,* vol. 426, 109th session, December 3, 1929, 3404.

17. Sollmann, SPD, *Reichstag,* vol. 428, 176th session, June 16, 1930, 5458.

18. Dr. Schreiber, Center Party, *Reichstag,* vol. 391, 234th session, December 12, 1926, 8067.

19. Dr. Steffens, German People's Party, Prussian *Landtag,* vol. 12, 239th session, May 7, 1923, 17025.

20. Dr. Heuß, German Democratic Party, *Reichstag,* vol. 391, 240th session, November 27, 1926, 8234.

deputy Schwering alleged that no "great artist" was emerging under the republic and expressed his hope that "such a figure will arise because that would also be of capital importance for Germany's political standing as a world leader."[21] His fellow party member Schreiber said that "the Germany of today in this postwar period, stripped to a large extent of weapons and the means to defend itself and no longer radiating power, is bound by its position in the world to proclaim its ethical and cultural strength on international cultural markets and thereby influence the peoples of this planet and the civilized world (cries of 'very good' from the Center Party). This is a new thought, this is a progressive thought."[22] Underlying Schreiber's remarks was the conviction that Germany was the intellectual capital of the world[23] and must remain so.

Another justification of cultural interventionism was the social transformation that had occurred in the aftermath of the war and inflation, especially the emergence of the new rich and their effects on German cultural life. According to Deputy Hoff of the German Democratic Party: "The social strata that for many decades patronized the arts and indirectly supported them are often no longer in an economic position to do so. . . . The new rich often lack an intimate understanding of the arts and the right attitude. . . . If the financially well-endowed showed some understanding of real art and supported it, we would be much further ahead."[24]

The desire for government intervention in culture was also due to the feeling in much of the well-educated bourgeoisie that it was waging a difficult, two-front war against popular culture on one hand and modern art on the other. This feeling aggravated the sense that German culture was threatened and needed to be defended. The struggle was against certain "signs of the times, in which pressure is exerted to force a so-called art on other people; signs of the times, in which the others just as consciously resist what is being forced upon them — and do so successfully, even if they need to fight!"[25] As can be seen here, the

---

21. Dr. Schwering, Cologne, Center Party, Prussian *Landtag,* vol. 12, 244th session, May 14, 1923, 17369.

22. Dr. Schreiber, Center Party, *Reichstag,* vol. 426, 109th session, December 3, 1929, 3410.

23. This is a only somewhat overstated interpretation of a passage from a speech by Schuster, German People's Party, Prussian *Landtag,* vol. 5, 102nd session, February 20, 1922, 7237.

24. Hoff, German Democratic Party, Prussian *Landtag,* vol. 12, 244th session, May 14, 1923, 17389.

25. Josef Buchhorn, German People's Party, Prussian *Landtag,* vol. 5, 105th session, February 23, 1922, 7461. Josef Buchhorn was a writer and the Berlin correspondent of the *Hannoversche Kurier.*

resistance was not only to popular culture but to modern art as well. Negative attitudes toward the latter tended to fall into two camps. Some people rejected modern art in toto, decrying it as pseudoart and the "decadence of German art." Others claimed that they were open to modernity and "healthy progress," in which there was some "continuity with the past," but that modern art was "exaggerated," "too or very modern," or still in an embryonic stage.[26]

Nobody wanted a Kulturkampf, but many felt that it had arrived.[27] The epithet "Kulturkämpfer" certainly resounded in the Reichstag, hurled by the Left at the conservative parties.[28] Not only the Left but also Dr. Theodor Bohner of the Liberal German Democratic Party, a writer and an assistant headmaster, spoke about the Kulturkampf being waged "by the other side," namely, the Center Party and the Right.[29] The Prussian minister of science, art, and adult education, Dr. Becker of the Center Party, hoped to forge a common front on cultural policy. In his view, cultural policy should be framed in such a way "that hopefully all constructive parties in this House and among the German people can cooperate."[30] (The party that he assumed would not be constructive was, of course, the Communists.) It was not easy to achieve a common front on cultural policy because the middle classes themselves were by no means unanimous. In a rough overview such as this, at least three groups can be distinguished: cultural conservatives, cultural nationalists, and cultural liberals.

Cultural Conservatives

Cultural conservatives were reformers who took an idealistic view of culture and tended to be culturally moralistic.[31] They directed their efforts toward curbing and altering popular culture, while strengthening traditional cultural practices as much as possible. There were cultural conservatives in all the middle-class parties, from the German Nationals

---

26. This is the essence of the research into the proceedings of the Prussian Landtag and the Reichstag. We will not provide individual examples at this point.

27. See Dr. Otto Boelitz, preparatory school headmaster (Gymnasialdirektor) and Prussian minister of science, art, and adult education, German People's Party, Prussian *Landtag*, vol. 4, 81st session, December 10, 1921, 5742.

28. See *Reichstag*, vol. 390, 205th and 206th sessions, May 19, 1926, 7327.

29. Dr. Bohner, German Democratic Party, Prussian *Landtag*, vol. 17, 355th session, March 14, 1928, 25348.

30. Dr. Becker, minister of science, art, and adult education, Center Party, Prussian *Landtag*, vol. 4, 91st session, November 3, 1925, 5712.

31. *Cultural moralism* was also a contemporary term. See Stiebler, "Kultur-Konservatismus," 105.

and the Center Party to the Economic Party, the German People's Party, and the German Democratic Party. However, most of the real activists were in the conservative German National Party and in the Center Party. Women played a relatively prominent role in the important debates in parliament because of the moral issues surrounding popular culture. Many women who took a particular interest in cultural policy belonged to the middle-class women's movement, which felt that it bore a special responsibility for questions of morals. In general, though, cultural conservatives acted out of a variety of motives and came from a variety of backgrounds. The influence that the churches exercised over cultural policy, especially the influence of the Roman Catholic Church over Center Party policy, was based on a particular religious and moral milieu that considered popular culture a challenge by the Zeitgeist to eternal ethical values. According to one speaker at the Catholic Conference in Essen in 1932: "The movies are still permeated with manifestations of a generally un-Christian attitude found among people in the big cities."[32] Cultural conservatives in the German National Party emphasized the decline of "good" German culture and plotted nationalistic counterstrategies.

Although cultural conservatives could be found throughout the middle class, they tended to be concentrated in the higher and middle strata and in the "cultural professions." Leading the way was the well-educated bourgeoisie (*Bildungsbürgertum*), from teachers to university professors, who perceived a threat to high German culture. A relatively large number of cultural conservatives were women. We should also mention the middle strata of the middle class, whether old or new, ranging from well-established master bakers to bank employees, notaries, and lawyers. Cultural conservatives were also relatively frequent among politicians, with women again out of all proportion to their numbers. The nobility too joined the ranks of the guardians of the moral order. Finally, there were those workers who lived in highly religious, middle-class milieus or in rural regions culturally dominated by the nobility.

Cultural conservatives differed as much in their motives as in their social origins. Some were involved in the Lebensreform or youth movements, while others were youth welfare workers or people with close ties to adult education, the churches, women's associations, or paramilitary units. About all that they could agree upon was that steps should be

---

32. I am indebted to David Foster for this reference. In the 1920s, popular culture was considered primarily a big city phenomenon and was interpreted as such. Cf. for instance Theodor Heuß, German Democratic Party, *Reichstag,* vol. 391, 240th session, November 27, 1926; Hermann Hofmann, senior teacher, Ludwigshafen, Center Party, *Reichstag,* vol. 393, 313th session, May 13, 1927, 10707.

taken to prevent society from becoming dominated by popular culture, which in any case needed to be reformed.

Cultural conservatives often shared the ideals of the well-educated bourgeoisie, combined with relatively rigid ethical values. They tended to take a normative view of morality and art and thought in terms of rather naive opposites such as "good" and "bad," "virtue" and "evil," "healthy" and "sick," "clean" and "dirty." They felt that lasciviousness, unbridled urges, and the pursuit of wanton pleasure were damaging to the individual, the family, youth, society, the German people, and the state. Leo Schwering, a secondary school teacher and Center Party deputy from Cologne, spoke like many other parliamentarians about a "general moral decay." "Times of moral decay," he continued, "have never engendered great art."[33] Artistic taste was declining, as could be seen not least of all in the hit musicals.[34] The alleged moral decay of the German people was often blamed on a "nervous attack," "overstimulation of the nerves of all *Volksgenossen,*" "heightened sexual sensitivity," "an almost sick compulsion to give free rein to one's impulses," and the "social and cultural distress of the German people."[35]

In the eyes of the cultural conservatives, the revolution of 1918–19 played an important part in the moral decline. Although they only referred directly to the alleged outpouring of "smutty and trashy products," the imagery they employed was ambiguous and often seemed to include the revolution itself in what was deemed to be "smut." "A spiritual cleansing" was allegedly necessary to produce "pure souls,"[36] and cultural policy should be guided by the "sentiments of the healthy-thinking population" and the "spiritual health of the *Volk.*"[37]

---

33. Dr. Schwering, Cologne, Center Party, Prussian *Landtag,* vol. 12, 244th session, May 14, 1923, 17369.

34. Schuster, German People's Party, Prussian *Landtag,* vol. 12, 244th session, May 14, 1923, 17407.

35. Emminger, Bavarian People's Party, *Reichstag,* vol. 423, 23rd session, December 1, 1928, 593; Hans v. Eynern, Oberverwaltungs-Gerichtsrat (retired), German People's Party, Prussian *Landtag,* vol. 4, 76th session, November 29, 1921, 5081; Stuhrmann, German National People's Party, Prussian *Landtag,* vol. 4, 77th session, November 30, 1921, 5219. Heinrich Stuhrmann was a pastor by profession and director of the German Protestant People's Union for the Public Mission of Christianity.

36. Dr. Köster, minister of the interior, *Reichstag,* vol. 354, 201st session, April 3, 1922, 6814.

37. Johann Leicht, dean of the Bamberg cathedral, Bavarian People's Party, *Reichstag,* vol. 425, 80th session, June 8, 1929, 2207; Artur Petzold, pharmacist, Economic Party, *Reichstag,* vol. 425, 84th session, June 12, 1929. Petzold also opposed "smut" and "trash" and was close to the Center Party in these issues; Ernst Martin, cathedral preacher, German National People's Party and later NSDAP, *Reichstag,* vol. 392, 289th session, March 18, 1927, 9680; v. Eynern, German People's Party, Prussian *Landtag,* vol. 4, 76th

Although cultural conservatives were often basically cultural pessimists,[38] many did not condemn popular culture in toto and felt it could be "refined" and made suitable for a modern, orderly, disciplined society.[39] They gave no thought to the norms underlying their attempts to refine popular culture and generally sought to achieve their ends through censorship. They were probably motivated largely by fear that the new popular culture would escape the norms and values of the middle class and threaten its cultural hegemony.[40] The would-be movie reformer Professor K. Lange wrote with great concern in 1920 that "We shall then have a cinema in which the wild, unbridled masses find fuel for their destructive urges. This cinema will be in the service of terror."[41]

Middle-class cultural conservatives tried not only to impose legal restrictions on popular culture but also to appeal to the reason of the masses and to enlighten the general population. Cultural conservatives advocated "clean" modernity and a new, "worthwhile" popular culture. Their attempts to make popular culture "worthwhile" were oriented for the most part toward "high culture," although with some concessions to the avant-garde and even popular taste.[42] This "refined" popular culture would be a positive influence on taste and mores or at least would not be detrimental. The attempts to improve popular culture should therefore not be seen solely as a reactionary strategy to restore the "good old days." What cultural conservatives wanted was a kind of steering mechanism within unbridled commercial culture that would help to rid it of its "trashy," "immoral" contents and promote those that, though easily digestible, still provided at least some intellectual nourishment.

---

session, November 29, 1921; parliamentary question of the Koblenz senior government counselor Dr. Heuß and others, Center Party, Prussian *Landtag,* vol. 15, 239th session, May 13, 1931, 20972.

38. We should point in this context to the influence of Oswald Spengler.

39. Cf. Detlev J. K. Peukert, *Grenzen der Sozialdisziplinierung: Aufstieg und Krise der deutschen Jugendfürsorge 1878 bis 1932* (Cologne, 1986), 180.

40. Cf. idem, *Jugend zwischen Krieg und Krise: Lebenswelten von Arbeiterjungen in der Weimarer Republik* (Cologne, 1987), 217.

41. Quoted in Helmut Korte (ed.), *Film und Realität in der Weimarer Republik* (Munich, 1978), 225.

42. This resulted both in "high culture" being made banal and crude and in "shallow" commercial culture being enriched with "worthwhile" content and style elements. Eco, who refers in turn to MacDonald (Dwight MacDonald, *Against the American Grain* [London, 1963]), analyzes the "midcult" that was envisaged as follows: "If a stylistic device came from a prestigious message, it has a certain density for audiences that are eager for genteel experiences. The midcult-product will therefore attempt to produce a new message (aimed mostly at triggering effects) in which that stylistic device refines and ennobles the context." Eco, *Apocalittici,* 88. "The audience is not offered the original messages but simplified ones that play on the style of messages that are famous for their poetic qualities." Ibid., 87.

Middle-class cultural conservatives wanted to provide alternatives to "shallow" popular culture and in so doing joined forces, at least to some extent, with the artistic avant-garde and leftist intelligentsia. One of the fruits of their joint efforts was the outpouring of educational and documentary films in Germany. These films were supposed to illustrate the "right" approach to modernity and provide training in "proper" selection from the mass media and "proper" use of leisure time. The emphasis was always on family life and further education. The new sensitivity to nature and one's body was supposed to improve health and advance the Lebensreform movement. Hiking and gymnastics in the open air were particularly encouraged, as well as such useful pursuits as Schrebergärten, or little gardening colonies on the edges of cities. It was said that women would gain a new grace, freshness, and naturalness from gymnastics and interpretive dance. A counterimage was thus established to the modernistic "new woman,"[43] although the counterimage was also rooted in modernity in many ways, for instance the rationalization of housework. State theaters and unaffiliated "people's theaters" were supposed to provide "good" programs, while "good literature" could be found in public libraries and the libraries of various associations.[44] It was no coincidence that Fritz Klatt pioneered the new field of leisure studies (*Freizeitpädagogik*) at this time, thereby turning the proper use of free time into a science. Although concepts of leisure time followed the trend toward scientific analysis, there was some concern that the masses might become too beholden to the scientific method. It was supposedly not good to cultivate the intellect in a one-sided way; instead people should be educated to have a Goethean sense of reverence, especially for all higher things, at least according to high school principal Dr. Wilhelm Steffens of the "liberal" German People's Party.[45]

Folk culture was also "marketed" as an alternative to popular culture, especially *Heimatspiele* (plays with local, rural settings), folk drama, folk choirs, and open-air theater.[46] When not eyeing "folk culture" for the deep roots it provided, cultural conservatives remained on the lookout for

---

43. The concept of the "new woman" brought together a number of elements in a social construct that only partially captured the real lives of women at the time. The quintessential "new woman" was fashionable, modern, self-confident or independent, enthusiastic about the new media, consumption oriented (including alcohol and cigarettes), youthful, eager to have a good time and go dancing, and to a great extent "Americanized."

44. We could mention in this context the Catholic Borromäusverein.

45. Steffens, German People's Party, Prussian *Landtag,* vol. 12, 239th session, May 7, 1923, 17030.

46. Dr. Leo Schwering, secondary school teacher from Cologne, Center Party, Prussian *Landtag,* vol. 12, 244th session, May 14, 1923, 17374.

"good and great art."[47] It is not surprising, therefore, that they constantly hearkened back to the classics, which moved to the forefront of cultural policy.[48] Folk culture and the classical culture may have been very different, but they served the same purpose in the eyes of cultural conservatives: the creation of a "*Volk* community as a cultural community."[49] General Superintendant Wilhelm Reinhard, a deputy of the German National People's Party wanted to provide "a healthy diet of art to the broadest strata of the people," a "healthy German diet."[50]

We still very much need research into how and the extent to which people changed the ways in which they spent their leisure time in the 1920s in response to popular culture. All we know for sure is that cultural conservatives certainly felt that there had been a major change. They pointed repeatedly to the experiences of the war as the turning point, meaning more the defeats of the war than the horrors. Another contemporary stereotype can be found in the frequent references to the great "nervousness" of the German people.

Film, Radio, and Pulp Fiction in the Eyes of Cultural Conservatives

Film

Cultural conservatives were most disturbed by the new medium of film.[51] There had already been local censorship of it before the First World War.[52] Film was viewed primarily from the standpoint of "public health," and much thought was given to ways in which it could be used to provide instruction for the masses. During the November revolution, film censorship was lifted, whereupon movie houses were allegedly

47. Helene Weber, department section head, Center Party, *Reichstag,* vol. 393, 312th session, May 12, 1927; Karl Troßmann, Bavarian People's Party, *Reichstag,* vol. 393, 313th session, May 13, 1927, 10702. Troßmann was the district manager of the Bavarian People's Party in Nuremberg.

48. Dr. Bohner, German Democratic Party, Prussian *Landtag,* vol. 9, 167th session, May 11, 1926, 11593.

49. Dr. Rudolf von Campe, lawyer, county manager (retired), Hildesheim, German People's Party, Prussian *Landtag,* vol. 4, 81st session, December 10, 1921, 5717; Friedrich Oelze, headmaster, German National People's Party, ibid., 5727; Otto Boelitz, minister of science, art, and adult education, ibid., 5742.

50. Reinhard, German National People's Party, Prussian *Landtag,* vol. 5, 102nd session, February 20, 1922, 7208.

51. For an introduction to the German movie business see Paul Monaco, *Cinema and Society: France and Germany during the Twenties* (New York 1973).

52. Cf. Emilie Altenloh, *Zur Soziologie des Kinos: Die Kino-Unternehmung und die sozialen Schichten ihrer Besucher* (Jena, 1914), 40ff.

flooded with erotic movies.[53] The middle-class parties demanded another censorship law and succeeded as early as 1920 in having the Reich Motion Picture Act passed.[54] Buoyed by this victory, cultural conservatives attempted in the following years to tighten the law, especially for youth. By the mid-1920s, 25 to 30 percent of all movies shown in Germany were closed to youths under eighteen years of age.[55] Germany was something of an anomaly in this regard because in France only 5 to 8 percent of movies were closed to youths.[56]

People inclined to take a moral view of culture joined together in the cinema reform movement, whose origins stretched back to before the First World War.[57] Educators, priests and ministers, theater critics, art historians, journalists, physicians, and lawyers worked side by side. The Popular society for the Preservation of Decency and Morality was formed, whose members viewed "dirty" movies and informed the state authorities, churches, and other organizations about what they had seen.[58] Even deputies in the liberal-minded German Democratic Party wanted steps taken against "kitsch films."[59] All these people feared that "sensationalistic kitsch movies"[60] encouraged an "intellectual and spiritual leveling" and threatened the soul, especially because of all the "images of criminal activity" and eroticism, which would spoil the imagination and make people nervous.[61] There was also a concern that movies would have a negative impact on middle-class culture in general. They allegedly encouraged a "quick and superficial view of things." Even

---

53. Korte, *Film*, 72.

54. According to the Motion Picture Act of 1920, films were to be refused authorization if the board found that "showing the film is likely to endanger public order or public safety, offend religious feelings, have a coarsening effect or lower public morals, or endanger Germany's prestige or its relations with foreign countries." Movies could not be refused authorization, however, solely on account of their "political, social, religious, ethical or philosophical bent." Korte, *Film*, 226. The phrasing of the act was therefore open ended, and censors had a great deal of latitude.

55. By 1920, 70 to 80 percent of all films that were shown were closed to youths under eighteen years old. Monaco, *Cinema*, 54.

56. Ibid., 54.

57. Korte, *Film*, 60; Erwin Ackerknecht, *Das Lichtspiel im Dienste der Bildungspflege: Handbuch für Lichtspielreformer* (Berlin, 1918).

58. Taken from *Reichstag*, vol. 393, 312th session, May 12, 1927, 10681. However, the comment was in reference to 1920.

59. Dr. Klausner, deputy for Berlin, German Democratic Party, Prussian *Landtag*, vol. 17, 359th session, March 17, 1928, 25687.

60. See Else von Sperber, no occupation listed, German National People's Party, *Reichstag*, vol. 393, 312th session, May 12, 1927, 10683.

61. As evidence for this assertion, reference was made to cases in which, according to newspaper reports, youths engaged in deviant sexual or criminal activities after allegedly having been overexcited by movies. Korte, *Film*, 61.

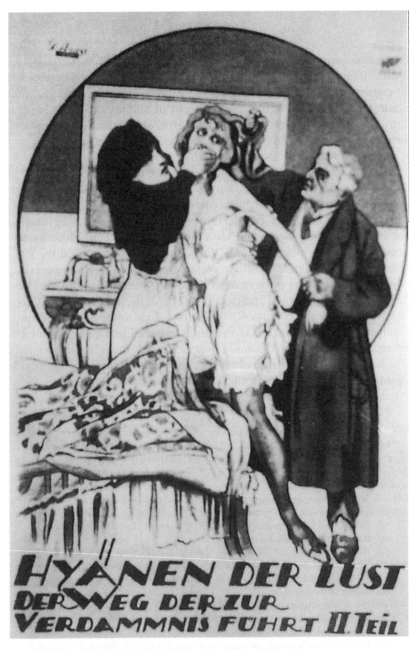

Fig. 9.   Advertisement for one of the so-called trash movies in the 1920s. (From
Geschichtswerkstatt Hannover [ed.], *Alltag zwischen Hindenburg und Haarmann: Ein anderer Stadtführer durch das Hannover der 20er Jahre,* 26 [Ham-
burg, 1987].)

comedies were considered "damaging to the broadest extent." Most movies were said to be inimical to art and culture and to impair aesthetic appreciation.[62] Dr. Külz of the German Democratic Party reportedly expressed his concern before the budget committee of the Reichstag that a movie could even provoke another revolution. The Social Democrat Carl Schreck, a carpenter by trade and an honorary member of the Bielefeld City Council, took great delight in excoriating the empty-headedness of this remark.[63]

In the eyes of cultural conservative reformers, the only true salvation lay in the nationalization of all movie houses.[64] Since this could not be done, they had to content themselves with more modest methods. They pushed municipal governments into organizing the German Picture Theater Union and setting up their own "model theaters," which could serve as forums for "the work of educating and informing the people." As early as 1910, the Popular Association for Catholic Germany had founded a film distribution company of its own, and in the 1920s another private Catholic company named Neuland was formed. The passage of the film censorship act in 1920 led eventually to the formation of so-called Lampe committees, named after the chairman, Professor Lampe, to review movies and issue appropriate recommendations.[65]

The middle-class cinema reform movement sought as well to provide alternatives, especially the cultural and educational films mentioned earlier. These films, which received favorable tax treatment, treated works by well-known writers, the lives of people in foreign countries, various natural wonders, and new technical or scientific breakthroughs. It is certainly no coincidence that German cultural and educational films were of very high quality at this time and were screened around the world.[66] It must have been depressing for cultural idealists, however, to

62. Quotations appear in Korte, *Film,* 60f. Cf. Reinhard Mumm, German National People's Party, *Reichstag,* vol. 426, 109th session, December 3, 1929, 3404.

63. Schreck, SPD, *Reichstag,* vol. 392, 289th session, March 18, 1927, 9686.

64. Korte, *Film,* 72.

65. These "Lampe committees" were much criticized, especially by the labor movement, because of their members, who were very close to the government bureaucracy, and because of their tendency toward informal censorship; cf. *Sozialistische Bildung,* no. 4 (1931): 110ff.

66. Cf. Walter Laqueur, *Weimar: A Cultural History, 1928–1933* (New York, 1974), 307. However, fairly frequently these cultural and educational films were packaged in a sensationalistic way; see in this regard Joseph Gregor, *Das Zeitalter des Films,* 3d ed. (Vienna, 1932), 185ff. Kracauer's criticism of certain educational films is also well known, for instance his criticism of *Berge in Flammen* (1931) with Luis Trenker and Leni Riefenstahl. Kracauer saw some prefascist elements in them, in particular the antirationalistic euphoria over cliffs and glaciers, which the Nazis later used for their purposes. I am

discover that these movies were not very popular with the public. The German National deputy Max Wallraf, a former minister of state and undersecretary of state for the interior, resigned himself to the elitist conclusion that "If you look at how the mass institution of movie houses has evolved and how patrons virtually flee films on scientific matters or beautiful landscapes but flock to those showing the familiar mixture of horrible sensationalism and false sentimentality, you realize the truth of the old saying that art is not everyone's cup of tea (*die Kunst ist ein Kräutlein nicht für alle Leutlein*)."[67]

Although the film industry continued to be criticized by cultural conservatives for its shallowness, the censorship law did not pose much of a problem. There was no law against kitsch, which could often be very successful at the box office.[68] Some discussions were held in 1929 about tightening the legislation and including restrictions on bad taste. Reinhard Mumm, a German National deputy and pastor from Siegen, perceived some of the difficulties inherent in censoring bad taste but claimed that, far from wanting to suppress other people's tastes, he just wanted to get rid of all the films that were "simply worthless from an aesthetic standpoint."[69] Some deputies from the Economic Party, such as Siegfried, expressed their opposition to such a step.[70]

Finally, cultural conservative reformers hoped that the movie industry would "refine" itself over the course of time.[71] This wish apparently went unfulfilled, although censorship did have some effect. In its own business interests, the industry generally avoided infringing the censorship laws, at least insofar as morality was concerned.[72] It is therefore not very surprising that the censors rarely had occasion to ban films outright and generally made only a few cuts.[73]

---

also indebted to Sabine Guckel-Seitz for insights into the ideology of cultural and educational films.

67. Wallraf, German National People's Party, Prussian *Landtag,* vol. 12, 244th session, May 14, 1923, 17375ff.

68. Cf., for instance, *Kulturwille* 7, no. 7–8 (1930): 132.

69. Mumm, German National People's Party, *Reichstag,* vol. 426, 109th session, December 3, 1929, 3404.

70. Siegfried, *Reichstag,* vol. 426, 109th session, December 3, 1929, 3407.

71. Cf. Schreiber, Center Party, *Reichstag,* vol. 354, 201st session, April 3, 1922, 6821.

72. Cf. Victor Szczesny, *Das Lichtspielgesetz vom 12. Mai 1920,* (Berlin, 1920), 8ff.

73. For instance, the censorship board in Munich announced in 1926 that it had not banned a single one of the 374 motion pictures it reviewed that year and had cut out only 142 meters of a total of 230,000 meters of film. Of the 3,000 motion pictures reviewed in 1928, only 37 were banned. Cf. Wolfgang Petzet, *Verbotene Filme* (Frankfurt, 1931), 109. Examples of the practices of individual boards can be found in Korte, *Film,* 226; for the

Radio

Since radio broadcasting was a mixture of private and state enterprise,[74] fewer conflicts arose between cultural conservatives and programmers. Radio was first developed before the First World War but did not become a continuously available mass medium until late 1923. From the outset, radio was taken under the wing of government, which used the new medium for its own purposes, especially during the Great War. The Radio Code of 1926 led to the establishment of supervisory committees and cultural councils[75] that censored material according to what were supposed to be "strictly nonpartisan" criteria.

Since the government always had a strong influence over radio, middle-class reformers found it relatively easy to implement at least some of their ideas for refining this medium and making it educational. Many radio programs were quite didactic in tone. However, as the *Weltbühne* commented in 1927: "There is certainly no effort to use radio to liberate the proletarian masses from their intellectual and material poverty or to adapt programs to the ideology of working people. . . . It is heartwarming to know that listeners are informed about foreign peoples almost exclusively by retired army officers. Working women are supposed to get some spiritual and intellectual nourishment from discussions of such topics as 'How to Set a Tea Table Properly' or 'Good Eating and Serving Manners'—the actual titles of two programs."[76]

Undaunted by such criticism, middle-class reformers saw the start-up of the first nationwide Deutsche Welle in 1926 as an opportunity to extend their influence. Much more than the regional stations, this national transmitter considered itself a kind of wireless "apolitical and nonpartisan" adult education center. It featured regular broadcasts about agriculture and economics, as well as specialized broadcasts for lawyers, civil servants, merchants, physicians, dentists, and even housewives and moth-

rest see Monaco, *Cinema*, 56. Laqueur is of the view, however, that film censorship in Germany was less severe than in other countries, although the censorship of left-wing views increased in the final phase of the republic; Laqueur, *Kultur*, 290.

74. Cf. in general Joachim-Felix Leonhard (ed.), *Programmgeschichte des Hörfunks in der Weimarer Republik*, 2 vols. (Munich, 1997); Lerg, *Rundfunkpolitik;* Peter Dahl, *Radio: Sozialgeschichte des Rundfunks für Sender und Empfänger* (Reinbek, 1983), 22ff.; Heide Riedel, *60 Jahre Radio: Von der Rarität zum Massenmedium*, 2d ed. (Berlin, 1987); cf. as well *Sozialistische Bildung*, no. 10 (1929): 299; *Weltbühne* 23, first half year (1927): 494ff.

75. The members of the supervisory committees and cultural councils were appointed by the respective state governments in cooperation with the Reich minister of the interior. In many cases, they were officials in the ministries; cf. in this regard Lerg, *Rundfunkpolitik*, 377, 394, 397, 400, 405.

76. *Weltbühne* 23, first half year (1927): 496ff.; cf. Dahl, *Radio*, 113.

ers.[77] Deutsche Welle also had programs about working-class life, although the information they provided was often extremely arrogant. For instance, the Deutsche Welle yearbook for 1928 contains the following: "The programs touch in some ways on questions of workers' lives. Insofar as workers' culture is concerned, there were discussions of good books to read and sensible appliances for workers' apartments. There are masses of workers. . . . We want to show these workers, who are among the listeners to the programs, how they should see themselves in relation to society, the state and the German people. At the same time, though, we have the related secondary aim of providing the middle class with some insight into what is happening in the depths of society."[78] There could be no clearer statement of the gulf between the classes and the cultural hegemony of the (well-educated) bourgeoisie. Far below, in "the depths" of society, lived uncultured masses that needed to be educated. The reformers had to make some compromises, though, in their efforts to provide enlightenment over the radio. Not everything could be "refined" — just some parts of the programming. On the radio as well, the flood of light, shallow entertainment could no longer be halted.

Pulp Fiction

Mass-produced pulp fiction was perceived as a threat to one of the main components of "high culture." As early as the nineteenth century, reformers had attempted to cure the masses of their dullness and brutishness, which was blamed, at least to some extent, on the trashy literature that they read. With the increasing availability of cheap pulp fiction since the late nineteenth century,[79] the battle over the "good taste" of the masses heated up. A Central Office to Combat Offensive Literature was established as early as 1911 within the Central Office for Social Welfare in Berlin. The Weimar constitution provided legal measures to fight "smutty and trashy literature."[80]

On December 18, 1926, the Act to Protect Youth from Trashy and Smutty Publications was passed by the Reichstag with the support of all the middle-class parties but over the opposition of the SPD and KPD. For a moment, a relatively solid middle-class cultural front again arose,

---

77. Ibid., 44. Angela Dinghaus, "Frauenfunk und Jungmädchenstunde: Ein Beitrag zur Programmgeschichte des Weimarer Rundfunks" (Ph.D. diss., University of Hanover, 2000).

78. Quoted in Dahl, *Radio,* 46.

79. The first great wave of crime and detective serials swept over the European youth between 1905 and 1910. Paul Samuleit and Hans Brunckhorst, *Geschichte und Wege der Schundbekämpfung* (Berlin, 1922), 10.

80. Cf. Articles 118 and 122.

which included the liberal parties as well.[81] The so-called Trash and Smut Act to protect youth prohibited the selling or advertising of this kind of materials.[82] The act failed to define "trash and smut," but it seemed to mean anything likely to "eradicate or weaken instinctive reactions of conscience, shame and decency or to diminish these reactions by making people unaccustomed to them."[83]

What qualified as "smut" could be deduced from moral standards that were still thought to be widely accepted, but it was harder to say what constituted "trash." A distinction was made between "trashy" and "smutty" literature.[84] "Trash" consisted of "mass products of no literary value"[85] — the cheap serials and pulp fiction. In general, "trash" meant kitsch. The close connection between trash and kitsch could be seen in an assessment of the state theater organizations, which, according to Deputy Klausner, fought "against trash, against kitsch."[86] However, cultural idealists soon made the bitter discovery that there was no consistent definition of "trash." Deputy Lang-Brumann of the Bavarian People's Party argued in favor of "refining the instruments of censorship" in the area of taste, hoping that some uniformity could be achieved despite the difficulties.[87] However, these hopes proved illusory. When Herman Hofman, a Center Party deputy from Ludwigsburg and a senior primary school teacher, railed against "kitsch and smut," he was interrupted by an interjection from the ranks of the Social Democrats: "But kitsch is not against the law!"[88]

Although the criticism concentrated on pulp magazines, it also

81. For this reason, Communist deputies in particular were always at pains to point out the class nature of the act in debates in the Reichstag; cf. for instance Hoernle, Communist Party, *Reichstag,* vol. 391, 241st session, November 29, 1926, 8270.

82. In the various states, censorship offices were set up consisting of experts from art and literature, bookselling and art dealing, youth welfare and youth organizations, as well as schools and adult education organizations, to decide whether particular works should be included on the "trash list." Their decisions were binding for the entire Reich. Objections to the inclusion of a book on the "trash list" could be raised with the chief censorship office in Leipzig.

83. In Stephan Reinhardt (ed.), *Lesebuch Weimarer Republik: Deutsche Schriftsteller und ihr Staat von 1918–1933* (Berlin, 1982), 144. The war on "dirt" was aimed primarily at erotic literature; cf. Peukert, *Sozialdisziplinierung,* 175.

84. Dr. Külz, minister of the interior, *Reichstag,* vol. 391, 240th session, November 27, 1926, 8257.

85. Mumm, German National People's Party, *Reichstag,* vol. 391, 239th session, November 26, 1926, 8218.

86. Dr. Klausner, Berlin, German Democratic Party, Prussian *Landtag,* vol. 4, 94th session, November 6, 1925, 6151.

87. Lang-Brumann, Bavarian People's Party, *Reichstag,* vol. 426, 109th session, December 3, 1929, 3411.

88. *Reichstag,* vol. 393, 313th session, May 13, 1927, 10707.

extended to detective stories such as the Nick Carter and Sherlock Holmes tales and to stories about American Indians and the Wild West, such as the Buffalo Bill stories. Interest was allegedly kept at a fever pitch by "depicting down to the last detail the most unbelievable, revolting crimes dreamed up by the most frightful imagination."[89] Cultural conservatives also opposed the serials for girls. The most successful serials published about a hundred thousand copies a week for years on end. They could be purchased not only in bookstores and at newspaper stands but also in barber shops, hairdressing salons, and cigar stores as well as at greengrocers. There was also a brisk trade in old, used installments.[90]

What riled cultural conservatives especially, though, was "smutty" literature. Women played a particularly prominent part in the campaign against it, often feeling that they had a special duty to act as "guardians of morality and order," in the words of female Center Party deputy Bachem.[91] Another female deputy named Scheidel from the German National People's Party made a point of the fact that the General German Women Teachers' Association and the Working Group of German Occupational Associations, to which four hundred thousand women belonged, would support the Trash and Smut Act, and she urged all female members of the Reichstag to follow their fine example.[92] This appeal for solidarity on the basis of gender failed when the female members of the working-class parties refused to go along, although there was widespread support among the female members of the bourgeois parties. Gertrud Bäumer, a very committed representative of the women's movement and member of the liberal-minded German Democratic Party, was particularly outraged over "trash capitalism," describing it as "the filthiest form of capitalism, which targets the pennies of the broad masses of young people."[93] She felt that "trash capitalism" was a "calamitous outgrowth of capitalism"[94] and hoped that the cultural sphere could be kept free, for the most part, from the "production of wares" or at least that controls and guidelines could be adopted. Similar arguments could be heard from Center Party deputy and department section head Dr. Helene Weber: "That which speculates on the lowest instincts and urges out of a lust for profit is not art but just greed and business (interjections from the Center Party and the Right: Very true). That is capitalism under the guise of art, both these publications for youth and these shows

89. Samuleit and Brunckhorst, *Geschichte,* 9.
90. Ibid., 9.
91. Prussian *Landtag,* vol. 9, 169th session, October 2, 1922, 12275.
92. *Reichstag,* vol. 391, 240th session, November 27, 1926, 8255.
93. *Reichstag,* vol. 391, 245th session, December 3, 1926, 8368.
94. Ibid.

and entertainments (interjection from the Social Democrats: Since when have you been opposed to capitalism?). I have always been opposed to this kind of capitalism."[95]

Some males joined this chorus of female voices criticizing capitalism, for instance Bäumer's fellow party member and minister of the interior Külz, who was preparing to do battle against this "disgusting capitalist aberration of trashy literature for the masses."[96] The German National Party joined the critique of capitalism, at least insofar as pulp literature was concerned. Deputy Lukassowitz, for instance, decried the "lack of business conscience."[97] Even the German People's Party, which often represented the interests of business, railed against "trash capitalism."[98]

The Trash and Smut Act did not appear on the surface to work very well. The procedures for banning works were long and complicated,[99] and the boards felt overworked and lacked the necessary financial resources. Most important of all, the legal situation was not clear.[100] However, Gertrud Bäumer and similarly minded people hoped primarily that the act would help to reduce the production of "bad" literature because it could not be sold as easily as before and because the "risk of winding up on the list and losing money or not making as much money as hoped" would make publishers "very cautious."[101]

The churches too joined the fray over pulp fiction. They kept bookstores and newsstands under surveillance and welcomed denunciations from alert citizens. The Central Working Committee of German Catholics to Promote Public Morality, founded in 1928, as well as Caritas (the largest Catholic welfare organization); the Protestant Central Committee of the Inner Mission; the Volkswartbund; the Protestant young men's associations, and the Protestant Central Office against Trash and Smut, founded in 1927, all did their best to foster a "clean culture," although they found themselves mostly tilting at windmills.[102]

---

95. Weber, Berlin, Center Party, *Reichstag,* vol. 393, 312th session, May 12, 1927, 10688.

96. Dr. Külz, minister of the interior, German Democratic Party, *Reichstag,* vol. 391, 239th session, November 26, 1926, 8212.

97. Lukassowitz, German National People's Party, Prussian *Landtag,* 110th session, March 8, 1922, 7879.

98. According to the school inspector (retired) and privy counselor Dr. Heinrich Runkel, German People's Party, *Reichstag,* vol. 391, 239th session, November 26, 1926, 8227.

99. Peukert, *Sozialdisziplinierung,* 189.

100. Ibid.

101. *Die Frau: Monatsschrift für das gesamte Frauenleben unserer Zeit* 34, no. 3 (1926): 173.

102. I am indebted to Klaus Petersen for pointing this out.

Almost all cultural conservatives felt that good reading materials would improve the conditions in which much of the working class lived. Some, such as Gertrud Bäumer, were even convinced that "trashy literature" was especially dangerous for people living in poor conditions.[103] Her fellow party member Theodor Hueß spoke accordingly of a "social policy of the soul," as was already mentioned in another context.[104] The primary purpose of this, as Gertrud Bäumer said, was to protect young people and refine their taste. It is not surprising, therefore, that the Trash and Smut Act was promulgated as a measure "to protect youth." After the lost world war, "human capital," especially youth, had supposedly become very valuable, and young people were "the most precious national asset."[105]

Cultural conservatives hoped to succeed at least in the realm of literature in imposing severe restrictions on the "harmful" pleasures of popular culture. Reading pulp fiction was already considered an indication that one's faculties had become shallow and trivial.[106] The antidote was "true, genuine education" informed by cultural norms often rooted in German classicism. No questions were asked about the class bias and historical nature of these norms; instead, the emphasis was on "eternal values."[107]

Finally, middle-class reformers claimed that "trashy and smutty literature" had a corrupting effect on the family, society, and the state. They feared that it posed a serious threat to the integrative function of predominately middle-class culture and that the "masses" might well show less and less respect for the middle-class values and norms found in "worthwhile culture."[108] "Shallow, superficial literature" would "undermine respectable society," it was felt, hasten the moral decline, and overstimulate the nerves of the masses.[109]

Cultural conservatives did not confine themselves to ensuring passage of the Trash and Smut Act. They devoted their efforts much more to altering the reading habits of the youth by means of presentations, exhibitions, pamphlets, and alternative literature as well as by constructing libraries. The antidote to "trash" was "good books." No one knew

---

103. According to Gertrud Bäumer, German Democratic Party, *Reichstag,* vol. 391, 245th session, December 3, 1926, 8368.

104. For example ibid., 8363ff.

105. In Reinhardt, *Lesebuch,* 144.

106. Cf. Peukert, *Sozialdisziplinierung,* 184.

107. In Reinhardt, *Lesebuch,* 151.

108. Cf. Korte, *Film,* 63.

109. Cf. for instance: Superior district court counselor Erich Emminger, Bavarian People's Party, *Reichstag,* 23rd session, December 1, 1928, 593; also Kube, *Völkisch* working group, *Reichstag,* vol. 391, 240th session, November 27, 1926, 8245.

for sure, though, what "good books" were because usually only undesirable aspects were mentioned and even then only occasionally. It was claimed, for instance, that good literature should not contain any extensive accounts of the murder of children.[110] This shows that cultural conservatives wanted not only to change the way in which literature was written but to suppress some topics as well.

One reason why cultural conservatives tended to focus their attacks on pulp fiction was that they themselves often came from the well-educated bourgeoisie, which was particularly steeped in traditional culture and ascribed enormous importance to the written word. They still nursed the illusion that the world of letters could be saved from industrial mass production or that at least some controls could be maintained.

Cultural Nationalists

One identifiable group within the cultural conservative camp was the nationalists on the right of the political spectrum. Although the ideological and strategic differences between the various middle-class groups were fluid and cultural conservatism attracted all kinds of middle-class politicians, some general distinctions can be drawn. The nationalists combined cultural moralism and idealism with aggressive chauvinism. Hugenberg was a typical representative of this group, but so was the German Women's Association to Fight the Degeneration in the Life of the German People. Nationalistic cultural conservatives emphasized the importance of *German* customs and culture: the "German spirit," the "German mentality," the "German character," the "German soul," the "German language," the "German family," and the "German sense of work." Germans, they said, were "a people of poets and philosophers." They encouraged the study of local homelands (*Heimatkunde*), "German art," "German morality," and "German faith."[111] Cultural policy, in their view, should aim primarily at strengthening the German way of life.[112] Ernst Martin, who preached in the Magdeburg cathedral

110. For instance Dr. Runkel, German People's Party, *Reichstag,* vol. 425, 81st–82nd session, June 10, 1929, 2261.

111. See Dr. Klamt, Economic Union, Prussian *Landtag,* vol. 17, 359th session, March 17, 1928, 25698; Reinhard, German National People's Party, Prussian *Landtag,* vol. 5, 102nd session, February 20, 1922, 7206ff.; von Kulesza, German People's Party, Prussian *Landtag,* vol. 6, 110th session, March 8, 1922, 7845. Anny Kulesza was an assistant headmistress and town counselor in Berlin-Lichtenberg, first president of the Union of German Women Public School Teachers, and a member of the chief censorship office for film.

112. According, for instance, to the teacher Ilse-Charlotte Noack, German People's Party, Prussian *Landtag,* vol. 5, 104th session, February 22, 1922, 7450.

and was a German National deputy, told the Reichstag that "all art must be rooted in the soil of the country, where the deepest sources of folk life run."[113] Only in this way, one might continue, could the allure of popular culture be countered.

In the eyes of the cultural nationalists, popular taste needed thorough reform, even in the realm of fashion. Center Party deputy Bachem complained that "you see vain, coquettish girls decked out in clothes that are not German and are not in keeping with our ways. (Interjections of Very good! and Exactly!) Something must be done immediately about these poor behaviors."[114] In opposition to the theory of the class struggle advanced by the Left, cultural nationalists promoted the idea of a *Volksgemeinschaft*, or a community of all Germans in respect not only to citizenship but to culture and education as well.[115] The distinctions between this and a *völkisch* or *völkisch*-racist cultural policy were rather fuzzy.

It was not only the German National Party and the *völkisch*-racist inclined people who sang the nationalistic tune but also the churches, the Center Party, and the German People's Party. The Protestant Central Office against Trash and Smut placed a great deal of emphasis on patriotism and on German customs and culture.[116] As can be seen in the preceding quotation, Center Party deputy Bachem saw the solution in the basic nature of Germans (*im deutschen Wesen*). The 1931 program of the German People's Party showed very little sign any more of a liberal approach to culture. It inveighed "against the un-German hustle and bustle, which is destroying the moral fiber of the nation, and the anticulture, trash and smut on the radio, at the theater and in movies" and called for "government protection."[117]

In the final phase of the Weimar Republic, the influence of cultural nationalists on the public debate and cultural life intensified. The German Women's Association Fighting the Degeneration of the Life of the German People issued a call in 1929 for "the protection and reconstruction of the German family and German culture," which was signed by all

---

113. Martin, German National People's Party, *Reichstag*, vol. 392, 289th session, March 18, 1927, 9680.

114. According to Center Party Deputy Bachem, Prussian *Landtag*, vol. 9, 169th session, October 2, 1922, 12277.

115. Lukassowitz, German National People's Party, Prussian *Landtag*, vol. 6, 110th session, March 8, 1922, 7879.

116. In general see Klaus Petersen, "The Harmful Publications (Young Persons) Act of 1926 [called in the current volume the Act to Protect Youth from Trashy and Smutty Publications]: Literary Censorship and Morality in the Weimar Republic," *German Studies Review* 15 (1992): 505–25.

117. In Dieter Langewiesche, *Liberalismus in Deutschland* (Frankfurt, 1988), 264.

well-known nationalistic organizations, including the Stahlhelm (a para-military unit).[118] The German nationalists, and most of all the National Socialists,[119] not only denounced "trashy literature" but did what they could to exclude those who thought differently from the debate by means of censorship. "Political censorship" and "cultural censorship" grew increasingly indistinguishable in the dying days of the Weimar Republic as a result of the steep decline in the power of parliament and the mounting influence of nationalistic and reactionary right-wing circles on the presidential cabinets and public opinion.[120] Action was taken primarily against left-wing publications,[121] and Communist literature for the masses was banned with increasing frequency.[122]

Film

Motion pictures also felt the trend toward stricter censorship. It had long been possible to suppress political films by combining the Reich Motion Picture Act of 1920 with the Defense of the Republic Act of 1922. During the period of presidential cabinets toward the end of the Weimar Republic, the Motion Picture Act was interpreted increasingly often in a politically reactionary direction and was even amended in 1931 to make it more restrictive.[123] Time and again during this period, there were cases of outright political censorship. Well-known examples are the Russian film *Battleship Potemkin* and the antiwar film *All Quiet on the Western Front*, which were prohibited for a while.[124]

In the later stages of the Weimar Republic, nationalists did not

---

118. In Reinhardt, *Lesebuch,* 151.

119. We cannot delve any further here into Nazi cultural policies.

120. This was based less, however, on the Trash and Smut Act than on the Defense of the Republic Act of June 26, 1922; the Presidential Decree against Political Riots of March 28, 1931; and even the Emergency Press Decree of July 17, 1931.

121. Cf. in this regard Reinhardt, *Lesebuch,* 129ff., 133; as well as Kurt Kreiler (ed.), *Traditionen deutscher Justiz: Große politische Prozesse in der Weimarer Zeit* (Berlin, 1978), 252.

122. Further information can be found in Michael Rohrwasser, *Saubere Mädel, starke Genossen: Proletarische Massenliteratur?* (Frankfurt, 1975), for instance 133.

123. Following this amendment, films were already banned if they endangered "vital state interests." We should point out in this regard that the co-opting of film by politically reactionary forces had a "long" tradition reaching back to the First World War.

124. However, as a result of a wave of public criticism, the movie *Battleship Potemkin* had to be released after certain cuts, at least for adults who were not members of the Reichswehr; cf. Reinhardt, *Lesebuch,* 145. In addition, closed showings of the movie *All Quiet on the Western Front* were finally allowed; Frank Heidenreich, *Arbeiterbildung und Kulturpolitik: Kontroversen in der sozialdemokratischen Zeitschrift "Kulturwille" 1924–1933* (Berlin, 1983), 100.

confine their activities to seeking bans on movies and attempted to extend their influence into the studios themselves. The German film industry had always churned out nationalistic and politically reactionary movies,[125] and many put a special emphasis on alleged German national characteristics. These trends grew more pronounced in the final years of the Weimar Republic, as could be seen in the following exhortation: "In the production of movies in German studios, there should be a bit more emphasis on German customs and German practices, German land-scapes and German history, German handicrafts and German industry, German manners and the traditions of the German people."[126] At the same time, some movies imported from abroad were criticized because they were produced by "peoples alien to us" — by which was meant especially the Russians but possibly the Americans as well — "who, far from understanding our national ways, are much more interested in our downfall."[127]

In the final years of the Weimar Republic, the leader of the German National Party, Alfred Hugenberg, succeeded in extending his media empire into the film industry when the Scherl publishing group he owned bought up Ufa (Universum Film AG). Thereafter, Ufa ceased distributing any Soviet films.[128] Newsreels too fell under the control of right-wing companies.[129] Although Hugenberg did not interfere directly at first in movie production, his activities resulted in Ufa being handed over to the leaders of the Third Reich in 1933 as their "crown jewel" in the film and publishing industry.[130]

Radio

Nationalistic and reactionary forces recognized the importance not only of movies but of radio as well, which they used for their own political purposes. Radio fell increasingly under their sway during the illiberal presidential governments in the twilight of the Weimar Republic. The Radio Code of 1932 introduced new regulations in the area of program-ming. Henceforth, German radio was supposed to serve the life's work of the German people, preserving and strengthening "the natural order-ing of people in their homelands, families, occupations and country."

---

125. Cf. Korte, *Film,* 88; Monaco, *Cinema,* 70ff.

126. In Korte, *Film,* 62.

127. Ibid.

128. Monaco, *Cinema,* 31, 58.

129. Laqueur, *Weimar,* 290.

130. Jost Hermand and Frank Trommler, *Die Kultur der Weimarer Republik,* 268 (Munich, 1978).

Radio was therefore supposed to address its listeners not just as individuals but as "links in the natural order of the German people."[131] Radio was expected to show respect for Christian ethics and convictions and uphold the "idea of the Reich" — the latter primarily a reference to ethnic Germans in foreign countries. Not only should radio "emphasize and cultivate the German spirit" but also help to "eradicate all foreign, un-German influences."[132] These included modern art, which was felt to be un-German. In a sign of the times, the trade magazine *Funk* printed complaints in 1932 that radio stations no longer had the courage "to nurture modern art, the production of living artists, out of fear of giving political offense."[133] Like motion pictures, radio was already heavily influenced by reactionary circles before 1933.

Pulp Fiction

At the end of the Weimar Republic pulp fiction also witnessed the emergence of more chauvinistic, *völkisch* writers, who romanticized the supposed "community of the front" during the war. Scherl Verlag published cheap brochures and paperbacks and thereby produced, at least in the eyes of the leftist intelligentsia and labor movement, the very sorts of "trash" that Hugenberg's party was so bitterly denouncing in the Reichstag.

Cultural Liberals

Cultural liberals could be found most often among the artistic avant-garde and leftist intelligentsia.[134] They defended individualism against the threat posed by mass society. Basing their ideas on the Enlightenment, they cultivated the idea of the self-determining individual who accepted the established ethical and moral norms of his or her own accord. Some "cultural liberals" harbored doubts, though, about whether such an ideal could be extended to the masses. These "cultural liberals" had one foot therefore in the camp of the cultural interventionists and were prepared to work with them to some extent under the right circumstances. The line between cultural liberals and cultural conservatives was accordingly blurred, a fact that posed particular dilemmas for a party like the German Democrats, which considered itself liberal and

---

131. In ibid., 96.
132. *Sozialistische Bildung,* no. 5 (1932): 151. Deutsche Welle was also strengthened as a journalistic "bulwark against Bolshevism." Dahl, *Radio,* 43.
133. In ibid., 97.
134. *Cultural liberalism* is also a contemporary term.

anticlerical. Elitist cultural liberals also often found themselves in a quandary. They had nothing in principle against "immoral" works, such as those about the life and doings of Casanova, so long as these works were not widely distributed.[135] They themselves did not need protecting, of course, but the "ignorant" masses certainly did.[136]

While cultural conservatives hoped ultimately to propagate the norms of the well-educated bourgeoisie and further its claim to cultural hegemony, cultural liberals (primarily the artistic avant-garde and the leftist intelligentsia) often had quite different motives.[137] Many of them hoped that the new popular culture would help to democratize culture and diminish the "deficit" of the lower classes. Some even nursed the illusion that popular culture could be used to foster conditions that would help set the stage for the transformation of the entire society. For a "historic moment," their long- and short-term goals came together in a desire to give an enlightening impetus to popular culture. However, it must have been very sobering to discover that their numerous attempts[138] to promulgate avant-garde works, ideas, and products as an alternative popular culture generally did not have very much appeal for the masses.[139]

---

135. For a concrete example see Hermann M. Popert, *Hamburg und der Schundkampf* (Hamburg-Großborstel, 1926), 7.

136. We cannot delve any further here into the consumption and appropriation of popular culture and therefore provide a few references in this regard. Eco is pressing ahead with his research into the actual reception of popular culture and is convinced that the masses respond in more independent, individualistic ways (i.e., behave less as masses) than intellectuals and the well-educated bourgeois tend to think. According to Eco, the masses are capable of understanding the scope and limitations of the messages they receive. Eco, *Apocalittici,* 157. In reaching this conclusion, Eco refers to Pierre Bourdieu and Jean-Claude Passeron. Although popular culture is certainly alienated, people still seem to see themselves in it to some extent and therefore more or less accept this kind of culture. Cf. in this regard the discussion in *American Historical Review* 97, no. 5 (1992): 1369–1431.

137. Absolutely no attempt is made here to analyze and comment critically on the multitude of ideas and views expressed by contemporary artists and intellectuals about popular culture, let alone to present their works. We only have space here to outline very generally the positions adopted by these groups or their representatives within the public discourse on popular culture. We should remember in this regard that two of the best-known essays of the interwar period were not published until 1934–35 and 1947, respectively, namely, Walter Benjamin, "The Work of Art in the Age of Mechanical Reproduction," in idem, *Illuminations* (New York, 1968), 219–69; and Max Horkheimer and Theodor W. Adorno, "Kulturindustrie: Aufklärung als Massenbetrug," in Max Horkheimer and Theodor W. Adorno, new ed. *Dialektik der Aufklärung,* (Frankfurt, 1971), 108–51.

138. See Hermand and Trommler, *Kultur;* Laqueur, *Weimar;* Peter Gay, *Weimar Culture: The Outsider as Insider* (New York, 1968).

139. This question is addressed in impressive fashion, at least insofar as architecture is concerned, in Peter Gorsen, "Zur Dialektik des Funktionalismus heute: Das Beispiel

Although the leftist intelligentsia and artistic avant-garde concurred in poking fun at the moralizing of cultural conservative reformers, they could never agree among themselves about popular culture and its effects. All that united them was their opposition to the Trash and Smut Act. Just as all middle-class parties favored it, the artistic avant-garde and leftist intelligentsia bitterly opposed it. Many organizations, with the German Writers' Union in the vanguard, attempted to form a counterfront on cultural policy. Well-known writers, publishers, and booksellers joined the effort, including Carl Zuckmayer, Alfred Döblin, and Heinrich Mann. The chairman of the Prussian section for letters, Wilhelm von Scholz, also took a stand against the bill.[140] Although cultural liberals certainly did not approve of cheap pulp fiction—quite the contrary—they worried that the new law would pose a threat to "artistic and cultural freedom." The fact that they did not have enough influence with the middle-class parties to stop the bill speaks volumes about the clout of the intelligentsia and artistic avant-garde in the Weimar Republic.

Although many cultural liberals looked down on "shallow popular culture" just as much as cultural conservatives, they differed enormously in the conclusions they drew. A writer such as Alfred Döblin could not support any steps against the cultural industry: "We must defend intellectual freedom, even when it ventures into troublesome, controversial, erotic or political areas. This is different from defending the capitalism of the publishers when they set out, without the slightest cultural ambition, to exploit particular sexual cravings. We have nothing to do with that kind of business. We do not moralize about it; it just does not interest us. In any case, we will continue to draw a sharp distinction between 'business capitalism' and 'cultural or intellectual aims.'"[141] The Letters Section of the Prussian Academy of the Arts opposed, this time with success, a draft "Act to Protect Youth at Public Entertainments."[142] What raised most concern was the possibility that such an act could be used in an underhanded way to censor the theater.

Some "shallow" popular culture (e.g., the crime thrillers of Edgar Wallace) was positively received by leftist intellectuals such as Siegfried Kracauer, Béla Balasz, and Bertolt Brecht, who felt that it helped to puncture traditional concepts of culture. In general, "the younger gen-

---

des kommunalen Wohnungsbaus im Wien der zwanziger Jahre," in Jürgen Habermas (ed.), *Stichworte zur "Geistigen Situation der Zeit"* (Frankfurt, 1979), 2:688–707.

140. Found in a speech by Mumm, German National People's Party, *Reichstag*, vol. 391, 239th session, November 26, 1926, 8219.

141. Quoted in Reinhardt, *Lesebuch*, 147.

142. *Reichstag*, vol. 393, 312th session, May 12, 1927, 10681.

eration was particularly enthusiastic about 'revolutionary' factualness, progress through rationalization and technology, and untraditional, 'American' forms of knowledge and entertainment such as sports, jazz and detective stories."[143]

Film

However, other parts of the leftist intelligentsia wanted nothing to do with popular culture, especially movies that only spread trivia in their view. This elitist, left-wing avant-garde included, for instance, Franz Pfemfert, the publisher of the magazine *Aktion,* who commented: "Trivia has dominated the situation [for decades]. . . . our great minds serve up anti-culture, usually unconsciously and often against their own will."[144] More influential than this kind of left-wing cultural elitism were the sociological critiques of one of the best-known journalists of the 1920s, Siegfried Kracauer. He was not opposed to movies per se but criticized their mendacity and tendency to ignore reality in favor of a rosy, idealized world. In Kracauer's view, audiences went to movies mainly as an escape from the problems of their everyday lives. He interpreted the fantasies in movies as the daydreams of society, which reflected the fragility of modernism, its contradictions and ambivalence.[145] The depth of Kracauer's insights into popular culture distinguished him from other left-wing journalists such as Kurt Tucholsky, who never completely overcame a condescending attitude toward the movies.[146] Intellectuals of this kind generally felt that movies were incapable of developing an aesthetic of their own.[147]

However, other members of the intelligentsia and artistic avant-garde took a positive view of the new mass medium of film, viewing it as

---

143. Schütz, "Medien," 391ff.

144. Quoted in Anton Kaes (ed.), *Kino-Debatte: Texte zum Verhältnis von Literatur und Film 1909–1929* (Munich 1978), 59.

145. For Kracauer see the recent work of Miriam Hansen, "Kracauer on Film and Mass Culture," *New German Critique* 54 (1991): especially 61, 63ff., and 76. We will not dwell any longer here on Kracauer's problematic gender-specific perspective.

146. Mayer, *Linksbürgerliches Denken,* 246.

147. This critical attitude toward movies on the part of some leftist intellectuals was probably related to the steep downturn in the market for books. Some of the avant-garde feared that if the cultural status of the cinema improved, even fewer well-educated bourgeois would read books than was already the case; see in this regard Anton Kaes, "The Debate about Cinema: Charting a Controversy (1909–1929)," *New German Critique* 40 (1987): 16ff. It is probably not just a coincidence that German films tended to be based particularly often on literary works and plays, in comparison for instance with the United States, where motion pictures developed without much reference to the education tradition. Hermand and Trommler, *Kultur,* 274.

a golden opportunity to reduce the "cultural deficit" of the masses.[148] They searched for the laws that this art form had developed for itself[149] and felt that the government should support the production and distribution of "progressive films."[150] Some, such as Bertolt Brecht, expected that a new popular culture borne by the proletariat would emerge, providing an opportunity to enlighten the masses about social realities and the fact that they can be changed.[151] The Bauhaus architect Adolf Behne said he hoped "that the proletariat, working together with the best artists, would create films of exemplary form and humanity."[152] However, little came of this declaration of cooperation between the artistic avant-garde and the labor movement: "Although leftist intellectuals and artists, including Anna Siemsen, Heinz Lüdecke, Erwin Piscator, Franz Jung, Hanns Eisler and Bertolt Brecht, promoted and experimented with such alternatives [i.e., grassroots alternatives] at various times throughout the period, they received little support and were often criticized by the political parties of the left. For the most part, they developed and practiced their models of artistic production and reception independently of the SPD's and KPD's cultural programs."[153]

In 1928, leftist intellectuals including Heinrich Mann and Erwin Piscator founded the People's Association for the Art of Film, later known as the People's Film Association (*Volksfilmverband*). Acting in a critical, enlightening spirit, they hoped to alter public taste, "work the public over," "wake it up," and "educate" it.[154] The issue of major concern to them was who would gain influence over the general public, that is, who would exercise cultural hegemony.[155] The founders of the association felt that most people were not particularly fond of "kitsch and trash" but had only grown accustomed to it. If they could only be properly enlightened, their tastes would change, and "trash" would yield to "good" entertaining movies.[156] However, the association still had only five thousand members in 1928. The magazine it published, known at first as *Film und Volk* from 1928 to 1930 and then as *Arbeiterbühne und Film* (Workers' theater and film) in 1930–31, had some success.[157] How-

148. Mayer, *Linksbürgerliches Denken*, 230.
149. Cf. for instance *Neue Schaubühne*, no. 4 (1921): 81.
150. Petzet, *Filme*, 141, 145.
151. Cf. Kaes, "Debate," 32.
152. *Kulturwille* 2 (1925): 226.
153. Bruce Murray, *Film and the German Left in the Weimar Republic: From Caligari to Kuhle Wampe* (Austin, 1990), 237.
154. *Weltbühne* 24, first half year, no. 13 (1928): 478.
155. Cf. for instance ibid., 477ff.
156. Cf. Kaes, *Kino-Debatte*, 172.
157. Hermand and Trommler, *Kultur*, 268.

ever, this kind of rational approach to culture based on the ideals of the Enlightenment was ultimately not very effective because it failed to come to grips with the real reasons why people watch trite movies.

Radio

Although the leftist intelligentsia required a considerable amount of time to develop a differentiated view of film, it was positively disposed toward radio from the outset. Bertolt Brecht, Alexander Döblin, Rudolf Leonhard, and others quickly recognized the opportunities afforded by this new medium. In 1925, an intense debate about radio broke out among writers—a debate made all the livelier by their assumption that, since it was public by law, considerable influence could be exerted over the programming. Publishers were primarily interested at first in using radio as a means of disseminating literary texts.[158] However some writers soon began to experiment with innovative literary forms such as *Hörspiele,* or plays written especially for the radio. The censors usually intervened, though, as soon as socially emancipating or even pacifist ideas clearly surfaced.[159]

According to Irmela Schneider, reactions varied to the emergence of the new medium of radio, ranging from euphoria to concern about the directions that civilization might be taking. Some people were particularly interested in how radio could be used to disseminate literature and science, while others hoped that it could be used to achieve a cultural balance among the social classes. Some became infatuated with radio plays as a new artistic form and speculated about the ability of radio to change the culture. Others developed various ideas on radio policy and theories of the media.[160]

All in all, the artistic avant-garde and leftist intelligentsia tended to fall between two stools. Their culturally liberal attitudes raised the ire of cultural conservatives, who accused them of making a fetish of intellectual freedom.[161] According to a German National deputy named Mumm, they demonstrated "Jewish libertinism."[162] While exposing themselves

---

158. Some writers, such as Döblin and Zweig, also hoped that radio could be used to "deepen the conception of the Reich and the republican state." Mayer, *Linksbürgerliches Denken,* 251.

159. Cf. *Weltbühne* 23, first half year (1927): 497.

160. Irmela Schneider (ed.), *Radio-Kultur in der Weimarer Republik: Eine Dokumentation* (Tübingen, 1984).

161. Center Party deputy Schreiber directed this reproach at the German Democratic Party, *Reichstag,* vol. 392, 288th session, March 17, 1927, 9637.

162. Mumm, German National People's Party, *Reichstag,* vol. 391, 239th session, November 26, 1926, 8217.

on the one hand to criticism from the powerful block of cultural conservatives, the artistic avant-garde and leftist intelligentsia found on the other hand that their attempts to shape and mold popular culture did not have much appeal for the masses.

The Labor Movement and Popular Culture

Within the labor movement popular culture was often considered an apolitical pleasure beyond any class considerations. The "goals it encouraged and the interpretations it gave to life were confined to individualistic struggles to get ahead and find private escapes and happiness in love and one's family and therefore ran counter to all demands for class action."[163] Both the Social Democratic and Communist labor movements had great difficulty accepting the fact that thrilling or erotic entertainments, though "shallow," had become an integral part of working-class life, about which little could be done.[164]

The Social Democratic Labor Movement

There was a widespread feeling within the SPD that German culture had changed substantially. In 1923, the writer Marie Kunert (formerly a member of the USPD and by then a member of the SPD) addressed an important part of this change, namely, the influence of the new rich and their "parvenu taste": "Mr. Raffke, newly rich, has virtually unlimited power. Even art is increasingly subject to his depraved instincts. Kitsch predominates." According to Kunert, art was becoming "a domain or

163. Kaspar Maase, *Leben einzeln und frei wie ein Baum und brüderlich wie ein Wald: Wandel der Arbeiterkultur und Zukunft der Lebensweise*, 2d ed. (Cologne, 1987), 70. Again we can only provide a broad outline of the attitudes expressed by labor organizations in the discourse over popular culture. More detailed, in-depth information can be found in the specialized literature. A good overview is Willi L. Guttsman, *Workers' Culture in Weimar Germany: Between Tradition and Commitment* (New York, 1990); cf. Adelheid von Saldern, "Der Wochend-Mensch," *Mitteilungen aus der kulturwissenschaftlichen Forschung* 15, no. 30 (1992): 5–33; Dietrich Mühlberg, "Modernisierungstendenzen in der proletarischen Lebensweise," *Mitteilungen aus der kulturwissenschaftlichen Forschung* 15, no. 30 (1992): 34–64; Adelheid von Saldern and Dietrich Mühlberg, "Kontinuität und Wandel der Arbeiterkultur: Ein Forschungsaufriß," *Mitteilungen aus der kulturwissenschaftlichen Forschung* 15, no. 30 (1992): 226–60.

164. The workers' parties also had difficulty accepting such enjoyable leisure pursuits as visiting fairs and pubs. The prewar Social Democrats complained incessantly about the "craze for pleasure" among workers. The beginnings of an international comparison can be found in Victoria de Grazia, "The Left Labour Movement in Europe and the Problem of Worker Leisure, 1918–1939," in Helmut Konrad (ed.), *Internationale Tagung der Historiker der Arbeiterbewegung: 16. Linzer Konferenz 1980* (Vienna, 1982), 165–81.

preserve of a narrow upper class" and "the health of the people" was "suffering from all the artistic trash." She criticized purely commercial theater for staging too much "garbage."[165] Nevertheless, Social Democratic deputies often tried to put the negative effects of "trash and smut" in perspective, emphasizing for instance that poor social conditons posed a far greater danger.[166] They also denounced the view that the rising tide of immorality was primarily a problem of the lower classes. "Propertied circles" were also affected, they pointed out, as could be seen by the simple fact that the "worst shows" were very expensive.[167] Deputy Sollmann claimed in 1930 that a "cultural crisis" had arisen in Germany, which he attributed to the decline of the old economic and social structures. The old authorities were faltering, the old cultural forms had been smashed, and a new worldview was just beginning to emerge, he said.[168]

Party members differed in their views on the condition of youth. Rudolf Breitscheid assured the Reichstag that the war and its aftermath had made the youth rougher and more callous,[169] but his fellow party member Mathilde Wurm, a social worker and later a writer, told the deputies that the working-class youth were no wilder and more wayward than before the war. The same could not be said, she added, of the "rowdies" on the political Right.[170] The Social Democratic leadership always emphasized all that the party was doing to assist in the training and education of working-class youth, thereby helping to save them from moral turpitude and contributing to their spiritual and cultural betterment.[171] The party continued to adhere to this approach, hoping that the socialist concept of culture would eventually foster the emergence of a "new Man," who would know the difference, not least of all, between worthwhile and worthless elements of popular culture, in addition to helping pave the way for socialism.[172]

165. Kunert, SPD, Prussian *Landtag,* vol. 12, 244th session, May 14, 1923, 17361; cf. Prussian *Landtag,* vol. 12, 244th session, May 14, 1923, 17362; Prussian *Landtag,* vol. 5, 105th session, February 23, 1922, 7468.

166. For instance Dr. David, SPD, *Reichstag,* vol. 391, 245th session, December 3, 1926, 8378.

167. Wilhelm Krüger, party secretary, SPD, Prussian *Landtag,* vol. 4, 75th session, November 25, 1921, 4986.

168. Sollmann, SPD, *Reichstag,* vol. 428, 176th session, June 16, 1930, 5458.

169. Rudolf Breitscheid, SPD, *Reichstag,* vol. 391, 245th session, December 3, 1926, 8362.

170. Wurm, SPD, *Reichstag,* vol. 393, 313th session, May 13, 1927, 10704.

171. Cf. *Reichstag,* vol. 391, 245th session, December 3, 1926, 8361.

172. For corresponding attempts of the prewar Social Democrats to "refine and uplift" see Brigitte Emig, *Die Veredelung des Arbeiters: Sozialdemokratie als Kultur- bewegung* (Frankfurt, 1980).

There were many workers' cultural associations in the 1920s with strong ties to the Social Democratic Party. The party felt that these associations, which were in their heyday at the time, provided the organizational basis for the "right" approach to popular culture and leisure time.[173] Young people (including some women) could usually find workers' cultural associations in which to pursue their leisure interests, whether gymnastics, sports, chess, singing, photography, listening to the radio, or much else. Some elements of popular culture entered the workers' cultural movement in this way, although attempts were made to ensure that these elements were always "worthwhile" and had a meaningful place within Social Democracy.

As important and successful as these cultural associations were from a qualitative point of view, they remained a minority interest. The attempts of the workers' cultural associations to provide an alternative to popular culture were therefore of limited success, despite some great triumphs.[174] These associations demonstrated little or only a restricted ability to attract new strata or groups of workers, especially the unorganized, youth, and women,[175] and thereby expand their cultural capacities.[176] In general, the SPD and probably the cultural associations themselves did not give enough thought to the ways in which popular culture had changed the environment in which Social Democratic cultural and leisure-time policies had evolved within the associations and among the grassroots, and all too few people understood the far-reaching implications of the changes.[177] If the communications between the working-class

173. See Wilfried van der Will and Rob Burns, *Arbeiterbewegungskultur in der Weimarer Republik: Eine historisch-theoretische Analyse der kulturellen Bestrebungen der sozialdemokratisch-organisierten Arbeiterschaft* (Frankfurt, 1982).

174. Cf. Langewiesche, "Freizeit," 244.

175. Cf. James Wickham, "Arbeiterpolitik und Arbeiterbewegung in den 1920er Jahren in einer Großstadt: Das Beispiel Frankfurt am Main," *SOWI* 13, no. 1 (1984), 22–29; Peter Friedemann, "Anspruch und Wirklichkeit der Arbeiterkultur 1891–1933," in Institut zur Geschichte der deutschen Arbeiterbewegung (ed.), *Fahnen, Fäuste, Körper* (Essen, 1986), 109. There is considerable controversy over assessments of the workers' cultural movement in the Weimar Republic; cf. Peter Lösche and Franz Walter, "Zur Organisationskultur der sozialdemokratischen Arbeiterbewegung in der Weimarer Republik: Niedergang der Klassenkultur oder solidargemeinschaftlicher Höhepunkt?" *Geschichte und Gesellschaft* 15, no. 4 (1989): 511–36; Hartmann Wunderer, "Noch einmal: Niedergang der Klassenkultur oder solidargemeinschaftlicher Höhepunkt?" in *Mitteilungen aus der kulturwissenschaftlichen Forschung* 15, no. 30 (1992): 277–82.

176. Cf. Heidenreich, *Arbeiterbildung*, 127.

177. Ibid., 108. For the entire context see as well Adelheid von Saldern, "Arbeiterkulturbewegung in Deutschland in der Zwischenkriegszeit," in Friedhelm Boll (ed.), *Arbeiterkulturen zwischen Alltag und Politik: Beiträge zum europäischen Vergleich in der Zwischenkriegszeit* (Vienna, 1986), 29–71.

parties and the cultural associations had been better, there might have been more discussion of these matters. However, party and union activists had a hard time understanding, despite their assurances to the contrary, that the workers' cultural associations were not just a distraction from the serious matter of politics.

The SPD also attempted to induce workers to take a greater interest in "high culture," partly as an antidote to popular culture. Organizations founded around the turn of the century to promote "people's theater" provided cheaper tickets for their members or even established theaters of their own. These organizations proved very successful and by 1920 had six hundred thousand members.[178] Most of these people, though, were already eager to improve their minds. According to Detlev J. K. Peukert, little thought was given to providing help with basic education or to forms of political agitation that would appeal to the masses and take advantage of their consumption habits. According to Peukert, the Social Democratic labor movement saw itself as a cultural movement that transcended class culture and wanted primarily to share in the high culture of the bourgeoisie. As a result, it grew increasingly estranged from the everyday world and life experiences of many workers, especially the unskilled and semiskilled.[179] SPD deputy Marie Kunert claimed, in her idealistic way, that attempts should be made to awaken the "artistic sense of the people" by staging "really good theater" and bringing the proletariat into "deep, heartfelt contact with great art." Attempts should be made to "cut the ground out" from beneath movies, "which, with their amply demonstrated excesses, are directly inimical to art."[180] A successful alternative, according to her fellow party member Rabold, was workers' culture, especially workers' cultural sections in newspapers.[181] Social Democrats were also not opposed to, and even encouraged, folk culture, especially folk music and folk song.[182]

Pulp Fiction

What the SPD did vehemently oppose was "trash," especially pulp fiction. It even went so far as to call for a law against it. In 1924, Heinrich

---

178. Guttsman, *Workers' Culture,* 212.

179. Peukert, *Sozialdisziplinierung,* 187ff.

180. Kunert, SPD, Prussian *Landtag,* vol. 12, 244th session, May 14, 1923, 17363. The physician Hermann Weyl of the USPD, for instance, also insisted on "good art." Prussian *Landtag,* vol. 4, 77th session, November 30, 1921, 5241.

181. Rabold, SPD, Prussian *Landtag,* vol. 4, 76th session, November 29, 1921, 5101.

182. According to the Cologne university librarian Heinrich Erkes, SPD, Prussian *Landtag,* vol. 5, 104th session, February 22, 1922, 7433.

Schulz crafted a bill to protect the youth by drawing up lists of "trashy writings" and placing restrictions on them. Experts from the fields of public education, literature, and art; the book trade; and the youth movement would be responsible for drawing up the lists. Only if the representatives of all four groups agreed would a piece of "trashy writing" be placed on the list. The law would be enforced on the federal level in cooperation with the Ministry of the Interior. However, when this bill was altered and then debated in the Reichstag two years later, the SPD opposed it, as mentioned earlier. The most important stumbling blocks were, first, the change in the requirement for a unanimous decision to a simple majority decision and, second, increased influence for the government representatives on state censorship boards, who would replace the federal board envisaged by Schulz. Schulz had seen the requirement for unanimity as the sole protection in the bill against abuse and felt that this shield was no longer provided under the changed provisions. The government had therefore gone too far in the eyes of the SPD, and it joined the trade unions and, most important, the Socialist Cultural Union in opposing the bill.

The Prussian minister of the interior Severing agreed fully with the middle-class parties that something needed to be done about "real smut and trash" and "sensation mongering."[183] He also advocated "combating degenerate outgrowths in literature."[184] While Severing's position was quite close to that of the middle-class cultural moralists, Breitscheid pointed out the problems that would arise in determining what "trash" and "smut" were in the context of the Trash and Smut Act. Politics often played a role, he said, in one's definition. He, for instance, considered *völkisch* literature to be "trash" but realized that the nationalists took a different view.[185] Considerable caution should therefore be exercised in regard to the ability under the act to summon the police. Severing warned against this and provided sage advice: "Not everything can be eradicated with billy clubs. It is much more effective to refine public tastes. That is what we should work toward."[186] Breitscheid then asked

---

183. Severing, minister of the interior, SPD, *Reichstag,* vol. 425, 83rd session, June 11, 1929.

184. Severing, SPD, *Reichstag,* vol. 4, 76th session, November 29, 1921, 5064. The use of the term *Entartung* (degeneration) by a Social Democrat is noteworthy.

185. Breitscheid, SPD, *Reichstag,* vol. 391, 245th session, December 3, 1926, 8362ff.; cf. Max Seydewitz, SPD (later Socialist Workers' Party), editor, *Reichstag,* vol. 391, 240th session, November 27, 1926, 8252. In his eyes, the works of Hedwig Courths-Mahler were also "trash."

186. Severing, SPD, *Reichstag,* vol. 425, 80th session, June 8, 1929, 2209. Similar comments also from Dr. Weyl, USPD, Prussian *Landtag,* vol. 4, 77th session, November 30, 1921, 5241.

whether his fellow deputies really believed that the Trash and Smut Act could help to "refine the taste of our youth."[187]

Film

The SPD faced similar questions in respect to motion pictures, especially since it initially took a rather dim view of this new mass medium. It is not surprising that the party even voted in favor of the Reich Motion Picture Act in 1920.[188] Only slowly and with much hesitation did the SPD begin to warm up to movies, thanks especially to Russian films; film adaptations of literary works; "art" films; and realistic, socially critical films. The Social Democrats attempted to gain some influence over the censorship boards but without much success.[189] Margarete Bauer complained in general about the movies that "Workers have long had economic cooperatives, their own press, their own libraries, and their own book clubs, and they have long put on plays and concerts. Only in this institution, of which they make such abundant use, do they have hardly the slightest right of codetermination."[190]

Walter Pahl (SPD) took the disparaging view that the popularity of movies was due to the feminine culture[191] of the Weimar Republic. "It is no accident that more women than men play heroic roles in movies. The inner lives of women are more closely bound to the vegetative laws of basic urges than those of men, in whom will and intellect play far more decisive roles."[192] He explained the fact that men too enjoyed movies by their need to let off steam and live out the fantasies that they suppressed in everyday life. Here we see massive sexist prejudice applied to the consumption of movies.

Early in the Weimar Republic, the Social Democrats demanded that the motion picture industry be nationalized or at least brought under the control of local authorities. When this approach failed, the party itself began to take an active role in the movie business beginning in the mid-1920s. It established its own central loan system, the Film and Motion

---

187. Breitscheid, SPD, *Reichstag*, vol. 391, 245th session, December 3, 1926, 8363.

188. The USPD demanded that the film industry be socialized. Korte, *Film*, 62. It was also opposed to the Motion Picture Act.

189. The SPD had hardly any representatives even on the "Lampe committees." *Sozialistische Bildung*, no. 4 (1931): 110–13.

190. Margarete Bauer, "Was ist das Kino dem Volk," *Kulturwille* 2 (1925): 227.

191. In feminist research into feminine culture, the desire of women to see and be seen is interpreted as a consciousness-building process. Patrice Petro, *Joyless Streets: Women and Melodramatic Representation in Weimar Germany* (Princeton, 1989). For earlier times see Miriam Hansen, "Early Silent Cinema: Whose Public Sphere?" *New German Critique* 29 (1983): 147–84.

192. In *Kulturwille* 2 (1925). I am indebted to Inge Marßolek for this quotation.

Picture Service; trained mobile teams to show movies; and provided the district educational committees with movie equipment.[193] The SPD and the labor unions in its orbit also made political films of their own, which were usually very simplistic and one sided.[194] These promotional films were sometimes shown by a traveling cinema known as Rotes Volkskino. The party had some success with political films, especially in rural areas, but on the whole these films were of limited effect.[195] The Social Democrats never succeeded in building up any sustainable movie production within their sphere of influence. They always contented themselves with much more modest plans than the KPD in this regard as well and simply produced a few exemplary movies that showed a progressive republican spirit in full bloom.[196] "The SPD's dedication to parliamentary democracy, its affirmation of traditional aesthetic models, and a lack of experience with film production led the Social Democrats to assimilate uncritically the dominant trends in production and reception," says Bruce Murray in a study published in 1990.[197] The party put more effort into selecting and promoting movies from the bourgeois studios that it deemed artistically and thematically "worthwhile."

Radio

In contrast to film, whose relevance to "culture" remained controversial, radio was always seen within the SPD and the labor unions close to it as basically a positive force.[198] However, views in the party differed in regard to whether radio was a suitable method of providing further education for workers. The party newspaper *Vorwärts* encouraged the use of radio for this purpose and felt that it would help to reduce the "cultural deficits" of the lower social strata and democratize cultural production.[199] The bourgeois avant-garde and leftist intelligentsia supported this general approach.[200] It was not unusual in SPD circles for people to break into utopian raptures over the potential of radio and to mystify and idealize it as a great force for cosmopolitanism.[201] Others in the party,

---

193. Heidenreich, *Arbeiterbildung*, 99.

194. Promotional films first showed miserable living conditions and then the lives and activities of boys and girls in the trade union youth portrayed in a very positive way. Cf. *Sozialistische Bildung*, no. 9 (1931): 275.

195. Further details in *Sozialistische Bildung*, no. 6 (1930): 180; no. 12 (1929): 368.

196. Korte, *Film*, 95.

197. Murray, *Film*, 236.

198. Cf. Korte, *Film*, 54.

199. Cf. Christoph Rülcker, "Arbeiterkultur und Kulturpolitik im Blickwindel des 'Vorwärts' 1918–1928," *Archiv für Sozialgeschichte* 14 (1974): 115–55.

200. Cf. Mayer, *Linksbürgerliches Denken*, 232.

201. Cf. Dahl, *Radio*, 106; Heidenreich, *Arbeiterbildung*, 101ff.

such as Anna Siemsen, cast doubt on radio's potential as a method of education because dialogue was impossible.[202] Occasionally, objections could be heard that radio took the pleasure out of art by making it so easy to appropriate.[203] The SPD recognized that radio was a source of entertainment for "masses of work-weary people"[204] and accepted, at least to some extent, the love that many showed for it.[205] It warned, however, that this new interest should not result in reduced political and cultural work within labor organizations—an argument that the party had already made under the empire in reference to its own workers' cultural associations.

The Social Democrats continued to try to gain influence over radio stations and censorship boards. Radio was not politically and religiously neutral, complained Deputy Sollmann in the Reichstag in 1926, because "99 percent of the intellectual offerings support the current social order." He felt that the "new intellectual stance of 'socialism'" should be represented on the radio as well. "We will carry on the struggle to ensure that we have our say on the radio just as much as other worldviews."[206] However, what the Social Democrats deemed a "new intellectual stance" (*eine neue Geisteshaltung*) beyond any particular political affiliation was considered by others to be simply party politics, from which radio was supposed to be generally free. This dispute highlights the disadvantages faced by the nonhegemonic culture and those who espoused it.

In order to participate more fully in radio, circles close to the SPD established an organization of their own in 1928, the Free Radio Headquarters. In 1929 it produced a catalog of demands on media policy, which did not come close to being implemented.[207] The Social Democrats

---

202. Cf. Heidenreich, *Arbeiterbildung*, 105.

203. *Vorwärts*, no. 84, February 18, 1928; Rülcker, "Arbeiterkultur," 147.

204. Ibid., 147.

205. Cf. Dahl, *Radio*, 106.

206. Sollmann, SPD, *Reichstag*, vol. 425, 79th session, June 7, 1929, 2166; there were also complaints, for example, from Meier, SPD, Prussian *Landtag*, vol. 2, 28th session, December 16, 1932, 2202ff., and from Kurt Löwenstein, SPD, *Reichstag*, vol. 391, 240th session, November 27, 1926, 8219.

207. Heidenreich, *Arbeiterbildung*, 106. The list of demands included the following: inclusion of leading representatives of the Social Democratic labor movement on the key bodies overseeing radio, extension of the function of the cultural councils from providing advice to an active and responsible part in shaping programming, equality for proletarian celebrations with morning broadcasts of religious services, more relevant programming (i.e., to the political issues of the day), a change in the status of radio companies from a mixture of private enterprise and public utilities to a full public utility under the control of parliament, reduction of the radio license fee, and free licenses for the unemployed and people receiving old age pensions or government income support. Ibid., 106.

continued to have very little influence over radio, despite the fact that they demonstrated their readiness to compromise by renouncing their demand for a station of their own, in contrast to the Communists. The "cultural conservative block" was simply not prepared to give an inch in the realm of popular culture. Occasionally, Social Democratic organizations held protests, for instance one in Frankfurt in March 1929, at which the local cultural alliance demonstrated against the reactionary state of broadcasting.[208]

In general then, the Social Democratic labor movement tended to view culture as class neutral and sought above all to ensure that workers had an opportunity to share fairly in classical high culture. The new sociopolitical conditions under the Weimar Republic were seen as an opportunity for workers to make up their historical deficit in this regard. The Social Democratic labor movement demanded an appropriate place for its representatives in all the agencies overseeing the new mass media but with disappointing results. Although its desire to uplift and refine the masses must be seen in the context of a vaguely envisaged socialist future, its actual cultural activities were in some respects not very different from those of the cultural conservatives.[209] These two groups were therefore even able to work together on some occasions.

The SPD seemed deeply divided and uncertain about laws to regulate popular culture. It flirted with legal restrictions but on the other hand often seemed more drawn toward cultural liberalism, especially in view of some of the reactionary views emanating from cultural conservative circles.

The Communist Labor Movement

The Communists also considered themselves opponents of the commercial popular culture springing up in capitalist Germany. They interpreted movies, for instance, primarily as ideological and economic weapons in the hands of the rulers of society and the state. Peter Maslowski, a writer and Reichstag deputy, described the interplay between culture and the class struggle as follows in 1929: "Now more than ever, cultural matters have also been drawn into the class struggle, matters like the cinema, radio, the theater, art, science and literature. All these are more disputed than ever by the two classes of the bourgeoisie and the proletar-

---

208. Rainer Stübling, *Kultur und Massen: Das Kulturkartell der modernen Arbeiterbewegung in Frankfurt am Main von 1925–1933* (Offenbach, 1983), 100.

209. For the Austrian Social Democrats, see the recent work of Helmut Gruber, *Red Vienna: Experiment in Working-Class Culture 1919–1934* (New York, 1991). Gruber comes to similar conclusions; cf. 184ff.

iat."[210] In Maslowski's view, class conflict was "far more intense than in prewar times."[211] In the early days of the republic, the Communists tended to advance primarily moral reasons for their rejection of commercial culture. Movies would not only distract from political work and sap one's energy but also "sully the soul" and "intensify sick urges," as Clara Zetkin said in 1919.[212] However, the longer the controversy over popular culture raged, the more the KPD based its opposition on the class struggle. "Whoever controls movies has great influence over the ideology of the great mass of the people,"[213] said Axel Eggebrecht in 1922 in regard to cultural hegemony. This assessment became widely accepted within the party. In 1929, Maslowski commented in the Reichstag: "[I]t is fraudulent to claim today of all times that smut and trash in movies are an especially important issue. In reality, the issues are much deeper and have much more to do with the political and class situations than with these empty words of moral outrage."[214] The KPD considered the efforts to censor "smut and trash" as mostly a sign of the intensifying class struggle. Maslowski's fellow party member Kurt Rosenbaum, a retail clerk by trade, spoke in this connection about the "black-blue cultural block in the German Reichstag," which opposed all progressive culture.[215] The Communists were convinced that any war on "smut and trash" would inevitably be extended to include proletarian and Communist culture as well. Communist deputies in the Reichstag often recounted cases of Communist culture being suppressed or treated unfairly or suffering from unjustifiable decisions. In this way, they tried to reveal the "hypocrisy" of the prevailing cultural policies and expose their underlying political intent.[216] Communist deputies made cutting remarks about the connection between capitalism and the "production of trash." As Rosenbaum said: "[I]f you want to fight smut and trash in capitalism, you have to fight capitalism itself."[217]

It was only logical, therefore, that the Communist labor movement would have nothing to do with the government agencies and boards that were supposed to steer and control popular culture. There was no question of adopting the SPD's strategy of "influence through participation,"

---

210. Maslowski, KPD, *Reichstag,* vol. 426, 109th session, December 3, 1929, 3405.

211. Ibid.

212. Quoted in Neue Gesellschaft für bildende Kunst (ed.), *Wem gehört die Welt: Kunst und Gesellschaft in der Weimarer Republik* (Berlin, 1977), 494.

213. Quoted in ibid., 495.

214. Maslowski, KPD, *Reichstag,* vol. 426, 109th session, December 3, 1929, 3405.

215. Rosenbaum, KPD, *Reichstag,* vol. 393, 316th session, May 17, 1927, 10771.

216. For instance Rosenbaum, KPD, *Reichstag,* vol. 391, 239th session, November 26, 1926, 8229. Even Georg Grosz's "ecce homo" had allegedly been banned.

217. Rosenbaum, KPD, *Reichstag,* vol. 391, 245th session, December 3, 1926, 8367.

quite apart from the fact that the other parties would never have accepted the Communists as legitimate interlocutors and partners in any case. Consequently, the Communists were much more inclined than the Social Democrats to turn their minds toward producing an alternative mass culture. The attempts of Communist sympathizers to build a counterculture far outshone the efforts revolving around the SPD, as could be seen for example in proletarian movies and proletarian pulp fiction. However, the Communists could not point to any major success in the area of radio.

Pulp Fiction

The "red one-mark novels" touched upon earlier should be mentioned again in the context of Communist literature for the masses, although they were not issued as serials until 1930.[218] The most successful venture in the realm of popular literature was the *Arbeiter-Illustrierte Zeitung,* with a circulation of some three hundred thousand.[219] It had a very modern layout for the times and tried to keep up with the new ways of seeing and perceiving by enabling workers to read and understand it quickly. It was calculated to appeal primarily to unorganized workers and had some success in this regard. Nevertheless, its achievements remained modest, not least of all because the KPD was always quick to mix partisan politics with culture. The *Arbeiter-Illustrierte-Zeitung* therefore acquired the reputation of a Communist paper that could only appeal to people who were not antagonized by its partisan affiliation.

Film

The course that proletarian movies would follow was set by the programmatic article "Conquer Film" written by KPD member Willi Münzenberg in 1925. Münzenberg was not just a good talker and was perfectly prepared to act. In 1925–27, he founded a company called Prometheus-Film GmbH., which imported movies from Russia and produced some of its own.[220] These proletarian movies usually stressed the poor living conditions of workers, exposed the class nature of social relations and the suppression of the working class, and suggested concrete political alternatives that would liberate the working class.[221] However, Prometheus-Film

---

218. Cf. Rohrwasser, *Saubere Mädel,* 132.

219. Schütz, "Medien," 390.

220. The films *Mutter Krausens Fahrt ins Glück* (1929) and *Kuhle Wampe* (1932) became especially well known.

221. While some leftists from the Communist ranks wanted to use film primarily for propaganda purposes — for instance the film interpolations used by agitation and propaganda troupes — others wanted more emphasis on film as an art form.

did not produce very many movies, partly because costs were already so high that it was impossible to enter the industry in a grand fashion.[222] The company finally went bankrupt in 1931.[223] Although its proletarian movies proved fairly popular, their overall impact on the general population remained quite limited.[224]

The Communists also attempted to institutionalize a proletarian movie criticism primarily to advance the struggle against "kitsch and trash" and against nationalistic propaganda and war films.[225] Communists and left-wing socialists worked together with members of the intelligentsia on the People's Film Union (*Volks-Filmverband*). A kind of popular front of film criticism was therefore created, although middle-class intellectuals were not drawn any closer to the KPD as a result.

Radio

The Communists approached radio in a similar way to the other media and attempted to develop alternative products, although mostly in vain. A great quarrel broke out with the Social Democrats over the issue of whether the working class should demand a radio station of its own. The Communists vehemently opposed the existing stations, claiming that they only helped to stabilize the existing capitalist system.[226] The Communist demand for a working-class station was by no means exceptional from an international point of view. The Austrian labor unions had their own station, and in Holland the national station was turned over at least one night a week to the Workers' Radio Association. In the United States, the American Federation of Labor, an umbrella group of labor associations, had a radio station of its own in Chicago.[227] However, the Social Democrats in Germany could not be persuaded because they were committed to the participation concept and felt in any case that there was little chance that demands for a working-class station would be successful in view of the power balance at the time.

The dispute between the two parties over a workers' radio station heated up in 1928, when the workers' radio movement split into two organizations oriented toward the Social Democrats and the Communists. The Communist organization founded the Free Radio Union of Germany in 1929, which sharply criticized current radio programming

---

222. Korte also gives the censorship of motion pictures and the splits in the labor movement as reasons why action was taken so late. Korte, *Film*, 93.

223. Ibid., 102.

224. Ibid., 88; cf. also Langewiesche, "Freizeit," 245; Stübling, *Kultur*, 114.

225. *Wem gehört die Welt*, 482.

226. Mayer, *Linksbürgerliches Denken*, 251.

227. Dahl, *Radio*, 44.

and organized listener groups for the German-language broadcasts of Radio Moscow.[228] It also protested against the size of the fee that listeners to radio were required to pay. However, the Free Radio Union remained quite small, with only three thousand members in 1931.[229]

In summary, the Social Democratic and Communist labor movements found many ways of trying to influence and shape popular culture but with only limited success. Although some of the attempts to create an alternative popular culture were quite successful, especially from the point of view of quality, they remained a small part of the market. The Social Democratic and Communist labor movements were disadvantaged in the realm of popular culture, each in its own way, by the lopsided distribution of influence and opportunity in Weimar society. The development of an alternative culture was also hampered by the mutual hostility of the two labor parties. Despite some admirable initiatives and individual successes, occasionally quite impressive, the labor movement never succeeded in creating an alternative popular culture that could appeal to the broad strata of the (lower) middle class as well, nor did it ever have much prospect of doing so for both internal and external reasons.[230]

Conclusion

The debate over popular culture focused for the most part on movies, radio, and pulp fiction. These particular media also played a central role in the attempts to refine popular taste of primary interest to us here. All sorts of approaches were tried, from censorship to efforts to enlighten the masses and provide them with alternatives based on a number of very different beliefs. The social distribution of the power to shape and mold popular culture was very unequal because of the cost and basic political and cultural structure of radio and movie production and to a lesser extent of pulp fiction.

German Particularities

The question of whether the discourse over popular culture was animated by concerns particular to Germany can only be answered in part and in the form of hypotheses because of a lack of comparative studies. Popular culture was obviously very controversial in other countries as well, for instance Great Britain. Here too, cultural elitism of various

228. Cf. Guttsman, *Workers' Culture*, 262.

229. Hartmann Wunderer, *Arbeitervereine und Arbeiterparteien: Kultur- und Massenorganisationen in der Arbeiterbewegung (1890–1933)* (Frankfurt, 1980), 182.

230. Murray, for instance, comes to a similar conclusion. *Film*, 234ff.

shades and hues came to the fore, and intellectuals associated the popular press, movies, and jazz with "lower instincts" and sensationalism. Here too, attempts were made to edify the masses in the spirit of the Enlightenment and "uplift tastes," especially through the cultural monopoly exercised by the BBC.[231]

However, the situation in Germany was different in some ways. First, the attempts to censor and "uplift" were probably more intensive. In the United States and Great Britain, there was more reliance on self-censorship and less on the heavy hand of legislation. Binding guidelines were developed in the United States, though, in March 1930 and were very similar to the German censorship laws.[232] The pronounced tendency in Germany toward legislated censorship and more intensive efforts to refine popular culture can probably be ascribed to the defeat incurred in the Great War, the experiences of the revolution, and the demise of Wilhelminian society and its cultural values — all of which left much of the middle class feeling insecure and uncertain. "Cultural pessimism" was deeper in Germany and colored the discourse about cultural decline in a way that was largely lacking in Great Britain for instance.[233] The more intensive attempts in Germany to intervene in popular culture could probably be ascribed as well to the greater social importance attributed to, or at least claimed by, the "well-educated bourgeoisie." There was a widespread feeling among Germans after the war that their country was at least still a first-class "cultural nation" and had to remain so[234] if it was ever to regain its old status or become a world power. Finally, the inclination in Germany to pass laws could also be attributed to the traditional emphasis in German culture on the role of the state. Commenting on popular culture in Great Britain between the wars, LeMahieu said: "This common culture helped define the collective identity of a broad cross-section of the British public. . . . Shared cultural experiences became one of many cohesive forces in British society."[235] The same could not be said about Weimar society, even in modified form. Although Charlie Chaplin's movies, for instance, provided a common experience that transcended the social classes in Germany, the effects soon dissipated under the combined pressures of a very divided and unsettled society and the workers' cultural movement, which was

---

231. D. L. LeMahieu, *A Culture for Democracy: Mass Communication and the Cultivated Mind in Britain between the Wars* (Oxford, 1988), 3, 101–225.

232. Cf. Petzet, *Flime,* 134; cf. as well on self-censorship Monaco, *Cinema,* 60.

233. LeMahieu, *Culture,* 3.

234. Victoria de Grazia, "Mass Culture and Sovereignty: The American Challenge to European Cinemas, 1920–1960," *Journal of Modern History* 61 (March 1989): 54.

235. LeMahieu, *Culture,* 333.

relatively strong. The attempts to refine and uplift focused more strongly on the youth[236] than was the case in France for instance.[237] This was probably due to the feeling, which gained currency after the lost war, that the youth were Germany's greatest cultural hope.

Another German peculiarity was the influence on popular culture of nationalists and political reactionaries. Although their power could be seen throughout the Weimar Republic, it culminated during the period of cultural upheaval beginning in 1930. In Germany, the great economic crisis of the 1930s became an all-enveloping crisis that affected culture as well. There were incessant attempts on the radio and in movies and pulp fiction to exploit popular culture for politically reactionary ends and to suppress anything that was socially emancipating. The political Right in Germany recognized from the outset the new opportunities afforded by the mass media. The efforts of German nationalists, reactionary conservatives, and even some prefascists to "uplift" popular culture are a testament to their strategic flexibilty in the cultural sector. The National Socialists were able to resume these efforts after 1933 in their attempts to squeeze popular culture into a new, fascist framework. They owed at least some of their success to the realization, primarily by Goebbels, that political indoctrination is more effective when leavened with "shallow" entertainment.

Naive Interpretations of the Influence of Popular Culture on Consumers

All the attempts in the Weimar Republic to refine popular culture were marked by what strikes us today as a naive belief that its effects on consumers were clear and obvious and could hardly be exaggerated. The current state of our knowledge leads us to conclude that people interpreted popular culture in many different ways and enjoyed it for many different and often conflicting reasons. Although popular culture was sold in the marketplace like any other merchandise, people did not lose their status as subjects when consuming it.[238] Popular culture was assimilated in the obvious, expected ways much less than critics thought and much more in ways that individuals determined for themselves depending on their particular dispositions, mentalities, and circumstances. A contemporary quotation illustrates the array of possibilities: "All these weekday evenings, especially in the winter! Then it [the

---

236. Cf. for instance the Trash and Smut Act but also the film censorship.
237. Monaco, *Cinema,* 54.
238. For a first overview see Lawrence Grossberg, Carry Nelson, and Paula A. Treichler (eds.), *Cultural Studies* (New York and London, 1992).

cinema] becomes a shelter for impecunious lovebirds, a warm spot for lodgers who can't afford to heat their little rooms, often the only place of relaxation and an ersatz theater for working men and women, and for thrill seekers, a modern Coliseum where you can see the most amazing things."[239]

The new mass media were not free of power relationships and ideology, of course. The mass media were often complicit in the attempt to preserve the cultural hegemony of the highly educated bourgeoisie, even in an age of popular culture, and to "refine" the tastes of the lower classes. However, consumers appropriated popular culture in many different ways that were impossible to determine in advance with any accuracy.[240]

Particular Characteristics of the Weimar Republic and Future Developments

What we have seen in the preceding discussion leads us to hypothesize that the attempts to refine popular culture were particularly varied and intense in the 1920s. The reason lies probably in the lack of experience with popular culture and anxieties about whether it could be integrated into the existing society. In addition, the educated bourgeoisie had not yet come to accept the fact that its traditional cultural icons and values had been relegated to the past and would no longer be the dominant force in public culture. Nevertheless, the educated bourgeoisie retained its influence over the official culture and certainly succeeded—from an objective perspective—in exercising enough control over popular culture that it remained generally compatible with the existing social and political system. However objectionable "kitsch and trash" may have been from an aesthetic point of view, they did little to undermine the existing power relationships, as had been feared, and usually did not exceed the bounds of the existing social system. While there was no real reason for concern, the well-educated bourgeoisie and reform bourgeoisie experienced this period subjectively as a time of immense cultural insecurity and confusion, weakness, and decline. They saw it as a time of radical cultural change, with senseless experiments by avant-garde artists who often came, horror of horrors, from their own ranks.[241]

The insecurities of the cultural conservative bourgeoisie were exploited by reactionary German nationalists and later National Socialists, especially during the period of all-enveloping crisis after 1930. In terms

239. *Kulturwille* 2 (1925): 226.
240. Cf. Eco, *Apocalittici*, 30ff.
241. Key phrase: *artistic avant-garde.*

that sounded quite modern to many people, the nationalists and National Socialists offered their own interpretations of reality and the future world, such as the need for a strong leader, a new elite, a return to the historical roots of the German people, and (racist) imperialism and chauvinism to solve the social and cultural crisis in Germany. Some elements of popular culture that seemed useful to the fascists were picked up and given an appropriate social and political spin.[242] As we have seen, much of popular culture was politically polyvalent and could therefore be used to help stabilize the existing system, in this case German fascism. One need only think of the important role that entertainment in movies and radio played in the Third Reich. On the other hand, popular culture could never be entirely politicized, and it provided many people in the Third Reich with what they remember as "happy times" because they often did not see, or did not want to see, the connection between popular culture and Nazi dictatorship.[243]

In the 1950s, cultural conservatives in the Federal Republic revived some of the ideas from the 1920s and strategies for intervening in popular culture. On June 9, 1953, the Act on the Dissemination of Literature Dangerous to Youth was promulgated. Once again the target was "smutty and trashy literature," especially pulp fiction with racy content. By now, though, Karl May's stories were considered "pure, clean adventure," and one of the main bugaboos was comic books.[244] The search was still on for "good literature" and "good books," as could be seen in the debates of the Landtag of Lower Saxony, especially the contributions of the far-right Socialist Reich Party. "Genuine, clean literary figures" were still in demand.[245] The Lower Saxon minister of education and cultural affairs, a Social Democrat named Voigt, dared to broach the old question of what "smut and trash" actually are before scurrying back to the search for "good literature" and issuing a call for "cleanliness

---

242. Cf. Adelheid von Saldern, "Cultural Conflicts, Popular Mass Culture, and the Question of Nazi Success: The Eilenriede Motorcycle Races, 1924–1939," *German Studies Review* 15, no. 2 (1992): 317–38.

243. However, "apolitical" popular culture also provided opportunities for some freedom from the Nazi regime and was therefore an ambivalent force.

244. Bernd Dolle-Weinkauff, *Comic: Geschichte einer populären Literaturform in Deutschland seit 1945* (Weinheim and Basel, 1990), 96ff. Adelheid von Saldern, "Kulturdebatte und Geschichtserinnerung: Der Bundestag und das Gesetz über die Verbreitung jugendgefährdeter Schriften (1952/53)," in Georg Bollenbeck and Gerhard Kaiser in cooperation with Edda Bleek, *Die janusköpfige 50er Jahre: Kulturelle Moderne und bildungsbürgerliche Semantik,* vol. 3 (Opladen, 2000).

245. Druck, Socialist Reich Party, *Verhandlungen des Niedersächsischen Landtags, Stenographische Berichte,* vol. 1, 16th session, January 24, 1952, 988, 991. Similar arguments could be heard at this session from Deputies Sehlmeyer of the FDP and Meyer-Oldenburg of the Bund der Heimatvertriebenen (BHE).

and order."[246] As in the 1920s, there was a broad social consensus, lasting into the 1960s, that cultural policy should serve primarily "high art," although in contrast to earlier times, this concept included modern art and especially the Weimar avant-garde. Organized labor, now consisting basically of the SPD and the trade unions, was considerably weaker from a cultural perspective as a result of the general failure after 1945 to reestablish the workers' cultural associations. It continued the Weimar policy of seeking primarily to democratize high culture.

Not until the late 1960s and 1970s did a trend set in toward the liberalization of popular culture, which was by now heavily Americanized.[247] At the same time, the traditional understanding of culture was challenged through approaches developed largely within the orbit of the student movement. "No longer did cultural policy focus on the work itself but on the social process by which it was created."[248] Everyday culture and grassroots public culture were said to be fundamental to democracy and to play an essential role in the development of the individual.

In the German Democratic Republic, the cultural policies of the 1950s were also frequently rooted in ideas and concepts from the Weimar Republic. Popular culture was generally freed from its ties to "capital and commerce," but, the legacies of German fascism and the long-Stalinized Soviet Union lived on in the form of government control over cultural organizations and a virtual government monopoly over cultural policy. This framework shaped the way in which the GDR's brand of socialist popular culture would evolve. In the words of the East German cultural historian Dietrich Mülhberg: "All in all, a program intended to uplift culture, but which, in combination with the departure of the old cultural elites, inevitably flattened it at a lower level. This socialist-conservative program for a cultured society was abandoned in principle in the early 1970s and gradually replaced by a program for a socialist industrial society able to modernize itself. This program included a more liberal view of what a socialist lifestyle was all about, and it 'permitted' cultural differentiation."[249] However, the bounds of what was allowed remained narrow — all too narrow in the eyes of many.

---

246. Voigt, Minister of Education and Cultural Affairs, in ibid., 993ff.

247. Kaspar Maase, *Bravo Amerika: Erkundungen zur Jugendkultur der Bundesrepublik in den fünfziger Jahren* (Hamburg, 1992). Maase points out that the vulgarization and greater informality of everyday culture in Germany were to a large extent the result of the influence of American popular culture (e.g., rock 'n' roll).

248. Gerhard Schulze, *Die Erlebnisgesellschaft: Kultursoziologie der Gegenwart* (Frankfurt, 1992), 500.

249. Dietrich Mühlberg, "Überlegungen zu einer Kulturgeschichte der DDR," in Hartmut Kaelble, Jürgen Kocka, and Hartmut Zwahr (eds.), *Sozialgeschichte der DDR* (Stuttgart, 1994), 62–94.

The liberalization of cultural policy did not (and of course never does) solve the problems that were (and are) inherent in "media civilization." The internal contradictions and ambivalence of modernity, including popular culture, have become an enduring part of the twentieth century, connecting the discourses of the past, as outlined here, with those of the present and future.

CHAPTER 10

"Art for the People": From Cultural Conservatism to Nazi Cultural Policies

Introduction

"The restriction and monotony of it [music] has become unbearable. How the Germans themselves can stand it year after year is a mystery; but the German mind is something that no other nation can hope to understand."[1] This comment, which appeared in the London *Sunday Times* in 1939, is part criticism and part bewilderment over cultural practices under the Nazis. The following is a contribution toward explaining the inexplicable, with particular attention to the support for Nazi cultural policies among the general public.[2]

The term *cultural conservatives,* which was used at the time, refers here to those people from all social strata who tended to be "cultural moralists," which was also a contemporary term. Cultural conservatives and moralists took an idealistic view of culture rooted in the traditions not only of the petite bourgeoisie but most important of the well-educated bourgeoisie. In some respects, they took a negative view of modernity, although in others they accepted what they deemed to be moderate modernization or modernization that left certain traditional values intact. They also frequently advocated state intervention

I am grateful to Kathrin Hoffmann-Curtius, Ines Katenhusen, Michael H. Kater, Carola Lipp, Inge Marßolek, Daniela Münkel, Monika Pater, Martin Rector, Uta C. Schmidt, Gerhard Schneider, Harald Welzer, and Silke Wenk for their input and criticism.

1. *Sunday Times* (London), cited in *Living Age* 357, no. 4479 (December 1939): 386.

2. In contrast to the analysis of political power, much still needs to be done in regard to this question; cf. Uwe-K. Ketelsen, "Kulturpolitik des III. Reiches und Ansätze zu ihrer Interpretation," in *Text und Kontext* 8, no. 2 (1980): 217. For the lead-up and for the term *cultural conservatism*, see chapter 9 in this volume.

in culture.[3] The label "cultural conservatives" does not refer, therefore, to any particular social strata or groups and includes more than just supporters of the conservative political parties.

Just as cultural conservatism was not confined to the conservative political parties, it was also not confined to people with particular attitudes or mentalities. The term is therefore more of an analytical construct used primarily to differentiate from "cultural liberalism" and "cultural socialism," which were also in common use at the time.[4] The Catholic Center Party figured prominently in attempts to strengthen "genuine culture," and churches of all denominations tended to back cultural conservatism. One cannot fail to notice as well how many politically active women were cultural conservatives, for instance Gertrud Bäumer, the devoted campaigner for women's rights, who was a member of the generally left-liberal German Democratic Party.[5] The public sphere was also influenced in a culturally conservative direction by the federal and state legislatures and by various magazines, leaflets, newspapers, and public addresses.

Cultural conservatism had a greater impact than one might think simply from reading the academic literature, even though cultural conservatives differed considerably in the intensity and extent of their desire for change and even though they were sometimes inconsistent and ambivalent. Researchers have clearly been impressed by the achievements and vitality of the cultural avant-garde in Germany, especially during the 1920s, and have tended to overlook many other aspects of culture and attitudes in the general public. Only the most prominent of the neo-conservatives have attracted much attention, for instance Ernst Jünger, the group around the Tatkreis, and a few others.[6]

Wilhelminian society was modernized under a political system that was actually extremely fragile, although in retrospect it may have seemed quite robust, at least from the perspective of the 1920s. The

---

3. See as well chapter 9 in this volume. Georg Bollenbeck, *Tradition, Avantgarde, Reaktion: Deutsche Kontroversen um die kulturelle Moderne 1880–1945* (Frankfurt, 1999).

4. Cultural liberals, who opposed censorship legislation, could be found primarily among the artistic avant-garde and the leftist intelligentsia. However, the line between cultural liberals and conservatives was fuzzy. Some culturally conservative ideas could be found in publications of the Social Democratic Party, although in different contexts and with different objectives in mind (the "new man," "cultural socialism") than those of bourgeois or petty bourgeois cultural conservatives.

5. For more see chapter 9.

6. See for instance Jeffrey Herf, *Reactionary Modernity: Technology, Culture, and Politics in Weimar and the Third Reich* (Cambridge, 1984); Klaus Fritzsche, *Politische Romantik und Gegenrevolution: Fluchtwege in der Krise der bürgerlichen Gesellschaft: Das Beispiel des "Tat"-Kreises* (Frankfurt, 1976).

bourgeoisie still had to share political power with the nobility and, even more important, with a very self-confident bureaucracy and emperor's court and often found themselves pushed aside. In the cities, though, where art and culture were most at home, the middle classes reigned supreme. Magnificent city halls, attractive art galleries, and impressive museums and theaters symbolized the confident conviction of the bourgeoisie that the art and culture of modern Germany were theirs.

The aftermath of the First World War brought dramatic change. Earthshaking experiences, some quite novel, filled much of the bourgeoisie with a sense of uncertainty and disquiet[7] and led to an "intellectual crisis" among the literary intelligentsia in particular.[8] These experiences included the lost war and the Treaty of Versailles; the revolution and virtual civil war that ensued; the emergence of what was called the "labor union state" and rule by "squabbling political parties" (in reference primarily to the increased power of the unions and the Social Democratic Party); and the series of economic crises in Germany, especially the great inflation of 1923 and the depression beginning in 1929–30. The debacles surrounding war loans and hyperinflation brought about deep change within the middle classes. Prominent old families were impoverished and vanished as influential purchasers on the art market. Other families profited from the war or the inflation and became very wealthy, although they were still looked down upon by old money and the well-educated bourgeoisie as vulgar "new rich" lacking in taste and a proper sense of obligation to the traditional cultural values of the bourgeoisie.

Much of the art and artistic life of the Weimar Republic was permeated by the avant-garde, and it took many more shapes and unpredictable forms than in the days of the empire.[9] It was also impossible to ignore the tremendous breakthrough of popular culture[10] and the extent

---

7. Art teachers in particular suffered from this sense of disquiet and uncertainty. Herbert Wilmsmeyer, "'Volk, Blut, Boden, Künstler, Gott': Zur Kunstpädagogik im Dritten Reich," in Peter Lundgreen (ed.), *Wissenschaft im Dritten Reich* (Frankfurt, 1985), 84ff.

8. Frank Trommler, "Inflation, Expressionismus, und die Krise der literarischen Intelligenz," in Gerald D. Feldman et al. (eds.), *Konsequenzen der Inflation* (Berlin, 1989); Anton Kaes, "Die ökonomische Dimension der Literatur: Zum Strukturwandel der Institution Literatur in der Inflationszeit (1918–1923)," in the same volume.

9. For the spread of modern art in the 1920s see the introduction provided by Jost Hermand and Frank Trommler, *Die Kultur der Weimarer Republik* (Munich, 1978); Peter Gay, *Weimar Culture: The Outsider as Insider* (New York, 1968); Walter Laqueur, *Weimar: Die Kultur der Republik* (Frankfurt, 1977); John Willett, *Explosion der Mitte: Kunst und Politik 1917–1933* (Munich, 1981).

10. No negative connotations are attached to this term here. We cannot delve any further here into the connections between popular culture and the artistic avant-garde.

to which it was changing both public and private life. One need only think of radio, movies, records, jazz, fashion, advertising, and professional and spectator sports. The ways in which people perceived the world were changing, as were their everyday habits, expectations, and aspirations. Some people affiliated with the old, closed social milieus were becoming more open, especially the youth. Cultural conservatives were bothered by the strong foreign influences in both avant-garde and popular culture. The avant-garde was particularly receptive to influences from the new Soviet Union, which were decried as "cultural Bolshevism," while popular culture was susceptible to "Americanisms."[11] Modernity, whether in the form of the artistic avant-garde or popular culture, was rightly considered to pose the great cultural challenge of the times. It was dividing the traditional cultural camps in new ways and provoking a crisis in the time-honored understanding of art and culture.[12] The concept of "modernity" is therefore understood here to include not only the artistic avant-garde but other phenomena as well, especially popular culture. Taking our cue from the series of radio lectures completed in 1989 and entitled "The Turn of the Century: The Emergence of Modern Society 1880–1930,"[13] we use "modernity" to designate the historical epoch when all areas of life began to be modernized. One of the initiators of the lecture series, Detlev J. K. Peukert, described the period of the Weimar Republic as follows: "In the years between the First World War and the Great Depression, classical modernity triumphed on a broad front, deepened its internal contradictions, and plunged into its worst crisis."[14]

The new times struck many bourgeois Germans as *ver-rückt* in all senses of the word (crazy, disarranged, disjointed). What seemed in retrospect like the stable touchstones of the Wilhelminian system no longer applied in many instances. In the midst of all the upheavals that followed the First World War, hostility toward modernity took on a new quality in comparison with earlier periods. In the new era of uncer-

---

11. For cultural anti-Americanism see Adelheid von Saldern, "Überfremdungs-sängste: Gegen die Amerikanisierung der deutschen Kultur in den Zwanziger Jahren," in Alf Lüdtke, Inge Marßolek, and Adelheid von Saldern (eds.), *Amerikanisierung: Traum und Alptraum im Deutschland des 20. Jahrhunderts* (Stuttgart, 1996), 213–45; Mary Nolan, *Visions of Modernity: American Business and the Modernization of Germany* (New York and Oxford, 1994).

12. Detlev J. K. Peukert spoke therefore in his book on the Weimar Republic about the crisis years of classical modernity; cf. idem, *Die Weimarer Republik: Krisenjahre der klassischen Moderne* (Göttingen, 1987).

13. August Nitschke, Gerhard A. Ritter, Detlev J. K. Peukert, and Rüdiger vom Bruch were responsible for the historical aspects.

14. Peukert, *Weimarer Republik*, 11ff.

tainty, crisis, and threat, many cultural conservatives placed their hopes in the youth and the cultural heritage, especially the German cultural heritage. Much thought was devoted to ensuring that the youth maintained this heritage, and those politicians who were anxious to steer young people down the "right" path certainly included the right cultural path among their concerns. This seemed even more necessary because popular culture was proving especially attractive to the youth, particularly to all those who were not integrated into either the youth movement or particular social and moral milieus.[15]

In these times of uncertainty and material loss, the culturally conservative middle classes (and especially the well-educated bourgeoisie) tried to take advantage of their inherited "cultural capital" (Bourdieu's term) in order to define the Zeitgeist and take culture in the public sphere under their wing.[16] "Culture," and especially German culture, needed allegedly to be defended against (American) "civilization," just as "intellect" and the "spirit" needed to be defended against the "masses."[17] This kind of thinking in loaded, stereotypical dichotomies — typical of modernity in Bauman's view — emphasized the differences between the two poles of the dichotomies and the significance of these differences.[18]

German culture was also seen as an instrument that could be used to help the fatherland recover its former strength, as ardently desired by most Germans, especially in the middle classes. But which German culture was meant? From our present perspective, we might well ask whether there could still be a quintessentially German culture at a time when international trade and contacts were skyrocketing.[19] The same

15. The term *social and moral milieus* was coined by M. Rainer Lepsius. It refers primarily in this connection to the Catholic milieu and the milieu of the workers' cultural associations, which reached their apotheosis in the 1920s. See Willi L. Guttsman, *Workers' Culture in Weimar Germany: Between Tradition and Commitment* (New York, 1990); for the Catholic milieu see the case study by Cornelia Rauh-Kühne, *Katholisches Milieu und Kleinstadtgesellschaft, Ettlingen 1918–1939* (Sigmaringen, 1991).

16. For the concept of public culture, see first of all Jürgen Habermas, *Strukturwandel der Öffentlichkeit: Untersuchungen zu einer Kategorie der bürgerlichen Gesellschaft* (Darmstadt and Neuwied, 1962); also Habermas's introduction to the new edition of 1990; for a critical view, see Craig Calhoun (ed.), *Habermas and the Public Sphere* (Cambridge, 1992), as well as Nicholas B. Dirks, Geoff Eley, and Sherry B. Ortner (eds.), *Culture/Power/History: A Reader in Contemporary Social Theory* (Princeton, 1994).

17. Helmuth Berking, *Masse und Geist: Studien zur Soziologie in der Weimarer Republik,* (Berlin, 1984), 177.

18. Zygmunt Bauman, *Modernity and Ambivalence,* 28ff (Cambridge, 1991). Thinking in terms of dichotomies (friend/enemy) also plays a central role in Carl Schmitt's work. See Carl Schmitt *Der Begriff des Politischen* (Hamburg, 1953), 7ff.

19. We should point out in this connection that the term *culture* was used at the time in a narrow sense in reference only to either "high culture" or "folk culture."

question arose in regard to a contemporary, "modern" art: could it still be national in character; could it still be quintessentially German? The same sort of critical thinking is needed in regard to what was called "art for the people." The tensions between artists and the general population who are supposed to respond to the art can hardly be resolved, even nowadays when the line between "high art" and popular culture has become much less distinct. Theodor W. Adorno even considered the dichotomy between high and low art an immutable fact.[20]

It is impossible to overlook the similarities on a formal level in the desire of both the left and right wings of the political spectrum to bring art closer to the people. They shared an irrational longing for role models and a discomfort with fragmented, conflicted culture, "whose pluralism they saw as the reason for its decline."[21] If one grants that there is a widespread feeling of fragmentation and alienation in the modern world, then attempts to promote a harmonious, pleasant aesthetic that is "liked" by the general public amount to a denial or blurring of reality. The issue of whether and to what extent "the people" really do want a harmonious aesthetic should be approached as a sociocultural and historical question and not as an anthropological constant, especially since there is no such thing as the "people" in the sense of a homogeneous block. Recent sociocultural studies—inspired first and foremost by Pierre Bourdieu—reveal the complex cultural significances of the social differentiation of taste in modern industrial societies. People develop their tastes in art primarily in order to position themselves within their "social space."[22]

We outline subsequently the leading ideas of cultural conservatives in the Weimar Republic and the Third Reich. General assertions are illustrated with concrete examples from various spheres in order to encourage further systematic studies. The section on the Third Reich concentrates on cultural policies that do not receive sufficient attention in many studies of the art and culture of this period, especially the attempts to popularize the classics and folk culture, encourage "cultivated entertainment," develop a particularly German brand of contemporary art,

20. Christa Bürger, "Einleitung," in idem et al., *Die Dichotomisierung von hoher und niederer Literatur* (Frankfurt, 1982), 14f. Bürger refers to Theodor W. Adorno, "Über den Fetischcharakter in der Musik und die Regression des Hörens," in Theodor W. Adorno, *Dissonanzen: Musik in der verwalteten Welt* (Göttingen, 1969), 14f.; Max Horkheimer and Theodor W. Adorno, *Dialektik der Aufklärung* (Amsterdam, 1955), 161; and Theodor W. Adorno, "Letter an Benjamin March 18, 1936," in Theodor W. Adorno, *Über Walter Benjamin,* ed. Rolf Tiedemann (Frankfurt, 1970), 129, 132.

21. Wilmsmeyer, "Volk," 95.

22. Pierre Bourdieu, *La distinction: Critique social du jugement* (Social distinctions), French ed. (Paris, 1979).

and overcome the alleged feminization of culture. In a few concluding remarks on cultural practices after 1945, we return to the fundamental issue of breaks and continuities with the past, which was already addressed in regard to 1933 and is now addressed as well in regard to the years after the Second World War.

Cultural Conservatism in the Weimar Republic

The basic thrust of all cultural conservative speeches and writings was the search for and cultivation of "good" or "great" art. We will briefly outline the main ideas of the cultural conservatives and their attempts to put these ideas into practice in order to gain ground from the avant-garde and popular culture.

"Classics" and "Old Masters"

Particular emphasis was placed on the "classics" and "old masters"[23] and making them more accessible to the people. "Classical works" were (and often are) considered repositories of timeless ideals for the edification of humanity, including, by this time, the lower classes. Wilhelm II had expressed a similar view before the First World War when he said that "art should also contribute and have an educational effect on the people." The foremost mission of the German people, he added, was "to tend these great ideas, cultivate them and continue them. Among these ideals is providing the toiling classes with an opportunity to take pleasure in beauty and to work themselves up and away from their other thoughts."[24] Cultural conservatives therefore encouraged art in which the people could share and that would "refine" them.

Despite the attempts to resist modernity by democratizing access to "high culture," this culture remained the chief rallying point of the well-educated bourgeoisie through which it identified and distinguished itself. This could be seen, for instance, in the often quoted "Appeal to the World of Culture," issued on October 4, 1914, and signed by fifty-six professors. The First World War was interpreted here as a war against

---

23. The term *classics* is used here in two ways, referring first to works from the age stamped in particular by Goethe and Schiller but also in an extended sense to what was meant by the contemporary term *the old masters,* that is, works that have long been recognized as great stemming mostly from the (classical) ancient world and the Renaissance.

24. Quoted in Rüdiger vom Bruch, "Kunst- und Kulturkritik in führenden bildungsbürgerlichen Zeitschriften des Kaiserreichs," in Ekkehard Mai et al. (eds.), *Ideengeschichte und Kunstwissenschaft: Philosophie und bildende Kunst im Kaiserreich* (Berlin, 1983), 332.

German culture, and Germans were called upon "to wage this struggle to the end as a cultured people, to whom the legacy of a Goethe, a Beethoven or a Kant is as sacred as hearth and home."[25]

There was still very widespread agreement in Weimar Germany on the importance of cultivating the classics. A left-liberal deputy named Bohner spoke for many in parliament when he said in 1926 that the classics must remain at the heart of all cultural policy "because we cannot do without the moral heights and inner freedom attained in the classics."[26] Achieving these same heights and inner freedom, he continued, should be the goal of adult education, which was especially popular in the Weimar Republic. The classics included in particular Weimar of the classical age, and it was alleged that cultivating the works of Goethe and his contemporaries would help to overcome the supposed intellectual crisis that gripped the nation in the aftermath of the First World War and the revolution.

However, the classical tradition was clearly a two-edged sword. "Referring to the culture of German classicism, when the thoughts of the people and the nation were voiced by social and political champions of the bourgeoisie, certainly provided the 1920s with solid notions of a well-ordered whole, but not very democratic ideas."[27] The veneration of German classicism certainly made it easier for many conservatives to justify their disdain for "politics," by which they meant primarily the system of competing parties and parliament.[28] In addition, the classics, and especially the ancient Greeks, encouraged the formation of elites, which many cultural conservatives found especially appealing in an age of "mass society" and popular culture.[29] In the waning days of the Weimar Republic, the classics were reinterpreted in a neoconservative direction, as can be seen in the 1932 celebrations marking the anniversary of Goethe's death. The great poet was subsumed into the cult of the irratio-

---

25. Cited in Georg Bollenbeck, *Bildung und Kultur: Glanz und Elend eines deutschen Deutungsmusters* (Frankfurt and Leipzig, 1994), 275.

26. Prussian *Landtag,* 167th session, May 11, 1926, 11593.

27. Horst Dräger, *Volksbildung in Deutschland im 19. Jahrhundert* (Braunschweig, 1979), 1:11.

28. We do not wish to imply that the classics always have to be understood in this way. However, we can assume — unless this is disproved by further research — that cultural conservatives generally did interpret them in this way.

29. For examples taken from the *humanistische Gymnasium* see Kathrin Hoffmann-Curtius, "Der Doryphoros als Kommilitone: Antikenrezeption in München nach der Räterepublik," in Rudolf Wolfgang Müller and Gert Schäfer (eds.), *Arthur Rosenberg zwischen Alter Geschichte und Zeitgeschichte: Politik und politischer Bildung* (Göttingen, 1986), 84ff.

nal, Dionysian, and pseudoreligious and declared to have a "true German nature" and a "German sense of mission."[30]

Folk Culture

Cultural conservatives also considered "folk culture" particularly worthy of support. *Heimat* (regional homeland) dramas, folk dramas, folk choirs, and open-air theaters had already received special support in Wilhelminian times, and this continued in Weimar Germany.[31] Implicit in this support was a certain unease with the direction that art had taken in the nineteenth century. The rise of the bourgeoisie brought increased attention to the arts, which it revered as the highest expression of humanity, far above the mundane, workaday world. In general, only the upper bourgeoisie and especially the well-educated bourgeoisie were initiated into all the mysteries of the arts, which were growing increasingly exclusive. Often it was claimed that the arts were absolute unto themselves, and artistic freedom was considered sacrosanct. However, a basic contradiction went unresolved: while artists deemed themselves the keepers of the national culture, they were cutting it off from the broad masses of the population.[32]

In reaction to "elitist aestheticism" and an exaggerated "l'art pour l'art" stance, a view arose around the turn of the century that the arts should be rooted in the cultural life of the people and their everyday activities.[33] Some of the efforts to reconcile art and the people were undertaken in a reformist, emancipatory spirit or even from a leftist, utopian perspective.[34] Although cultural conservatives pursued the same aim of bringing art and the people closer together, the ultimate synthesis

30. Rainer Nägele, "Die Goethefeiern von 1932 und 1949," in Reinhold Grimm and Jost Hermand (eds.), *Deutsche Feiern* (Wiesbaden, 1977), 102ff.

31. There is still no thorough research into this.

32. Similarly Bürger, "Einleitung," 12. Bürger refers in this regard to the intelligentsia.

33. See in this regard for instance the polemical comments of Richard Müller-Freienfels in the final years of the Weimar Republic: "Looking at intellectual history from a sociological viewpoint, one would have to say that the arts were a cultural factor only when they avoided pure aestheticism and were carried not only by a few snobs but by broad strata of society." Richard Müller-Freienfels, "Künstlertum und Kunstpublikum," *Kölner Vierteljahrshefte für Soziologie* 10 (1931–32): 82.

34. The artistic avant-garde was also eager to bring the arts closer to the "people," especially the futurists, dadaists, and early surrealists. The Bauhaus also pursued this goal at first. These attempts reached their conceptual and organizational peak at the time of the revolution of 1918–19. Suggestions about how to do this can be found in many manifestos of the Workers Council for the Arts.

that they sought was quite different. The controversy about educating the people was touched off by the publication of Julius Langbehn's *Rembrandt als Erzieher* (Rembrandt as an educator) in 1890. It was very influential and led among other things to the founding of the Dürerbund, an association to which mostly clergy and elementary school teachers belonged, in 1902. The Dürerbund not only attempted to popularize the "old masters" but also organized numerous exhibitions of folk art and arranged speeches on such topics as "The Arts in Everyday Life" and "The Value and Art of Living," in which handicrafts and *Heimatkunst* were highlighted.[35] The Dürerbund was actually a middle-class attempt to take peasant art forms and lifestyles and formalize and revitalize them in an effort to combat both the emerging popular culture and the workers' cultural movement, which was urban, proletarian, and socialist in orientation.

The periodical *Kunstwart,* which was close to the Dürerbund and edited by Friedrich Avenarius, attempted to counteract the supposed "flattening" of artistic life in Germany and propagate a new aesthetic-ethical culture with nationalistic and imperialistic streaks.[36] The *Kunstwart* sought to foster the emergence of a *deutscheigentümliche Modernität* and a *deutscheigentümliche Kunst* (a specifically German modernity and a specifically German art).[37] In another implicitly judgmental comparison based on a false dichotomy, German art was said to be fundamentally "content art" while French art was "form art." Ideas of this kind became entrenched during the 1920s and in some cases were inflated into sweeping theories that were usually reactionary and highly nationalistic. At the same time, the opposition to "modernity" grew more venomous.[38]

For many years, historians focused on either avant-garde or working-class culture in the Weimar Republic, with the result that we still know very little about folk culture. It was certainly more concentrated in rural

---

35. Gerhard Kratzsch, *Kunstwart und Dürerbund,* (Göttingen, 1969), 351. For the Heimat protection movement, see Werner Hartung, *Konservative Zivilisationskritik und regionale Identität: Am Beispiel der niedersächsichen Heimatbewegung 1895 bis 1919* (Hanover, 1991).

36. Wolfgang J. Mommsen, "Die Herausforderung der bürgerlichen Kultur durch die künstlerische Avantgarde: Zum Verhältnis von Kultur und Politik im Wilhelminischen Deutschland," *Geschichte und Gesellschaft* 20, no. 3 (1994): 436ff. However, the ideological direction of this journal was not clear because various points of view were expressed, including both *völkisch* and culturally pessimistic views.

37. Gerhard Kratzsch, "'Der Kunstwart' und die bürgerlich-soziale Bewegung," in Ekkehard Mai et al. (eds.), *Ideengeschichte und Kunstwissenschaft: Philosophie und bildende Kunst im Kaissereich* (Berlin, 1983), 381.

38. See in this regard among others Nanny Drechsler, *Die Funktion der Musik im deutschen Rundfunk 1933–1945* (Pfaffenweiler, 1988), 161ff.

areas than urban and in the older generation rather than the younger. However, folk culture aroused a certain interest even in Social Democratic circles, despite the flourishing workers' cultural associations.[39] Kurt Huber, a professor of psychology with roots in the bündische Jugend (who later became a member of the White Rose resistance group to the Nazis), also took an interest in folk songs long before 1933 and carried out research.[40] The Reichszentrale für Heimatdienst was founded in 1918 to strengthen and preserve "Germanness," especially in the territories and borderlands, as well as among ethnic Germans in foreign countries. Many cultural institutions encouraged the reading of *Heimatliteratur,* alongside the classics, as a "healthy" alternative to popular culture and a way of "refining" the morals and artistic taste of the general population.[41] In addition, the Kulturring, an umbrella group founded in 1923 of all the associations in Lower Saxony devoted to local folk cultures, did its best to encourage initiatives related to these cultures.[42] The promotion of traditional folk culture reached its peak at the huge Trachtenfest held in Berlin in 1931, when thousands of Germans dressed up in their regional costumes came together.[43]

We still do not know much about the appeal of folk culture to various social groups and whether exhibitions of it were partially "modernized" for the new era of popular culture. More work needs to be done as well on all the organizations that fostered traditional folk practices, including not only those whose purpose was to preserve and encourage local cultures (*Heimatpflege*) but also the various clubs, such as archery clubs and choirs. We also do not know much about the effects of folk culture in the 1920s. It is usually and probably quite rightly assumed that the cultivation of folk culture strengthened regional or local identities. However, many nationalistic politicians on the federal level evidently hoped that folk culture would also strengthen a sense of German national identity based on the twin pillars of the *Volk* and the community. A minority, at most, felt that cultivating local traditions and customs would contribute to a more democratic, republican political culture.

---

39. For instance, the local Hanover association sent out invitations in 1924 to a folk festival, whose program included folk dancing as well as songs and gymnastics. We should also note that the illustrated supplement to the *Hannoversche Volkswille* was called for a time *Heimat und Kultur.*

40. Michael H. Kater, "Carl Orff im Dritten Reich," *Vierteljahrshefte für Zeitgeschichte* 43, no. 1 (1995): 27.

41. A study of the Palatinate was done by Celia Applegate. Celia Applegate, *A Nation of Provincials: The German Idea of Heimat* (Berkeley, 1990), 175.

42. Kulturring Hannover (ed.), *Kulturelles Leben: Aus der Arbeit hannoverscher Vereine* (Hanover, 1956). I am grateful to Ines Katenhusen for pointing this out.

43. Applegate, *Nation,* 193.

"Refinement" and "Enoblement"

Another option for cultural conservatives was to attempt to "refine" and "ennoble" what they considered "shallow" popular culture. Wilhelm Reinhard, a German National deputy in the Prussian Landtag, stated for instance in 1922 that "healthy artistic fare" should be provided to "the broadest strata of the *Volk*."[44] Cultural conservatives turned up their noses not only at the popular dime novels but also at westerns and stories about American Indians, such as the tales of Buffalo Bill, or detective stories, such as the Nick Carter and Sherlock Holmes stories, sometimes because of their content and sometimes for more aesthetic reasons. "Shallow" or even "dangerous" films were also rejected. In their place, cultural conservatives encouraged products that, though easily understandable, were still "uplifting": "We want and must provide refined entertainment."[45] It was no coincidence that cultural and educational films received strong support in Germany. Radio stations, adult education centers, and public libraries were also expected to provide alternatives to "trash" and "smut."[46] Cultural conservatives also attempted to influence the reading habits of the youth by holding readings, lectures, and exhibitions and by distributing flyers and leaflets. Cultural conservatives always lauded "good books," although no one seemed to know for sure what they were. Cultural conservatives were better at specifying what was bad, for instance literature that contained lengthy descriptions of the murder of children.[47] Attitudes were particularly vague in regard to products considered trite but harmless. It was virtually impossible in a democratic society with a free market to influence commercial culture in particular aesthetic directions, and realistic cultural conservatives therefore felt forced to make concessions to so-called popular taste and not aim too high in their attempts to "uplift" and "refine."[48]

---

44. Prussian *Landtag,* 102nd session, February 20, 1922, 7208.

45. Ernst Kantorowics, "Bemerkungen über das öffentliche Musikleben Hannovers," *Das Hohe Ufer* 1 (1919): 50. I am grateful to Ines Katenhusen for pointing this out.

46. For more see chapter 9 in this volume.

47. Reichstag 81st–82nd session, June 10, 1929, 2261.

48. "Popular taste" is not understood here, of course, as an ontological phenomenon. For theoretical considerations see Umberto Eco, *Apocalittici e integrati* (Milan, 1964), especially 88. For the late nineteenth century see for instance Jürgen Reulecke, "'Veredelung der Volkserholung' und 'edle Geselligkeit': Sozialreformerische Bestrebungen zur Gestaltung der arbeitsfreien Zeit im Kaiserreich," in Gerhard Huck (ed.), *Sozialgeschichte der Freizeit: Untersuchungen zum Wandel der Alltagskultur in Deutschland* (Wuppertal, 1980), 141ff.

"Moderate Modernity"

Another strategy of cultural conservatives was to support "moderate modernity." Some, of course, dismissed all modern art as "pseudoart" and the "decadence of German art," but this attitude was not typical. Much more common were mixed feelings of distaste and open-mindedness. Many cultural conservatives did not desire at all to return to the nineteenth century and wanted to be up-to-date, even "modern" — but just not "too modern." This was the stance of the journal *Die Kunst für alle* (Art for all), which did not hesitate, for instance, to pay homage to the painter Max Liebermann in an issue from 1913. He was supposedly deeply rooted in the soil of his local homeland but at the same time was a modern German with an international following.[49]

Cultural conservatives advocated what they called "healthy progress" and criticized modern art for being "unhealthy," "excessive," "too modern," "very modern," or at least "immature" and still in the early stages of development.[50] Large parts of the middle classes also considered modern art a fad[51] that should not be taken too seriously. Cultural conservatives were disturbed by the disjointedness of modern art, its experimental nature, and the rapidity with which one stylistic movement supplanted another.[52] However, in the realm of architecture, for instance, they did consider the housing built in Hamburg and Hanover "a moderate path to modernity."[53] Middle courses of this kind were generally welcomed by the urban middle classes, whereas only a small portion of them (or of workers, for that matter) could warm up to the Bauhaus, which was considered the height of modernity. The situation in theater was similar. The Social Democratic Freie Volksbühne Hannover complained that "mainly old theater" was offered and there was "virtually no sign of contemporary theater."[54] It was no coincidence that only a few

---

49. See *Die Kunst für alle* 18, no. 1. (1913): 217ff.

50. See chapter 9 in this volume.

51. Peter-Klaus Schuster, "München: das Verhängnis einer Kunststadt," in idem (ed.), *Die "Kunststadt" München 1937: Nationalsozialismus und "Entartete Kunst"* (Munich, 1987), 24.

52. Ibid., 24ff.

53. For Hamburg see the epilogue from Hermann Hipp in Fritz Schumacher, *Das Werden einer Wohnstadt: Bilder vom neuen Hamburg* (1932; reprint, Hamburg, 1984), 159ff.; for Hanover see Adelheid von Saldern, *Neues Wohnen: Wohnungspolitik und Wohnkultur im Hannover der Zwanziger Jahre* (Hanover, 1993).

54. Uta Ziegan, "'Die Kunst dem Volke': Die 'Freie Volksbühne' Hannover in den Zwanziger Jahren," in Adelheid von Saldern and Sid Auffarth (eds.), *Wochenend und schöner Schein: Freizeit und modernes Leben in den Zwanziger Jahren: Das Beispiel Hannover* (Berlin, 1991), 81.

modern artists had works on display at the Great Art Exhibition in Munich in 1930, accounting for about 10 percent of the total.[55] Among writers, it was not works by Kafka or Döblin that sold well but *Die Biene Maja,* Walter Flex's *Wanderer zwischen beiden Welten,* and Hermann Löns's *Werwolf.*[56]

Some cultural conservatives advocated not only a reasonable, moderate modernity but also a German, or at least Germanized, modernity. The search for a German modernity had already begun before the First World War. One group that should be mentioned in this connection is Deutsche Werkbund, which, in keeping with the imperialistic views of the time, even wanted "world-power status for German taste."[57] This kind of attitude could be found most frequently on the nationalistic Right, but even some journals that were quite open to modernity took a "cool to dismissive"[58] view of new movements in literature and the arts that they considered "un-German" and threatening. The movements denounced as "un-German" were primarily those that seemed to conflict with the values traditionally espoused by well-educated *Bildungsbürgertum.* They saw "no German feeling and yearning" in the Secessionists, whose art was decried as an "import." Even before the First World War, the middle classes had sensed that the avant-garde was a threat to them and had denounced it as un-German and "alien."[59] If it was true that foreign cultural influences could no longer be avoided in an age of mass communications, then those that were problematical or undesirable could at least be Germanized, that is, made to conform with what was generally thought to be quintessentially German in each case. This applied to such very different realms as jazz, movies, and advertising on the one hand and the rationalization of work and housekeeping on the other.[60]

More-right-wing cultural conservatives were particularly disturbed by alleged foreign and Jewish influences. Deputy Koch was cheered on by the German Nationals in the Prussian Landtag when he commented in 1930 that if he had to choose an appropriate term for the current

---

55. Rob Burns, "Prefigurations of Nazi Culture in the Weimar Republic," in Michael N. Dobkowski and Isidor Wallmann (eds.), *Towards the Holocaust: The Social and Economic Collapse of the Weimar Republic* (Westport and London, 1983), 305.

56. Marianne Weill (ed.), *Werwolf und Biene Maya: Der deutsche Bücherschrank zwischen den Kriegen* (Berlin, 1986), preface, 5ff. However, there are also contrary examples: Thomas Mann, *Die Buddenbrooks* (Berlin, 1904); Erich Remarque, *Im Westen nichts Neues* (All quiet on the western front) (Berlin, 1929).

57. Gert Selle, "Weshalb keine Geschmackserziehung?" in Michael Andritzky and Gert Selle, *Lernbereich Wohnen* (Hamburg, 1979), 1:241ff.

58. For this and what follows see vom Bruch, "Kunst- und Kulturkritik," 330, 333.

59. Mommsen, "Herausforderung," 443.

60. For more information see von Saldern, "Überfremdungsängste."

cultural era, like the "Renaissance" or "Rococo" for earlier times, he would call it "the Jewish-Negroid epoch of Prussian art."[61] The record of parliamentary proceedings contains the comment "laughter and animated interjections from the Left" but apparently nothing from the middle of the House. The left-wing parties firmly rejected any descriptions of modernity that seemed to stem from extreme artistic nationalism with racist overtones, but why were the liberals in the middle of the House so quiet? One should not read too much into the interjections noted in the record of proceedings, but this incident certainly reinforces the general impression one gains from the record that the "liberal" parties in parliament did not contain many cultural liberals who championed modernity — or at least that these cultural liberals did not have very much to say, in contrast to their more conservative counterparts.

Another reason for the search for a so-called German modernity lay in the previously mentioned desire to see Germany return to the ranks of the great powers. This desire often went hand in hand with the belief that Germany was the cultural capital of the world, because of all its great classical composers, artists, and writers, and steps had to be taken to ensure that it remained so. The question was how this could be done in the modern era.

"Cultural Feminism"

Cultural conservatives also resisted what they considered the feminization of the arts and the cultured public, or so-called cultural feminism. Popular culture was threatening to change traditional gender roles. The new wave of female employees in low-level positions, the saleswomen, clerks, and secretaries, was often seen as the herald of massive cultural change. While popular culture expanded the range of experiences open to women, women were also advancing on the political stage after gaining the right to vote in 1919.[62] The modern ideal of the "new woman" was

---

61. Prussian *Landtag,* 157th session April 4, 1930, 13462.

62. See in this regard Eve Rosenhaft, "Lesewut, Kinosucht, Radiotismus: Zur (geschlechter-)politischen Relevanz neuer Massenmedien in den 1920er Jahren," in Alf Lüdtke, Inge Marßolek, and Adelheid von Saldern (eds.), *Amerikanisierung: Traum und Alptraum im Deutschland des 20. Jahrhunderts* (Wiesbaden, 1996), 119–43; Patrice Petro, *Joyless Streets: Women and Melodramatic Representation in Weimar Germany* (Princeton, 1989). For the early period: Miriam Hansen, "Early Silent Cinema: Whose Public Sphere?" *New German Critique* 29 (1983): 145–84. The classic text in this regard is Siegfried Kracauer, "Die kleinen Ladenmädchen gehen ins Kino," in Siegfried Kracauer, *Der verbotene Blick* (1927; reprint, Leipzig, 1992), 156–71; for the criticism see Heide Schlüpmann, "Die nebensächliche Frau: Geschlechterdifferenz in Siegried Kracauers Essayistik der zwanziger Jahre," *Feministische Studien* 11 (1993): 38–47.

promoting greater independence for women, especially economic independence, as well as a more assured, self-confident bearing in public.[63]

Certain aspects of the "new woman" clearly appealed to the middle-class women's movement so long as they did not pose any threat to the family, which was generally considered the foundation of society and a particular responsibility of women. These aspects included not only participation in political life but also, and most important, greater material independence. Ever since the emergence of the middle-class women's movement in the mid–nineteenth century, it had demanded more occupational training and opportunity for women, although the emphasis was primarily on spinsters who were no longer supported by their families.

There was never any shortage of warnings, though, about the danger of going too far and making things worse. The greatest danger lay in so-called *girl Kultur,* which was considered youthful, Americanized, superficial, and obsessed with dancing and fashion, as well as inclined to heavy makeup and displays of the body, for instance in girlie shows, or even dissolute sexual lives. The deep sense of insecurity reached far beyond *girl Kultur* however. There was a fear that modernization could take on a life of its own and, in particular, that uncontrolled consumption of the new popular culture would eventually have a negative impact on women as the cultural guardians of the family. Many male politicians feared as well that traditional gender roles — especially the hierarchical division of labor — would dissolve in the face of the modernization of life and new opportunities for women. These cultural conservatives looked with concern and even horror at the example set by the United States. They criticized the increased influence of women in American public life; frequently equated greater independence for women with a loss of femininity; and denigrated American women, often in cliché-ridden ways, as trite and superficial. "America's civilization is female civilization to the extent that civilization is equated with feminism: the taming of males by females."[64] German culture was allegedly masculine and should remain so, especially in an age of popular culture, which was often thought to be especially feminine. No one said specifically how German culture could be kept masculine, but the goal was clear: basically no changes in traditional gender socialization and gender roles, which were supposedly equal in value but polar opposites. Cultural conservatives were especially worried about the "feminization of boys" that they saw in the United States and were quick to defend the "healthy

---

63. See Katharina Sykora et al. (eds.), *Die neue Frau: Herausforderung für die Bildmedien der 20iger Jahre* (Marburg, 1993).

64. Rudolf Hildebrandt, "Feminismus in Amerika," *Eiserne Blätter: Wochenschrift für Politik und Kultur* 10, no. 16 (1928): 261.

mind and spirit of our men."[65] Concerns about gender roles were especially widespread in the Stahlhelm (a paramilitary unit) among the "generation of front soldiers," and in religious circles but appeared elsewhere as well. For instance, a 1927 edition of the magazine *Sport und Sonne* (Sport and sun) contained the following observation: "German women should become involved in sports . . . in order to discover and experience for themselves how to raise their sons to be German men, who will bring a better future to their impoverished country."[66] In other words, women should play sports primarily in order to raise a strong new generation of men. Female sports, with the exception of gymnastics, remained very controversial among cultural conservatives, who worried about their effects on young women. Conservative ideas on ways to maintain the "proper" roles of the sexes tended therefore to concentrate on other cultural areas.[67]

Efforts to Shape Culture

All the efforts discussed previously to limit the influence of both the avant-garde and popular culture stemmed from a desire to steer culture in what were deemed appropriate directions through cultural policy or even direct state intervention. In other words cultural conservatives, and especially their radical wing, wanted to influence cultural life not only by means of government promotion of certain kinds of cultural expression but also by means of active discouragement, especially prohibitions. Prohibitions were usually opposed not only by the left-wing bourgeois intelligentsia and artistic avant-garde but also by the working-class parties.[68] Cultural conservatives fought on, though, arguing that since the state pursued an activist social policy there was no reason why it could not and should not pursue an activist cultural policy.

"Cleanliness" and the need to "clean up" became central concepts and, as Bauman above all has shown, a constituent element in modern thought. Cultural conservatives claimed repeatedly that anyone who valued order, health, and morality should actively oppose "smut" and "trash," which only cause illness. There was much rhetoric in the state

---

65. Cited in Manfred Buchwald, "Das Kulturbild Amerikas im Spiegel deutscher Zeitungen und Zeitschriften 1919–1932" (Ph.D. diss., Kiel, 1964), 209.

66. "Deutscher Frauensport marschiert," *Sport und Sonne,* no. 8 (1927): 467. I am grateful to Heike Hanisch for pointing this out.

67. We cannot delve any further here into the areas of politics or economics, especially the "dual-income campaign" directed against married women who held jobs. For an introduction see Ute Frevert, *Frauen-Geschichte: Zwischen Bürgerlicher Verbesserung und Neuer Weiblichkeit* (Frankfurt, 1986).

68. However, the SPD did vote in favor of the film censorship law of 1920.

parliaments, the Reichstag, and elsewhere about the "moral collapse of the German people" and *moralische Entartung* (moral degeneracy). The term *Entartung* even began to appear occasionally in Social Democratic circles and in the mouth of a modern artist such as Franz Marc, who described the big city of Berlin as *entartet* even before 1914.[69] The term was used on a regular basis, though, by political conservatives of all stripes. *Moralische Entartung* stood at the core of the discourse over cleanliness. People needed supposedly to be "cleansed of impurities."[70] A "spiritual cleansing" was necessary to produce "pure souls," and cultural policy should be guided by the "sentiments of the healthy-thinking population" and the "spiritual health of the *Volk.*"[71] From this point of view, there was considerable continuity before and after 1933. At the time of the passage of the Act to Protect Youth from Trashy and Smutty Publications in 1926, all the middle-class parties came together in a movement to form a solid and ultimately successful front against the SPD, KPD, and nonparliamentarian opposition of left-wing intellectuals and the artistic avant-garde. The literary historian Klaus Petersen concludes: "What had made the campaign into a movement was its emphasis on activism. Its emphasis on youth, its practice of blacklisting books, and particularly the recruitment of workers for its well-organized system of surveillance of bookstores and public libraries anticipated important characteristics of the Nazi drive for a 'total culture' and the effective control of literary and artistic output after 1933."[72]

National Socialist Cultural Policies

While government had intervened only occasionally in the cultural sphere before 1933 (the Motion Picture Act of 1920, the Act to Protect Youth from Trashy and Smutty Publications of 1926, and some regulations issued under the presidential governments), the Nazis instituted a full "cultural dictatorship." There was some continuity with the past in the sense that the Nazis had the means to implement everything that cultural conservatives could have wanted. However, there was an impor-

---

69. Schuster, "München," 27. Max Nordau wrote a book in 1892–93 entitled *Entartung* (Degeneration). He was referring to the sense of decadence and the fin-de-siècle atmosphere in European capitals. Ibid., 26.

70. See chapter 4 in this volume.

71. For citations see chapter 9 in this volume.

72. Klaus Petersen, "The Harmful Publications (Young Persons) Act of 1926: Literary Censorship and the Politics of Morality in the Weimar Republic," *German Studies Review* 15, no. 3 (1992): 521. (Elsewhere in the current volume the Gesetz zur Bewahrung der Jugend vor Schund- und Schmutzschriften is translated as the "Act to Protect Youth from Trashy and Smutty Publications.")

tant break with the past in the sense that the cultural interventionism of the Nazis was no longer based on free decisions by parliament.[73] Cultural conservatives, and especially their nationalistic wing, had always felt under the Weimar Republic that the law did not provide government with nearly enough power to intervene in culture and channel it. As anti-republicans, or at most *Vernunftrepublikaner* (republicans by rational conviction), they did not have many complaints about a cultural dictatorship so long as the results were more or less what they wanted. In the final years of the Weimar Republic, many educated people sympathized with National Socialism not least of all for cultural reasons, feeling that the Nazis, with their extraordinary vigor and vitality, would bring about decisive change. "It is an experiment that we are entering. Let us hope that it succeeds. It is our only hope, the way things are now."[74]

The Nazis were able to pick up directly on the concerns about "German culture" and the ideas and plans for intervention laid out in the 1920s. They did not need to develop any artistic forms or theories of their own and to some extent never had any intention of doing so.[75] In comments about the new German dance, for instance, they let it be known that the "goal of National Socialism is not to create or even dictate a new art form. . . . National Socialism sees its task much more as acting as an honest broker of genuine German culture, supporting and fostering all healthy artistic movements and watching very strictly to ensure that all unhealthy excesses are avoided."[76] The old prejudice that intellect is bad for the soul and all that is natural in humanity now became official government doctrine, with an admixture of various racist conceptions. Opposing opinions were silenced, and the artistic avant-garde was rigorously suppressed.[77]

Government cultural policy was advanced primarily through the NS-Kulturgemeinde (Cultural Community), which was quite successful

---

73. For this reason it was no coincidence that cultural interventionism, for instance in radio and film, became more intense under the presidential governments (1930–33).

74. According to Otto Schumann in a letter from March 26, 1932, cited in Georg Bollenbeck, *Bildung und Kultur: Glanz und Elend eines deutschen Deutungsmusters* (Frankfurt and Leipzig, 1994), 288. The expectations of cooperation between the right-wing, nationalistic bourgeoisie and the Rosenberg wing were explored in the journals *Deutsche Kultur-Wacht* and *Mitteilungen des Kampfbundes für deutsche Kultur.* I am grateful to Michael Kater for pointing this out.

75. Cf. Drechsler, *Funktion,* 162, in which the author refers to Bazon Brock.

76. Siegfried Bergengrün, "Der Tanz im Dritten Reich: Grundsätzliches über die Stellung der nationalsozialistischen Kulturinstitutionen zum Tanz," *Der Tanz* 6, no. 12 (1933): 5, cited in Hedwig Müller, "Die Begründung des Ausdruckstanzes durch Mary Wigman" (Ph.D. diss., Cologne, 1986), 201.

77. Cf. Wilmsmeyer, "Künstler," 108, in which the author reflects on the continuing effects of Nazi art pedagogy after 1945.

from a quantitative point of view. By 1935, total membership had risen to 1.5 million in two thousand different organizations, and it could be found in the remotest corners of the Reich.[78] Insignia were distributed as an expression of the cultural will of the "entire nation." The NS-Kulturgemeinde published the journal *Kunst und Volk,* built up a circle of record lovers, and supported puppet shows and literary works. In 1935, it organized almost sixteen thousand events, including eleven thousand theatrical presentations. The magazine *Ich lese* was founded to foster regular contacts with poets and writers.[79]

Artistic Freedom and the Public Sphere

In their battle against "trash and smut," the National Socialists picked up on the views of cultural conservatives, that is, a large part of the well-educated bourgeoisie. The leader of the NS-Kulturgemeinde in Marburg commented, for instance, that it wanted "in the long run to create a *Volk* community for clean cultural work."[80] No one found the term *"Volk* community" (*Volksgemeinschaft*) especially shocking since the longing for a harmonious community with no room for partisan political rancor had long been a staple of cultural conservative dreams. This feeling was all the stronger in the wake of the lost world war and the Treaty of Versailles, which had badly damaged national self-confidence and pride. Culture would be the cement that bound the new *"Volk* community" together. The liberal lawyer Rudolf von Campe of the German People's Party said for instance in 1921 that the idea was to create a *"Volk* community as a cultural community"[81] — a view that was advocated in an increasingly aggressive way in the final years of the Weimar Republic.

Modern art was considered by many to be a kind of snobbism or even a fraud. Hitler summarized the negative attitude as follows: "An art that does not have the most joyful, heartfelt consent of the broad, healthy people but relies on small cliques, which are either jaded or promoting their own interests, is unbearable."[82] The National Socialists

---

78. Ulrike Gruner, *Musikleben in der Provinz 1933–45: Beispiel: Marburg: Eine Studie anhand der Musikberichterstattung in der Lokalpresse* (Marburg, 1990), 68. This is, however, a self-description. The Kulturgemeinden were headed by people in whom the Nazis had confidence but were otherwise largely left to themselves to do what they wanted. In 1937–38, the NS Kulturgemeinde became the cultural department of the Kraft durch Freude organization. Ibid., 96.

79. Werner Wien, "Dichter in ihrem Volk," *Kunst und Volk: Neue Folge der Zeitschrift Die NS-Kulturgemeinde* 4, no. 6 (1936): 232.

80. In Gruner, *Musikleben,* 93.

81. Prussian *Landtag,* 81st session, December 10, 1921, 5717ff.

82. Cited in Schuster, "München," 25.

attacked modern art in the same ways that cultural conservatives had prior to 1933. The new government was eager to suppress art that it considered disjointed, exaggerated, and degenerate and particularly associated with Jews.

The National Socialists used the selection and exclusion of certain people as a key method of social and cultural control.[83] Many artists found themselves treated in this way, including large numbers of Jews. The cultural clearance sale in Germany left many blank spaces, which the National Socialists hoped to fill with their own "language of fascist forms." However, all their efforts in this direction failed to impress, and it remained more effective for them to demonstrate their own greatness by suppressing what was "alien" and "different." Underlying this strategy was a desire to resolve the ambivalence that seemed to be inherent in modern art (Zygmunt Bauman's term), which many cultural conservatives had also found annoying before 1933. Clarity and explicitness were now desired, and after the "cleansing" had taken place, they would contribute to a "vital *Volk* community." Art was classified and selected, and the "weeds" were removed from the garden.[84] Not only the artistic avant-garde was exterminated but at least some parts of popular culture. Eventually, people too were put through a selection process and the "noxious" ones were eliminated, in a further step that was not inevitable but possible.

We cannot examine in detail here the efforts in the cultural realm to categorize, select, and exclude[85] and will have to content ourselves with a few examples. The extent of the selection can be seen in the print media, where 3,298 newspapers and magazines were shut down after 1933 in the course of *Gleichschaltung* (coordination).[86] The difficulties that the authorities sometimes faced can be seen in the record business, where, according to one Nazi politician, "good and bad, worthwhile and totally reprehensible are all mixed up together."[87]

---

83. For the organizational basis of the exclusion process see inter alia Alan E. Steinweis, *Art, Ideology, and Economics in Nazi Germany: The Reich Chambers of Music, Theater, and the Visual Arts* (Chapel Hill and London, 1993), especially 103–47.

84. See Bauman, *Modernity.* For another analytical approach in comparison with Bauman see Fritz Stern, *Kulturpessimismus als politische Gefahr: Eine Analyse nationaler Ideologie in Deutschland* (Munich, 1986).

85. See in this regard the usual literature. For recent work, see Peter Reichel, *Der schöne Schein des Dritten Reiches: Faszination und Gewalt im Faschismus* (Munich, 1991); and Harry N. Abrams, *National Socialism and Art* (New York, 1992).

86. *Living Age* 349, no. 4330 (November 1935): 272. Further prohibitions and "self-dissolutions" followed.

87. "Amtliche Mitteilungen der NS-Kulturgemeinde," *Kunst und Volk* 5, no. 2 (1937): 61.

The selection process carried out with dictatorial powers did leave a certain variety, although it is surprising how few empirical studies have been done of the range of cultural practices that remained. One of the rare studies concluded that "on the whole, very little actually changed in the traditional areas of emphasis in the musical life of Marburg."[88] It is possible that this study took a narrow view of traditional musical life and disregarded some aspects, such as the widespread workers' choral societies that were dissolved by the Nazis; however, it is clear that we should be very careful not to exaggerate the reduction in the range of cultural attractions.[89]

A study of public libraries in the Third Reich drew the conclusion that a considerable variety of books remained on the shelves, despite all the "cleansing" and space taken up by titles on "racial anthropology."[90] The remaining "variety" should not be confused, however, with what would have been available under a free, pluralistic system. "Readers did not encounter the clearly National Socialist worldview that the earliest propagandists had demanded." However, the remaining book stocks were piecemeal in their approach "because of the political limits that were imposed," and they did not offer any opposing views.[91] The essence of genuine pluralism — a free opposition — was lacking. It would be just slightly exaggerated to say that the effects of the "cleansing" only become clear when the "remaining variety" is fully understood. Many people were apparently quite satisfied with what remained. If this assumption can be confirmed through further research, it might explain why so many "cultivated" people from the middle classes were quite content with cultural life under the Nazis, even though they did not like official Nazi art.

Do the attendance figures for the Exhibition of Degenerate Art in

---

88. Gruner, *Musikleben,* 120. Cf. Rudy Koshar, *Social Life, Local Politics, and Nazism: Marburg 1880–1935* (Chapel Hill and London, 1986).

89. See in this regard the differentiated analysis of Günter Katzenberger, "Zur Situation einer 'unpolitischen Kunst': Überblick über das Musikleben im Dritten Reich," in Heinrich Bergmeier and Günter Katzenberger (eds.), *Kulturaustreibung: Die Einflußnahme des Nationalsozialismus auf Kunst und Kultur in Niedersachsen* (Hamburg, 1993), 35ff.

90. Cf. Reichel, *Der schöne Schein,* 334. Under the Nazis, the number of public libraries and Popular Education Centers (Volksbildungsstätten) increased. Margaret F. Stieg, *Public Libraries in Nazi Germany* (Tuscaloosa and London, 1992), 128, 130; Engelbrecht Boese, *Das Öffentliche Bibliothekswesen im Dritten Reich* (Bad Honeff, 1987), 238, 246; Helmut Keim and Dietrich Urbach, *Volksbildung in Deutschland 1933–1945* (Frankfurt, 1976), 26. One of the most important topics was supposed to be "German Cultural and Intellectual Life."

91. Boese, *Bibliothekswesen,* 271.

Munich in 1937 not demonstrate that the general population had actually become quite attached to modern art by this time? After all, 2 million visitors came, which was more than the number of people who went to see the counter-exhibition organized in the same year, the first Great Exhibition of German Art. Only recently have increasing doubts been expressed about the meaning of the number of visitors.[92] It is estimated that about 90 percent of the visitors to the Exhibition of Degenerate Art belonged to the lower middle classes and were people who otherwise never went to exhibitions and were genuinely outraged over what they saw (although it must be admitted that the exhibition was consciously arranged in a way that would elicit this response).[93] A contemporary observer, Paul Ortwin Rave, described his impressions as follows: "The dense crowds kept their silence throughout. Many people made notes. Some, mostly older gentlemen, shook their heads or made noises of astonishment. There were also many youths in attendance. Those who were a little older often talked guardedly among themselves, but most just looked around in utter bewilderment; only the rougher types, who seemed to have just descended from the mountains, laughed with incomprehension."[94]

It was not only the "rougher types," however, who demonstrated their incomprehension. Many educated people were nonplussed as well, for instance Karl Korn, who wrote as follows in the *Berliner Tageblatt* of July 21, 1937: "The first impression one gains as a visitor to the new Munich exhibition on 'Degenerate Art' is one of alienation and shock. We have probably never had so many documents from this past period gathered together at one time. . . . A George Grosz, who mocks Christ as a repulsive cripple with staring eyes and signs of epilepsy, or a Professor Gieß can certainly never be compared to the great representations of the suffering of the Son of God depicted so shatteringly by our German painter, Matthias Grünewald. We want to be a people with healthy life instincts, and therefore have no use any more for the collages of the dadaists, or the topic of whores, or the cold, spiteful fury in the paintings of cripples by someone like Dix. Kandinsky, Kirchner, Kokoschka,

---

92. See for instance Schuster, "München." The ban on the works of Schönberg, Hindemith, and Stravinsky affected only a relatively small audience. Cf. Drechsler, *Funktion,* 41.

93. Mario-Andreas von Lüttichau, "'Deutsche Kunst' und 'Entartete Kunst': Die Münchner Ausstellungen 1937," cited in Peter-Klaus Schuster (ed.), *Die "Kunststadt" München 1937: Nationalsozialismus und "Entartete Kunst"* (Munich, 1987), 98.

94. Quoted in von Lüttichau, "'Deutsche Kunst,'" 98. Huge numbers of spectators also gathered at the book burning in Berlin in May 1933, which created the "impression of a folk festival." Josef Wulf, *Literatur und Dichtung im Dritten Reich* (Gütersloh, 1963), 44.

Chagall, Katz, Klee and Beckmann are all people who were not only part of something that has now been overcome but actually created it."[95]

There are many indications that Nazi policies against the avant-garde were actually quite popular at the time. Large numbers of people preferred pleasant, affirmative art that conveyed a feeling of security and did not raise any disturbing questions. As Korn's article shows, many were scandalized by the antireligious streak in the artistic avant-garde. The Nazi regime seized on the widespread desire for "harmony," "completeness," "purity," and the "sublime" and tried to connect these ideas on the aesthetic level with its policies and ideology.[96]

Popularizing the Classics

The extent of the Nazi effort to popularize "high art," especially the classics, is particularly striking.[97] By associating themselves in the public mind with works that had long been held in high esteem, the Nazis implied that they could be trusted to incorporate into their future world what were alleged to be the eternally valid elements of the past. They encouraged reverence for the classics and hoped that some of this esteem would rub off on themselves, who made it all possible. People were encouraged to show respect for "higher things" (but not to recognize how the Nazis perverted them), to assume their places modestly in the given order, and to be prepared to make sacrifices if necessary on behalf of these "higher things." The strategies underlying the promotion of the classics therefore went far beyond the Nazis' proclaimed goal of "art for the people." The Nazis hoped to demonstrate how cultured they were and thereby counteract their reputation among intellectuals and the well-educated bourgeoisie as philistines and lowbrows.

The financial and organizational support provided by the Nazis for traditional and classical culture are now believed to have been quite large. They went to great lengths to market Dürer, Goethe, and, most of all, Wagner as German masters.[98] The artistic postcards common at the

95. Cited in Richard W. Eichler, "Die bildende Kunst von heute im Fadenkreuz der Kulturrevolutionäre," in Pierre Krebs (ed.), *Das unvergängliche Erbe: Determinanten zum Prinzip der Gleichheit* (Tübingen, 1981), 398.

96. Cf. Kathrin Hoffmann-Curtius, "Die Kampagne 'Entartete Kunst': Die National-sozialisten und die moderne Kunst," in Monika Wagner (ed.), *Moderne Kunst: Das Funkkolleg zum Verständnis der Gegenwart* (Reinbek, 1991), 482ff.

97. Cf. Burns, "Prefigurations," 308. "The utopian demand that the arts should be incorporated into everyday life, often formulated in Marxist aesthetics," was taken up in perverted form. Drechsler, *Funktion*, 161.

98. For Nazi cultural policies in the years before 1933 see for instance Dennis E. Showalter, "'A Tidal Wave of Degeneracy': National Socialism and Cultural Politics in

time depicted not only sculptures done under the Nazis but also many works from classical antiquity.[99] The government organized lectures, literary presentations, "musical evenings," readings by authors, "theater days," "culture trips," book groups, exhibitions, and much more[100] to popularize the classics. The famous Dresden Boys' Choir was given a subsidy.[101] The Reich Symphony Orchestra was founded to popularize classical music, and it went on extensive tours to reach "thousands of workers."[102] The Reich Symphony Orchestra was supposed to "proclaim the cultural will of National Socialist Germany."[103] The *Beethoven Weeks of 1934* were broadcast all over the world, and the announcements for the series expressed suitable pride. In this way, hundreds of thousands of people supposedly learned to appreciate "high culture."[104] The radio also carried operas by Wagner and, later, works by Bach and Händel. Presentations of great artistic works were packaged as major social occasions, combining art with new technical know-how.[105] The Nazis not only presented cultural events as grand occasions, they also wanted to package themselves as a Wagnerian *Gesamtkunstwerk* with a corresponding effect.[106]

The Nazis used the classics and all the festivals that were staged in order to reflect positively on themselves. This was especially true of the Bayreuth Festival, which had fallen on rather hard times during the Weimar Republic. After the Nazis came to power, the opening ceremonies were trumped up into virtual state occasions. Salzburg, Munich, Dresden, and Zoppot also organized festivals that were widely acclaimed for their outstanding productions of classical works.[107] All the

Nürnberg, 1923–33," *South Atlantic Quarterly* 83 (1984): 289. The NSDAP received strong support in Thuringia precisely because of its cultural policy. Uwe-K. Ketelsen, *Literatur und Drittes Reich* (Schernfeld, 1992), 289.

99. For the function of artistic postcards in the Third Reich see Silke Wenk, "Völkskörper und Medienspiel: Zum Verhältnis von Skulptur und Fotografie im deutschen Faschismus," *Kunstforum* 114 (July–August 1991): 226ff.

100. Wolfgang Kraus, *Kultur und Macht*, 2d ed. (Munich, 1978), 41ff.

101. Helmut Stiehl, "The Dresden Boys' Choir," *American-German Review* 4, no. 3 (March 1938): 12ff., 53ff.

102. Cited in Gruner, *Musikleben*, 58ff. The Deutschlandfunk was especially partial to the classics, despite the letters from listeners expressing their objections; Drechsler, *Funktion*, 85.

103. Cited in Gruner, *Musikleben*, 59.

104. E. Hadamomovsky, quoted in Drechsler, *Funktion*, 58.

105. Ibid., 108.

106. See in this regard Modris Eksteins, *Rites of Spring: The Great War and the Birth of the Modern Age* (Boston, 1989), 312.

107. Arthur Burkhard, "Music Festivals in Germany," *American-German Review*, no. 2 (December 3, 1936): 34ff.

Fig. 10. The Führer at the third concert of the Reich Bach Festival in Leipzig, 1935. (From Thomas Schindköth, *Musikstadt Leipzig in NS-Staat*, 362 [Altenburg, 1997].)

festivals, whether old or new,[108] helped to portray National Socialism as a movement of allegedly cultivated people who appreciated the arts.

Big business also increased its support for the arts, in cooperation with the new authorities. The head of Siemens's social policy department, Karl Burhenne, stated that the firm had a duty to make "all Siemens employees supporters and guardians of the cultural heritage . . . that our fathers have bequeathed to us, beginning with the healthy bodies of our children and via a lively experience of our local homelands to the intellectual riches of German art in word, picture and sound."[109] Under the Nazis, Siemens greatly increased its spending on films, concerts, and presentations for its workforce. Employees living outside Berlin were taken on excursions to the museums in the capital, in cooperation with the Kraft durch Freude organization. Siemens's workforce was particularly impressed by the factory concerts that were provided, for instance the concert staged in Berlin-Siemensstadt in 1943 by the Vienna Philharmonic under the direction of Furtwängler.

Beyond the factory gates, the classics were promoted through *Kunst und Volk,* the magazine of the NS-Kulturgemeinde, which contained enlightening pictures and texts in every edition. The reinvigorated record circle of the NS-Kulturgemeinde offered, as if only naturally, the "great works of our classical music, which in this way will find new friends."[110] The theater classics were also heavily promoted.[111] In the 1933–34 season in Düsseldorf, for instance, the classics accounted for 38 percent of all stage productions.[112]

The Nazis used the classics to foster a new sense of national identity with strong heroic streaks. The classics also served to legitimize the "*Volk* community" and place it on elitist, racist foundations suffused with the autocratic *Führerprinzip,* which underlay the political and social structure of the Third Reich. The Nazis encouraged veneration of

108. Michael Meyer, *The Politics of Music in the Third Reich* (New York, 1991), 282ff.

109. Quoted in Carola Sachse, *Siemens, der Nationalsozialismus, und die moderne Familie: Eine Untersuchung zur sozialen Rationalisierung in Deutschland im 20. Jahrhundert* (Hamburg, 1990), 200ff. The talks and shows organized at Siemens in the framework of its cultural program seldom revolved explicitly around racist or other Nazi themes, if one is to judge by their titles.

110. "Amtliche Mitteilung," 61.

111. Cf. Thomas H. Dickenson, "Inside a Great German Theater," *American-German Review* 1, no. 1 (September, 1934): 39. This journal was quite pro-German and must therefore be read with a skeptical attitude.

112. Furthermore, 29.5 percent were works with Nazi ideology, and 32.5 percent were light entertainment. Walter Rischer, "Die nationalsozialistische Kulturpolitik in Düsseldorf 1933–1945" (Ph.D. diss., Düsseldorf, 1972), 52. In Hanover, there was a larger percentage of *völkisch* plays. I am grateful to Ines Katenhusen for this information.

the timeless genius that had created the classics, in the expectation that some of the sense of awe would carry over to that other great German genius, the Führer. In the 1920s, there had already been a heavy emphasis on the *German* classics, especially in music, and there was nothing new to this aspect of the Nazi program. After 1933, however, the classics "were given an ideological streak."[113] The Nazis undertook to familiarize the people with the great heroes of German music in a lively, entertaining way, free from all "intellectual nit-picking," as they always put it. This deintellectualization of the reception of the classics reflected the general devaluation of the mind by the Nazis. From a functional standpoint, it was part of the widespread devaluation of all that was considered feminine and Jewish and the increased appreciation of physicality and German maleness.[114]

The price that bourgeois connoisseurs had to pay for all the productions of the classics was the fascist slant frequently given to them. There is some doubt, though, whether many people were terribly upset. Another price was probably only noticed by those who opposed the Nazi regime in principle. The emphasis on the classics made the Third Reich seem like a "normal" regime[115] that was cultivating Germany's cultural traditions, a most praiseworthy undertaking in the eyes of most. The Nazis appeared to have a real sense for all that was good, noble, and eternally valid in form and content.

It seemed only natural, therefore, that the Nazis would organize a lavish ceremony in Weimar in 1934 to mark the 175th anniversary of the birth of Friedrich Schiller and the 15th anniversary of the founding of the Goethe Society. Seated alongside the connoisseurs of the classics were the leading lights of the *völkisch* movement, people such as Hans Grimm.[116] Furthermore, the theater director in Weimar was the father of none other than Baldur von Schirach, the leader of the Reich Youth.[117] Barbarism had carved out a place for itself at the heart of classical culture, as symbolized in 1937 by the construction of the Buchenwald concentration camp near Weimar. The intimate connection between classical culture and Nazi barbarism is often overlooked in

---

113. Gruner, *Musikleben*, 120.

114. I am grateful to Uta C. Schmidt for pointing this out.

115. Fraenkel only plumbed the depths of the right-wing sphere, however, in distinguishing the "Normative State" from the "Prerogative State." Ernst Fraenkel, *The Dual State: A Contribution to the Theory of Popular Culture* (New York, 1941).

116. Jane F. Goodloe, "Some German Poets at Home," *American-German Review* 4, no. 4 (June 1938): 8. The "Goethe year" was already in 1932, to be sure. Grimm published his book *Volk ohne Raum* in 1926. By the mid-1930s, sales had reached half a million. Burns, "Prefigurations," 302.

117. I am grateful to Gerhard Schneider for pointing this out.

works on the Third Reich. In fact, the dominant impression seems to be that the classics — like so much else — only flourished thanks to the non-Nazi bourgeoisie, an impression that is at least partially mistaken.[118] Karl Böhm, for instance, said once that he always tried "to give of my best, regardless of what the audience looked like."[119] But in terms of an analysis of the system as a whole, this opinion is untenable; dictatorships do not allow anything they are not willing at least to tolerate. Classical culture was not only tolerated by the National Socialists but actively encouraged — even in concentration camps.[120]

"Weimar" symbolized not only German classicism but humanism as well. Although much of the well-educated bourgeoisie considered itself loyal to the humanist tradition, it did not produce any broadly based ethical opposition to the Nazi regime,[121] despite some belated insights and disappointments.[122] This failure was partly due to the lack of any structural connections between (humanistic) thought and (political) action. In addition, the Nazi state was not generally perceived as criminal. Finally, there was definitely a snobbish, antidemocratic streak to the humanistic tradition as practiced in the Weimar Republic. Humanism was rooted in what was allegedly "good" and "noble" and was the opposite of "bad" and "evil." But what happens when, in modern times, evil no longer requires evil people? Modernity, according to Zygmunt Bauman, "has created the means by which cruel things can be done by people who are not cruel."[123] The aestheticization of barbarism was evidently part and parcel of the creation of moral indifference. The horrible was taken out of the horror, which was then even lent a certain fascination.

Concentration camps, such as the one in Buchenwald near Weimar, served the new social order being built on the hubris of modernity that only things defined as "valuable" have any right to exist. In the Third

---

118. Cf. Hanns-Werner Heister, "Nachwort: Funktionalisierung und Entpolitisierung," in idem and Hans-Günter Klein (eds.), *Musik und Musikpolitik im faschistischen Deutschland* (Frankfurt, 1984), 313. People often speak all too quickly in this regard of "inner emigration." Ketelsen, *Literatur,* 391.

119. Quoted in Heister, "Nachwort," 313.

120. See Fania Fenelon, *Playing for Time* (New York, 1976).

121. Cf. Bollenbeck, *Bildung,* 300.

122. We should point in particular here to those conservatives who finally came together in opposition to Hitler (July 20, 1944).

123. Zygmunt Bauman, "Das Jahrhundert der Lager?" *Kommune: Forum für Politik, Ökonomie, Kultur* 11, no. 12 (1993): 46. Rüdiger Altmann, a conservative journalist, still maintained as late as the 1950s that the concentration camps were clearly rooted in the state of emergency that was declared but also "an important instrument of modern social engineering." Rüdiger Altmann, *Das Erbe Adenauers: Eine Bilanz,* 2d ed. (Munich, 1963), 123; and idem and Johannes Groß, *Die neue Gesellschaft: Bemerkungen zum Zeitbewußtsein* (Stuttgart, 1958), 129ff.

Reich, even official charities operated according to this principle. The Winter Assistance Program exemplified an exclusionary brand of "humanism," in which the universality of the humanist ideal was discarded. Nevertheless, there was always a seductive, superficial continuity with the humanism of the past. On the whole, the Nazi regime was characteristically quite successful in co-opting classical culture and the ideals associated with the city of Weimar and thereby eliminating any possibility that Weimar could serve as a symbol and cultural basis for deep-seated political criticism or opposition. Here too one can see the subtle co-opting, integrative effect of encouraging the classics.[124]

Speaking in retrospect after 1945, Thomas Mann was one of the few who strongly criticized the use of the classics to aestheticize barbarism. How, he asks, could the classics have been staged — he speaks in this context of "culture" — "while all around that which we know too well was happening. Depravity was being gilded, crime decorated. . . . How is it possible that Beethoven's *Fidelio,* this lofty, festive opera for the day of German self-liberation, was not banned in the Germany of the 12-Year Reich? The scandal is that it was *not* prohibited and there were even highly cultivated productions of it: singers were prepared to sing it, musicians to play it, and audiences to watch it. What mindlessness was needed in Himmler's Germany to hear *Fidelio* and not cover your face in your hands and flee from the hall!"[125]

Finally, there is another way of viewing the link between the Nazi dictatorship and the classics. The London *Sunday Times* got to the heart of it when it wrote: "[I]f a German could not say just what he thought about the petty tyrant who ruled him, he could at all events express his sentiments about freedom through the mouth of a dramatic character like William Tell."[126] In addition, the revered "old masters" such as Dürer and Cranach, as the journal the *Listener* pointed out, were "not so much Germans as Europeans, and their work is not especially national but belongs to the general tradition of 'Western civilization.'"[127]

---

124. That devotees of the humanistic tradition were by no means immune to National Socialism can be seen, for example, in the behavior of most librarians, who went along with the system. Boese, *Bibliothekswesen,* 352.

125. Quoted in Heister, "Nachwort," 314. For the aestheticization of politics in the Third Reich see the standard work by Walter Benjamin, "Das Kunstwerk im Zeitalter seiner technischen Reduzierbarkeit," in Walter Benjamin, *Illuminationen: Ausgewählte Schriften* (1934–35; reprint, Frankfurt, 1977); and Anson G. Rabinbach, "Die Ästhetik im Dritten Reich," in Ralf Schnell (ed.), *Literaturwissenschaft und Sozialwissenschaften,* vol. 10, *Kunst und Kultur im deutschen Faschismus* (Stuttgart, 1978), especially 74ff.

126. Ernest Newman in *Sunday Times* (London), cited in *Living Age* 357, no. 4479 (December 1939): 387.

127. Herbert Read, "Hitler on Art," *Listener,* September 22, 1937, p. 607.

Cultivation of the "old masters" and traditional great works provided some relief from total domination by the Nazi system and may accordingly have been an expression and consequence of "inner emigration."

"Folk Culture"

Not only classical culture was especially favored after 1933 but "folk culture" as well. Folk music, folk song, and folk dancing were fashionable and — like classical culture — were deemed expressions of *das Allgemein-Menschliche* (the universally human). "We have probably never needed to imbibe spiritual health from the clear, pure spring of folk song as much as we do today. The universally human, which finds such wonderful expression precisely in folk song, must be restored to its ancient place."[128] Comments like these were predicated on a particular view of the "folk" as a great mass of creative potential and the bedrock on which high art could build without ever losing its connection to the people.[129] For instance, the aforementioned Kurt Huber, who later participated in the German resistance to the Nazis, advocated "music rooted in the soil" in order to "maintain the purity of the real substance of the German people."[130]

Much was done after 1933 to advance "folk culture." For example, instruction in folk art was expanded, and a German School for Folk Music and Dance was founded in 1935–36. In addition, the study of folklore was encouraged. Amateur artists received strong support, and those who worked for various companies were asked to display their works in the factories. In 1936, the Museum for Folk Art in Berlin put so-called peasant art on display for the first time.[131] In music classes in schools, more emphasis was placed on folk songs. New round dances and dance songs were composed for recorder and fife to "complement" the traditional works and expand the repertoire in a National Socialist direction.[132]

The associations that cultivated various kinds of folk art did not change much after 1933 so long as they were not associated with the workers' cultural movement. Their prestige soared, though, as well as the opportunities afforded them, as can be seen in the case of the three

128. Cited in Gruner, *Musikleben,* 119 (newspaper report from 1933).

129. Wilmsmeyer, "Künstler," 86.

130. Quoted in Kater, "Carl Orff," 27ff.

131. Konrad Hahm, "The Museum of German Folk Art in Berlin," *American-German Review* 3, no. 1 (September 1936): 35.

132. See Kater, "Carl Orff," 16. Carl Orff also became somewhat involved in this; cf. as well Jutta Lambrecht, "'Nicht jede Musik paßt für jeden . . .': Anmerkungen zur Musik im Dritten Reich," in Bazon Brock and Achim Preiß (eds.), *Kunst auf Befehl? Dreiunddreißig bis Fünfundvierzig* (Munich, 1990), 145ff.

male choirs in Marburg. These "apolitical" choirs shared a common interest with the Nazis in traditional German songs.[133] The Nazis announced that "the times when male choirs were considered reactionary nonsense have passed for good. The current political leadership recognizes the importance of male song, and the participants are proud to sing about love and fidelity, German soul and German ways."[134] These words of praise should not obscure, however, the considerable inconsistencies that existed in some areas between the ideas and mentalities of the Nazis and those of the choirs. For instance, the choirs often loved to wallow in a luxurious, sentimental style that was far removed from the Nazi preference for firm expression of male martial virtues.[135]

For the most part, the associations practiced their old-new cultural ways within the narrow confines of their homelands. However, some grandiose exhibitions were organized to capture the attention of the entire nation and possibly the outside world as well. The first Great Exhibition of German Art in 1937, conceived as the antithesis of the Exhibition of Degenerate Art, was supposed to be a thought-provoking demonstration of "art for the people" in the so-called Year of German Festivals. The Munich Festival Summer of 1937 began with a huge, pompous parade, four kilometers long, illustrating "Two Thousand Years of German Culture." In an obvious attempt to implement Hitler's call for "art for everyone," thirty floats with scenes from various cultural eras paraded through the streets of the city.[136] Even Henri Nannen was impressed by this "tremendous demonstration of the life and will of the German people." He downplayed the political significance of the parade, describing it as less a National Socialist event than a "celebration of real Munich *joie de vivre*," particularly because of the "dancing in the public squares."[137] Further examples could be added. Although very few studies have been done of the reaction of the general public to this

---

133. Gruner, *Musikleben,* 37.

134. "Cited in ibid., 38. In the musical life of Marburg, events that directly served Nazi propaganda purposes were extremely rare. Ibid., 121. Changes occurred only as the number of light entertainment events and military concerts increased. Ibid., 91, 93. After 1936–37, the Nazi organization *Kraft durch Freude* assumed responsibility for ensuring a "rich program." Ibid., 70.

135. Dietmar Klenke, "Bürgerlicher Männergesang und Politik in Deutschland," *Geschichte in Wissenschaft und Unterricht* 40, no. 9 (1989): 547ff.

136. Von Lüttichau, "'Deutsche Kunst,'" 88. The staging of parades and scenes with elements of folk culture was not new by any means, but it acquired a particularly programmatic and propagandistic aspect under the Nazis.

137. Quoted in Reichel, *Der schöne Schein,* 362; Hoffmann-Curtius, "Kampagne," 473.

cultural policy,[138] one may safely assume that a large portion supported it, although not without reservations and certainly not always assimilating it in the ways in which the Nazis wished.

"Refined Entertainment"

While the attempts to ennoble "shallow" popular culture had been politically and socially diverse before 1933,[139] the Nazis focused narrowly on how compatible particular products were with their own ideology and interests. Anything deemed inimical was excluded, although it was not always easy to know how particular products would be viewed because of conflicting views on culture within the Nazi hierarchy and overlapping jurisdictions within the bureaucracy.[140]

The efforts to integrate compatible popular culture into the Nazi system did not generally go so far that everything was wholly or even largely politicized, apart from during the earliest days. Popular culture was less directly politicized than one might conclude from reading the academic literature. Movies, records, and radio programs that were intended to be entertaining were generally perceived by consumers as entirely apolitical. Under the Nazis, entertainment seemed to remain "pure entertainment." The years after 1932 were a time when radio gradually entered a phase of "absolute entertainment, increasingly free of intellectual problems and as void as possible of content."[141] There were two noteworthy innovations in radio around 1935: nonstop music programs without voice interruption and musical request programs, which proved especially popular.[142] The movie *Wir machen Musik,* directed by Erich Käutner, established pure entertainment as virtually a genre of its own, thereby indirectly supporting the policies of the minister of propaganda, Joseph Goebbels. The hero in the movie fails in his early attempts at

---

138. Hermann Bausinger makes the same observation in "Folk-National Work during the Third Reich," in James R. Dow and Hannjost Lixfeld (eds.), *The Nazification of an Academic Discipline: Folklore in the Third Reich* (Bloomington and Indianapolis, 1994), 89.

139. This involved both trivializing and coarsening "high culture" and enriching "shallow" commercial culture with "worthwhile" contents or style elements. Cf. Eco, *Apocalittici,* 87ff.

140. For the overlapping jurisdictions and competing views in the Nazi conception of culture see Reinhard Bollmus, *Das Amt Rosenberg und seine Gegner: Studien zum Machtkampf im nationalsozialistischen Herrschaftssystem* (Stuttgart, 1970).

141. Heinz Schwitzke, "Der U-Teppich: Marginalien zur Geschichte der Unterhaltung," in Alois Rummel (ed.), *Unterhaltung im Rundfunk* (Berlin, 1980), 28ff.

142. Ibid., 29. We should also recall the film *Das Wunschkonzert* in this connection. I am grateful to Silke Wenk for pointing this out.

serious, very demanding music but goes on to great success composing sophisticated popular music.

The Nazis eventually used those elements of popular culture that were deemed acceptable to make the general population feel comfortable with the new system. In the early years, though, popular culture was heavily politicized, even spectator sports, as can be seen in the Eilenriede motorcycle races.[143] Ceremonial speeches were larded with Nazi slogans. After about 1936, though, direct infiltration of this event was confined to the symbolic level (e.g., Nazi flags and symbols and the presence of Nazi officials and uniforms) and to short ceremonies related to the races (e.g., the roll call of cyclists and the honoring of the victors). Even libraries expanded the realm of "apolitical" literature "in a way that was totally regime compatible."[144] They relaxed somewhat their traditional efforts to steer patrons toward serious literature and placed greater emphasis on light fiction, especially during the war. Holdings of this kind were expanded, and Goebbels searched assiduously for "cultivated light fiction." Walter von Hollander published eleven didactic but "apolitical" popular novels, including *Das Leben zu Zweien* (Life as a couple) and *Der Mensch über Vierzig* (People over forty).[145]

It seems paradoxical at first that a dictatorship that "cleansed" and censored so ruthlessly would encourage public libraries simply to serve their patrons without attempting to reform or refine them.[146] The authorities were not motivated by a sudden urge to liberalize culture but rather by raw political calculation, and it was no coincidence that their efforts in this direction peaked during the war. An artificial "variety" of choice was maintained in light music as well, but it only highlighted the fact that only a fraction of the public was willing to switch to marches and folk dances in place of the new German light music. The dilettantish attempts of the Nazis to create a popular culture of their own, for instance *Thingspiele* (The Germanized theater), were even less successful.

The Nazis tried to ban modern American dancing but with only modest results. Many people still liked to dance to swing music, a fact that well illustrates the limitations on the ability to shape popular cul-

---

143. Adelheid von Saldern, "Cultural Conflicts, Popular Mass Culture, and the Question of Nazi Success: The Eilenriede Motorcycle Races, 1924–39," *German Studies Review* 15, no. 2 (1992): 317–38.

144. Boese, *Bibliothekswesen*, 271.

145. Lu Seegers, "Rundfunk, Technik, und Familie: Die Programmzeitschrift Hör Zu! und ihre Vorläufer (1931–1965)" (Ph.D. diss., Hanover, 2000). New dime novel series were also published. Hainer Plaul, *Illustrierte Geschichte der Trivialliteratur* (Hildesheim, 1954), 231.

146. Boese, *Bibliothekswesen*, 352.

ture. "When you go to many nightclubs that have dancing, . . . you cannot escape the feeling that you are in America! The band rattles off one foreign dance after the other; there's no end to it!"[147] This quotation from 1937, when American dances were officially forbidden, shows that public willingness to accept the "cultural dictatorship" of the Nazis had its limits, especially in the musical sphere, and many people circumvented the directives. The authorities devoted considerable effort to suppressing jazz because of the "dangerous excesses" that seemed to accompany it, especially body movements. In the eyes of cultural conservatives and National Socialists, dance partners were supposed to be held at a dignified distance in the "proper" way for Germans.[148] Although American jazz was officially scorned, it became very popular in a Germanized, often tamer version called the "new German dance music," which even enjoyed government approval.[149] The range of "modern" dance music played on the radio and especially in nightclubs was apparently "very diverse,"[150] even though jazz and swing were frowned upon. This "diversity" should not blind us, however, to the fact that crucial forms of contemporary culture were simply missing.

Entertainment was especially important during the war. The Nazis were concerned about the general frame of mind of the population and eager to provide distractions from the troubles of everyday life. While the connection between entertainment and the war was obvious to any thoughtful person, the connection between entertainment and the reign of terror against "inferior" civilians was harder to discern and generally only realized by people who recognized the fundamental barbarity of National Socialism, regardless of any cultural opportunities that it afforded. Entertainment not only provided people with an escape from the reality of their lives or an emotional outlet after they had faced great dangers and made tremendous sacrifices, but it also lent a patina of normality to society beneath which the terrorist Prerogative State could carry on.[151] To this extent, entertainment fulfilled the same function as the devotion to the classics or the same function, one might add, as the smooth operations of the bureaucracy, through which horrors, especially the annihilation of Jews, were being perpetrated.[152]

147. Christian Frederic Hippmann (1937), quoted in Joseph Wulf, *Musik im Dritten Reich* (Frankfurt, 1983), 299.

148. Cf. Bausinger, "Folk-National Work," 92.

149. Cf. Michael H. Kater, *Different Drummers: Jazz in the Culture of Nazi Germany* (New York and Oxford, 1992), 52.

150. Drechsler, *Funktion,* 130.

151. See Fraenkel, *Dual State.*

152. See in general Bauman, *Modernity.* Bauman's comments do not refer directly, however, to the arts.

The Search for a German Contemporary Art

The architect Paul Schultze-Naumburg was a well-known member of the Lebensreform movement around the turn of the century and then, in the 1920s, a leading figure in the conservative reaction to the Bauhaus. "Art and the people" could again be reconciled, he evidently thought, "if whores and idiots are no longer presented as paragons but heroic individuals instead."[153]

Although the Rosenberg wing[154] of the NSDAP looked to "folk culture" and the *Heimatkultur* of old, the Goebbels wing was interested in developing "a contemporary German art."[155] The Nazis themselves had a hard time deciding what this might be, if not a continuation of the modernism of the 1920s, or whether it could even exist. Instead of adopting a theoretical approach, they relied on the energy and vitality of the Nazi party and its character as a movement. The call went out for artists whose work was not like much-despised "degenerate" art but nevertheless had a "contemporary" feel, without being "modern" in the 1920s sense of the term.[156] Goebbels was evidently seizing on ideas expressed before 1933 by the nationalistic cultural conservatives when he said that "National Socialist Germany . . . wants a German art again."[157] The classics, folk art, and bits and pieces of popular culture could not ultimately satisfy the Nazis, who were bent on building a great cultural empire as well. One of the effects of the search for a "contemporary German art" was that the word *German* became a cheap descriptive attached to virtually any new work.[158] There were paintings of "German" landscapes, "German" earth, "German" forests, "German" oak trees, and even a "German" summer's day. Many painters in the Third Reich also tried to appeal to public tastes through a sense of romantic yearning or longing.[159]

---

153. Quoted in Kratzsch, *Kunstwart,* 435.

154. At first Alfred Rosenberg headed the Kampfbund für deutsche Kultur, and then in 1934 he became the head of the "Rosenberg Office" responsible for "overseeing the entire intellectual and practical schooling and training of the Party and of all "forced into line" (*gleichgeschaltete*) organizations such as *Kraft durch Freude.*"

155. Geobbels was minister of popular enlightenment and propaganda and at the same time president of the Reich Chamber of Culture.

156. According to Heinz Drewes, cited in Kater, "Carl Orff," 35.

157. Quoted in Schuster, "München," 25. The result was an amalgam of naturalism and classicism. Walter Grasskamp, *Die unbewältigte Moderne: Kunst und Öffentlichkeit* (Munich, 1989), 87.

158. Labeling things as "German" or "French" had a long tradition reaching back to the nineteenth century. I am grateful to Silke Wenk for pointing this out.

159. Abrams, *National Socialism,* 305. *Völkisch*-romanticizing products were encouraged by official circles.

The Nazis actually embraced many modern innovations, although they were usually packaged in traditional ways. One example was the Bauhaus. It was stamped out as an institution and symbol of the avant-garde, but its functional innovations were often preserved in industrial buildings and even housing. Steep, traditional-looking roofs were usually added, though, in the case of housing. We should point in particular in this context to Ernst Neufert and the architectural norms that were introduced.[160] Recent research has been especially interested in the connection between modernity and fascism, connections that extend well beyond the well-known links between futurism and Italian fascism.

Another consequence of the search for a contemporary German art was that certain artists and their works were seen as embodiments of the modern German spirit. For instance, Hindemith's music was praised in 1934 as modern, in the positive sense for the Nazis, before he was finally forced to emigrate after all and his music was proscribed.[161] Werner Egk's music was lauded as tonal, German, and "modern" in the Nazi sense of contemporary and new.[162] For a while, Richard Strauss became the cultural badge of the regime. He eventually fell out of favor with the party grandees, although his music continued to be played. "The search for the new music after 1936, which would be rooted in and again related to the community, was no longer restricted to *völkisch* composers but involved the entire spectrum of compositional activity, as everybody had learned to rationalize composition in Nazi terms either (1) by explicit texts or (2) by reference to the spiritual experience said to be captured in the musical work."[163]

This did not hold true, however, in this way for Carl Orff. Once an admirer of Brecht, he too managed despite all the criticism and hostility directed at him to build a brilliant career, especially during the war years. "Orff's idea of 'music-theater' and the theatrical nature of his productions involving massive orchestras and choirs, if possible, combined with the primitive, organicistic structure of his music could conjure up visions of a Nazi *Thingstätte* cult."[164] He is considered from our present perspective as "the utmost in modernity produced by the music of the 'Third Reich.'"[165]

160. Wolfgang Voigt, "'Triumpf der Gleichform und des Zusammenpassens': Ernst Neufert und die Normung in der Architektur," in Winfried Nerdinger (ed.), *Bauhaus-Moderne im Nationalsozialismus: Zwischen Anbiederung und Verfolgung* (Munich, 1993), 179–93.

161. *Die Sendung* 11, no. 37 (1934).

162. Cf. Kater, "Carl Orff," 35.

163. Meyer, *Politics,* 289. We cannot try to assess the music here.

164. Kater, "Carl Orff," 34.

165. Ibid., 35.

In cities such as Marburg, there were more concerts under the Nazis featuring works by contemporary composers, especially during the war, and the audiences were apparently quite interested.[166] The record circle of the NS-Kulturgemeinde also offered its members "contemporary music," whatever was understood by this term.[167] Special prizes were awarded for new compositions. Radio too provided a showcase for contemporary art, broadcasting works by Orff for example.[168] Lavish series were also presented on the radio, with works by Richard Strauss, Hans Pfitzner, and Paul Graener. Beginning in 1935, there were national broadcasts of new compositions that went on for two weeks at a time (although the programs did not start until 11 P.M.).[169]

Similar attempts were made to foster a "contemporary" but still quintessentially "German" dance, meaning modern German interpretive dance as it had developed since the turn of the century under Rudolf von Laban and Mary Wigman. "This dancing, often known as the Central European Dance, is really German,"[170] wrote a journalist in the *Listener.* This opinion was largely shared by Laban and Wigman. While Laban took a racist view, Wigman defined the new German dance more as an expression "of the nature of Germans," as a willingness to experience the world in "deep," irrational ways, and as the typical German striving for organic harmony with nature.[171] A lavish international dance festival was held at the time of the Olympic Games in Berlin, and fourteen nations took part. According to a 1936 edition of the *Listener:* "So great is the German passion for dancing that Germany's three greatest choreographers led group dances at the opening of the games."[172]

The compulsive search for a "German" kind of modernity was one side of a coin whose other was the exclusion and, in some cases, destruction of everything alleged to be "un-German." Here too, the intimate connection between culture and terror becomes all too apparent under the Nazi regime.

---

166. Gruner, *Musikleben,* 120, 130.

167. "Amtliche Mitteilungen," 61.

168. Kater, "Carl Orff," 22. What the National Socialists found attractive was apparently the "conventional, simple, diatonic tonality of Orff's compositions," as well as the at times "elemental, even primitive nature of the musical forms," the "heavily accentuated, often ostinato rhythms," and the "constant repetition of monorhythmic sequences." Ibid., 32ff.

169. Drechsler, *Funktion,* 89.

170. Kathleen Monypenny, "Modern German Dances," *Listener,* October 7, 1936, p. 684. This statement is then qualified, however, in what follows.

171. In general: Müller, "Begründung," 193ff. However, some dancers were persecuted in the Third Reich.

172. Monypenny, "Dances," 684.

Opposition to the Feminization of Culture

Heroic individuals, such as those mentioned by Paul Schultze-Naumburg in the earlier quotation, were always considered males, just like geniuses. The Nazis looked to great heroes to help overcome the alleged feminization of culture. Beethoven was deemed particularly suited to the task of remasculinizing culture and was often portrayed as a heroic, combative male artist.[173] This emphasis led to greatly increased public interest in his personality, in direct continuity with German classicism. The pianist Elly Ney, who sympathized with the Nazis in many ways, encouraged the hero worship of the great composer when she said at the Hitlerjugend's Beethoven festival in Wildbad in May 1938: "Nordic music is by nature heroic. This can be heard here in every sound. The human side of our *Meister* was also simple and heroic. . . . This sacred fire should inflame the hearts of the youth, arouse their sense of responsibility, steel them in their struggles, and console and raise them up in their sorrows. So come, ye German youth! Leave everyday life behind! In these days and hours we want to open ourselves together to the rivers of spiritual strength in the German people. May this render our deeds in the service of the Führer great and luminous."[174] We can clearly see here how even artists used the classics and classical composers such as Beethoven to inculcate in the youth a highly aesthetic approach to life, on the basis of which they could be integrated all the more easily into the Nazi system through all that is masculine, heroic, sublime, and suffused with elemental power.[175]

Further examples can be seen in the sculptures of Arno Breker and Josef Thorak, in which everything soft and weak has literally been hammered away. The naked male body is seen through the prism of a heroic, mystical aesthetic and portrayed as firm and solid. Breker and Thorak also took a heightened view of the female body, although in a somewhat different way as a vision of harmony and order. The upright female body was both related functionally to males as a symbol of the "healthy body of the people" and also transported into otherworldly, deathless realms. The female body gently floating away was considered a symbol of war and the victory of a pure race.[176]

---

173. See Drechsler, *Funktion,* 66ff.

174. Quoted in Fred K. Prieberg, *Musik im NS-Staat* (Frankfurt, 1982), 248ff.

175. Schiller's *Wilhelm Tell* and Kleist's *Hermannsschlacht* also lent themselves to a very masculine, heroic interpretation. Burns, "Prefigurations," 302.

176. For an introduction to this see Reichel, Der *schöne Schein,* 366ff.; see also Silke Wenk, "Aufgerichtete weibliche Körper: Zur allegorischen 'Skulptur im deutschen Faschismus,'" in Neue Gesellschaft für bildende Kunst (ed.), *Inszenierung der Macht: Ästhetische*

Summary

Nazi cultural policy concentrated more than we generally realize on the same points that had been close to the hearts of cultural conservatives in the Weimar Republic, namely, the classics and "folk culture," the search for a "German" path to modernity, resistance to the alleged "feminization" of culture, and efforts to "refine" popular taste by encouraging "worthwhile" art and culture and permitting only a select popular culture that was compatible with the system and posed no threat to it. In the academic literature, Nazi aesthetics and policies are often equated with the *völkisch* approach advocated by Rosenberg and others of his ilk. This intentionally limits the question of continuities with the past and obviates any inquiries into the attempts of the Nazis to appear modern. However, there were clearly many continuities between National Socialism and cultural conservatism in particular. Insofar as ethnology and folk culture are concerned, the continuities were summarized as follows: "It was this conservative-nationalistic stance which contributed to the conservative development of German *Volkskunde* and its effectiveness before 1933, and which was apparently not only integratable but even ideologically useful for German fascism."[177]

Our emphasis on continuities should not blind us, however, to the clear breaks with the past. These lay (*a*) in the change from cultural interventionism to a fascist cultural dictatorship and (*b*) in the radicalization, monopolization, and "ideologization" of art and culture policies, in which racial exclusion and extermination played important roles.

If we wish to understand why Nazi cultural policies seemed to work quite well, it is not very helpful simply to dismiss the opponents of modern art as lowbrows and petty bourgeois philistines, as the intellectuals and the artistic avant-garde were often prone to do (although with good reason). It is more enlightening to start from the crisis precipitated by modernity and the Kulturkampf that erupted with renewed vigor, after a prelude

---

Faszination im Faschismus (Berlin, 1987); Anne Meckel, "Animation und Agitation: Frauendarstellungen auf der 'Großen deutschen Kunstausstellung,'" in *München 1937–1944* (Weinheim, 1993); for the symbol of death see also Saul Friedländer, *Kitsch und Tod: Der Widerschein des Nazismus* (Munich, 1984). For the lasting effects of Nazi aesthetics as they related to the two sexes see Silke Wenk, "Hin-Weg-Sehen oder: Faschismus, Normalität, und Sexismus," in Neue Gesellschaft für bildende Kunst (ed.), *Erbeutete Sinne: Nachträge zur Berliner Ausstellung "Inszenierung der Macht, ästhetische Faszination im Faschismus"* (Berlin, 1988), 17ff.

177. Hermann Strobach, "'. . . But When Does the Prewar Begin?' Folklore and Fascism before and around 1933," in James R. Dow and Hannjost Lixfeld (eds.), *The Nazification of an Academic Discipline: Folklore in the Third Reich* (Bloomington and Indianapolis, 1994), 60.

in Wilhelminian times, as a result of the many-faceted breakthrough of classical modernism and popular culture in the 1920s, at the same time as the political and economic foundations of the German state seemed particularly weak.[178] When the National Socialists came to power, they brought this Kulturkampf to a forced and violent conclusion, not least of all by means of blacklists. They also seized on the widespread animosity toward intellectuals. Nazi cultural policies supposed that artists may need a certain amount of leeway in order to be productive[179] but not real freedom. The question of artistic freedom was being discussed elsewhere in the world as well. The magazine the *Criterion* concluded an article about Nazi art, which was actually quite critical, with the following words: "[M]odern artists may have all the 'freedom' they want, but if they do nothing with it, they cannot be surprised if their freedom is taken away from them; they deserve to lose it, but they do not deserve to be replaced by Herr Ziegler and his kind."[180]

Under the Nazis, art was supposed to be close to the people. "Culture was a matter of people, the *Volk,* not of intellectuals."[181] However, cultural policy was not so much concerned with the past as with the creation of a new world. As Eksteins points out, the Nazis understood their own cultural policies as very progressive. The intent was "to create a new type of human being, from whom would spring a new morality, a new social system, and eventually a new international order."[182] Modern rulers have the power to make art and culture serve new social orders, in this case a racist, aggressive order. The importance of artistic freedom only becomes fully apparent in the context of this power.

The Nazis sought to stage-manage a rapprochement between "art and the people," but the connection between them was so tightly controlled through exclusion and static regulations that both art and its connection to the general population were greatly deformed and diminished. The NSDAP considered itself the mouthpiece of the cultural desires of the people. The "solution" it found consisted of a tenuous, forced synthesis of "art and the people," in which exclusion

---

178. Cf. Peukert, *Weimarer Republik;* Cornelia Klinger, "Faschismus: Der deutsche Fundamentalismus?" *Merkur* 9–10 (September–October 1992): 782ff. Contemporaries also occasionally used the term *Kulturkampf* before 1933, although with the understanding that they did not want to have one.

179. Those who enjoyed the confidence of the Nazis, for example Brecher, Riefenstahl, Gründgens, and Furtwängler, were sometimes given considerable latitude.

180. Roger Hinks, "Art Chronicle: Freedom and the Artist," *Criterion* 18, no. 70 (October 1938): 68. The artist Adolf Ziegler served as president of the Chamber of the Fine Arts and specialized in allegorical, overly naturalistic female nudes.

181. Eksteins, *Rites,* 327.

182. Ibid., 303.

and extirpation played major parts. In the forced synthesis of the Nazis, art and culture were considered an expression of *"Volkskörper* that is close to nature and forms what one might almost call a biological body, a unified whole, a manifestation of natural harmony in a world free from internal contradictions."[183]

When we say that the Nazi synthesis of art and the people was forced and illusory, we do not mean that many people at the time perceived it in this way. In fact, Nazi cultural policies were fairly popular, including with some workers. This was because of the flair the Nazis lent to cultural conservatism and because, within the confines of the racist "folk community," they allowed certain elements of modernity, such as the new media—although often trying to give them new meanings or shape them.

The Legacy of Nazi Cultural Policies

The two parts into which Germany was divided after 1945 drew differing conclusions from their shared historical experiences. Many people in the GDR thought as late as the 1970s and 1980s that it was perfectly sensible and necessary to have a "cultural dictatorship" that would guide culture in a different, socialist direction and keep it abreast of historical progress. In their attempts to forge a national identity, restore the humanist foundations of society, and lend socialism a pan-German air, the authorities in the GDR turned once again to the classics and the national heritage. In the Goethe anniversary year of 1949, they set out to familiarize the "widest possible circles" with the "greatest" of German writers.[184] The fixation on classical culture continued longer than in West Germany and produced, in actual practice, a theater life that seemed at first glance bourgeois.[185] A stuffy, anti-modern "heritage cult" emerged as a result of "the attempt to include Goethe and German classicism in the regime's strategy for legitimizing the 'real-existing socialism' of the GDR."[186] This cult resulted, as late

---

183. Wilmsmeyer, "Künstler" 88.

184. Nägele, "Goethefeiern," 117ff.

185. For an introduction see Christoph Kleßmann, "'Das Haus wurde gebaut aus den Steinen, die vorhanden waren': Zur kulturgeschichtlichen Kontinuitätsdiskussion nach 1945, *Tel Aviver Jahrbuch für deutsche Geschichte* 19 (1990): 174; idem, "Relikte des Bildungsbürgertums in der DDR," in Hartmut Kaelble, Jürgen Kocka and Hartmut Zwahr (eds.), *Sozialgeschichte der DDR* (Stuttgart, 1994), 254ff.

186. See Karl Robert Mandelkow, "Der 'restaurierte' Goethe: Klassikerrezeption in Westdeutschland nach 1945 und ihre Vorgeschichte seit 1870," in Axel Schildt and Arnold Sywottek (eds.), *Modernisierung im Wiederaufbau: Die westdeutsche Gesellschaft der 50er Jahre* (Bonn, 1993), 549ff.

as the mid-1970s, in a practice of "historical faithfulness to the work." Fealty to the "old masters" was complemented by special support for folk art, folk song, and folk music,[187] also in the hope of indirectly strengthening "GDR socialism." The GDR's cultural policies of the 1950s therefore revived many ideas and concepts from the Weimar Republic. According to the East German cultural historian Dietrich Mühlberg, these policies were intended to uplift culture but, "in combination with the departure of the old cultural elites, inevitably flattened it at a lower level."[188]

Similar in this way to the Nazis, the Socialist Unity Party (SED) considered itself the mouthpiece of the cultural will of the "working people." As such, it launched a highly polemical debate in the early 1950s over "formalism," "cosmopolitanism," and "decadence" in the West. Like the Kremlin after 1932, it encouraged "socialist realism" as the alternative. In its search for literary models, the SED looked not to the proletarian, revolutionary tradition of the Weimar Republic but once again to classicism, which was thought to set an artistic standard above all time and place.[189] The aesthetic encouraged by the SED continued in many ways the sorts of perceptions to which people had grown accustomed in the Third Reich. For instance, many paintings and sculptures depicted an ideal world generally free of conflict (although on the level of content this world was very different of course from the Third Reich). People who had lived through the Third Reich were also accustomed to a monumental, stylized aesthetic full of symbolism.[190]

In the late 1950s, an attempt was undertaken to strengthen the connection between art and the masses and put it on a strong socialist footing. Reviving traditional socialist theories of culture, plans were made at the Bitterfeld Conference in April 1959 to bring the "socialist cultural revolution" to literature by means of a two-pronged approach. Not only were writers expected to go to the factories and work with the "brigades" there, but workers were encouraged to take up the pen themselves.[191]

---

187. Sigrid Meuschel, *Legitimation und Parteiherrschaft: Zum Paradox von Stabilität und Revolution in der DDR* (Frankfurt, 1992), 80.

188. Dietrich Mühlberg, "Überlegungen zu einer Kulturgeschichte der DDR in sozialgeschichtlicher Perspektive," in Hartmut Kaelble, Jürgen Kocka, and Hartmut Zwahr (eds.), *Sozialgeschichte der DDR* (Stuttgart, 1994), 62–94.

189. We should point in this connection to the influence of Georg Lukács. For an introduction to this see inter alia Wolfgang Emmerich, *Kleine Literaturgeschichte der DDR* (Darmstadt and Neuwied, 1981), 77ff.

190. Cf. Martin Damus, *Sozialistischer Realismus und Kunst im Nationalsozialismus* (Frankfurt, 1981).

191. Emmerich, *Literaturgeschichte,* 84ff. Here we see traditions from the workers' cultural movement of the 1920s being revived.

In the western zones of Germany after the Second World War and then in the Federal Republic, the cultural perversions of the Third Reich deterred any great upsurge of artistic innovation[192] and abetted a revival of interest in Western traditions. Humanism and the classics of the ancient world, the Renaissance, and the age of Goethe were all in demand, as if they had passed through the Nazi era safe and sound, free from all contamination. The artist still functioned as a great creator and representative of national heroes.[193]

Eventually, the public turned to abstract art out of a desire for renewal and novel forms of artistic expression. People naturally wanted to distance themselves from the Third Reich as much as possible and accomplished this on an aesthetic level by turning their backs on representational art. Henceforth, they would not have to deal at all with the art of the Nazi era. As the Cold War deepened, it became even more important to distance oneself from the representational art of "socialist realism."[194] In some ways, the revival of the classics paved the way for the acceptance of abstract art since both encouraged a highly aesthetic approach and interpretations that emphasized the work itself without outside references.[195] "Classical modernity," once so disparaged by cultural conservatives, was officially rehabilitated—although in a cleansed, depoliticized form, as could be seen in the case of Bauhaus architects. Classical modernity was soon interpreted as the only "true modernity" and a symbol of artistic freedom, although it continued to interest only about 5 percent of the population. Not only did classical modernity become a weapon in the Cold War struggle against "socialist realism," but it was also used increasingly as a sign of aesthetic modern-

192. Hans-Joachim Manske, "Anschlußsuche an die Moderne: Bildende Kunst in Westdeutschland 1945–1960," in Axel Schildt and Arnold Sywottek (eds.), *Modernisierung im Wiederaufbau: Die westdeutsche Gesellschaft der 50er Jahre* (Bonn, 1993), 567.

193. See Silke Wenk, "Pygmalions moderne Wahlverwandschaften: Die Rekonstruktion des Schöpfer-Mythos im nachfaschistischen Deutschland," in Ines Lindner et al. (eds.), *Blick-Wechsel: Konstruktion von Männlichkeit und Weiblichkeit in Kunst und Kunstgeschichte* (Berlin, 1989), 70ff.

194. Ibid., 582; Anselm Doering-Manteuffel, "Die Kultur der 50er Jahre im Spannungsfeld von 'Wiederaufbau' und 'Modernisierung,'" in Axel Schildt and Arnold Sywottek (eds.), *Modernisierung im Wiederaufbau: Die westdeutsche Gesellschaft der 50er Jahre* (Bonn, 1993), 537; Jost Hermand, *Kultur im Wiederaufbau: Die Bundesrepublik Deutschland 1945–1965* (Munich, 1986), 484.

195. Doering-Manteuffel, "Kultur," 537ff. The author speaks of the widespread attitude of "no longer wanting to look"; cf. Jost Hermand, "Revolution und Restauration: Thesen zur politischen und ästhetischen Funktion der Kunst-Ismen nach 1918 und nach 1945," in Gerald D. Feldman et al. (eds.), *Konsequenzen der Inflation* (Berlin, 1989), 331–49. However, the trend toward abstract art certainly cannot be explained entirely by the desire to repress the past.

ization appropriate to the economic rise and the Westernization of West Germany.[196]

Although influential social circles encouraged an open-minded attitude toward modern art, many critical voices were heard.[197] The general population still often looked askance at abstract art. According to one young artist who watched the visitors to an exhibition in Celle, they were on the verge of attacking the works on display.[198] The Nazis had activated many people with their exhibitions of "degenerate art" and incited them to visit displays of modern art with a view to expressing their outrage. For instance, the Exhibition of Degenerate Art in Munich in 1937 had included the selling prices of the works on display and stickers that read "Paid from the tax pennies of the laboring German *Volk*." Despite the Nazi way with words, such statements had their effect,[199] and many people took this attitude into exhibitions of modern art even after the war. "The organizers could not complain about a lack of visitors, but it turned out that the reason for the large crowds was by no means just hunger for an art that had long been missed but a desire to feel outraged again. Even small galleries found that people came in and inquired about the prices of the works on display in order to get steamed up over how high they were."[200]

Another example shows that the reactions of the citizens of Celle were no exception in the postwar period. At an exhibition of "modern painters" held in Augsburg as early as December 1945, questionnaires were distributed to the visitors, and their answers were published by Erich Kästner in the *Neue Zeitung*. "One person wanted to have all the pictures in the exhibition so that he could 'burn them all up.' Another dipped a sheet of paper in an inkwell and wrote on it 'Study in Blue.' Someone else wrote that 'these artists should be eliminated without further trace. Concentration camp.'"[201]

196. Hermand, "Revolution und Restauration," especially 349. We cannot delve any further here into the years immediately after the war and the cultural searching peculiar to them.

197. Werner Bührer, "Der Kulturkreis im Bundesverband der Deutschen Industrie und die 'kulturelle Modernisierung' der Bundesrepublik in den 50er Jahren," in Axel Schildt and Arnold Sywottek (eds.), *Modernisierung im Wiederaufbau: Die westdeutsche Gesellschaft der 50er Jahre* (Bonn, 1993), 594.

198. Christine Hopfengart, *Klee: Vom Sonderling zum Publikumsliebling* (Mainz, 1989), 126.

199. Even a man like Max Liebermann attacked Ludwig Justi of the National Gallery in Berlin in 1932 for purchasing a van Gogh for 250,000 R.M. Schuster, "München," 24.

200. Ibid., 126.

201. Cited in ibid., 127.

Even a person such as Adolf Behne, who had nothing to do with National Socialism, used the idea of Nazi aesthetics in trying to persuade his fellow citizens of the importance of modern art. In a speech at the opening of the Wilmersdorf adult education center in July 1945, he claimed that "all these so-called degenerate artists were actually and without exception hearty, vigorous, magnificently well-developed human specimens. I can scarcely imagine any more German natures than those of Franz Marc, August Macke, Paul Klee, Schlemmer and Morgner. There was nothing in any of them of that wan aestheticism and pale coffee-house geniality. They were as healthy as horses in body and soul; they were joyful and optimistic. You can only laugh bitterly that a satanic, malignant man like Goebbels of all people could deride these magnificent natures as 'degenerate.'"[202] Not all opponents of "smut and trash" lost their taste for book burnings after 1945,[203] and the occasional bonfire was lit. However, most of even these strong opponents objected to such extremes because of the book burnings in the Third Reich.

The Third Reich was often described in the Federal Republic as the "cultural terrorism of the petite bourgeoisie." Thus the traditional elites absolved themselves of all responsibility for the cultural perversions under the Nazis, as Thomas Mann once pointed out.[204] Ethnologists and many of their colleagues from the well-educated bourgeoisie developed the theory that two folk cultures had existed in the Third Reich, one that was a Nazi perversion and another that just continued long traditions.[205] At the same time, many cultural conservatives carried on their battle against "mass society" and "popular culture."[206] They attempted to reconcile classicism and humanism with modernity, and Weimar once again played a prominent role in their efforts. Gropius and "his" Bauhaus were "cleansed" of all their former social and political implications and closely identified with Goethe. All were put on a pedestal as representatives of pure humanism.[207] Buchenwald was expunged from general Ger-

---

202. Ibid.

203. Cf. Petra Jäschke, "Der Kampf gegen Schmutz und Schund," in Klaus Doderer (ed.), *Zwischen Trümmern und Wohlstand: Literatur der Jugend 1945–1960,* 3d ed. (Weinheim and Basel, 1993), 385.

204. Ludwig Fischer, "Zur Sozialgeschichte der westdeutschen Literatur," in Axel Schildt and Arnold Sywottek (eds.), *Modernisierung im Wiederaufbau: Die westdeutsche Gesellschaft der 50er Jahre* (Bonn, 1993), 561.

205. For a critical view of this see James R. Dow and Hannjost Lixfeld, "Epilogue," in idem, *The Nazification of an Academic Discipline: Folklore in the Third Reich* (Bloomington and Indianapolis, 1994), 288.

206. For the Weimar Republic, cf. Berking, *Masse.*

207. See Paul Betts, "Die Bauhaus-Legende: Ein amerikanisch-deutsches 'Joint-Venture' des Kalten Krieges," in Alf Lüdtke, Inge Marßolke, and Adelheid von Saldern

man cultural and social history and compartmentalized in another separate history — or just forgotten.

When the question arose of whether Goethe's house in Frankfurt should be rebuilt after its destruction in the war, the journalist Walter Dirks raised some thoughtful objections, although they too were quickly pushed aside. According to Dirks: "There was a certain bitter logic to the destruction of Goethe's house. It was not the result of some oversight, which needed to be corrected, or historical mistake. There was some sense to this destruction, and it should be recognized. . . . The notion that beloved things which have been lost can be forced back is either just sentimentalism or impotent revolt against the judgment that has been passed."[208] The literary scholar Richard Alewyn commented in a similar vein: "Between us and Weimar lies Buchenwald. We cannot get around it."[209] But there was little interest in this kind of approach to history. Instead, interpretations and memories concentrated primarily on the Christian, Western tradition, in which the religious element played a particularly prominent role. Conservation and restoration were the hallmarks, not least of all because of psychological repression of what had happened in the Third Reich.[210] "The return to an 'apolitical' aesthetic could not undo the fact that the leading representatives of German culture had been co-opted by *völkisch* thought, but it could help to erase this fact from the cultural consciousness."[211] The Third Reich was dismissed as a time of no culture at all and safely deleted from cultural history. Karl Korn, who in 1937 had expressed his outrage over modern art, as we saw earlier, apparently changed his mind and had a successful postwar career at the culturally liberal *Frankfurt Allgemeine Zeitung*.

In the 1950s, cultural conservatives in the Federal Republic picked up again on the attitudes toward popular culture expressed by their counterparts in the 1920s. By now, Karl May stories had entered the realm of "good clean adventure," and one of the main bugaboos was the rapidly spreading phenomenon of comic books.[212] Once again the search was on for "good literature," "good books," and "genuine, clean literary works," for instance in the Landtag of Lower Saxony, especially among

---

(eds.), *Amerikanisierung: Traum und Alptraum im Deutschland des 20. Jahrhunderts* (Wiesbaden, 1996).

208. Quoted in Werner Durth and Niels Gutschow, *Architektur und Städtebau der Fünfziger Jahre* (Bonne, 1987), 34.

209. See Mandelkow, "Goethe," 545, 548.

210. Fischer, "Sozialgeschichte," 561.

211. Doering-Manteuffel, "Kultur," 535.

212. Bernd Dolle-Weinkauff, *Comics: Geschichte einer populären Literaturform in Deutschland seit 1945* (Weinheim and Basel, 1990), 96ff.

the ranks of the radical right-wing Socialist Reich Party.[213] The Social Democratic minister of education and cultural affairs in Lower Saxony, Voigt, posed the old question of what actually constitutes "trash and smut," before joining the search for "good literature" and standing up for "cleanliness and order."[214] Not until the late 1960s and 1970s did attitudes toward popular culture, which by then was even more strongly Americanized, begin to liberalize.[215] At the same time, the traditional understanding of culture began to be challenged, especially in student movement circles. "No longer did cultural politics focus on the work itself but on the social process by which it was created."[216]

Entertainment for the "people" became ever more commercialized. Although leading politicians in the Federal Republic were quick to distance themselves from the tight state controls on popular culture in the GDR, they resorted once again to censorship in order to influence cultural tastes in the Federal Republic. The *Volkskörper,* as they still said, should not suffer any detrimental consequences.[217] Attempts were made to "refine" pulp fiction and even rework comics into good, "clean," child-friendly products.[218] However, the 1953 Act on the Dissemination of Literature Dangerous to Youth turned out to be the high-water mark of narrow cultural moralism and interventionism and the deliberate revival of policies pursued in the Weimar Republic.[219]

The continuities in popular taste from the Third Reich to the 1950s

213. Deputy Druck, Socialist Reich Party, *Verhandlungen des Niedersächsischen Landtags, Stenographische Berichte,* vol. 1, 16th session, January 24, 1952, 988, 991. Deputies Sehlmeyer of the FDP (Free Democratic Party) and Meyer-Oldenburg of the BHE (Bund Heimatvertriebener) made similar arguments at this session.

214. Minister of Education and Cultural Affairs Voigt, in ibid., 993ff.

215. Kaspar Maase, *Bravo Amerika: Erkundungen zur Jugendkultur der Bundesrepublik in den fünfziger Jahren* (Hamburg, 1992). Maase thinks that popular culture became more entrenched and informal, particularly because of the influence of U.S. popular culture (e.g., rock 'n' roll). The runaway commercial success and ideals created by popular culture made the rigid, old control mechanisms of the established elite obsolete.

216. Gerhard Schulze, *Die Erlebnisgesellschaft: Kultursoziologie der Gegenwart* (Frankfurt, 1992), 500.

217. *Landtag* of Lower Saxony, 16th session, January 24, 1952, 1001.

218. Edgar Selke, "Die Schmutz- und Schundliteratur in der Bundesrepublik der fünfziger Jahre" (master's thesis, University of Hanover, 1994), 79.

219. Jäschke, "Kampf," 321. The Bundesprüfstelle singled out a total of 8,579 works between 1954 and 1978. Irene Ferchl, "Zensurinstitutionen und Zensurinitiativen," in Michael Kienzle and Dirk Mende (eds.), *Zensur in der BRD: Fakten und Analysen,* 2d ed., (Munich and Vienna, 1980), 208. For more information see Adelheid von Saldern, "Kulturdebatte und Geschichtserinnerung: Der Bundestag und das Gesetz über die Verbreitung jugendgefährdeter Schriften (1952/53)," in Georg Bollenbeck and Gerhard Kaiser in cooperation with Edda Bleek, *Die janusköpfige 50er Jahre: Kulturelle Moderne und bildungsbürgerliche Semantik,* vol. 3 (Opladen, 2000).

can hardly be ignored. Although jazz became acceptable in the 1950s, and even embraced in leading social circles, popular taste was oriented more toward polka music, as suggested by the lyrics of a popular song of 1949: "people are playing the flute now, instead of the jazz trumpet" and "we are dancing the polka again, because the polka is going to be in vogue."[220] Had the once-familiar song from the Third Reich with the programmatic title "A *Hitlermädel* dances the Polka" already been forgotten? The polka music of the 1950s best symbolized the restorative tendencies and modernized "folk culture" of the times, along with the emphasis on both *Heimat* (regional homeland) and exotic locales, such as South Sea romanticism, and songs with a strong streak of folk music, such as "Die Fischerin vom Bodensee" (1951). "Not even the rock 'n' roll generation forgot the polka, although it was pushed aside for a while."[221] The forms taken by folk culture have been constantly modernized, right up to the popular folk music telecasts of today, which typically occupy prime time.

There were some continuities as well in more "cultivated" forms of entertainment. "The suites, overtures, intermezzos, medleys and *volkstümliche* melodies played on more cultivated programs did not fade away and are still played on the radio today."[222] Continuities with the period before 1945 could be seen not only in the musical request programs, which remained popular, but also in songs that were composed during the war but not produced until afterward for economic reasons, such as the song about the fishermen of Capri. The distribution of commercial light music on the radio and in recordings expanded enormously during the Third Reich, and we can safely assume that the preferences and tastes established then became entrenched and continued in much of the population far into the post-1945 era.

---

220. Hans B. Bruns, "Wir tanzen wieder Polka," in Bernhard Schulz (ed.), *Grauzonen Farbwelten: Kunst und Zeitbilder* (Berlin and Vienna, 1983), 438.
221. Ibid., 443.
222. See ibid., 435, 437.

CHAPTER 11

Entertainment, Gender Image, and Cultivating an Audience: Radio in the GDR in the 1950s

Introduction: The Relevance of Research into Radio

"Radio plays a major part in family life today, and the radio set is one family friend equally cherished by everyone in the house. If suddenly deprived of radio, countless listeners would not know any more what to do with themselves in their spare time, especially on glum, rainy evenings."[1] This observation from the 1930s shows what an important part of everyday life radio had become. It had significant political uses as well. The Third Reich certainly employed radio to cast itself in a dramatic light. Politics and everyday life, the public sphere and the private sphere were becoming intertwined in new ways thanks to radio. It certainly became *the* new medium of the early twentieth century because of the major role it played in both politics and everyday life, and its star did not fade at all after the war in either the western or Soviet occupation zones. In the earliest postwar days — the summer of 1945 — radio stations in all the occupation zones functioned as cultural headquarters[2] because of the lack of paper for newspapers and magazines. This "golden age of radio" lasted from about 1930 to 1960 and drew to a close only when television took over.[3]

---

1. Werner Hensel and Erich Keßler, *1000 Hörer antworten . . . Eine Marktstudie* (Berlin, 1935), 46.
2. Interview with Hans Mahle, in Edith Spielhagen (ed.), *So durften wir glauben zu kämpfen: Erfahrungen mit DDR-Medien* (Berlin, 1993), 32.
3. Historical research into twentieth-century societies generally needs to be conducted on two levels that need to be meshed: the primary, real level and the level of "media realities."

The following study, which was part of a larger research project,[4] examines the connections among radio, power structures, and everyday life and is intended as a contribution to the history of mentalities, understood as collective, long-term attitudes and thought patterns.[5] Mentalities and the structurations of everyday life[6] do change, of course, but usually only very slowly. They are not very responsive to abrupt changes in political systems,[7] like those of 1945. For people wary of Communism, it was already an enormous political and cultural leap to abandon the attitudes encouraged during the years of Nazi rule and quickly adjust to a centralist, Communist state. The tendency to cling to the familiar in the apparently apolitical domain of everyday life was therefore hardly surprising, if only to the harmless-sounding hit songs of earlier days. In such times of enormous change, traditional mentalities collided with new experiences, habits, perceptions, and expectations. The impulses for change coexisted with a longing for continuity or intermingled with it in a conflicted whole.

We intend here to examine the medium of radio with a particular view to its interaction with society and power structures. This approach is rather unusual in Germany, where radio has been analyzed primarily as a political and institutional medium at various points in its history. Literary historians have also taken some interest in radio plays, and there has been at least some historical research into radio audiences.[8]

---

4. This project, funded from 1994 to 1996 by the Volkswagen Stiftung, was published in two volumes: Inge Marßolek and Adelheid von Saldern (eds.), *Zuhören und Gehörtwerden: Zwischen Lenkung und Ablenkung,* vol. 1, *Radio im Nationalsozialismus,* and vol. 2, *Radio in der DDR der fünfziger Jahre* (Tübingen, 1998). The authors Daniela Münkel, Monika Pater, and Uta C. Schmidt carried out a great part of the research work. I am grateful for all the fruitful discussions and for access to the materials in the archives of the Deutsche Rundfunkarchiv Berlin (especially I 54, 56, 57, 58, 59 and personal effects no. 14). I refrain to some extent from individual references and just refer to these materials. I would also like to thank Ines Katenhausen for comments and advice.

5. We should point in this connection to the French "Annales" tradition. For an introduction to this, see Michael Erbe, *Zur neueren französischen Sozialgeschichtsforschung* (Darmstadt, 1979). Bourdieu tried to develop a more complex approach to the development and effects of mental "dispositions" by means of his concept of habitus. See Pierre Bourdieu, *Outline of a Theory of Practice,* translated by Richard Nice (New York, 1977). We cannot delve any further here into the conceptual differences between the theoretical concepts of "mentality" and "habitus."

6. The term *structuration* is meant to eliminate the static quality inherent in the term *structure.* See in this regard Patrick Joyce, "The End of Social History," *Social History* 20, no. 1 (1995): 73–91.

7. For the staying power of attitudes and behaviors see Bourdieu's comments on habitus. Bourdieu, *Outline of a Theory of Practice.*

8. For research into the listeners to radio see Hansjörg Besseler, *Hörer- und Zuschauerforschung* (Munich, 1980).

The few media studies that touch upon social constructs of the relationship between the genders deal primarily with the print media, not radio.[9] Historical research into the uses to which radio was put and the listeners' reception of what they heard is still in its infancy. The source materials are not very good, and many scraps of information have to be tracked down and fitted together to form a picture. In the place of empirical evidence, we often have to resort to plausible deductions, which are accepted if they seem sufficiently convincing. The difficulties are only aggravated by the fact that radio scripts are often meant to elicit a variety of interpretations, and listeners frequently hear and understand them in different ways. Audience reception of the media is neither a passive process nor one that is necessarily filled with manipulation, dreaming, and distraction from the real issues. As shown by the new approaches developed in connection with "cultural studies" in the English-speaking countries in particular,[10] the use of the media should be seen as a social act.[11]

---

9. Ina Merkel, . . . *und Du: Frau an der Werkbank* (Berlin, 1990), Irene Dölling, "Continuity and Change in the Media Image of Women: A Look at Illustrations in GDR Periodicals," in Margy Gerber et al. (eds.), *Selected Papers from the Fourteenth New Hampshire Symposium on the German Democratic Republic,* Studies in GDR Culture and Society, vol. 9, (Boston and London, 1989), 131ff.; Christian Schmerl, *Das Frauen- und Mädchenbild in den Medien* (Opladen, 1984). For radio and gender see Kate Lacey, *Feminine Frequencies: Gender, German Radio, and the Public Sphere 1923–1945* (Ann Arbor, 1996); Angela Dinghaus, "Frauenfunk und Jungmädchenstunde: Ein Beitrag zur Programmgeschichte des Weimarer Rundfunks, Ph.D. diss. (Hanover, 2000).

10. Geoff Eley described "cultural studies" as a "still-emergent cross-disciplinary formation [that] comprises a varying miscellany of influences — sociologists, literary scholars and historians in Britain (but interestingly rather few anthropologists); mass communication, film studies, literary theory, reflexive anthropology in the USA, with a supportive institutional context in programs in Women's Studies, American Culture, and so on." Geoff Eley, "Is There a History of the Kaisserreich?" in idem (ed.), *Society, Culture, and the State in Germany, 1870–1930* (Ann Arbor, 1996); see also the introduction in Nicholas B. Dirks, Geoff Eley, and Sherry B. Ortner (eds.), *Culture/Power/History: A Reader in Contemporary Social Theory* (Princeton, 1994); David F. Crew, "Who's Afraid of Cultural Studies? Taking a 'Cultural Turn' in German History," in Scott Denham, Irene Kacandes, and Jonathan Petropoulos (eds.), *A User's Guide to German Cultural Studies* (Ann Arbor, 1997).

11. For the criticism of traditional research into the influence of the media, see Jan-Uwe Rogge, "Gegenstandsbereiche und Probleme einer vergleichenden Kommunikationsforschung: Dargestellt am Bild der 'BE-ER-DE' in den Kinder- und Jugendmedien der DDR," in Karl Friedrich Reimers et al. (eds.), *Zweimal Deutschland seit 1945 im Film und Fernsehen,* vol. 2, *Audiovisuelle Medien in der politischen Bildung* (Munich, 1985), 226. The methodological consequences are quite great. Rogge, who studies communications, formulated them in the following way in regard to the GDR: "Anyone who equates what should be with what is misses any chance of a differentiated analysis of everyday culture and media culture in the GDR, becomes an exegete of the officially ordained reality."

Gender relations exert a powerful influence on the ordering and structuring of society in general and hence everyday life, the world of work, and power relations. The media are affected as well. At the same time, power relations, everyday life, and the media produce or reproduce social constructs of the genders and the relationship between them. The main reason for including light entertainment in this research project was our desire to move beyond women's studies to gender studies. We were interested, therefore, in more than just areas in which one particular gender (usually women) tended to concentrate and for which suitable sources could be found, for instance women's radio, which had existed since the Weimar Republic and reappeared in the GDR and Federal Republic. Our interests included or even concentrated primarily on broadcasts that were not directly related to women alone; instead, we were interested in determining the social constructs of gender relations that appeared in these shows.

One logical conclusion of this new approach is that subjects should no longer be studied exclusively from gender points of view because it is possible that social constructs of gender played only a part in them. In order for the research results to justify all the effort, our subject must be broadened to include such matters as generational questions, particular social strata and groups, general social practices, and mentalities that are not gender specific. The advantage of this approach is that it integrates gender history into general history, where it belongs, apart from some specialized studies that are needed. The drawback is that questions of gender might be included only in some parts of the research. This possible drawback can be overcome by combining gendered sources, such as women's radio and certain advice programs aimed primarily at women, with sources of a general nature, such as light entertainment. It is precisely through the comparison of both kinds of sources that differences can be determined in the treatment of gender-related issues and informative conclusions can be drawn about mentalities and everyday life.

A major source for this research was broadcast scripts and some sound recordings that were sampled and evaluated.[12] The selected scripts were for a variety of programs, with special emphasis on light entertainment. In all cases, the programs were not political in the narrow

---

Rogge, "Gegenstandsbereiche," 137. Appropriations of the media are therefore multidimensional, relational processes, involving the relations among the communicator, the recipient, and the social situation. The text alone is just a part of the whole.

12. Sound recordings and broadcast scripts do not reflect reality, of course, but are the so-called secondary reality, the media reality. They make sense of the world in various latent and overt ways.

sense.[13] These "apolitical" broadcasts were nevertheless much influenced, of course, by the ruling system and therefore by politics, and they contained interpretations of everyday life and society, and therefore of gender, that were quite explicit in some cases and more subtle in others. However, the ideas presented in these programs about the behavior of men and women and gender relations with one another were intended primarily to be entertaining.

In the first part, we address the problems that entertainment programs posed for the political authorities and in the second part, the images of gender conveyed in advice programs, women's programs, and light entertainment. In the third part, we look at the attempts of government institutions and the radio stations themselves to improve audience relations and gain regular listeners for the state-operated radio, including for programs that were not just entertaining, in order to build support for a socialist society.

Entertainment

In the Weimar Republic, radio was thought to have enormous potential for informing and educating the masses, and there were many efforts to use it to this end. However, early listener surveys already indicated a preference for music and light entertainment, and attempts were made within certain limits to cater to this desire. The National Socialists made the first systematic effort to develop and expand light entertainment — after an initial phase dominated by propaganda — and incorporate it into their strategies for maintaining power.[14] While the radio broadcasts on May 1, 1933 and 1934, bristled with direct political propaganda and descriptions of the events being staged, the broadcast on May 1, 1935, was a huge show of light entertainment lasting from 6:30 in the morning to 3:00 at night. Political messages were inserted but only as a kind of break. Politics and entertainment were therefore intertwined in the belief that amusement and diversion would make the listeners more receptive to

13. For a general introduction to light entertainment on the radio, see Klaus Neumann-Braun, *Rundfunkunterhaltung: Zur Inszenierung publikumsnaher Kommunikationsereignisse* (Tübingen, 1993). However, it does not contain any particular gender-specific analysis.

14. The Allgemeine Deutsche Unterhaltungsrundfunk (General German Light Entertainment Radio) was founded as early as 1923. Its purpose, as stated at the time, was to cheer up the German people, who had become joyless because of all their worries, and thereby increase the pleasure they took in their work and enhance their productivity. Nevertheless, there were great hopes that, under the Weimar Republic in particular, radio programs could be developed to educate the general population.

political propaganda. It was the Minister of popular enlightenment and propaganda, Joseph Goebbels, who advocated the interweaving of politics and entertainment. He was adamantly opposed to inundating listeners with political speeches, as other Nazi leaders were inclined to do, because he realized that radios could simply be switched off. The National Socialists eventually achieved relatively high levels of light entertainment, which posed a challenge for the Communist leaders after 1945, who felt that they had to match the standard or risk losing listeners.

This was the problem faced by the Communists when they assumed control of the media,[15] especially in respect to light entertainment. They had difficulties not only with technical expertise and the tastes that the public had already developed but also and most important with implementing Lenin's conception of the media. According to Lenin, the media should be put to good use as organs of agitation, organization, and propaganda on behalf of the working class and the Communist Party. The media were supposed to educate and inform, taking their cue not least of all from Bertolt Brecht.[16] Both the Soviet Military Administration and the German Communists around Walter Ulbricht felt in the years immediately after 1945 that one of the central purposes of radio had to be the political and moral education of the people. They needed to be "enlightened" about the "true facts" and "reeducated" on the basis of some combination of humanism and Stalinism.[17] The people required the "right" kind of education and a corresponding understanding of culture, including in particular their heritage of the "German national culture." Entertainment did not figure very prominently in this concept of radio.

The earnest socialist attempts to educate and enlighten were not as successful with the general population as had been hoped. The problem

---

15. The new program producers evidently lacked experience. In addition, people working in radio in these early times were expected to fill a number of roles. The Adolf-Grimme-Institut of the Deutsche Volkshochschulverband e.V. (ed.), *Unsere Medien — unsere Republik: Selbst- und Fremdbilder in den Medien von BRD und DDR* (Marl, 1992), 1:35. The continuities in light entertainment are striking. The most popular broadcasts under the Nazis and in the early GDR and FRG had names like *Musical Requests, Variety Evening, Merry Ride over the Waves,* and *Our Little Treasure Box.* Artists such as Johannes Heesters, Ilse Werner, and Marika Rökk managed to continue the careers they had launched in the Third Reich, hardly missing a beat.

16. Examples were the merry factory evenings and village evenings that were organized.

17. See in this regard Gerd Dietrich, "'. . . wie eine kleine Oktoberrevolution . . .': Kulturpolitik der SMAD 1945–1949," in Gabriele Clemens (ed.), *Kulturpolitik im besetzten Deutschland 1945–1949* (Stuttgart, 1994), 225ff.

could be seen in the listener mail, of which quick summaries were made as early as the summer of 1947. Listeners seemed highly critical of the programming because it did not consider the needs of working people, who were looking for light music, humor, and entertainment after a hard day's work. In a way, the radio audience had been "spoiled" under the Nazis. Mentalities, customs, and tastes are deep seated and change only gradually, certainly much more slowly than political views.

The listener surveys in 1951 produced similar results. Audiences wanted more comedy, variety shows, and radio plays. Talk shows should be shorter and not so dry. The audiences also wanted more folk music and light music. Adults often disliked jazz, requesting "proper German dance music" and "no crazy American jazz." Many listeners wanted to hear melodies from old operettas. Soviet music, especially choruses, was quite popular. There was probably some progovernment spin on the way in which the survey was interpreted, for instance in the disapproval of U.S. influences and the encouragement of friendship with the Soviet Union, but this does not adequately explain the coolness toward jazz. The traditional tastes of a certain part of the population surfaced here quite clearly, as they did in the Federal Republic as well as in the 1950s.[18]

By the late 1940s, radio was already a mass medium in the GDR, and by the mid-1950s it was ubiquitous.[19] In the years before 1949, when radio was still in its developmental stage, the Mitteldeutsche Rundfunk was the most popular station because it had a lot of musical programs. Eventually, though, the other broadcasters[20] were forced to follow suit and devote more and more time to light entertainment. The New Course announced on June 9, 1953, marked a turning point. It was supposed to reverse the changes that had been made to society and the economy since 1952 in an effort to hasten the transition to socialism. The changes were having a negative impact on the standard of living, and the population was becoming agitated. The New Course was meant to remedy the situation (although it failed to forestall the revolt of June 17), and radio was called upon to play its part. Even government leaders were admitting by 1953 that they had failed so far to "drive out RIAS [the station in

---

18. Young people were apparently more open to jazz. See the subsequent discussion.

19. Rolf Geserick, *40 Jahre Presse, Rundfunk, und Kommunikationspolitik in der DDR* (Munich, 1989), 56.

20. They were the Berliner Rundfunk, Radio DDR I, and the Deutschlandsender (beginning in 1949). There were also two secondary stations, Berliner Welle and Radio DDR II. For an overview see Heide Riedel, *Hörfunk und Fernsehen in der DDR: Funktion, Struktur, und Programm des Rundfunks in der DDR* (Cologne, 1977).

the American sector of Berlin] by means of the superior programming on our radio."[21] A decision was made, therefore, to improve light entertainment programs. The connection is clearly visible here between improving light entertainment and strengthening the government's hold on power.[22] Warnings were issued, though, against too much light entertainment at the expense of propaganda or at the expense of "revolutionary music" and well-known labor songs in the case of music programs. In the end, the recommendation was for a skillful blend of light entertainment and politics. At the same time, the increasingly plentiful variety shows were criticized for lacking "political spice."[23] "We have to provide more light entertainment. . . . See if you can combine it with all-German ideas, that is, with the struggle for German unity."[24]

By expanding its light entertainment and musical shows, the GDR still had not come to grips with its second enduring problem in the realm of radio: how to create a socialist brand of entertainment that was different from that of its archenemy to the west. "What we need is the humor of *our* social order, the path to socialism."[25] A few suggestions were made to increase the overall attractiveness of GDR radio. There were to be no more dry talk shows on the radio or long sentences with a multitude of clauses. All sound-production techniques were to be employed, and texts had to be written in a popular style, though still in "proper High German." Further suggestions called for more local color and lively, interesting descriptions of daily life and economic success stories in the GDR. This task was more suited to local stations, which were supposed to provide a skillful mix of reporting, commentary, and music.[26]

In the late 1950s, programmers set out to show that light entertainment was actually one of the arts. It was, they said, "a genre of its own among the arts, perhaps just a function of the arts as well."[27] Formal

---

21. According to Fred Oelßner, *Über die Verbesserung der Arbeit der Presse und des Rundfunks: 16. Tagung des Zentralkomitees der Sozialistischen Einheitspartei Deutschlands, 17. bis 19. September 1953* (Berlin, 1953), 44.

22. A very different example of the interrelationship between politics and light entertainment is the fact that the party leaders were never very fond of political satire as a major entertainment genre. Gunter Holzweißig, "Medienlenkung in der SBZ/DDR," *Publizistik* 39, no. 1 (1994): 66.

23. Oelßner, "Über die Verbesserung," 37, 44.

24. Interview with Krickow on October 24, 1995, in connection with the radio project (see footnote 4).

25. *Der Rundfunk* 17 (1953).

26. Oelßner, "Über die Verbesserung," 37.

27. Olaf Leitner, "Stimmungskanonen für die Kämpfe der Zeit: Die Unterhaltungskunst der DDR 1984 zwischen Resignation und Reorganisation," in Karl Friedrich Reimers et al. (eds.), *Zweimal Deutschland seit 1945 im Film und Fernsehen,* vol. 2, *Audiovisuelle Medien in der politischen Bildung* (Munich, 1985), 226.

demands were accordingly made at the Fifth Party Congress in 1958 to "reunite culture and light entertainment and put them at the service of building a socialist consciousness."[28] The "edification of socialist man" was also updated at this congress. Light entertainment was supposed to lead eventually to "cultured entertainment" in an atmosphere of conviviality and "the development of the socialist personality." Light entertainment was thus upgraded on the ideological level and legitimized as a staple of radio broadcasting.[29] All of this had no effect on the control exercised over light entertainment and all other programming by the State Radio Committee, established in 1952, and the Press and Radio Section of the Central Committee of the SED.

Images of the Genders

We will now look at three areas in which gender codes, whether obvious or latent, could be found in radio broadcasts: gendered spheres of competence, social constructs of "normal gender types" and the exclusion of "otherness," and government patriarchy.

Gendered Spheres of Competence

In media communications of gendered spheres of competence, three stand out in particular: private life, including so-called reproductive tasks, the world of work, and public life and politics. We look subsequently at some sample women's programs, advice programs, and light entertainment on the radio.

Women were the primary targets of the scores of recommendations in women's programs and advice programs about housekeeping, marriage, the family, food, and clothing.[30] It was taken for granted that women would continue to bear most of the responsibility for this entire sphere.[31] There were no fundamental changes in comparison with former times, and any differences from the Federal Republic were likely not very great. For example, a women's program broadcast in the Soviet Occupation Zone in 1946 provided advice for mothers on how to raise

---

28. Cited in Wolfgang Böttcher and Siegfried Schmidt, "Unterhaltung und Sprache im sozialistischen Journalismus," *Theorie und Praxis des sozialistischen Journalismus* 12, no. 6 (1984): 383.

29. The book by Horst Slomma, *Sinn und Kunst der Unterhaltung* (Berlin, 1971), is very informative, especially 82ff.

30. See for example the radio program *Aus unseren Tagen: Zeiten der Erfolge*, March and April 1950.

31. Susanne Diemer, *Patriarchalismus in der DDR: Strukturelle, kulturelle, und subjektive Dimensionen der Geschlechterpolarisierung* (Opladen, 1994), 55.

"their boys and girls to be healthy, peaceful, thoughtful people." The fathers of these children (who in many cases did not exist at all because of the war) were mentioned only in passing at the end: "Games with lead soldiers are forgotten because Father has brought home a shovel for him [the son]." A report in a women's program about conversations heard while one was waiting in line at the grocer's included only women expressing their views on the reasons for the shortages. Another report for a women's program, based on a script two and a half pages long, was entitled "We Go Shopping." Again it was only women who did the shopping and related their experiences. A further report of one and three-quarter pages was called "Women as Consumers."

These kinds of broadcasts were related to the power structure in ways that were typical of both the times and the system. In the early 1950s women were often encouraged to identify with the GDR especially in their role as housewives. For example, in the program *Aus unseren Tagen—Zeiten der Erfolge* (The days of our lives—times of success) broadcast in March–April 1953, a housewife with a job outside the home as well says: "It's a real pleasure nowadays. In the past when we looked at our households, which are basically our responsibility, we housewives in particular found that we couldn't buy many of the things that we urgently needed." In other words, housekeeping was becoming enjoyable because the GDR was doing quite well and life was improving. Housewives should therefore feel especially inclined to identify with their new country.

The multiple burdens on women were usually taken for granted, although occasionally the ability to stand them all was portrayed as a great achievement. Any recognition of this achievement was usually presented, though, in a way that held it up as something that other women should emulate. In a broadcast of *Aus unseren Tagen—Zeiten der Erfolge,* this time from March–April 1950, a female reporter inquires: "And so you go to work and also take care of the housekeeping at home?" The woman being interviewed not only did all this but was active in political organizations as well and could therefore be portrayed as an admirable role model for others.

Although traditionally gendered competencies, in this case housekeeping, were certainly thrust upon women, many saw them as positive cultural practices and contributed in various ways to ensuring that housekeeping, for example, remained their domain. Women had a hand in planning and writing these broadcasts. The attribution of housekeeping to women was part of the Zeitgeist to some extent (in both east and west), but we would also postulate that women often felt that it enabled them to put their own stamp on life in the home—an increasingly significant power as private life became more and more important for people in the GDR. Women received social recognition for their work in the home, especially in view of the double burden they often bore, while receiving less than their share of appreciation for work performed elsewhere. Although most women held jobs outside the home sooner or later, they were disadvantaged in many ways in comparison with men. We assume, therefore, that women did not feel any less responsibility for their households because they had outside jobs. Instead, they generally accepted their dual task[32] and asked only that it be recognized. The internalization of the dual role for women can be seen, for instance, in the strong support they gave to retention of the paid day off for housework in the GDR, a benefit that only women could claim.[33] However, many women must often have felt torn by their dual role and must have had problems in their personal lives because of it.[34]

While women were fulfilling their dual role, men lived more one-dimensional lives revolving primarily around their jobs. They played a correspondingly minor role at home,[35] helping out only under unusual circumstances, as could be seen for instance in the entertainment program *Heinz und Ingeborg.* In a show called "Chats about Culinary Delights," broadcast on January 16, 1954, Ingeborg gets her companion Heinz to do some shopping because they are expecting guests that evening. Speaking directly to the listeners, she adds: "maybe you are interested in knowing what *our* preparations are." The word *our* is stressed, showing clearly that male help was considered natural only on special occasions. Even when men helped out, there was no change in who was

---

32. For the dual socialization of women see Gudrun Axeli Knapp, "Zur widersprüchlichen Vergesellschaftung von Frauen," in Ernst-H. Hoff (ed.), *Die doppelte Sozialisation Erwachsener: Zum Verhältnis von beruflichem und privatem Lebensstrang* (Munich, 1990), 17–52.

33. The fact that the traditional areas of competence were maintained at least to some extent with the active approval of women and not always against their wishes can be seen, for instance, in the requests of women in the Weimar area in 1951 for more programming tailored to the interests of housewives. There were also requests for more programs for rural women and an expanded role for women's radio. The tradition of diversifying programs (also for farmers, young people, and children), as practiced in the Weimar Republic and Third Reich, was continued. Despite their legal and economic equality, women were seen as a different, special group, and their lives and experiences needed to be discussed in separate broadcasts. These special programs had ambivalent effects.

34. We still do not know very much about any effects specific to the GDR of the dual role and dual socialization of women.

35. See Klaus Wilhelm, "Frauenbilder im Programm des DDR-Fernsehens: Konzepte, Konstruktion, und Realität," in Karl Friedrich Reimers et al. (eds.), *Zweimal Deutschland seit 1945 im Film und Fernsehen,* vol. 2, *Audiovisuelle Medien in der politischen Bildung* (Munich, 1985), 206.

mainly responsible. The situation in the Federal Republic was not very different in the 1950s.

The traditional gender codes communicated in many radio programs stood in curious contrast to the changes actually under way in the relations between the sexes. Women were expected to contribute to the economic reconstruction of the country and were therefore granted a number of rights that diminished the status of husbands and fathers. Fathers no longer had the right to determine where the family would live, and parental rights were divided between the father and the mother. The fathers of children born out of wedlock had duties but no rights. Divorce laws were eased, and various programs were initiated to assist women in particular. Women generally became legally independent of their husbands. However, the model "new family" in the GDR faced a population that was still quite traditionally minded.[36] The tension between the old and the new needs to be kept in mind when radio scenes are interpreted. The media seemed to continue reproducing those parts of the gender order that were difficult to change by legal fiat. However, the forms of the programs were contemporary. For instance, there were no programs on male dominance of the family hierarchy and assigning household tasks to women. Especially in the later 1950s, programs depicted the ideal marriage as an equal partnership in which husbands acted responsibly and were devoted to their families, especially in regard to raising the children.[37] Marriage and the family remained private realms and symbols of individual happiness. This individual happiness was extolled in many popular songs in the GDR based on family-centric ideals.

Radio depicted both the new occupations that were opening to women and the traditional gender hierarchy, although in different types of shows. One women's program called *Concise Guide for the Inexperienced* lauded the new independence and "freedom" of women, due not least of all to jobs outside the home and their ability "to think for themselves," which was in the "interests of everyone." This program was meant to be educational, and the main figures in it were named Olly and Friedl. In general, it is clear that the greater the emphasis on entertainment, the less equality there was between the sexes. Traditional mentalities were portrayed in traditional comical ways in order to be humorous

---

36. Robin Ostow, "Die volkseigene Familienromanze: Arbeitende Mütter und entrechtete Väter in der Deutschen Demokratischen Republik, 1949–1989," in Dagmar Reese et al. (eds.), *Rationale Beziehungen? Geschlechterverhältnisse im Rationalisierungsprozeß* (Frankfurt, 1993), 348.

37. Deutsches Rundfunkarchiv (DRA) Berlin, BR 58, no. 1344, 31.12.1958; BR 57, no. 96, 29.1.1957.

and entertaining.[38] The popular show *Da lacht der Bär,* for example, was highly gendered. The leading characters were men, while women appeared only as their helpmates, with the exception of the great female star, a figure who could be traced back through the Third Reich and beyond. In a show about a vacation (1961), a woman is portrayed as a stand-in for her husband and not someone who is independent or initiates activities.[39] Although entertainment programs tended to preserve the hierarchical, gendered roles of the past, these roles were portrayed in more brittle, subtle, conflicted ways. In contrast to women's programs, light entertainment often resorted to *Schadenfreude* and disparaging remarks about the incompetence of the other sex, as well as condescending offers of help when one sex pushed into areas of life traditionally reserved for the other.[40] Men were accordingly shown as being all thumbs at housekeeping and women as incompetent at mechanical problems.

In the show *Heinz und Ingeborg,* Ingeborg is busy in one scene portraying Heinz as a typically inept man who cannot even hide his wife's birthday present properly. Suddenly, Heinz begins to set her straight in a way that extends far beyond the scope of the original conversation: "We men aren't all that primitive any more, and besides, you're so old-fashioned you don't even know that packages don't fall out of pockets nowadays. You can put a nylon blouse in your vest pocket . . . and three pairs of monofilament stockings fit quite nicely into a case for eyeglasses." In other words, there has been a lot of technological progress in the GDR, about which men instruct and inform women. What sounds ironic in retrospect, was certainly meant seriously at the time. As was mentioned previously, the authorities wanted comments of this kind woven into various kinds of broadcasts. For example, during the first Five Year Plan from 1950 to 1955, publicity for new chemical products was woven into various programs, apparently as a reminder of the efficiency and productivity of the GDR.

Political equality for women also meant participation in mass organizations. The advice programs tried to make women more aware of their

38. One cannot exclude the possibility that one thing or another might have been meant ironically. It is inevitable that texts can be read differently.

39. There was also a joke about stand-ins: "What is the difference between government ministers and husbands? The former know their stand-ins and the latter don't." Housewives were supposed to be controlled but no longer could be. The desire to control wives, seen as property, surfaces in the concern about potential lovers. The inability of men to control their wives was thought to be humorous. One could conclude from this joke that affairs outside the bonds of marriage were increasing, but it is hard to say to what extent there were allusions here to the political situation (ministers and their stand-ins).

40. Ina Merkel, "Kumpeline, Mutter, Ehefrau: Frauenbilder in DDR-Zeitschriften der 50er Jahre," *Unsere Medien: Unsere Republik,* no. 3 (November 1992): 11.

new role in a socialist society. On a more elevated plane, there were the officially approved role models of certain revolutionary women who were trotted out once a year on International Women's Day or in broadcasts commemorating figures such as Klara Zetkin, "Hilde Coppi—a German Woman" (1956), or Danielle Casanova (1957).[41] The scripts were reminiscent in structure of the lives of the saints and in content of the Marian ideal of modest, caring, motherly women who had learned the lessons of the past and were henceforth doing all they could to build a socialist future.[42] These characteristics can be seen in an interview in the previously mentioned program *Aus unseren Tagen,* in which the interviewee had a paid job, did the housekeeping at home, and was also active in mass organizations. In describing why she did all this, she said: "Well, how should I put it, the lesson that we, that one had to draw from the past obliges one to do the right thing now for the future."[43] Women's programming attempted in various ways to convey gender-specific political views such as these about the past, present, and future. It was precisely in the years of reconstruction immediately after the end of the war that the social function of women's traditional role as housewives was duly recognized: "[W]e know as women that great things can only come from small, from the care provided every day, from picking up and cleaning up."[44] According to a program called "The Political Work of Women in the World," written by Susanne Drechsler about the International Democratic Women's Federation, "German women . . . know what their responsibilities are." Elsewhere in the same program, it was said that "the women of Germany are on their way to exterminating the mistakes of the past." Unfortunate linguistic continuities with the Third Reich crept in here as well. No one, and especially no one working in the media of an "antifascist state," should have still been using the unspeakable term *exterminate (ausmerzen).*

Another tradition was carried on in the women's programs, especially in the early years of reconstruction: there was little talk of politics, and, at most, current events of the previous day would be mentioned. The broadcasts tended to be a collage, and the comments, according to one woman who worked on these broadcasts, were kept short and superficial. One cannot help noticing that the reports in all kinds of women's

---

41. DRA Berlin, DS 56, no. 315; personal effects 14.

42. I am grateful to Uta C. Schmidt for pointing this out.

43. DRA Berlin, NL 10, "Hörfolge aus unseren Tagen." This program was broadcast on April 30, 1950. One wonders whether programs like this contributed much to building a positive identity for women in and together with the GDR.

44. DRA Berlin, NL 14, "Gespräch über Frauenlisten," n.d. (approximately the end of August 1946).

programming lasted only from three to five minutes.[45] For example, a script about the lists of female candidates for political office was only about two pages long. It was entitled "Three Women Chat about the Lists of Female Candidates" and depicted the women as talking in a very casual manner, even though the subject was highly political. Perhaps this was an attempt to adopt a style that was in keeping with the ephemeral nature of the medium. Politics were handled in these broadcasts in the form of short scenes blending entertainment with information. There was accordingly some continuity in this regard with women's programming in the Third Reich and the Weimar Republic.

The hierarchical nature of the communications in entertainment programming is also noteworthy. The figure of Heinz is reminiscent of a teacher as he doles out praise or criticism to Ingeborg. Women had particular spheres of competence, at least in matters of everyday life, but were often depicted as learners. This was not always the case, though, and there was some latitude for showing women as independent.[46]

New perspectives mix with old in the scripts. Women are and feel needed, and a female tractor driver symbolizes their entry into male-dominated jobs. However, the tasks carried out by women remain complementary to those of men. Men are the driving force; it is they who are primarily responsible for the reconstruction of the country and therefore for its future.

Constructs of "Normal Gender Types" and the Exclusion of "Otherness"

Standards for the behavior of the sexes and their relationship with one another were predicated on what was implicitly assumed to be "normal." People and practices that fell outside the norm did not exist insofar as radio was concerned. The exclusion of "otherness" was certainly typical of the times and of the Federal Republic as well in the 1950s; however, this kind of exclusion proved more enduring in the GDR. Standards of "normal" behavior were based on a curious mixture of

45. Maria Dahms, "Aus dem ff . . . Vom Wirken der Frauenfunk-Redaktion Leipzig," *Beiträge zur Geschichte des Rundfunks* 1, no. 1 (1967); 73ff. This concept did not change, according to Dahms, until after 1961. However, the scripts that we have suggest a more differentiated view and qualify Dahms's perspective. We should also inquire whether the opinions of women were taken sufficiently into account in political broadcasts for the general public, for instance the opinions of the Deutscher Frauenbund (German Women's Union).

46. For more information see Monika Pater, "Rundfunkangebote," in Inge Marßolek and Adelheid von Saldern (eds.), *Zuhören und Gehörtwerden*, vol. 2, *Radio in der DDR der fünfziger Jahre: Zwischen Lenkung und Ablenkung* (Tübingen, 1998), 249ff.

socialist and national cultural traditions, as can be seen for instance in the kind of wedding ceremonies encouraged by the state. In the run-up to the Fifth Party Congress, there were more broadcasts than usual about socialist wedding ceremonies, which were made as attractive as possible in order to detract from the appeal of church weddings. The result looked remarkably similar to the petit bourgeois idea of a perfect marriage, complete with the wedding march from Wagner's *Lohengrin*. In an effort to win acceptance of the new, socialist ceremony, many familiar elements from the past were included, including in this case the wedding march from an opera popularized under the Third Reich.

Although women were making many advances in the world of work, including in jobs previously considered exclusively male domains, the authorities in the GDR did not attempt to call into question, let alone revolutionize, the norms of gender relations. There was a fear, quite to the contrary, that women might become too masculine and men too feminine, and the media were expected to help counteract this trend. Radio continued, therefore, to emphasize virtues traditionally considered feminine, such as care and solicitousness,[47] and "moms" became role models for GDR women. Both men and women were still depicted, though, in a variety of ways. For instance, the "new" kind of father was shown as taking an interest in his family, helping out with the housekeeping, and feeling some responsibility for the raising of the children.[48] The images remained within certain bounds, however, and were very hierarchical in nature. "Otherness" was systematically ignored, and people were depicted as much more uniform than they really were, apparently in an attempt to create a new norm rather than reflect reality.[49] Whether specific GDR mentalities emerged as a result in the medium run and long run is difficult to determine. In any case though, the systematic exclusion of "otherness" stifled the development of more liberal, tolerant attitudes in both the political sphere and the supposedly apolitical sphere of everyday life and entertainment. There were continuities, therefore, in this regard as well with the Third Reich and similarities with the Federal Republic under Adenauer. Cultural exclusion and

---

47. We could also mention the greater modesty and selflessness ascribed to women. Were the ascetic ideals (Merkel) of the GDR Arbeitsgesellschaft not aimed in particular at women, who were supposed to apply their insights into what was needed at each particular time in the family? In other words, the social construct of "normal women" contained many clichés and many more or less covert assumptions.

48. Merkel, "Kumpeline," 159ff.; DRA Berlin, BR 58, no. 1344, December 31, 1958. Even in the Third Reich there were a number of different images of women, although they were ordered according to a clear ranking.

49. Cf. Kornelia Hauser, *Patriarchat als Sozialismus: Soziologische Studien zur Literatur aus der DDR* (Hamburg, 1994), 122.

relatively rigid norms remained a part of German life after 1945, quite openly in some cases and more covertly in others. The years of Nazi dictatorship left a strong imprint on both German states, which could be seen in the tenacity of a mentality colored by cultural conservatism.[50]

Government Patriarchy

Government patriarchy was personified by the almost exclusively male elite that dominated senior positions in the government and the party. Walter Ulbricht saw himself as a kind of father of the nation, in imitation of Stalin.[51] Radio stations too were dominated by men.[52] Women may have been equal in a legal sense, but in practice a gender hierarchy remained in effect. Women succeeded in breaking out of lower-level jobs and advancing into the middle echelon, but they remained rare at senior levels, whether in radio or elsewhere. The number of women working in radio was actually relatively high because of a deliberate policy to include them, although they remained scarce among senior decision makers.[53] There were many reasons for this: traditional self-conceptions, networking among powerful men, differences in education, and the burden that women bore because of their dual role at home and on the job and their resulting tendency to sacrifice their careers. The gender hierarchy existed not only in society but in the media as well. Radio audiences therefore experienced the power and dominance of males twice over, probably with mutually reinforcing effects, and their understanding of the relationship between the sexes was naturally affected.

More than anyone else on radio, Gerhart Eisler helped to project the image of the state as a kindly father figure. He held a number of positions, including head of the Information Office. In his broadcasts, he conveyed the impression that he could and would assist individual listeners, and he and his colleagues did take their task of answering listener mail very seriously. As he said on the radio in 1958: "If anyone among you, dear listeners, is having problems or knows anybody who is, whether they are his own fault or the fault of someone else, or the result of his own or someone else's lacking of understanding, every one of us

---

50. The 1960s were a particularly important decade for changes in mentality.

51. It was possible to write to Ulbricht and pour out one's heart. It did not cost anything, and some people were even helped through unofficial channels.

52. For the recruitment of personnel for radio, see Daniela Münkel, "Produktionssphäre," in Inge Marßolek and Adelheid von Saldern (eds.), *Zuhören und Gehörtwerden*, vol. 2, *Radio in der DDR der fünfziger Jahre: Zwischen Lenkung und Ablenkung* (Tübingen, 1998), 45ff. Any research into the GDR elites that ignores gender-specific issues is overlooking an important aspect.

53. The proportion of women in 1953 was 51 percent.

here on democratic radio is always ready to jump in and help in a very discreet way." Eisler ensured that the complaints raised in his listener mail were followed up, often over the heads of local authorities and party functionaries.

The significance of government patriarchy must be seen in the context of actual developments. Women and children became more independent of family fathers, but on the other hand, family relationships were destabilized, and women and children became the objects of government intervention, from day care to the promotion of working women. Individual well-being depended on the government, and it was the government that became "the driving force and socializer."[54] People could pursue their own interests only insofar as they did not conflict with government doctrine and plans. Women were expected, for instance, to work outside the home, and their labor was essential if the various government plans were to be fulfilled. Outside jobs were therefore the price that women had to pay, regardless of whether or not they wanted them, in order to avoid conflict with the state, which provided for them and took care of them. It is not surprising that radio and women's programs were conscripted to urge women to do their duty.[55] As in the Third Reich, "we" came before "I," and individual wants and desires were expected to take a backseat (even though the demands of the state were for totally different purposes in the GDR).

Listener Loyalty

Radio can be switched off and on, and other stations can be tuned in — much to the chagrin of dictators whose ability to control what is heard is therefore limited.[56] The problem of listener loyalty was especially vexatious in the GDR, where most people could and did listen to western stations. It is no longer possible to determine exactly how much of the population tuned in to western radio, but estimates for the late 1950s range from 70 to 90 percent.[57] Many people listened to both eastern and western radio, depending on the program.

54. Ostow, "Die volkseigene Familienromanze," 356.

55. Dahms, "Vom Wirken," 70.

56. Switching to foreign broadcasters or, in the case of the GDR, West German broadcasters always posed a particular problem. Listening to foreign broadcasters was important to many people in the Third Reich and the GDR, as well as in the Federal Republic in its early days, although for very different reasons. The standards set by Western programs posed a permanent challenge to the GDR, both for radio-related processes and the reactions of many listeners.

57. Geserick, *40 Jahre Presse,* 157. However, according to a survey in 1957, the rate was much lower at 35 percent.

Attempts were made in the GDR to influence the habits of listeners and dissuade them from turning their radios off all too quickly or switching to western programs. A Listener Relations Office was established for this purpose and then, in 1956, a Scientific Division for Research into Listener Opinion. Beside the attempts described earlier to use light entertainment as a way of habituating people to GDR radio, listening in large groups was also encouraged through such mass organizations as the Association of Free German Trade Unions (FDGB) and factories. Even smaller factories had at least one radio loudspeaker in the canteen and a microphone for information and announcements. Schools and holiday resorts were equipped as well with centrally controlled sound systems. More research needs to be done into the extent to which people in the GDR listened (or were forced to listen) to radio in groups.[58] We should also mention that the radio equipment had the further advantage of operating as a bugging device when it was turned off.

"Group listening" was only practical, though, in very limited circumstances, and the State Radio Committee placed greater hopes in its concept of *Massenverbundenheit,* or closeness to the masses. Just as a "new kind of party" had been created in the GDR, a "new kind of medium" would be established. Attempts had already been undertaken elsewhere to bring radio closer to the people, notably in the Third Reich (with the important distinction that the Nazi efforts were predicated on the racially exclusive ideology of the "*Volk* community"). We could point in particular to the *Volkssenderaktionen* and the *Gaufunktage* (mobile radio stations that went to individual cities or areas to do live recordings and interviews). The attempts in the GDR to bring radio closer to the people were predicated on very different political and ideological convictions and looked for direction to Lenin's writings and the experiences of the workers' radio movement in the 1920s.[59]

In the GDR, as elsewhere, the efforts to bring radio closer to the masses focused mainly on the use of mobile radio stations. Similar stations had existed in the Third Reich, but now many more reporters roamed the countryside, organizing the local people and using broadcast vehicles to transmit live events and interviews from all across the GDR. These programs proved very popular, especially in rural areas. Women's programs also used broadcast vehicles.[60]

There were also initiatives to broaden the number of people involved in radio through the recruitment of suitable (including politically

58. In the Third Reich, people had to listen to Hitler's speeches even in private spaces. This was not true of Ulbricht's speeches in the GDR.

59. There is considerable disagreement over the extent to which the latter was true.

60. Dahms, "Vom Wirken," 72.

suitable) amateurs from the general population. These initiatives were especially common during the first period of reconstruction after the war. Even before the founding of the GDR, searches were conducted for talented writers. As early as 1946, a prize was announced for radio plays, and twelve hundred responses were received.[61] Courses were also established in 1946 for aspiring radio journalists, and a School of Radio was opened in Berlin-Grünau in 1950. Its mandate was to recruit talented people, professionalize the new medium of radio, and develop a management group. The degree of emphasis on each of these aims was constantly shifting.[62]

The plans to bring radio closer to the masses focused also on so-called radio correspondents.[63] There is some debate over whether this approach was inspired mainly by similar undertakings in the Soviet Union or in the Communist labor movement during the Weimar Republic. The first correspondents took up their positions as early as January 1946. They served in an honorary capacity, reporting on their workplaces or on other aspects of their daily lives and sometimes on other subjects of their own choosing. They provided advice and suggestions,[64] as well as information about the reactions of their colleagues to the programming. In some cases, regular circles of radio listeners were also organized. Not least among the tasks of the radio correspondents was keeping headquarters informed about the opinions of the listeners, including going so far as to spy on them. In 1950, the network of radio correspondents was extended, as was the network of *Volkskorrespondenten* working for newspapers. In the fall of 1951 the radio correspondents received their instructions from a central headquarters.[65] They were told which broadcasts they should listen to and the criteria by which to judge them.

The monthly reports of the Radio Correspondents Department

---

61. The idea was to get the entire people involved in cultural reconstruction. Cf. *Beiträge zur Geschichte des Rundfunks* 17, no. 3 (1983): 95. There were precursors in the Third Reich as well for this kind of attempt to attract and activate people. Many competitions were held, for instance on the occasion of the radio exhibition of 1935, including special competitions for radio announcers.

62. For more information about the radio school, see Münkel, "Produktionsspäre," 48ff.

63. The first radio correspondents took up their duties in 1947. Here too, prizes were offered. There has not been any research yet into the extent to which women were involved.

64. If similar initiatives in the Third Reich could be found at all, then possibly in regard to radio plays, in that prizes were also offered.

65. The bimonthly *Der Funkkorrespondent* was first published in the summer of 1951.

show that the producers did not hold the contributions of these people in very high regard. Of the 757 reports that were filed in August 1953, 81 were broadcast, 36 were rejected, and the information in 472 of them was at least evaluated. The disinterest was especially great in news departments. Of the 191 reports filed with them, 139 were evaluated, but only 41 were actually broadcast. One radio correspondent reported, for instance, about an exchange of letters between workers in Zittau and winners of the Stalin Prize in Liblina, near Moscow. However, the report was never broadcast, and the correspondent was told "no possibility of report because of changes in the program."[66] By 1959, there were about a thousand radio correspondents. We do not know how many of them were women. Source materials are poor, and there are still no thorough studies of these radio correspondents or of their reports.

In the 1960s, the number of radio correspondents declined, but a solid core began to develop and become professionals.[67] Their reports were supposed to provide authentic slices of life, but in reality they were staged and arranged in advance.[68] They attempted to give the impression that the general population had a real say in the "new kind of radio" in the GDR, but in actual fact the dialogues were manipulated in an attempt to hide the fact that the radio programming was undemocratic and controlled from above by the party and the government. All in all, the radio correspondents fell between two stools: they did not succeed in becoming the voice of the people, nor were they much appreciated by their superiors.

The attempt to bring radio closer to the listeners also included amateur productions of broadcasts. This approach too was not new and had already been tried, at least to some extent, in the Weimar Republic and the Third Reich, for instance in youth programming. In the GDR, so-called lay producers were responsible for programs originating from large factories in particular. As early as 1949, many large concerns had their own radio equipment, and "factory radio producers" put together broadcasts for the breakfast and lunch breaks. More research needs to be done into these broadcasts, not least of all in respect to their place in

66. Oelßner, "Über die Verbesserung," 37ff. Oelßner provides a very critical account of these events.

67. Sigrun Richter, *Die Volkskorrespondenten-Bewegung der SED-Bezirkspresse: Theorie, Geschichte, und Entwicklung einer Kommunikationsstruktur* (Frankfurt, 1993), 314ff.

68. According to Geserick, who is referring just to the phony reports that were actually written by editors or other people. Rolf Geserick, *40 Jahre Presse*, 119, cited in Sigrun Richter, *Die Volkskorrespondenten-Bewegung der SED-Bezirkspresse: Theorie, Geschichte, und Entwicklung einer Kommunikationsstruktur* (Frankfurt, 1993), 318. In my view, the term can also be used in a broader sense.

factory culture and gender issues. The broadcasts encompassed both stories about particular factories, produced on the spot, and retransmissions of central programming.[69] In 1952, a rather successful program was created called *Zwei bunte Stunden für die Werkspause* (Two variety hours for the company-wide break), consisting of a mixture of such things as short reports, conversations, congratulations, and lots of music.[70] In addition, reports from individual factories became quite common. Factory radio was also used for internal denunciations. In a number of firms, there were live broadcasts of general meetings of workers and staff "at which enemies were unmasked."

Although factory radio was fairly important in everyday life on the factory floor, its producers were largely left to their own devices. The political authorities complained that the party organizations within the factories did not provide enough guidance. The authorities also commented, rather self-critically, that the Central Committee (Agitation Division) and the district administrations should pay more attention to factory radio. Reading such comments against the grain, we can conclude that the producers of factory radio had some latitude to do what they wanted and made use of it in a variety of ways.

Finally, radio was brought "closer to the listeners" by means of listener mail and radio magazines, which carried letters from their readers. Between 1945 and 1949, radio stations received half a million letters, and thereafter the numbers only increased.[71] The Listener Relations Office of the State Radio Committee produced monthly reports on listener mail, and some of it was quoted on the air. Most mail came from urban areas and from pensioners or young people. The letter writers were also primarily male.[72] When women sent in mail, they tended to describe their current difficulties in the context of their entire lives. Letter writers often expressed the feeling that Gerhart Eisler was their

---

69. Geserick, *40 Jahre Presse,* 62; Karl-Heinz Moosgraber, "Zur Entstehung und zur Wirkungsweise des Landessenders Potsdam," *Theorie und Praxis des sozialistischen Journalismus* 14, no. 6 (1986): 396. Most of the factory-level producers of radio programs served in honorary capacities, and often they were also radio correspondents. Moosgraber, "Entstehung," 396.

70. Moosgraber, "Entstehung," 397. There were also precursors in the Third Reich.

71. Michael Straßer, "Der DDR-Rundfunk als Tribüne des gesellschaftlichen Erfahrungsaustausches: Dargestellt am Dialog mit dem Hörer, das heißt an der Nutzung und Beantwortung von Hörerzuschriften in ausgewählten Senderreihen der Inlandsprogramme" (Ph.D. diss., Berlin, 1984), 4. The listener mail was assessed on a systematic, confidential basis, and, although it cannot be seen as representative, it provides some information about the appropriation of the broadcasts and some insights into living conditions. We cannot go any further into this here.

72. Seventy-five percent of the letters.

last hope. It is difficult to determine why women did not write listener mail as often as men. Perhaps it was because the attention of women was usually divided when they listened to the radio, while men were more likely to pay close attention. Women treated radio differently than men, using it as company in the background while they did housework. They were therefore less inclined than men to be critical, especially when it came to going so far as to write letters.[73]

We should also touch upon the various events that were organized around radio, as well as the listener meetings that proved quite successful with the general population. For instance, a "Radio Day" was held, on which radio celebrated itself at a number of large, family-oriented events held in various locations and attended by between two hundred thousand and five hundred thousand people. Thousands also accepted invitations to listener meetings, which were held in the relevant radio station or in a restaurant or House of Culture (Houses of Culture were centers for cultural events).[74] For example, thirteen listener meetings were held in the various districts of the GDR between August 17 and September 30, 1953. The studio managers worked together with the Listener Relations Office on preparations for the meetings, although one report noted that these preparations were often inadequate. The ideal meeting was thought to involve between thirty and fifty people, especially delegates from factories who had already held discussions with their fellow workers and could report on the general response to the radio programs. The success of these meetings depended largely on the individual speakers. The aim was to establish "real contact" with the listeners. The seriousness with which radio stations took these meetings can be seen in the fact that even senior managers went and spoke. However, there were still complaints that "these comrades" did not yet fully appreciate "the political importance of relations with the masses."[75]

According to the minutes of the meetings, a variety of topics were addressed, including reception problems and requests that stations avoid repetition and coordinate programs better with one another. Also mentioned were the nature of the early morning programs, how current the news programs were, and the proper proportion of light and serious music. Very little was said about political broadcasts, much to the disap-

---

73. Uta C. Schmidt, "Radioaneignung," in Inge Marßolek and Adelheid von Saldern (eds.), *Zuhören und Gehörtwerden*, vol. 2, *Radio in der DDR der fünfziger Jahre: Zwischen Lenkung und Ablenkung* (Tübingen, 1998), 323.

74. *5 Jahre demokratischer Rundfunk* (1950): 25. In the early days, the cultural union also wrote reports about what it listened to and discussed the contents. This was probably a continuation of similar practices in the Weimar Republic.

75. Bundesarchiv Potsdam, DR 6, no. 231.

pointment of the State Radio Committee, which had hoped to determine by the nature of the questions "the chief emphasis of enemy propaganda in various districts." In conclusion, we should point out that although the listener events were staged as dialogues between radio stations and their listeners, the results of the dialogues were never considered binding on programming. There was no fundamental change to the express view of the authorities that radio could not possibly be governed by the taste of the majority. The staged dialogues influenced programming only insofar as the authorities in the SED wished. Listener mail, for its part, served primarily as a way for the authorities to keep abreast of the general mood in the country and learn a little about how a "socialist consciousness" and "socialist culture" were progressing.

One Listener Meeting and Three Letters from Listeners

The following examples are not meant to be representative, but they do provide some insight into what the sources are like and what can be found there. Let us look in particular at one listener meeting held in HO Restaurant Sanssouci in Ludwigsfelde near Berlin on August 28, 1956, from 7:30 to 11:00 P.M.[76] Three hundred and fifty people came, mostly workers, white-collar employees, and young people from the factory in Ludwigsfelde. Seven people came from various departments in the radio station in Potsdam, including two or three women. On the agenda for the evening were the news program, a show called "10:40 P.M. on Alexanderplatz," music programs, reception of the station's signal, and assessments of its programming. The discussions were summarized in two and a half pages.

Nine people spoke about the news program, and as far as can be determined from the minutes, they asked technical questions such as whether the news was taped. They also criticized some details, such as the way in which programs were announced, and there was some discussion of voices and the way in which people spoke. Finally, someone complained that the news was occasionally "too one sided." This person went on to provide innocuous, apolitical examples, in a way that seems typical of the criticisms that were provided. The person pointed out that there were "a lot of stories about storm damage in West Germany but none, or very few, about individual examples of damage in the GDR." The recording secretary wrote down that the speaker "wanted extensive information about the effects of storms, accidents, etc., in the GDR." We can assume that the person who raised this complaint was actually

---

76. For what follows see Bundesarchiv Potsdam, DR 6, no. 548.

speaking figuratively, whether consciously or not, sticking to innocuous examples but really criticizing distorted reporting in general. More veiled criticism of the authorities came to the fore in the comments about "10:40 P.M. on Alexanderplatz." One man said: "You get the feeling in many reports that people have things put into their mouths or imputed to them. In any case, it sounds artificial and is offensive. This is especially true of interviews." It is impossible to determine whether these critics had the political and social contents of the reports in mind or simply felt that the media were particularly inept at handling ordinary people. However, one suspects that this criticism often included the contents. The recording secretary likely knew very well what was actually meant, as did the people who read the minutes, but no one dared to say openly what everyone thought. One needed to be very aware of how one was expressing oneself, a talent that people had already developed under the Third Reich.

The problems and difficulties of everyday life also came up for discussion. As can be seen in the listener mail, people often turned to the radio to vent their frustrations with daily life. Complaints of this kind were recorded as follows in the minutes: "The people present also insisted that the city reporter or a reporter from 'Pulse of the Times' (*Pulsschlag der Zeit*) should go to Ludwigsfelde sometime and see what things are actually like there and do something to help, for instance the shortage of articles for sale and the women standing in line for hours in front of stores. (The *Tagesfragen* Office, Berlin Radio, is asked to follow up on the wish of the inhabitants of Ludwigsfelde as soon as possible. Please announce arrival at the workers' entrance to the Ludwigsfelde Industrial Works!)" These notes show that the people who attended listener meetings succeeded in drawing attention to their complaints, and the notes even included a demand for action in response to the wishes of the people of Ludwigsfelde. Finally, we might add that the traditional gendered division of labor is again apparent in the easy assumption that women do the arduous work of shopping in the GDR.

The discussion turned next to the Potsdam radio station itself, especially the poor reception of its signal and the need for more cooperation with producers of folk art and amateur theater groups. The latter topic was broached again when the discussion shifted to music and fourteen people took the floor. One person complained that when West German music was broadcast on "democratic radio," as he or she said, it was played by East German bands. According to the minutes, a number of speakers wanted the music broadcast at noon to be less heavy and monotonous, and one criticized the constant repetition. Some young people said how much they appreciated the series of jazz programs with introductory comments but expressed their desire to hear some foreign bands and not always local groups. They pointed out the fact that jazz bands had been formed in some of the people's democracies, especially Poland and Czechoslovakia, and said: "Please report about them because there is a lot of interest among young people." In the official view, it was apparently acceptable to listen to jazz occasionally in the framework of educational broadcasts. However, these broadcasts always sounded a warning note and were evidently intended to win the youth over eventually to "good music." A Mr. Zimmermann of the Light Music Office explained how important this task was, and the audience apparently accepted his clarification, although it is hard to know for sure. Particularly noteworthy in the minutes is the strong interest expressed by the youth in jazz and broadcasts of foreign recordings. Radio seems to have represented the wider world for them, both as a medium and because of the culture found there. Only very slowly, if at all, could the mentalities of young people in the GDR be molded by the narrowness of their country and its policy of cutting itself off from the west, which gave it an air of stuffy provincialism. The construction of the Berlin Wall gave both symbolic and very real expression to the government pressure to be narrow and limited.

We will now turn to three letters from listeners,[77] which arouse particular curiosity because they are so lengthy. The writers all refer to earlier times in their lives and describe the current difficulties that prompted them to turn to Gerhart Eisler, who encouraged his listeners to do so both directly and indirectly. Two of the letter writers did not want any material assistance, just Eisler's opinion about matters of deep concern to them, while the third hoped to get a raise in her wages. The first woman wrote on November 3, 1958, and described for Eisler her fate in the Third Reich. She had become engaged to a foreigner from Czechoslovakia in 1934, but they were not allowed to marry. After they had three children, her fiancé was denounced and sent to a concentration camp. When she visited him in the camp, he slipped her a note to the consulate describing his suffering. A neighbor discovered the note and denounced the woman, who was also sent to a concentration camp. Her children were split up and sent to foster homes. Her fiancé was then deported back to Czechoslovakia and never heard from again. By 1939, she wanted to marry another man, but this marriage too was quashed because, as she now discovered, one of her grandparents was Jewish. Her new male friend was drafted into the army, and she was forced to undergo sterilization. "Since that time," she continues, "I have been

---

77. For what follows see Bundesarchiv Potsdam, DR 6, no. 542.

unable to work because of a nervous disorder. After the war, a Jewish doctor who had returned from the concentration camp said . . . that he too could not do anything for my health. I implore you, dear Mr. Eisler, to state your views about these facts. Sincerely yours." What did this woman hope that Eisler would say? What could he say? This example of the letters to him, though perhaps extreme, shows the impact that experiences under National Socialism were still having on everyday lives in both the GDR and the Federal Republic. Apparently, the GDR did not do much to help this woman. Was this an isolated case?

In another, quite different letter, a woman reviewed her husband's life for Eisler over a total of eight pages. The father of her husband had been killed in the First World War. His mother had gone to work in a factory, and although he had suffered many deprivations in his life, he finally succeeded in becoming the chief clerk in a textile factory. He was a member of the NSDAP from 1933 to 1939 but still helped Jewish families to escape. When the war broke out, he was drafted and served as a paymaster. He was then charged with expressing contempt for members of the Reich government. Consequently, he was denied all future promotions and sent to the front, where he was eventually captured by the Russians. According to credible information provided by his wife, he worked hard after the war on the reconstruction of the new state and finally joined the Kasernierte Volkspolizei, the precursor of the East German army, at the age of forty-seven. He was promoted to captain, but then he was dismissed in 1959 after being accused of not having done enough to combat militarism. His past had apparently been dredged up and used against him. His wife said in her letter that she simply could not understand the behavior of the authorities. She had personally brought up her children and grandchildren "in the spirit of our Weltanschauung," as shown by the list of organizations they had joined. She was now writing to Eisler because he had said on the radio that all that mattered in the GDR was what you did now and that everyone would be helped to overcome his or her past. She said that she was not complaining but just wanted to "provide an example of how things that are reviewed and evaluated quite correctly by the leading comrades in our state actually play out or are carried out 'down below,' so to speak." She concludes with the following statements: "As a woman, who perhaps thinks things through more deeply, I would appreciate it very much if you could find time in your crowded schedule to express your opinions about my husband's case. Your views might bring some relief to my husband as well, who takes it all very hard."

One striking aspect of this woman's depiction of her husband's plight is the distinction she draws between the government leaders "above" and those who carried out instructions "below" on the local level. This was a traditional way of thinking, which had become ingrained not least of all in the Third Reich, as evidenced by the common expression "If only the Führer knew!" It does not seem very likely that the letter writer was motivated primarily by a tactical desire to flatter Eisler. In any case, this couple's belief in the new, socialist Germany was severely shaken. The letter writer mentions at the end that her husband was eventually given another job, although it does not seem to have made them forget the injustice that was done.

This letter also demonstrates a fact that is well known from the academic literature, namely, that loyalty to the new regime depended to a large extent on occupational advancement. This couple hoped that the husband's membership in the NSDAP would be forgotten, but in actual fact it was dug up twenty years later, if one assumes that the woman's description of the situation is accurate. This was not an isolated case, as is well known from the literature. We do not know why the husband was released from the Volksarmee — apparently age was not a factor. All we know for sure from the letter is that both the man and his wife found the treatment accorded him very hurtful and they could not understand it. Also noteworthy is the wife's belief that, as a woman, she would think matters through more deeply than men, although the comparison remains implicit in the letter. She felt entitled, accordingly, to write on behalf of her husband and put herself in his shoes. She says very little about herself, just that she raised the children and put in her hours on National Reconstruction despite being sick.

The third letter writer complained to Eisler in 1959 about her low wages. She was a worker in a large factory and was often asked to work in the factory kitchen and kindergarten as well. She complained that she and 150 people like her were paid the lowest wages (216 marks plus another 34 for the cost of food); she was not in any wage category; and she had not received any raises, even though her work was physically exhausting: "[I]t is very hard to lift the big pots and all the potatoes and vegetables in the kitchen or clean up in the kindergarten." She had spoken to the union and then to the party leaders, but everybody just put her off until later. This woman also wrote about her past, this time not in respect to the Third Reich but to her membership in the SPD as far back as 1922. Her great disappointment came later: "[I]n 1932 we had a frightful awakening when our comrades died coming out of meetings." Exactly what she meant by this is unclear. The letter concludes with the question, "Will I get an answer?" The writer was a simple working woman who, if one judges by her highly critical remarks about the West German SPD, probably supported the regime in the GDR but could not understand why she was paid so little for her demanding work. Was this too an isolated case?

Of the three letter writers seen here, two were dissatisfied with the regime for very different reasons, and one was still suffering from her treatment under the Nazis and from the fact that nothing much was done in the GDR to help her. The fact that all three went to the trouble of writing long letters shows that they had not broken with the regime and hoped somehow to reach the people in power. All the letters were very personal. As the recipient of letters like these, Gerhart Eisler gained useful insights into what people were thinking, their deepest concerns, and how they constructed their arguments. His knowledge of the society was deepened, and he was able to play all the better on human emotions in his broadcasts, while dissembling the role that his dialogues with listeners played in helping to stabilize the regime.

Conclusion

We have tried to show in the preceding discussion that there was a mix of continuities and breaks with the past in GDR radio. The continuities with the period before 1945 are generally considered to have been primarily in the areas of propaganda, misuse of information, and government attempts to steer and control the media.[78] However, other issues emerged as well in connection with continuities and breaks with the past. First, the effort devoted to the multifaceted concept of listener loyalty shows how interested producers were in intensifying the relationship between radio and the general population and encouraging amateurs to participate. Although the dialogue that ensued was staged and instrumentalized, it saved radio from being ruled "from above" in a uniform, one-dimensional way and engendered some complexity. The attempts to ensure listener loyalty were only partly successful from the point of view of the authorities. Least appreciated of all was the work of the radio correspondents. However, it was important that so many people participated in radio in one way or another and helped thereby, whether intentionally or not, to ensure the survival of the state-run system. The criticisms that surfaced were often ambiguous and could be interpreted as mundane and politically innocuous, even when they drew some comparisons with the West, for instance in the complaints about programming.

There was a certain complexity as well to the image of the genders communicated on radio. In some ways, the program producers seemed

---

78. Cf. Kay Laudien, "Propaganda als Machtsicherungsmethode: Die Kontrolle der Medien," in Ludger Kühnhardt (ed.), *Die doppelte deutsche Diktaturerfahrung* (Frankfurt, 1994), 64ff.

to act as if they realized that the enormous political, economic, and social changes in the GDR must be very unsettling for the general population and that the best thing they could do was to provide some continuity by accepting and reproducing traditional and apparently proven stereotypes. One area in which there was considerable continuity with the past was the relationship between the genders in "apolitical" entertainment programs. These programs were a subtle way of helping people to get their bearings in the new regime. Some forms of government patriarchy played a role in this as well.

On the other hand, "official" broadcasts reflecting government policy promised women plenty of support and proclaimed their liberation. A considerable discrepancy arose therefore between the gender relations in "official," "serious" broadcasts and in light entertainment. The latter continued to propagate the old clichés and traditional norms, although in contexts and in a packaging peculiar to the GDR, for instance all the references to the economic and technological achievements of the new state. Entertainment programs were therefore a hodgepodge of continuity and breaks with the past.

We should mention again the social tensions that arose from the exclusion of all "otherness." The exclusion of "otherness," including in relations between the genders, was rooted both in the National Socialist (and cultural conservative) past and in the socialist conceptions from the 1920s of the "new man," at least in general trend.[79] Nevertheless, it was the Nazi dictatorship that hardened and legitimized the inclination of many people toward intolerant behaviors and mentalities. The effects of this unfortunate cultural legacy could be seen in both parts of Germany in the 1950s. In the Federal Republic in the 1960s and 1970s, strong new impulses emerged in the direction of greater civility, democracy, and Americanization, thanks in large part to the new media and despite the deadening effects of the Cold War. These impulses were not felt to the same extent in the GDR, and the illiberal cultural legacy became further ingrained in everyday life, although in political and ideological contexts that were specific to that country. As a result, the tendencies in German society toward authoritarianism and the exclusion of "otherness" and insistence on narrow petit bourgeois norms became more firmly entrenched in the GDR.[80]

---

79. We are thinking here not only of the attitudes instilled by the Nazis but also of cultural conservative attitudes. In addition, there were the attempts of the Social Democrats in the 1920s to inculcate the "new man." Although this concept was based on people's own "insight," some illiberal tendencies managed to worm their way into it, especially in regard to people who did not want to accept the norms.

80. Although there were radical differences between the two systems in regard to both their theoretical and conceptual origins and their political contents and backgrounds,

Finally, radio did much in the GDR to enrich private life, a realm that grew increasingly important after the late 1950s.[81] Withdrawal into private life could also be seen as a continuation of behaviors that had become entrenched under the Nazis and in some ways stretched even further back in time.[82] The emphasis on private life detracted from political activism on behalf of socialism and was therefore hardly an ideal development from the point of view of the authorities. However, it did not pose a direct threat to them, especially since the unofficial employees of the State Security Service provided some degree of control over private life and people realized that they might well be punished for "inappropriate behavior." This was generally enough to instill caution in most of the population.

While radio — and later television — epitomized the ability of the state to penetrate private life, listening to western broadcasts meant constantly flouting the rules laid down by the government and reaching out beyond the limits of its authority. The history of radio in the GDR is characterized by this duality, which reminds us of the complex relationship between power structures and the everyday lives of the people.

---

some continuities in deeper mentalities and tastes cannot be overlooked — continuities that could also be seen, again in very specific ways, in the Federal Republic under Adenauer. Only slowly does a picture emerge of the more deep-seated after-effects of the Nazi dictatorship.

81. This is not true, however, of everyone. Youths and people intent on rising into the new "government bourgeoisie" were particularly inclined to join a kind of "other family," the "family" of the party and its suborganizations. See Dorothee Wierling, "Is There an East Germany Identity? Aspects of a Social History of the Soviet Zone/German Democratic Republic," *Tel Aviver Jahrbuch für deutsche Geschichte* 19 (1990): 200. Wierling speaks of the party as a kind of mother and of Stalin as a father figure.

82. Dorothee Wierling expresses a similar idea in the following words: "the political experience of the 1950s in many ways took over and readopted an older, but still fresh, experience from National Socialism. For some, this meant converting to socialism and thereby retaining one's authoritarian needs. For most East Germans, however, this experience affirmed the already strong depoliticization of their existence, which had aided them in living through National Socialism, had helped them to reorganize after the war and now was meant to compensate for the harm that was being done to them in a Stalinist society. Yet while National Socialism could count on considerable consent from the German majority, being rather successful and profitable up until the final years of the war, the social consent we find in the GDR, in contrast, did not emerge from official politics, but rather was pitted against it." Ibid., 201.

Index

Social History, Popular Culture, and Politics in Germany
Geoff Eley, Series Editor

(continued from pg. ii)